CASEY & MR. McGRAW

By
JOSEPH DURSO

Published by
The Sporting News

Published in the United States by THE SPORTING NEWS Publishing Co., 1212 North Lindbergh Boulevard, St. Louis, Missouri 63132.

ISBN: 0-89204-307-5
10 9 8 7 6 5 4 3 2 1

First Edition

Contents

MR. McGRAW

CASEY

Foreword

If New York is the big stage, to say nothing of the Big Apple, then they were the longest-running act on Broadway.

With one or two interruptions, it was an act that began on July 19, 1902, when John Joseph McGraw made the lineup of the New York Giants for the first time as the 29-year-old shortstop and manager. And it closed on July 25, 1965, when Charles Dillon Stengel fell and broke his hip and left the cast as the 75-year-old manager of the New York Mets.

Between those milestone dates, they dominated the sporting scene, at times the speakeasy scene and probably even the social scene, and they did it because they were explosive personalities who were superstars in the most dramatic vehicle in town: big league baseball.

One was the master; the other, the pupil. One came as a manager who already had been a famous player; the other came as a player who later became a famous manager. One was outrageously bellicose; the other, outrageously slapstick. Both were virtuosos of the art of commanding the public's pride and passion.

They did this whether they were winning or losing, but they both knew that it was easier to do when they were winning. And they were winning most of the time.

John McGraw was manager of the Giants for 31 years. They finished in first place 10 times, in second place 11 times, in third place four times. That's 25 years in the race, and in the money. Casey Stengel was manager of the Brooklyn Dodgers for three unsuccessful years, but then became manager of the Yankees for 12 spectacularly successful years: They were first 10 times, second once, third once. Then he became the first manager of the Mets and, for three and a half years, lost battles but won wars for the money and minds of the fans.

Between them, they were the managers of all four New York teams in this century, they won 20 pennants, they ran second 12 times, they won the World Series 10 times and Stengel even hit two home runs for McGraw's Giants when they played Babe Ruth and the Yankees in the 1923 World Series. That was the third straight Series played by the Giants and Yankees in a historic Battle of Broadway that led to what you might call the Babe Ruth reign between the managerial eras of McGraw and Stengel.

The clamor of those times was told in a pair of volumes a generation ago, just before the act closed for good. They were separate but related biographies, starting in 1967 with *Casey: The Life and Legend of Charles Dillon Stengel*. It was followed two years later by *The Days of Mr. McGraw,* also published originally by Prentice-Hall, also written by this author.

The idea for *Casey* came naturally while I was covering Stengel for *The New York Times,* which was a little like covering a typhoon. The idea for the next book came when I got to wondering who had fashioned this mad genius and eventually asked Casey who had been *his* teacher, tutor and hero and the best of the bunch. And he replied: "McGraw."

Now it is 20 years later, and about 100 years since John McGraw arrived in Baltimore as a teen-aged professional ball player, and about 100 years since Casey Stengel arrived as a newborn child in Kansas City, Mo. A century of McGraw and Stengel. And, says Richard Waters of *The Sporting News,* it is time to combine them into a century of baseball history and American history.

The only change we're making this time is to reverse the sequence. After all, genealogically speaking, Mr. McGraw begat Dr. Stengel. And together they begat generations of *joie de vivre.* One of the disciples was James Cagney, who was a dynamo catcher on the streets and sandlots of New York in the days of Mr. McGraw and who could have portrayed the Little Napoleon of the Polo Grounds during his own days as a superstar of the screen. On September 10, 1969, he wrote from his farm in Stanfordville, N.Y., that the biography of John McGraw had shaken down the memories, and he added:

"I've been a music lover all my life, but the 'bok' of a bat meeting a baseball carried more music to my young ears than a Warsaw concerto."

You can also shake down the memories if you happen to be near Jimmy Cagney's home in Beverly Hills, Calif., and drive up the freeway to Casey Stengel's old home in Glendale. There, on a grassy hillside in Forest Lawn Cemetery, you will find the graves of Casey and his wife, Edna, the onetime silent-screen actress who was his constant companion on the baseball trails.

It's a quiet manicured spot not far from the house where they lived for their half-century together, and I made a kind of pilgrimage there late in the summer of 1988 with Arthur Richman and Harry Minor of the Mets and Father Dan Murphy of New York, who sometimes travels with the Mets in the post-Stengel era.

Don't think the Old Man's spirit doesn't rule the hillside, either. A few yards from the grave markers, the city of Glendale has put up a large bronzed plaque on the stone wall of a memorial building. It shows Stengel's craggy face smiling out between crossed baseball bats, and it carries this inscription:

"Charles Dillon Stengel, Casey. For over 60 years, one of America's folk heroes who contributed immensely to the lore and language of our country's national pastime, baseball."

The inscription closes with this quote from Casey: "There comes a time in every man's life—and I've had plenty of them."

He had plenty of them, all right. As he said at Cooperstown in 1966 when he was retracing the steps that took him there:

"I got $2,100 a year when I started in the big league, and they get more money now. *** And Grover Cleveland Alexander pitched in a bandbox in those days and still won 30 games. *** And there was Walter Johnson, who could pitch for a second-division club. *** I chased the balls that Babe Ruth hit."

Yes, and John McGraw called the pitches that Babe Ruth hit, or missed. And that Christy Mathewson threw, and Bill Klem called, and Damon Runyon described, and Graham McNamee dramatized.

If there is a message to be taken from these two uncommon spirits, it is probably this: They were *driven* to compete, to attain and mostly to perform, driven by a love for life that was more of a lust for life, never bored or blasé, always involved, immersed and impassioned, *Casey and Mr. McGraw,* splendid and fairly amazin'.

—Joseph Durso

MR.
McGRAW

"O, it's great to be young and a Giant."
LARRY DOYLE,
who was both.

"Stoutly knit, as game as a pit-bird, he was very much in earnest when socking time was declared."
GENE FOWLER.

"His very walk across the field in a hostile town was a challenge to the multitude."
GRANTLAND RICE.

"In Mr. McGraw I at last discovered the real and most authentic Most Remarkable Man in America."
GEORGE BERNARD SHAW.

"The main idea is to win."
JOHN J. McGRAW.

Chapter

Mob Town

In August of 1891 a train pulled into Baltimore from the West carrying an eighteen-year-old country boy named John Joseph McGraw of Truxton, New York. He bounced down from the day coach and stepped into a new and tumultuous world that would make him rich, famous and hated, and he would be fought every foot of the way. He was toting a box suitcase and a baseball glove.

McGraw, a graduate of the Iron and Oil Baseball League, was arriving from Cedar Rapids, Iowa, and he found Baltimore a spectacularly busy and noisy place. It was a town of dogs in houses, chickens in backyards, Civil War veterans, high-tariff Republicans, Grover Cleveland Democrats, Gladstonian collars, cigar-store Indians, policemen in helmets and H. L. Mencken.

It was world-famous for the roughness of its cobblestones, the quality of its crab cakes and the terseness of its *Baltimore Sunpaper,* which reported on page 1 with remarkable restraint one day in 1888: "Berlin, March 9—William I is dead aged 91."

It was a town of famous churches, like the Watch Your Step Baptist Temple. It was a town of famous saloons, like the one that Jake Kilrain opened on Baltimore Street after losing to John L. Sullivan in 1889 and where he now reigned as a local demigod. It was a place that took its heroes seriously, as when Joe Gans, the Negro fighter, died and they had to hold his funeral in three phases in three churches to accommodate the waves of mourners.

It was a place where school children not much younger than John McGraw recited out of McGuffey's Readers. The kind of hometown where bands of youngsters roved the streets playing loud games that all seemed to involve singing or shouting, where they blew horns for weeks at Christmastime and exploded firecrackers for weeks before the Fourth of July, and then until August. A clamorous place where circus parades wound past City Hall with elephants and spangled girls, and sometimes even Buffalo Bill's Wild West Show with "bloodthirsty Indians."

Baltimore was not only loud but also tough, as it had been from the days thirty years before when the Massachusetts regiment heading south had to fight its way through town. And later when the Confederates heading north were, with passionate bipartisanship, tarred and feathered. It was known with good reason as Mob Town.

"Baltimore, by 1890," Mencken recalled a little unkindly, "was fast degenerating, and so was civilization."

Still, it was a tumultuous time of opportunity when the Common Man of the next century began to rise up out of the Machine Age of this century, and began to outmaneuver and outvote the uncommon man. He certainly began to outnumber him, and in that generation from 1880 to 1900 the population of the United States was skyrocketing by 50 percent, from 50 million persons to 75 million.

Conversely, the symbols of the frontier were fading from view. In 1866, General Philip H. Sheridan calculated that 100 million of the great American bison roamed the plains of Kansas and the Indian Territory alone. Now as the country rattled into the eighteen-nineties only 1,091 of the one-ton buffalo were reported alive on the planet.

Washington, Montana, and North and South Dakota had just joined the Union. The last armed conflict between the white man and the Indian had just been fought at a place called Wounded Knee Creek. The Census Bureau declared there no longer was a land frontier.

Like McGraw, America was moving from the frontier to the city, and machines were beginning to upstage and sometimes to upset men. Thomas B. Reed, the Speaker of the House of Representatives, a 300-pound "czar" of the national life and a distinguished wit and sage from Maine, was asked what was the greatest problem facing the American people at the time. He replied: "How to dodge a bicycle."

It was twenty-six years since Lincoln had been assassinated, and the frontier during that quarter-century had been relentlessly overrun by the marvels of the Machine Age. The typewriter, reinforced concrete, the Westinghouse air brake, celluloid, barbed wire—all made the scene in the decade after the Civil War.

Then in 1876 came Bell's telephone, and in 1884 Mergenthaler's linotype and Parsons' steam turbine. Edison started lighting the cities in the eighties, Daimler produced his high-speed internal combustion engine in 1886, Eastman his hand camera in 1888 and Otis his electric elevator a year later.

In Manhattan, brush arc lamps were replacing the gas lights, cable cars were chasing the stage coaches off Broadway and the Third Avenue Elevated was already rocking the sidewalks of New York with trains that coughed up storms of black smoke over the cobblestone streets. And in Baltimore, in the months before John McGraw arrived, H. L. Mencken's father had installed the first steam-heating equipment in the row houses along Hollins Street.

The man in the street was being fed, housed, heated, entertained and transported as never before—and courted by politicians as never before.

Theodore Roosevelt, upon entering the public life of the loud new age a few years earlier, had been ridiculed by "men of cultivated and easy life." They told him that politics was becoming a low craft run by "saloon-keepers, horse-car conductors and the like," and warned that he would find them "rough, brutal and unpleasant."

Later, after he had become a public hero himself, Roosevelt in turn was upbraided by Mark Hanna as "that damned cowboy." And Henry Adams' oldest brother, John, who had made a fortune in the Union Pacific Railroad, recoiled from the new politics. He reflected that he had "all he wanted—wealth, children, society, consideration," and he scoffed at the picture of sacrificing himself in order "to get cheers from an Irish mob."

It was a time when public influence was certain to be commanded by national-action types like Captain A. T. Mahan, the president of the Naval War College. He had spent many hours sitting in the Astor Place branch of the New York Public Library doing research for a book. It was published in 1890 with the title, *The Influence of Sea Power on History,* and it was read "straight through" by Teddy Roosevelt.

It was a time when the imagination of the crowd was captured by impresario types like Phineas Taylor Barnum, the promoter of the folk heroes General Tom Thumb and Jenny Lind, the Swedish Nightingale. Barnum's world of fantasy even grew to encompass his No. 1 rival, James Anthony Bailey, with whom he merged in 1881 to form the great traveling circus.

And though Barnum died in 1891, the year John McGraw reached Baltimore, a new era of flamboyance was opening that craved his type of flair and talent for beating the drum. McGraw didn't know it as he stepped off the train that August day—and Baltimore certainly didn't know it—but the country boy was the right man in the right place at the right time.

★　　★　　★

Truxton is a hamlet in the Finger Lakes region of New York State, fifteen miles south of Syracuse and west of Cooperstown, on a stream called the Tioughnioga River. John McGraw's father moved there in 1871. He had left Ireland in the fifties, which was when Casey Stengel's father was leaving Germany for the Midwest. Father McGraw was a short man with a long shock of black hair. He was a widower with one daughter, and he worked as a maintenance man on the Elmira, Cortland & Northern Rail Road. He worked sixty hours a week and was paid $9.

John McGraw Sr. met and married Ellen Comerfort, whose family had long since settled in upstate New York in the Mohawk Valley. They had eight children, and No. 3 was John Joseph, who was born April 7, 1873.

Across the country, in 1873, the cable cars were being installed for the first time on the steep streets of San Francisco. Across the world, a supercool science student named Sherlock Holmes was embarking for the first time—as far as anybody could deduce—on a case where the game was afoot, "The Gloria Scott." Across the state, the public conscience in New York City was catching up for the first time with William Marcy Tweed.

Tweed was the Tammany Hall leader who had been bankrupt at the end of the Civil War eight years earlier but who now owned a mansion at Madison Avenue and Fifty-ninth Street, a yacht and a collection of immense diamonds which he wore gloriously on his watch chain, his shirtfront and his fingers.

What caused this remarkable change in fortune? The answer was supplied chiefly by two men: George Jones, the editor of *The New York Times,* and Thomas Nast, who drew his first "Tammany Tiger" cartoon for *Harper's Weekly* on November 11, 1871.

New York was a growing city of about one million persons then and was blessed, or maybe afflicted at times, by a corps of editors from the sticks. Henry Jarvis Raymond of *The Times* was born in Lima, New York, in Livingston County, not far from McGraw's hometown. He once worked for Horace Greeley for $8 a week. Greeley was from Amherst in rural New Hampshire. George Jones, the bête noir of Boss Tweed, came from Poultney, Vermont.

The politics of Tammany Hall—the Democratic organization of New York County—would play an important part in John McGraw's career thirty years later. But none of the later shenanigans ever quite lived up to the rollicking robbery of the days when the Tweed Ring rode highest.

Cuspidors for the City Council chamber were sold for $190 apiece. Police jobs and transfers went for anywhere from $300 to $15,000 (captain, midtown). The City Controller, Richard B. Connolly, the man who supposedly held the civic purse strings, was universally known as Slippery Dick. The Council was appropriately nicknamed "the Forty Thieves."

Jones, who succeeded Raymond as editor of *The Times,* exposed the Tweed Ring and its "honest graft" that had corrupted a whole city. He found that Tweed, a onetime chairmaker, had stocked the city's armories with phantom chairs and other phantom services costing one million dollars. He was no piker with a tab; he billed the city $170,729 for chairs alone and $431,164 for carpentry. *And* $2,870,000 for plastering in a new county courthouse.

Now, in April of 1873, while the McGraws of Truxton were christening John Joseph, the irrepressible Tweed was being convicted in that same unplastered county courthouse. He was sentenced to twelve months in jail and a fine of $12,500, and got off lightly. He served the twelve months and paid only $250, but $500,000 went in fees to the lawyers who had arranged it all.

Two years later, Tweed was arrested again and was taken to the Ludlow Street Jail, another of his white-elephant construction jobs. But he escaped one night when the warden and the turnkey took him in a carriage to his Madison Avenue mansion so that he could dine in his accustomed splendor. He wound up in Spain. However, he was identified there by a Nast cartoon, returned home on a Navy cruiser and died in April of 1878, when Johnny McGraw was just turning five.

Life in the David Harum country was a little tight economically but otherwise was relaxed, innocent and pastoral—until the winter of 1884-85. Then an epidemic of "black diphtheria" swept through the valley and in a few weeks' time took Ellen McGraw, who was then in her thirties, and four of her children—John's sister of eight, stepsister of thirteen, brother of four and an infant brother. Half the family was gone, and his father never quite recovered from the devastation.

The four surviving children were sent to live with their mother's relatives —except for John, who stayed with his distraught father and who almost immediately became embroiled with him in a running tug-of-war about railroading, farming and the other paths of righteousness.

He did drive cows for neighbors on the dairy farms of the Southern Tier. He even let his father nudge him onto the railroad as a candy butcher when he was a 105-pound runt of sixteen in 1889. But by then he was living at the Truxton House Hotel with the Goddard family and tending horses—and playing baseball.

Baseball in 1889 was romantic but chaotic, and two things that McGraw's father did not need more of in 1889 were romance and chaos.

It was a game that had been played for exactly half a century on the corner lots and lawns of a country that had a tradition of hitting balls with sticks, whether the precise form was cricket, rounders, town ball, one o' cat or baseball.

It was played on corner lots like the one at Madison Avenue and Twenty-seventh Street in Manhattan, where Alexander Joy Cartwright and the other fashionable young sports played for the Knickerbocker Baseball and Social Club, and played in the early days until somebody scored 21 runs. Or, on historic lots like the Elysian Field across the Hudson River in Hoboken, New Jersey, where the Knickerbockers played the first match on record, a four-inning joust umpired by Cartwright and won—perversely enough—by a rival club, the New York Nine, by the untidy score of 23 to 1.

Or, on country lots like the one where the Truxton Grays played their games in the Finger Lakes and where John McGraw finally resisted his father's arguments once and for all and became a baseball player. He had given the railroad and the farm a whirl, not much of a whirl, kind of half-hearted but dutiful. And now, in 1889, he started pitching for the town nine, filling in at second base, third base, even shortstop. He was only sixteen, and skinny and short, but he had taken the step.

He took an even bigger step a short time later. He was offered $2 a game to pitch for the team in nearby East Homer, whose most distinguished celebrity and athlete had been the legendary David Harum. He was suddenly a professional.

He was a professional with a problem, too: East Homer was five miles from Truxton, transportation was thin and paying for transportation was unthinkable. True, he had heard all about Hans Wagner and his fourteen-mile

walks from Mansfield, Pennsylvania, to Allegheny City near Pittsburgh just to
see Cap Anson play first base for Chicago at Exposition Park. Very heroic,
McGraw admitted. But he soon displayed the McGraw flair for solving problems with the resources at hand.

He simply walked the five miles over and back, twice in fact. He pitched
and won games both times, and then made a really clever pitch: He held out
for $5 a game plus hack fare both ways. His timing was good and his aim
flawless. Being a "hot" pitcher at the moment, he did not have too much
trouble conning the manager into meeting his demands, and so his price more
than doubled, with fringe benefits extra.

Being a crowd-pleaser in East Homer, New York, probably meets most
definitions of starting small. But McGraw already had the useful talent of
approaching the job at hand with a one-track mind of concentration, and let
the chips fall where they may. And sure enough, an even bigger offer came his
way that fall from the Olean club of the New York and Pennsylvania League, a
team that had eleven baseball players and one mustachioed manager.

The mustache belonged to Bert Kenney, who owned a hotel in Truxton
but who complicated his off-hours life by running the Olean team. He never
had to look far for reinforcements for his ball club, and this time there was
McGraw, the home-grown hero at sixteen, commanding $5 every time he
pitched for East Homer.

Bert Kenney put it to McGraw in unmistakable terms. He would graduate
from the semi-professional sandlots to "organized baseball" and he would be
paid $40 a month plus room and board. His father, making a kind of last
stand, objected. But McGraw resorted to impenetrable logic. "Dad," he replied,
"I'll be making $3,500 a year before you know it." And he snapped up Ken-
ney's offer.

The New York and Pennsylvania League, also known as the Iron and Oil
League, was not crowded with players. Olean, for example, carried only eleven.
The economics of meeting the payroll kept the roster from expanding. One of
Olean's eleven was a pitcher, and so McGraw immediately suffered the indig-
nity of being switched to third base, and the indignity grew.

"I could field the ball all right," he recalled, "but on the throw I couldn't
hit the first-baseman or anything near him. I was quite a bust in my start as a
third-baseman. I played six games there and we lost every one of them."

They lost six straight games, all right—his first six in organized baseball—
and in one of them he broke defensive records all over the place by making
nine errors. His throwing arm, even for a pitcher, was just too hurried and
erratic. A week later he began riding the bench. But he couldn't sit still as a
sideline scatter-arm, and gradually became a respectable infielder by working
out in the morning several hours before games—a tactic that his own teams
copied in a later day in a much more demanding league.

He had just turned seventeen in the spring of 1890, and with Kenney's
blessing started to hop around a bit among the clubs nearby. The same thing
was going on in the major leagues, too, with the National League fighting the

American Association for players and both in turn fighting the Players League. The irony of it all was that the free-for-all broke out as a protest against the National Agreement of 1882, a baseball code drawn to *end* the raiding of talent among major league clubs.

All this seemed pretty remote in Olean, but it was getting less remote very quickly. McGraw hopped from Olean to Hornellsville to Canisteo that summer, and finished at Wellsville, where his friend Al Lawson was the manager. McGraw, at least, always dated his professional career from Wellsville, and it was probably easy to understand why. It was his first rung of the ladder, and the memory was a lot brighter than the memory of all those wild throws across Bert Kenney's infield.

Wellsville, thirty-two miles east of Olean, was in the Western New York League. McGraw played third base and pitched against teams like Hornell and Bradford, and in 24 games went to bat 107 times, made 39 hits, scored 40 runs, made 12 sacrifice bunts and batted .365. The ratio of runs and sacrifice bunts to times at bat—the ratio of advancing base-runners—cast a long shadow toward a career that would become dedicated to scrounging runs.

It was a strange world for a seventeen-year-old. He was paid $60 a month, he lived in a hotel in Wellsville and he became locally famous as Johnny McGraw the ball player. He was cutting the strings to Truxton.

Then Lawson organized a team for an exhibition tour of Florida and Cuba in the winter of 1890-91, and invited his rookie. They were billed as the American All-Stars, a slight exaggeration. McGraw was paid $60 a month plus a share of the team's split of any money collected in Cuba. But his greatest reward came after they had boarded the train at Wellsville as the winter's cold set in, and the train carried him—for the first time—to New York City.

He was there only a few days before heading south to Jacksonville and Ocala, and he got to know all those railroad towns in Florida where he would later bring his big teams for spring training. Then to Tampa, where Al Lawson's American All-Stars boarded a ship for Havana—a city filled with Spanish soldiers eight years before Teddy Roosevelt went charging up San Juan Hill.

Baseball had been brought to Cuba a few years before the Finger Lakes heroes had been brought there. The contact man was Frank Bancroft, an old burlesque and baseball man, who had started the ball rolling by importing two teams of minor leaguers from the mainland. Lawson's team played 17 games against other American teams that also were touring the island as well as a few Cuban clubs, and won 14 of them.

Lawson had taken the precaution of inserting half a dozen ringers into his ranks, former big leaguers who played the game like pool sharks trimming the hayseeds. The All-Stars made a big splash from the moment they took the field, chiefly because they were wearing yellow uniforms. And none made a bigger splash than the slender, fast, scurrying teen-ager at shortstop, the baby of the team. *El mono amarillo,* he was dubbed by the Cuban writers and crowds—the yellow monkey. And even in his grandest days thirty years later, he still would be called that in the newspapers of the Caribbean.

When they returned to Tampa in the early spring of 1891, Lawson gave *el mono amarillo* his due, and also gave him a firm push toward the kind of distinction he never could have reached in the hotel lobby back home in Wellsville.

"The best player on my team," Lawson said, "is Johnny McGraw. He is a hard, left-handed batsman, a fine shortstop, a good baserunner and, last but not least, a gentleman. He is one of the coming stars of the profession."

Instead of rushing his heroes back home to the snows of upstate New York, Lawson then took them on a barnstorming tour of Florida. They played for meal money and cigars, and at Gainesville one day they played a fateful game. It was March 26, 1891, and Lawson's country boys took on Pat Tebeau's Cleveland Indians, who had just arrived for spring practice and were looking for exercise: Cy Young, John "Dirty" Doyle, Charlie "Chief" Zimmer, Clarence Algernon "Cupid" Childs, George Davis, Chippy McGarr, Big Ed McKean and Leon Viau.

Taking the bull by the horns against this distinguished bunch, Lawson not only characterized his own boys "the champions of Florida" but even pitched against Viau himself. The "champions" lost the game, 9 to 6, contributing eleven errors to Cleveland's cause. But the seventeen-year-old boy at third base was a whirling dervish with four hits in five times at bat and three runs scored.

"They were a bit raw," McGraw said later, "having had only a few days' practice, while I was as spry as a kid could be. Viau was a good pitcher in those days, but of course he didn't have a seasoned arm, so he just lobbed the ball up to the plate. I got three doubles and a single, and it proved the start of my career.

"A few days later I was receiving telegrams from all over the country. The funny thing was, nobody ever got on to the fact that the pitcher was just lobbing them over the plate.

"Some offered me $60 a month. I kept putting them off, though, until the Cedar Rapids team wired me an offer of $125. I didn't even stop to take off my uniform, but ran all the way to the telegraph office to accept."

The number of offers, as a matter of fact, rose to twenty-eight and the number of shrieks of protest rose almost as high. He was claimed not only by Cedar Rapids but also by Fort Wayne, Davenport and Rockford, among other towns. And Rockford even hired a lawyer to "teach him a lesson" on the subject of inspiring, and presumably "accepting," a flurry of cash offers.

McGraw later went to some length to dispel any insinuation that he might have pocketed some of the advance money from clubs that were not so lucky as Cedar Rapids. For $125 a month, $75 in advance and transportation, Cedar Rapids at least got a baseball player. But in any event, his afternoon's work in the Florida sun against the Cleveland Indians had made him one of the most courted young athletes in the country, less than twenty-four months after the first game with the Truxton Grays.

He took the train west to Cedar Rapids in the farm country of the Illinois and Iowa League. It was an eight-team league that included Joliet, Quincy,

Ottawa, Aurora, Rockford, Davenport and Ottumwa. The towns ranged from five thousand persons to about twenty thousand, and they seemed to live for the summertime thrill of seeing a famous baseball team on tour, like Anson's Chicago White Stockings. In one of the towns, Kansas City, an infant named Casey Stengel was one year old—if anybody can imagine Casey Stengel being one year old.

There were no written contracts to bind players or teams then, and leagues tended to fold after July 4 had come and gone with its last big crowd of summer. McGraw got right to work, playing in 31 games in quick succession and before long, sure enough, the league was tottering.

Still, he made friendships that lasted a lifetime and that followed him eventually to New York. There was Henry Fabian in right field, a man who would become the groundskeeper at the Polo Grounds a generation later. And Dick Kinsella, who later prowled the minor leagues and sent good young prospects toward McGraw back East—prospects like Carl Hubbell.

He even had one more brush with the titans of baseball, as he had in Gainesville a few days earlier. That was the day the White Stockings came to town behind Cap Anson, the 6 foot 3 inch, 215-pound giant with yellow hair, still the world's most renowned baseball player at the age of forty. And Bad Bill Dahlen, later Casey Stengel's first manager in the big leagues, was at shortstop.

But the high moment came when Anson, in his twenty-first year in a baseball suit, hit a line drive toward third base and McGraw caught it. McGraw's team lost the game, 2 to 0, but two eras had crossed paths in Cedar Rapids that sunny spring afternoon.

"It was the first time I had played in a class that I thought I was entitled to," McGraw said later with no false modesty. "I made up my mind that I would show up that big league club, and I felt confident that I could do so. 'Say, old-timer,' I said to Anson as I ran past him, 'so that's what you call big league pitching, eh?'

"Anson looked at me in astonishment. My impudence almost took his breath away. You can imagine how that must have sounded coming from a kid of eighteen years who weighed but 120 pounds. Before the day was over I had three hot arguments with him, but finally he saw the humor of it and smiled at me.

"At shortstop, I accepted eleven chances that day and led our team at bat. It was a big day for me. After the game, Anson, forgetting my freshness and impudence, said some nice things about my playing—actually asked how I would like to play for Chicago sometime. That went to my head immediately. All thoughts of the Illinois and Iowa League and things like that went out of my head. I would be a big leaguer or nothing."

He didn't have to wait long. Bill Gleason, an oldtime shortstop for the St. Louis Browns, had ended his career in the majors and was playing with one of the clubs in the league. He wrote a letter about McGraw to Bill Barnie, the manager of the Baltimore Orioles of the American Association, which then was challenging the National League at the top of all baseball.

"I got a letter from Billy Barnie today," Gleason said to McGraw one day.

"Yeah," replied the child prodigy of Cedar Rapids, "what did he have to say?"

"He wants to know how good you are," Gleason said.

"Tell him," McGraw said, "that I'm as good as they come."

Gleason wrote exactly that, and in a few days McGraw received a telegram and a railroad ticket to Baltimore.

"I packed my bag," he recalled, "and went out of Cedar Rapids with a running jump."

When the train finally crossed the eastern half of the country and deposited him in Baltimore, the eighteen-year-old *mono amarillo* from Truxton, New York, stepped into the new and turbulent world of the big leagues and Mob Town. He walked from the depot to Barnie's office and "announced myself." The manager of the Baltimore Orioles stared at him in amazement "for a whole minute," McGraw remembered, and said:

"Why, you're just a kid. Can you play ball?"

Chapter

2

The Main Idea

Baltimore in the eighteen-nineties was a city to be reckoned with. It had the strength of the North, the bustle of the East, the grace of the South and the roughness of the West. It was called Crab Town for the quality of its seafood, and Mob Town for the quality of its mobs.

So an exceptional marriage of true minds took place in 1891 when John McGraw arrived from the West and reported to his new employer, the Baltimore Orioles baseball team of the American Association.

"Henry Fabian told me," he recalled with satisfaction in later years, "that when I showed up at Cedar Rapids I was the freshest and cockiest kid that ever broke into a ball game. I sassed everybody."

McGraw had just turned eighteen, but was so irreverent that he idolized brashness. He gloried in the blithe spirits of the day, like Arlie Latham, the baseball pioneer, who had achieved a spectacularly memorable "first day" in the major leagues—by McGraw's standards—by the following feats: He antagonized everybody on the Buffalo team, he made a monkey-face at the manager as he went to the plate to bat, he bowed to the pitcher with insulting courtliness and he belted a triple over the centerfielder's head.

It took McGraw no time to realize that Baltimore craved precisely such spirits, and with passion. It was a jumping town that drank it straight. Beer cost $1.20 for a case of 24, whiskey traded at $4 a gallon and blends were regarded with suspicion. Henry L. Mencken said he could not recall ever having seen his father drink a highball.

Baltimore stoked its passion with some of the tastiest food on the Eastern

Seaboard, chiefly because of the treasures of Chesapeake Bay. Mencken remembered prime hard crabs, blue in color and eight inches long, with snow-white meat as firm as soap. They were hawked in Hollins Street at ten cents a dozen, and the supply seemed endless, even in the polluted waters of the Patapsco River, which stretched fourteen miles from the bay to engulf the city's canneries and fertilizer factories. Any good man, the sage of Baltimore said, could go down to the river armed with no more than a length of stout cord, a home-made net on a pole and a chuck of cat's meat—and go home in a couple of hours with enough crabs to feed his family for two days.

Soft crabs, of course, cost more: two and one-twelfth cents each. Mencken recalled his mother's anger when the fishmongers began to *sell* shad roe instead of tossing it in with the fish. And when a 20-inch shad went from forty cents to fifty cents, his father predicted gravely that the Republic would not survive the nineteenth century.

The most celebrated crab cook in town was Tom McNulty, the sheriff of Baltimore, which said a great deal for the municipal esprit de corps. And General Ferdinand C. Latrobe, the Mayor of Baltimore for seven terms, never failed to rise to the occasion as the oratory demanded. He became famous for his speeches at picnics and outings, where he catered sensationally to the ethnic groups involved. Mencken, who was just stepping across the threshold of youth into his career as a writer and critic, heard Latrobe claim "not only Irish, Scotch, Welsh, Dutch and other such relatively plausible bloods, but also Polish, Bohemian, Lithuanian, Swedish, Danish, Greek, Spanish and even Jewish."

"The best he could do for the Chinese, who were then very few in Baltimore," he recalled, "was to quote some passages from the Analects of Confucius, which he had studied through the medium of a secretary."

Baltimore also was known for its proper legions of butlers, who wore blue-and-white checkered aprons as they swept the front steps clean and polished the marble stairs in front of the tidy row houses.

But one of its most enduring contributions to the American scene in those days was undoubtedly the "Wecker," or, freely transcribed from the German, the common hot dog. Mencken, a relentless guardian of the public idioms and mores, once read of the death of "an Irishman" in New York who supposedly was renowned as the inventor of the hot dog—"his epochal invention in the year 1900 or thereabouts, first marketed as consumers' goods at the Polo Grounds."

"All this made me smile in a sly way," he said, "for I devoured hot dogs in Baltimore way back in 1886, and they were then very far from newfangled. They contained precisely the same rubbery, indigestible pseudo-sausages that millions of Americans now eat, and they leaked the same flabby, puerile mustard. Their single point of difference lay in the fact that their covers were honest German *Wecke* (or *Wecken*) made of wheat-flour baked to crispness, and not the soggy rolls prevailing today."

With this historic bridge to the sporting life of the day, it was no surprise that Baltimore went the whole hog in its pursuit of competition. The newspapers had not yet realized the economic beauties of late-sports editions then, much less of baseball editions. So the town's saloons installed telegraph wires, received the news directly and then wrote the scores on blackboards—the high-toned saloons, that is.

Kelly's oyster house on Eutaw Street supposedly had the fastest and slickest telegraph operator around. He sat on a little balcony halfway up the wall, posting the scores for the hordes of imbibing customers below, and if the Orioles happened to be having a particularly good afternoon at the park that day, he'd be treated to maybe thirty beers before the ninth inning had come and gone.

The center of baseball in nearby Washington, meanwhile, was a cigar store at Seventh and G Streets owned by Mencken's father, August, as a branch of his establishment in Baltimore. His father even became vice president of the Washington ball club, and immediately found himself in a running series of fights with the railroads over their rates for transporting ball players. He considered it outrageous when they charged $30 apiece for thirteen players on a western trip from Baltimore to Cincinnati to Columbus to Louisville to St. Louis and back to Baltimore.

The public was becoming so imbued with baseball as the great intercity jousting match of the day that the game attracted attention like an immense magnet. Once August Mencken toyed with the idea of grouping a pitcher named Matt Kilroy and his eight brothers into a baseball team and sending them on tour around the country. Instead, though, he decided to name a five-cent cigar for Kilroy and even conscripted his Washington catcher, Sam Trott, to sell it. Sam was otherwise famous as a catcher who scorned a mitt. He would watch a throw from the outfield come whipping in to home plate, toss his catcher's glove aside with bravado and handle the throw bare-handed. He soon was a five-cent cigar salesman with ten gnarled fingers.

"The one sport my father was really interested in," H. L. Mencken said, "was baseball, and for that he was a fanatic."

He was not the only fanatic who doted on baseball, nor the only businessman who fawned over it as a public prize. The Baltimore club, for example, had been organized in 1882 by Harry Von Der Horst, a beer wholesaler who saw the adventure as a good chance to sell beer through the ball club (not unlike the companies who combined beer and baseball on television seventy-five years later).

Von Der Horst leased a lot at Huntingdon Avenue near Greenmount and built Union Park with six thousand seats, an upper deck and, predictably, a beer garden. In his second year of operations, he made $30,000 as crowds of fans swarmed from the horse-cars into his stadium. The tab at first was five cents, there was no Sunday performance and he even staged a doubleheader in 1884 and got twenty-five cents a head.

Professional baseball was in a chaotic state of warfare in those days. The National League, formed in 1876, was being challenged by the American Association and both were being challenged by the Players League. The Orioles belonged to the American Association. But in 1890, rather than buck the new and troublesome Players League, Von Der Horst deserted the association and joined the weaker Atlantic Association. A few months later he jumped back into the American and replaced Brooklyn, which had defected to the National.

All the while, he kept hinting that financial conditions were so precarious that he might use the park for carnivals instead of baseball games. He was taken literally, as things turned out, and a syndicate was almost organized to promote Baltimore into the National League under the aegis of those cigar-making baseball fans, August Mencken and his brother Henry.

However, in December of 1891 the National League got out from under the tangle of warring leagues and stepped into the clear—taking with it Baltimore, Louisville, Washington and St. Louis and expanding from eight cities to twelve. It was able to do this because the Players League had disbanded after the 1890 season and the American Association after the 1891 season.

The Players, or Brotherhood, League was a brief excursion into self-management by players who felt the two other leagues paid low salaries. The league actually outdrew its rivals during its one season. It played before 980,887 customers while the National League drew 813,678 and the American Association about 500,000. But it found that the financial straits that Von Der Horst and other owners always griped about were real enough, and it withdrew from the war of the leagues. However, it had stayed long enough to provide a footnote to history. Three-quarters of a century later, taking their cue from the Brotherhood, professional athletes in almost every major sport formed labor associations to fight their economic battles.

In any event, when John McGraw reported to Von Der Horst's little beer-and-baseball empire in 1891, the club was only a few months away from joining the National League—the mecca of his two-year pilgrimage from Truxton, New York.

Nor did it take him long to find out why Bill Barnie had flinched at his appearance fresh from the Illinois and Iowa League in the Corn Belt. He was eighteen years old, weighed 121 pounds and was a boy among men. (The Boston Nationals had just taken a "census" of their players and learned that the youngest was twenty-two and the average was twenty-eight.) In his first time at bat, he struck out with the bases full.

But the Orioles won that day, 6 to 5, with the country boy playing second base against the Columbus Senators. He even got a hit later in the game, scored a run, executed one sacrifice bunt properly and handled five ground balls without any catastrophe. Maybe it wasn't the National League, the really big league, but it was a *big* league and Mob Town, was his home for the next eleven years.

He batted only .245 that summer in the thickening competition. But, that winter, while Al Lawson was back in Havana telling the Cubans that *el mono amarillo* was a professional in the North, McGraw arrived in the magic National League when it absorbed the Baltimore team as the American Association collapsed.

Nobody knew it at the time, but Baltimore was about to climb out of the Middle Ages of its baseball history into a full-blown Renaissance. One reason was the teen-aged infielder McGraw. Another was Ned Hanlon, who arrived the following spring from the Pittsburgh club and succeeded Barnie as manager. Another was Hughey Jennings, a shortstop from Louisville who became a lawyer, a lifelong friend of McGraw and a player and manager of distinction himself.

Baltimore badly needed a baseball renaissance, too. Despite its public passion for such things, it never had won a championship, although cities like Chicago and Boston already had won half a dozen in seventeen years. Even in 1892, when the National League split its season and conducted two pennant races, the Orioles won neither. And when the league held a popularity contest to arouse some excitement, the winners were Buck Ewing, Ed Williamson, Mike Kelly and Cap Anson—none of whom played for the Orioles.

But all the public indexes, as the politicians say, were pointing toward Baltimore. For one thing, Hanlon was a decisive, imaginative sort and he promptly surrounded himself with an extraordinary troupe of ball players. For another thing, baseball was first in the hearts of his countrymen and the Orioles faced no competition or distraction for the public attention once Hanlon's troupe started to operate.

The chief reason was that people had neither the time nor the money for other sports, and usually did not have the weather for other sports once baseball pre-empted the summertime scene. Golf, boating and horse racing were beyond the mass reach of the public. Basketball was not introduced until 1892, and then was considered a stopgap between the football and baseball seasons, and a "sissy sport," at that. Football was still pretty much of a college man's grind and it seemed more like a military exercise of charging the Maginot Line.*

Baseball seemed to have just the right mixture of violence and finesse for mass appeal, and it started to create hero legends for country boys like John McGraw and city boys like H. L. Mencken.

It also wasted no time enshrining pioneers like A. J. Reach, who reportedly became the first professional player in 1864 when he took money to defect from the Brooklyn Atlantics to the Philadelphia Athletics and who later be-

---

*Actually, football grew parallel to baseball, but about two generations later. Columbia University organized a team in 1870, Yale in 1872 (beating Columbia, 3 to 0), Harvard in 1874 and Cornell a year later. It was still an experiment, and a primitive one, at that. Harvard played McGill in 1875, one half under soccer rules and one half under rugby rules. The confusion resulted in a 0-to-0 tie, with nobody scoring under *either* set of rules.

In 1876, the year the National League came to baseball, something called the American Intercollegiate Football Association came to football. It consisted of Yale, Harvard, Columbia, Princeton and Rutgers, and later added Pennsylvania. But in 1894, the year the Orioles started to panic the National League, the football league was wrecked by the withdrawal of Harvard and Penn. A touchdown and field goal each were worth five points then, probably accounting for the rise of drop-kicking and reflecting the fact that scoring a touchdown could be a grueling, brutish, losing proposition.

came an equipment maker whose name was inscribed on all baseballs used in the American League. Or like Eddie Cuthbert of the Philadelphia Keystones, who was observed "stealing" a base in 1865 and even sliding to get there—both pioneering efforts, according to the lore. Or like Dickey Pearce of the Brooklyn Atlantics, who in 1866 laid down a bunt "deliberately."

Then, three years later, the Cincinnati Red Stockings came along, a whole team of pioneers as the first admittedly professional club. They had just switched to knickers and were laughed at, but then they went on tour and won 55 games without losing while paying their players as much as $1,400—and now nobody laughed at them.

In 1870, the curveball came along—or, at least was confirmed—and even science was getting into the act. Henry Chadwick, on August 16, 1870, reported as follows in *The Brooklyn Eagle*:

"Yesterday, at the Capitoline Grounds, a large crowd assembled and cheered lustily as a youth from New Haven, Connecticut, Fred Goldsmith, demonstrated to the satisfaction of all that a baseball could be so manipulated and controlled by throwing it from one given point to another, as to make a pronounced arc in space."

To clinch his point, Goldsmith drove a pair of eight-foot poles into the ground—one halfway from the pitcher's mound to home plate, the other just to the right of the plate. Six times he pitched a ball outside the first pole, and bent it around toward the second one, "and that which up to this point seemed an optical illusion and against all rules of physics was now an established fact."

Six years later, all the pioneers and their "trick" pitches had a home, the National League. It was formed with eight cities in this order of admission: Chicago, Boston, New York, Philadelphia, Hartford, St. Louis, Cincinnati and Louisville. Its constitution was drawn by a judge from St. Louis, Orrick C. Bishop. The cost of a franchise was $100—a raging bargain compared with the price of $10 million that was to be paid by Montreal and San Diego ninety-two years later.

Memorable dates followed like the tide.

In 1878, as far as anyone can establish, turnstiles were introduced, although three years later only twelve persons went through them to see Chicago play Troy in a driving rain on the last day of the season.

In 1882, a real milestone: Umpires were told to stop soliciting the views of players and spectators, and to make up their own minds.

In 1888, DeWolfe Hopper recited "Casey At The Bat" for the first time on the stage. And, in a second move that spread the game before the public. A. G. Spalding took two teams on a tour of Hawaii, Australia, Ceylon, Egypt, Italy, France, England and Ireland.

Even the colleges were joining the fun, and their baseball teams were doing considerably more scoring than their football teams. As early as 1859, Williams had played Amherst at Pittsfield, Massachusetts, and Amherst won, 66 to 32. That was exactly ten years before Princeton and Rutgers played the first football game, with Rutgers winning, 6 to 4.

Still, people were insisting that baseball could use more punch. The pitching distance was moved steadily back—from 45 feet to 50 feet in 1881 and finally to 60½ feet in 1892, just after McGraw became a Baltimore Oriole. (At that, the precise distance was set by accident. It was supposed to be 60'0" but a surveyor with weak eyes misread the blueprint for 60'6" and that was that.) And whereas a pitcher in 1879 could throw eight balls off the plate before being charged with a walk on the ninth, by 1889 he was in trouble with his third stray pitch and the batter was on base with his fourth.

So that was the state of the art in 1892, when Ned Hanlon took over the Baltimore Orioles as a $4,000-a-year player and manager, and began to make ripples.

The first ripple that Hanlon made was in the direction of the front office. He bought stock from Von Der Horst and became president of the Orioles as well as manager. Von Der Horst finally was relieved of the great burdens he had complained about constantly. But, as happens with chronic complainers, he seemed to miss them once they became Hanlon's burdens. No longer the father-confessor to the club and to a widening circle of the city's sporting life, the old beer baron took to wearing a huge button on his coat at the ball park. It read, morosely: "Ask Hanlon."

People who asked Hanlon anything were likely to get a snappy reply. He became the absolute boss of the Orioles, and immediately impressed his youngest employee, McGraw, with his iron will. In fact, when he tried to farm McGraw out to Mobile for some experience, McGraw impressed him with *his* iron will. He just refused to go, and Hanlon finally relented and kept him as a utility infielder.

McGraw, to keep his end of the bargain, stayed on the move and tried to outwit his elders when he couldn't outhit them. He even enrolled at Allegany College after the 1892 season and became a kind of visiting professor of baseball tactics. The school was situated back in his home country between Olean and Allegany, New York, and later became St. Bonaventure. By the time spring training rolled around, the students had had a winter of baseball practice in the cellar of the biggest hall on campus, the Franciscans had a baseball program in full swing, and McGraw had four months of thinking, exercising and executing in the one activity that towered over all the others in his nineteen-year-old mind.

It paid off for him, too. The Orioles in 1893 ran eighth in the 12-team league, but McGraw turned a corner of sorts as an individual. He played in 127 games, got to bat 475 times, made 156 hits, scored 123 runs, hit .328 and led the club with 40 stolen bases. The kid who had appalled Bill Barnie had matured into a young professional who pleased Hanlon and the unusual bunch of ball players he was gathering around him in Union Park.

"McGraw," commented the Baltimore *Sun,* "is one of the youngest and most promising youngsters in the business, and undoubtedly has a brilliant baseball future. He is as lively as a cricket."

Thus anointed, the cricket tucked himself away at Allegany College again after the season, and this time he was joined by Jennings. Between them, they represented the left side of the Baltimore infield—Jennings at shortstop and McGraw now at third base. And they spent the winter instructing the college boys on "Oriole baseball."

★   ★   ★

Oriole baseball, as it flourished in 1894, was a combination of hostility, imagination, speed and piracy.

It also embraced one of the great, roistering, hellbent gangs of men who ever played baseball on the same field at the same time with the same purpose.

"The main idea," McGraw said, "is to win."

In pursuit of this simple, clearcut goal, Hanlon's troupe never hesitated to arrive for batting practice at 8 o'clock in the morning. It made for a long day, since the games normally didn't start until late afternoon—not until 4:30 in Washington, for example, in order to "get the crowd" from the Federal departments as they left work. But the Orioles spent the long pre-game hours in perfecting their skills, strategies, tricks and outright crimes.

The team had finished last in 1892 and eighth in 1893, but now was about to begin a spectacular rise to the top. They were young, they were tough, they became skilled to an exceptional degree. But mostly they were driven—by the crusty will of Hanlon and the strategic curiosity of McGraw and Jennings. And when William Henry Keeler joined the club from Brooklyn during spring training in Macon that March of 1894, they also were reinforced by one of the best, beady-eyed, left-handed hitters in the National League.

Dan Brouthers, the first-baseman, and Heinie Reitz, the second-baseman, also were heisted from other clubs, so the entire infield was new. In fact, the infield they played *on* was new, too. At McGraw's urging, the mustachioed groundskeeper, Tom Murphy, built up the third-base foul line so that bunts would roll down-slope and curl fair.

Then Murphy manicured the path from home plate to first base so that it tilted slightly away, giving the Oriole sprinters a downhill start. The outfield grass, on the other hand, was kept nice and high—something like a rye field. It was also suspected that the Orioles kept an extra ball or two hidden in the grass for emergencies. Once, Arthur Daley later reported in *The New York Times,* Joe Kelley made a perfect throw from left field to McGraw to retire a runner at third base, only to see Steve Brodie chase the batted ball to the centerfield fence and, to the Orioles' embarrassment, fire it back to the infield.

But their real trademark was something called "inside baseball." They became fanatics for techniques like the hit-and-run play. The base-runner started running with the pitch and the batter swung at the pitch automatically, trying to punch it through the infield—ideally through the spot vacated by an infielder who had moved over to cover the base against the runner.

The bunt, the stolen base, the Baltimore chop, the cut-off throw from the outfield; like burglar's tools, all these devices were developed, invented or emphasized as major ingredients of the Orioles' brand of inside baseball.

They rehearsed their slippery tactics, too, like the Lavender Hill Mob. During the long practices, they would clock base-runners in both directions— diving back into first base or roaring into second. During the long winters, McGraw would station Jennings up against the batting screen at St. Bonaventure so he couldn't back away from the plate, then would pitch him fastballs by the hour. Jennings, who had been a shy man at bat, grew conditioned to stepping in the only direction open, namely into the ball.

McGraw always stood on the inside corner of third base as a runner approached, forcing him to swing wide around McGraw rather than pivot on the bag itself. Sometimes,, when a runner tagged up at third base so that he could score after a fly ball, McGraw would hook him by the belt. During one stretch, they worked the hit-and-run play successfully thirteen straight times and John Montgomery Ward, the manager of the New York Giants, said:

"That isn't baseball the Orioles are playing. It's an entirely new game."

Another time, though, Ward got so exasperated with their tricks that he threatened to bring Hanlon before the league office on charges of chicanery on the diamond. But Hanlon was only the front man of the conspiracy.

"Jennings, Kelley, Keeler, Wilbert Robinson and myself organized ourselves into sort of committee," McGraw recalled. "We were scheming all the time for a new stunt to pull. We talked, lived and dreamed baseball. We met every night and talked over our successes and failures. If it was a trip to the theater, all of us went and sat together. Every year later on we had a reunion. The players even looked after each other for years afterward. It was like an old college football team."

They were as physical as a college football team, too. McGraw remembered going ten weeks without a rubdown in those unpampered early times. Keeler once saved a game in Washington by chasing a long drive to the outfield fence, plunging his hand through a barbed wire on top of it and making the catch—though his arm was ripped to the elbow. Joe Corbett once missed spring training because he was the sparring partner of his big brother, Gentleman Jim the heavyweight champion, and Jim even suggested that Joe give up baseball because it was growing too rough.

When the 1894 season finally opened, it looked as though all of Mob Town had turned out to see the rollicking brand of "Oriole baseball" in its debut against the New York Giants. It was April 19, and 15,000 fans had jammed the park and strained against the ropes that had been strung around the perimeter of the outfield to hold back the standing overflow.

The Giants, who had trained at Charleston, arrived with reinforcements, too. They were escorted by hundreds of fans from New York and by a dozen newspaper writers, as though the Army of the Potomac was besieging Baltimore. These were the Giants of Amos Rusie and Jouett Meekin, rated sure pennant-winners. But, said McGraw with maddening self-assurance, "Keeler and I stood them on their heads right off by pulling the hit-and-run play."

They stood the Giants on their heads for four straight days, in fact, and also stood Mob Town on its head by sweeping the series. And McGraw, who was absorbing a massive education in the arts and sciences of winning baseball games, learned a lesson from the performance that he harped on for the rest of his career: be off and running, because games in April count exactly as much in the standings as games in September.

After the Giants had left town, the Orioles made it five in a row by knocking off Boston, which had won three straight pennants. And now they had swept the two best teams in the National League.

Outside of Dan Brouthers, who was thirty-six years old, they were a young bunch and they cut dashing figures with their pell-mell style and great handle-bar mustaches (eight on the club). They could hit, too. This was the Orioles' batting order in 1894 and this is what it did:

	Position	Age	Average
John McGraw	3b	21	.340
Willie Keeler	rf	22	.368
Joe Kelley	lf	22	.391
Dan Brouthers	1b	36	.345
Hughey Jennings	ss	25	.332
Steve Brodie	cf	26	.369
Heinie Reitz	2b	26	.306
Wilbert Robinson	c	30	.348

When they got on base, they were no slouches, either. Jennings stole 36 bases that season, McGraw 77, Kelley 45 and Brodie 50. At no time during their heyday did the team steal fewer than 350 in one season.

With all these things going for them, the Orioles marauded through the league all summer and then ended the season as riotously as they had started it. They won 18 straight games in September, lost one, then won 6 more in a row—giving them 24 out of 25 and the National League pennant.

"We would've won all 25," McGraw commented, not completely satisfied, "if Robbie hadn't slipped in the mud chasing a foul fly. The big lummox."

Still, when they returned home from the West with the pennant, they were greeted at the Camden Street Station by a roaring celebration. It was only three years since McGraw had stepped off the train from Iowa and had made his solitary way to Barnie's office. This time, he had plenty of company, including the big lummox and the little hero, Wee Willie Keeler, a child-like figure standing only 5 feet 4½ inches who already was renowned for his ability to "hit 'em where they ain't."

A dozen carriages rolled up to the platform to whisk the Orioles through the streets of a town gone wild. National Guardsmen, armed with bayonets, were called, along with the entire police force, to restrain the crowds surging around a ten-mile-long parade with 200 floats that took two hours to wind through downtown Baltimore. And finally, in full evening dress, the Orioles were lionized at a bubbling civic banquet.

McGraw, who was twenty-one years old and already as imperious as Napoleon, was shocked rather than dazzled. He considered the season only beginning, since the two top teams in the league were scheduled to compete in a post-season series for the Temple Cup, which had just been donated by the president of the Pittsburgh club, William C. Temple. Besides, the No. 2 team was the New York Giants.

"It is a disgrace to baseball," he said in his most sanctimonious style. "I have kept myself in trim for these games, notwithstanding the temptations that have beset me every hour since our return to Baltimore. The team is not in fit condition to play, and we should forfeit the Temple Cup to New York."

He had a point, as the Giants immediately proved by sweeping all four games behind the relentless pitching of Rusie and Meekin. They simply alternated the two, winning 4 to 1 and 9 to 6 in Baltimore and then 4 to 1 and 16 to 3 at the Polo Grounds in New York. The townspeople of Baltimore, though, were as forgiving in defeat as they had been jubilant in victory. They realized that baseball contracts ran from April 1 to September 30 and that the players had been paid thinly for the Temple Cup series. So they staged benefits at Ford's Opera House and the Music Hall to raise the players' post-season ante and to reward "Oriole baseball" at the source.

The three years that followed were just as turbulent, noisy and successful. In 1895, the Orioles won the pennant again, but again were foiled in the Temple Cup series—this time by Cleveland and the great righthander, Denton True (Cy) Young. In 1896, they won the pennant for the third straight year and this time satisfied even McGraw by overpowering Cleveland for the Temple Cup. And in 1897, they not only survived a rock-throwing, punch-throwing summer's work but also took the cup, this time from the Boston club, which had beaten them out for the pennant.

McGraw by now was being recognized as the field leader of the Orioles in the way that Hanlon was recognized as the bench leader. He had arrived as a child and had grown up during those four seasons of solid, bullying success. Even his nickname reflected violence: Muggsy. It attributed to him the noble characteristics of a pure mug, and he hated it. His rivals used it to taunt him and his fans used it to glorify him, and he resented both groups on both counts.*

---

*Years later, McGraw offered the following explanation for the nickname "Muggsy" and for his explosive distaste for it: "When I first went to Baltimore, there was a roughneck ward politician in the town named McGraw, who was called Muggsy. In some way it was rumored that I was his son, and one of the newspapermen called me Young Muggsy McGraw. And the name caught on. Soon the 'Young' was dropped and I was just Muggsy in the papers. I paid no attention to this, not knowing who Muggsy McGraw was. As soon as I found out, I asked the newspapermen not to call me that anymore, and they stopped. But some of the fans in the other towns who didn't like me had picked up the name and, knowing I didn't like it, took delight in yelling it at me every time I appeared on the field. Since then every bastard who doesn't like me has called me that."

This recollection, while colorful as a piece of personal history, somewhat glossed over the violent connotation of "Muggsy"—a connotation not lost on McGraw's contemporaries. Connie Mack used to recall the "horror" of advancing as far as third base in a game and confronting McGraw, who stood there "guarding" the bag.

As long as the Orioles kept winning, though, McGraw could carry a chip on his shoulder like a badge of honor. He was making $2,100 a year now, as he turned twenty-two, and he was earning it with a busy bat as well as a provocative personality.

After hitting .340 in 1894, he went to .374 the following season, then to .356 and then to .326. Joe Kelley had a four-year stretch of .391, then .370 two years in a row and finally .389. Keeler kept hitting 'em where they weren't, going in a spectacular climb from .369 to .365 to .394 and then all the way to .432.

The first lull in McGraw's activity crept in during the season of 1895, after he had stolen 69 bases and the club had led Cleveland down the home stretch. He was benched by a siege of influenza late in the season, then later got the word that his "flu" really had been malaria. Then, as the spring of 1896 came and the Orioles went into training at Macon, he lapsed into typhoid fever and didn't play until August 25.

At that, he got into the lineup for 18 games and stole 13 bases as the Orioles won the pennant by ten games over Cleveland, taking 20 of their last 26. This was the year that the Orioles finally turned the trick and won a Temple Cup series, though the public taste for the playoff was dulled a bit by two things: The Cleveland club got involved in a railroad crash en route and arrived in Baltimore four days late. And the crowds were growing somewhat bored by the fact that the two teams had been rivals all season long anyway, a fact that really represented a built-in weakness for the playoff idea.

Each Baltimore player was paid $200 for winning the series that year and each Cleveland player was paid $117 for losing it.

When the season finally ended, McGraw took a good long look at himself and made two decisions. First, he skipped the customary winter's trip to St. Bonaventure so that he could get back his strength. Then he decided to branch out professionally and, with Wilbert Robinson as his partner, opened the Diamond Cafe. It was a three-story restaurant, saloon and hitching post on North Howard Street across from the Academy of Music, and he installed pool tables, bowling alleys, a reading room and lithograph posters of athletes, including American stars of the first modern Olympiad, which had been held in Greece the summer before.

Then he made an even more important decision. He married Minnie Doyle, the daughter of a newspaper printer, Michael Doyle, and was a family man as well as a business man by the time the season of 1897 began.

It was a fateful season, too, because it was the fourth and final one in the Orioles' monumental days of dominating the scene. It even started a little ominously when Joe Corbett's brother lost his heavyweight title to Bob Fitzsimmons in the fourteenth round at Carson City, Nevada, on St. Patrick's Day. Then the bell rang for the baseball season, and the Orioles came out punching.

They had one particularly memorable afternoon on August 7 in Boston. The umpire, Tom Lynch, was jockeyed to distraction by John "Dirty" Doyle, the Baltimore first-baseman, until Lynch finally threw him out of the game. So Doyle insulted him, whereupon Umpire Lynch responded with a right to the head. Joe Corbett and Joe Kelley cheerfully got into the melee at that point, and immediately were joined by howling hordes of Boston fans. The police had to break it up, but all the way back to the hotel afterwards the Orioles had to fight a desperate rearguard action against snipers who pelted their convoy of carriages with rocks from the sidewalks and houses.

The Orioles could hit pitchers as well as umpires. In one game that season, Keeler and Doyle each got six hits. Keeler finished the year with 243 hits (199 of them singles), and he did it in 128 games. During one stretch, he hit safely in 44 straight games, and it took nearly 45 years before a young San Franciscan named Joe DiMaggio broke the record by hitting in 56.

Five Orioles stole a total of 321 bases that year, with McGraw cashing in 42. Five hit more than .350. Five scored a total of 500 runs among them. They kept up the hitting right through the Temple Cup series, too, scoring 54 runs in five games and overwhelming Boston, four games to one.

But the public's disenchantment with an intramural series took a serious turn. The rivals were over-exposing their rivalry. They even played exhibition games at places like Worcester and Springfield on the idle days of the Cup series. And by the time they wound it up in Baltimore, only 1,600 persons paid to see each of the last two games.

Rough-house had become such a way of life to the Orioles, though, that Jack Doyle and Joe Corbett even got into a fight with each other. It was so rough that the Orioles traded Doyle to Washington and Jim Corbett prevailed upon his brother to quit baseball.

McGraw and Robinson, meanwhile, did the opposite. At least, they were still twenty years from their knockdown fight. They bought adjoining houses on St. Paul Street, three blocks from the ball park, and settled down to the good life as demigods of Baltimore.

Then came the turning point, and it came from events outside the game as well as from the growing indifference within.

For the second year in a row, in 1898, the Orioles ran second to Boston, with whom they had pretty well monopolized the league during the nineties. But the ball-park crowds had begun to fade, and war was brewing between Spain and the United States. On February 15, the day the battleship *Maine* exploded in Havana harbor, McGraw and Robinson were teaching "Oriole baseball" in the gymnasium at Johns Hopkins. Other members of the team, oddly enough, had followed their rough-and-tumble leader and were busy in similarly peaceful jobs at similarly peaceful campuses. Jennings was tutoring at the University of Georgia, Joe Kelley at Georgetown and Bill Clarke at Princeton.

They all were back in baseball uniforms by the time the season started, but a few days later, on April 24, war was declared. Then the ball-park crowds really disappeared, and a runaway race by both Boston and Baltimore did nothing to bring them back. The Orioles one afternoon in Cleveland played before 75 cash customers.

The Louisville club was the first to fold, though it was quickly bought by Barney Dreyfuss, later the impresario at Pittsburgh and the nemesis of Casey Stengel. Then Chris Van Der Ahe, who had built the St. Louis club from his saloon days, was pursued and jailed by his creditors and his ball park was sold from the courthouse steps. In Brooklyn, Charles H. Byrne died late in 1897 and Charles Ebbets—a onetime office boy, ticket-taker and schedule-maker—was elected president.

In New York, the Giants had been spiraling into this pit of poverty for several reasons. Their original owner, John B. Day, had been beset by a variety of money problems, not the least of which was the pressure of a professional team that played its games on Manhattan Field, next door to the Polo Grounds. Thrashing around for help, Day exchanged stock with Albert Spalding of the Chicago club and John T. Brush of the Cincinnati club, which in turn "sold" him the Indianapolis club. Even Arthur H. Soden of the Boston club held shares in New York, and Giants' stock was scattered all over the landscape. The Giants, in effect, were a National League co-op.

More than that, though, they were the victims—or the beneficiaries, depending on your viewpoint—of "syndicate baseball." And syndicate baseball became the great issue of the day in professional sports. Before it was settled the pattern of baseball had been revolutionized and McGraw had left his little empire in Baltimore.

The trigger was pulled by Von Der Horst in Baltimore. In the winter of 1898-99, as the war strained the economy of professional sports along with the economy in general, he bought an interest in the Brooklyn club. His aim was to move Hanlon there with most of his best players, reaping the benefits of Brooklyn's growing population, and to operate the becalmed Orioles as a kind of farm team.

Hanlon duly switched over to Brooklyn, and took with him the heart of the great Oriole teams—Keeler, Kelley, Jennings and three pitchers who had been 20-game winners. They set up shop in Brooklyn's new Washington Park and had everything—except McGraw and Robinson.

The two partners simply refused to switch. They were stubbornly, unyieldingly Orioles. And besides, they owned the Diamond Cafe and were in no position to move *that*. They put up such a fight that they prevailed and McGraw, who then was twenty-five years old, won his revolt. Von Der Horst agreed to let him stay. He would be manager of the Orioles and he would have Robinson as his deputy.

He also sent McGraw four hitters from Brooklyn, none of whom had batted more than .298 the season before, and three pitchers who had won a total of 13 games. McGraw realized he had got the short end of the exchange of talent but he didn't rock the boat further. "The main reason for the deal," he said, "was to make Brooklyn the dominating power in New York baseball, and we sure did."

He still had a couple of tricks up his sleeve, though, and he played them cleverly. He executed a three-club finesse to pry his old pal Jennings back to Baltimore, and he successfully concealed a new pitcher from the Indian Territory, Joseph Jerome McGinnity, a blond giant who, as Iron Joe, became one of McGraw's gold nuggets.

McGraw's only problem, outside of living with the war and the ravages of syndicate baseball, was living with something called the Brush Resolution. It was drawn by the western clubs through the well-intentioned John Brush, and its purpose was to make baseball more salable by making it more orderly, a dubious proposition. It also called for no swearing, no drinking and no Sunday baseball.

McGraw collided with the resolution almost as soon as the season began. On April 29 he was fined $5 after the entire Baltimore club had swarmed onto the field at the Polo Grounds. McGraw was on base at the time and Jimmy Sheckard hit a home run in the ninth inning to beat the Giants—only to have the umpire call it a foul ball. Later in the season Sheckard was called out while stealing second base against Brooklyn, and attacked the umpire. And in all, 700 batters were hit by pitches that season. It was a trying year for the Brush Resolution.

The Orioles, driven by a belligerent manager who still played a rough third base, refused to take the back seat that had been plotted for them in the restructured league. In fact, they briefly became the rage of baseball again while their "varsity" team at Brooklyn faded. McGraw once reached base safely nine straight times in a doubleheader on five hits and four walks, and he stole four bases besides. McGinnity won 20 games. The Orioles became the best road show in baseball. Von Der Horst, as though he had planned it all that way, beamed toward McGraw and said: "I wouldn't take ten thousand dollars for his contract."

By 1899, though, the league was wallowing in absolute confusion. The Louisville park burned. The Cleveland club disintegrated and won only 20 of 154 games after the players had been arbitrarily switched to St. Louis. Dreyfuss already was negotiating to buy the Pittsburgh franchise. Brooklyn was struggling to get the upper hand promised for it by the syndicators.

In the midst of all this, McGraw kept skyrocketing along and made himself the most talked-about man in the league. He hit .390 and stole 73 bases, and the Orioles drew 123,416 admissions—more than Brooklyn.

Then, a shattering sadness. On August 30, Minnie McGraw died of an inflamed appendix. While trying to recover from that shock, he received another. The National League, facing a new threat from the Western League, had decided to pull in its horns and drop four clubs, and one of them was Baltimore.

The Western League was a minor league, but it had a major-league mind behind it—Byron Bancroft Johnson. He had been a sportswriter on *The Cincinnati Commercial Gazette* and was a longtime critic of the Cincinnati owner, John Brush, who thereupon suggested sarcastically that Johnson take over the Western League and straighten it out. Which is precisely what Johnson did in

1894 at the age of twenty-eight. Later in the decade, he began to aim higher. He picked up the pieces of several National League fiascos, annexed the Cleveland territory to his league, moved his St. Paul Club to Chicago with Charles A. Comiskey in control, got Connie Mack to run the Milwaukee club and—as the *pièce de résistance*—wanted John McGraw to direct Baltimore as a new entry in his new league, the American League.

McGraw in fact was having the rug pulled out from under him at Baltimore, when the franchise was dropped by the National League at the end of 1899. He and Robinson were being told that they had been sold to St. Louis. But again they revolted. Even when he was offered the manager's job at St. Louis, McGraw refused to go and stayed north while the clubs went south for spring training in 1900.

A month after the season began, he received another call from St. Louis and this time he was willing at least to go through the motions. His terms were $100 a game and no reserve clause—that is, his services were not to be reserved to St. Louis after that season. He wanted to be a free agent, and he was three-quarters of a century ahead of his time in challenging the binding tie of a professional contract.

So McGraw and Robinson went along to St. Louis and they fooled away the summer there, not playing particularly well, and getting thrown out of enough games to make the racetrack across the street a worthwhile neighbor.

Their manager at St. Louis was Pat Tebeau, who had been with the Cleveland team in McGraw's fateful game at Gainesville ten years earlier. The club finished fifth and McGraw, despite his indifference, hit .337 with 28 stolen bases. Rumors even arose that he would replace Tebeau as manager. But when the season ended, he and Robinson hurried back to Baltimore.

Besides, in June of that year, McGraw had been invited to a blueprint meeting convened by Ban Johnson in Chicago. He was impressed by Johnson's approach, namely: "The National League is being administered to death. The American League is the only thing that can keep baseball alive."

The National League also was busy convening meetings, and McGraw was invited to these, too. In fact, he was summoned to sessions in New York and Philadelphia by the owners, was chided for having left St. Louis and was assured that he had a bright future—even though Baltimore no longer had a ball club. At least, it had none in the National League. But when Johnson announced his new American League in 1901, Baltimore had a club in the new league—and its chief stockholder and manager was the old Oriole, J. J. McGraw.

"A real baseball war was on," McGraw recalled. "We immediately started a raid on the National League and I managed to get most of the players that I had wanted of my former Baltimore club."

He got Joe McGinnity in particular, plus Mike Donlin from St. Louis and Jimmy Williams from Pittsburgh. In fact, when the American League took the field in 1901, about 85 percent of its players were refugees from the National League.

The new league opened on April 24, with ceremonies in Chicago and with clubs also in Milwaukee, Cleveland, Detroit, Washington, Boston, Baltimore and Philadelphia. The inaugural fiesta was rained out for two days in Baltimore, but it finally was started after Ban Johnson had thrown out the first ball before 10,371 customers. The Orioles beat the Boston Red Sox, 10 to 6, and the war was on.

But McGraw's honeymoon with Ban Johnson was short and turbulent. Johnson ruled with an iron fist, which made it certain that he would soon collide with McGraw. Then his first memorandum made it doubly certain. It said: "Clean ball is my main plank. I will suspend any manager or player who uses profane language to an umpire."

The acute issue between them, though, arose over one economic fact of life in the war between the leagues: The American League needed a team in New York. The expectation was that it would establish one, with McGraw in command. But as the league's first summer passed, the gulf between him and Johnson widened—and then he began to get new overtures from the National League.

As early as June, McGraw had been sounded out about his possible return "under ideal conditions," and to make the possibility even more alluring, he had been sounded out by the owners of the New York Giants. By August, though, he was still playing third base for Baltimore and batting .352, with the Orioles placed third behind Chicago and Boston. Then he pulled the tendons in his right knee and returned from the West with his leg in a cast while the Orioles faded to fifth place.

Both leagues now were losing money in the war, and Johnson was in no mood for palace intrigue. He immediately issued a statement accusing McGraw of "crimes" like dickering with his enemies and said in melodramatic tones: "We want no Benedict Arnold in our midst." McGraw replied, mixing historical plausibility with bitterness, "So the Julius Caesar of the league calls me a Benedict Arnold, does he?"

McGraw was engaged that fall to marry Blanche Sindall, the daughter of a contractor, James W. Sindall of Baltimore, who remembered him as "a young man of indestructible confidence." They were married the following January 8 in St. Ann's Church, while great crowds surged around the streets hoping to catch glimpses of famous guests like Keeler, Brodie, Robinson, Jennings and Joe Kelley.

It was one of the last public reunions of the old Baltimore Orioles. Before the next baseball season was half over, McGraw completed his complex negotiations with the owners of the Giants, left the scene of his greatest battles, deserted the new American League, jumped back into the old National League and fired this parting salvo at Byron Bancroft Johnson: "He picked on me—and I couldn't stand his umpires."

Chapter

The Polo
Grounds Gang

When John McGraw left the Baltimore Orioles in July of 1902 to become manager of the New York Giants, his first impression on arriving in Manhattan was that the baseball situation was desperate. He was right.

"The club at that time," he noted, "was in last place by 14 games—a good, safe margin. The attendance was almost nothing. And when I first walked onto the field to see my team, I found Christy Mathewson playing first base."

He had decamped from Baltimore because he sensed that "someone would be left holding the bag" there and he wanted to make sure it wasn't McGraw. He was twenty-nine years old then, already famous, with twelve years behind him as a major league third-baseman, two and a half years as a manager, and a towering reputation as an unbending sort who did not beat around the bush.

McGraw was a square young man with a formidable appearance, and he did not consider subtlety the shortest distance between two points. He had black hair parted left of center in a fish-hook style over his forehead. He wore high starched collars, four-in-hand ties and a fleur-de-lis pin perched grandly in the center. He had his shirts and shoes made in Havana, and he had such short arms that he needed to have his suits tailored. In the winter, he would bury himself in a fur-collared greatcoat and beaver hat, and would look more immovable than ever.

His second wife, Blanche Sindall, remembered him as a mellow person deep down. The type who was fond of family singing bees in the parlor on Sunday evenings and who would raise his voice for "Silver Threads Among The Gold," or "Break The News To Mother," "Mama's Boy," and even "Blue

Bell." He enjoyed light musical comedies and vaudeville, evidently finding them a relief from the melodramas he battled through on the baseball field every afternoon.

The things that most people remembered about McGraw, though, were those steady blue eyes, that don't-tread-on-me toughness and the uncringing determination not to be left holding the bag.

Consequently, his first impulse upon finding the Giants at the bottom of the barrel was to take firm command to make certain at least that their problems would be cast in his own image, and not somebody else's. He signed a four-year contract that gave him "absolute control" of the players on the field and of any trades he might plot. Then he set about the job of getting them out of last place, of attracting people into the Polo Grounds to watch them, and of switching Mathewson off first base to the pitcher's mound, where McGraw surmised that he belonged.

He did all this like a strutting bantam, and was pictured by the intrigued New York papers as an arresting figure of 5 feet 6½ inches and perhaps 155 or so pounds. And, McGraw interjected, "They might have added that I didn't have a gray hair on my head."

It was not that McGraw was so unique in his strong-arm approach to challenges, nor that baseball players as a group intimidated a timorous public. They all operated well within the forthright style of the day in personal relations, a style that seemed to follow a national mood embodied by the new President himself, Theodore Roosevelt.

It was a kind of frontier style that had spilled over into the twentieth century. Indeed, even the brawling street gangs of Manhattan, who mobilized as many as fifteen hundred bare-fisted fighters for important occasions, were impressed by it. And whenever Bat Masterson would make the rounds of the West Side bars—a bald, middle-aged figure in a black derby hat, no longer the scourge of Dodge City as he had been a generation before—he instantly received silent homage, respect and attention as the real McCoy.

The frontier influence was so revered that the Fourth of July show in 1902 at Sheridan, Wyoming, featured a "lifelike reproduction of the slaughter of General Custer and his men." The slaughter had taken place twenty-six years before, but the replay still attracted a remarkable cast and heavy coverage by the press. In it, the "heroic Seventh Cavalry" was besieged by fifteen hundred Crows and Cheyennes in "hideous warpaint who swooped down upon the 200 men from Fort McKenzie and surrounded, cut down and annihilated them in the presence of thousands of spectators."

Even city folk still were firing from the hip. *The New York Times* reported "an increase of hostility toward automobiles." One farmer shot at a passing automobile because it was frightening his horses. In Manhattan, "automobilists" were trying to win an increase in the legal speed limit from the present 8 miles an hour to 12 or even 15, but citizens formed vigilante committees to forestall the threat. And in Winnetka, a suburb of Chicago, things were getting so bad that the Mayor stretched a rope across the street and began timing cars with a stop-watch.

A young country judge from Texas named John Nance Garner joined the House of Representatives for the first time that year and later recalled: "When I entered Congress the autocratic leaders of the Democratic party thought I was just another cow thief from Texas." In point of fact, Garner had spent much of his time fighting the railroads in Texas on behalf of his constituents, who were mostly farmers. And when he wasn't doing that, he was principally interested in baseball, pecan-growing and poker, a game at which he became so skilled that his winnings in some sessions of Congress exceeded his pay of $10,000 a year.

As a rookie in Congress, though, Garner found the frontier spirit already in full flower when he arrived. In particular, Texans were all over the place flexing their muscles. A page 1 story in *The Times* told of their adventures one day under a restrained headline that read: "Mr. Bailey Attacks Senator Beveridge." The report then began in remarkably colorful language:

WASHINGTON, June 30—"Do you retract?"

"No."

"Then, damn you, I'll make you," shouted Senator Bailey of Texas, bursting all at once into a tremendous rage. He and Senator Beveridge of Indiana had been sitting side by side. He sprang to his feet, towering over Mr. Beveridge, who is a much smaller man, and seized him by the throat. His two fists crushed into the Indiana man's neck, and Mr. Bailey seemed about to shake him like a rat.

Before Mr. Bailey could carry out his evident purpose of throwing Mr. Beveridge across the desk behind him, Senator Spooner and Doorkeeper Layton sprang to the rescue.

The report noted that this was actually the second fight "of its kind" in the current session. The first was between Senators Tillman and McLaurin, and "in that case both men did their share of the fighting." Tillman struck the first blow, but McLaurin inflicted the most damage. In the latest round, unfortunately, "Bailey did all the fighting." The argument, in case anyone cared what had set two Senators at each other's lapels, involved "the neglect of interests of American citizens in Mexico."

Even the stock market reflected the earthy state of affairs. One of the highest prices on the New York Stock Exchange was commanded by American Snuff at $123 a share. And, as a result of the Boer War, new words were creeping into the language with a campaign flavor, words like "trek" and "veldt" and "commando."

Such was the temper of the times when McGraw bolted the Baltimore baseball club that July and caused a sensation by defecting to the New York Giants of the National League. The times suited him fine, too. He aroused all the frontier passions in people—love, hate, fear, revenge, loyalty and suspicion.

The National League owners deluged him with cheers for a *coup d'etat* against Ban Johnson, the president of the American League. Johnson denounced him as a traitor. The fans in New York girded for better days. And the fans in Baltimore watched in some horror as their team spiraled down, especially when McGraw hurried back to Baltimore on a hit-and-run raid and kidnapped Roger Bresnahan, Jack Cronin, Joe McGinnity, Dan McGann and Steve Brodie, signing them to contracts that he wrote in longhand on his father-in-law's stationery.

The date was July 16, and it was an important one in determining the pattern of the games that Americans would be watching for the next half-century. It was a day that triggered a lot of changes in the "national pastime." It brought McGraw to New York, it breathed life into the Giants, it induced the American League to plant a team in Manhattan alongside the Giants, it knocked Baltimore out of the major leagues for fifty years and within six months it helped end the war between the two big leagues—or, at least it polarized their positions as rival but co-existing big leagues.

It was a war that was fought at the box office, in the courts and in the political clubhouses whose members controlled the warring baseball teams.

When Connie Mack signed college stars like Eddie Plank of Gettysburg and Christy Mathewson of Bucknell, he stole a march on the National League. But when Mathewson failed to report and jumped instead to the Giants in New York, the Nationals stole a march on Connie Mack.

A season later, in 1902, when Napoleon Lajoie switched to Mack's team in the American League, a Philadelphia court refused to grant an injunction blocking the switch. But the Supreme Court of Pennsylvania reversed the ruling and upheld the validity of the National League contracts in Philadelphia. As a result, the American League went to theatrical lengths to protect Lajoie and its other stolen goods. It assigned him to the Cleveland club, putting him outside the range of Pennsylvania's judicial edicts. Then, whenever Cleveland would play in Philadelphia, it would slip Lajoie past the process-servers, stow him aboard the Camden ferry and hide him out in Atlantic City until the club ended its series in Philadelphia.

The chaos between the feuding leagues was reflected in gyrating attendance figures. In 1901, when the American League fired its opening shots, it was outdrawn at the gate—1,920,031 for the established Nationals and 1,683,584 for the challenging Americans. In 1902, though, the Nationals slipped to 1,688,012 while Ban Johnson's boys sold 2,206,457 tickets.

The ultimate battleground, everybody agreed, had to be New York City, which had the biggest population but only one team of consequence, Brooklyn. The Giants, who played across the East River in Manhattan, were dormant. The American League had no team there at all. So it was natural that Johnson plotted an invasion of New York. He plotted it, though, without McGraw. He planned—or, at least, McGraw suspected that he planned—to transfer the Baltimore franchise into New York. And that's when McGraw decided, in 1902, that he and the other Oriole stockholders would be left in Baltimore holding the bag without a team or a league.

So on July 16, McGraw burned his bridges behind him in Baltimore,

turned over his half of the Diamond Cafe to Wilbert Robinson, raided his own
club of half a dozen Oriole players and bolted to Manhattan with a guarantee
of "absolute control" over the New York Giants.

★   ★   ★

Nobody was quite sure how the New York baseball team came to be
known as the Giants. One legend was that Jim Mutrie, the manager during the
eighteen-eighties, had become so emotional during a rally by the team that he
jumped off the bench exclaiming: "My big fellows. My *Giants*."

New York was the eighteenth team admitted to the National League. It
took the step in 1883, inheriting the vacancy and the roster of the franchise at
Troy, New York. From the start, the New York "Nationals" were big not only
physically but also politically. Their original owner, John B. Day, was an
active tiger of Tammany Hall, the Democratic organization of New York
County. Day's brother-in-law, Joseph Gordon, had owned the New York Metropolitans even before the Giants were organized.

For a while, the Giants were the nomads of New York baseball. They
played before packs of gentlemen who watched their games in striped trousers
and silk hats, and they played wherever space could be found: Sometimes at St.
George on Staten Island; sometimes in Jersey City, sometimes even in Brooklyn.

Most of the time, though, they played on James Gordon Bennett's polo
field at Fifth Avenue and 110th Street, while Bennett was busy downtown
running *The New York Herald.* "Forever after," recalled Meyer Berger in one
of his glimpses of New York's history, "the Giants' stadiums were called the
Polo Grounds."

From the beginning, the Giants showed their knack of capturing the
town's imagination. As early as May 2, 1883, right after they took the field just
north of Central Park for the first time, their activities were reported on page 2
of *The New York Times* under a headline that read: "A Fine Game At The Bat."
They got more space that day than the item about General George Crook's
cavalry chasing the Apaches down to the Mexican border and much more
than Harriet Beecher Stowe as she toured the South.

They played that afternoon before a remarkable crowd of 15,000 persons
—mostly men in tall hats—and, *The Times* recorded, "the largest number of
persons that ever assembled on a ball ground in this city." When the game
ended, the score was New York 7, Boston 5. Grafulla's Seventh Regiment Band
played "See The Conquering Hero Comes," and the players were carried from
the field on the fans' shoulders.

In 1889, the Giants had moved their festivities uptown to Coogan's Hollow, at Eighth Avenue between 155th and 157th Streets. The hollow was a
remnant of a farm granted by the British Crown in the seventeenth century to
John Lion Gardiner, whose family later settled Gardiners Island off Long Island.

Harriet Gardiner Lynch inherited the farm along the Harlem River from her mother, a great-granddaughter of one of the early Gardiners. It became the Coogan estate when she married James J. Coogan, a Bowery upholsterer with genteel tastes who became the city's first borough president in 1899 through his friendship with Richard Croker, the Chief Sachem of Tammany Hall.

For a time, Coogan staged open-air horse shows in the hollow beneath the bluff overlooking the estate. He even considered importing a troupe of English actors to New York to stage bits of Shakespeare there. He was discouraged from that venture, though, and meanwhile the stage was pre-empted for good by John Day's baseball team.

The Polo Grounds stadium that eventually rose there was described in real estate directories simply as a "four-story structure on City Plot 2106, Lot 100." It was 740 feet long and 519.8 feet wide, and later was valued at more than a million dollars. But the dimensions that made it an exciting, sudden-death kind of baseball field were the foul-line measurements from home plate to the grandstand: 257 feet to right field, 279 feet to left field. And so the Chinese, or semi-gratuitous, home run was born.

In 1895, the team was bought by Andrew Freedman, a real estate lawyer without much personality but with impeccable Tammany Hall connections. He had been the best man at the wedding of Croker, who had caught the roving eye of Boss Tweed way back in the sixties. Freedman and Croker also were instrumental in the election of the first mayor of a consolidated New York—Robert A. Van Wyck, another Tammany team-mate. Freedman even induced August Belmont, another lodge brother, to help finance the Inter-borough Rapid Transit subway line. Ultimately, Belmont and Freedman called the shots for the subway as it was built and pushed across the river into Brooklyn, and it was no accident later that the Fourth Avenue line in Brooklyn sped *past* the new Ebbets Field.

However, by 1902, Freedman's political drag was being overpowered by his peevish personality. He fought umpires, insulted other National League owners, fired managers arbitrarily and even barred critical newspaper writers from the Polo Grounds.

He removed Horace Fogel as manager, named his shortstop George Smith to the job, kept Fogel around as a kind of deputy to Smith and then noticed that there were not many fans around watching the show anyway. Finally, Ban Johnson was threatening to invade the town with an American League team on the Giants' doorstep.

Under these depressing circumstances, Freedman played a trump card. He offered his manager's job to McGraw, who had been fighting Johnson in Baltimore and who was fretting through the rumors that he was about to be left holding the American League bag in Baltimore.

Actually, the trump card was played for Freedman by somebody else, John T. Brush, the owner of the Cincinnati club. Brush had held stock in the Giants since the middle of the eighteen-nineties, when "syndicate baseball" meant interlocking control of teams by other teams. Now he was preparing to exert even stronger control over the famished Giants, and playing a high card for Freedman was the first step.

Brush called McGraw to Indianapolis, where he lived in a large comfortable house on eight acres of forest. It had been named Lombardy by James Whitcomb Riley, "the Hoosier poet," in a toast to Brush's wife, the former Elsie Lombard. The setting was pastoral, and secretive. McGraw was instructed to reach Indianapolis by a train that would arrive before dawn, then to walk quickly from the depot to a street corner a couple of blocks away. There, Mrs. Brush picked him up in a carriage and whisked him off to Lombardy.

"All this," recalled John B. Hempstead, the son of Brush's son-in-law, "so that neither the press nor the baseball world would discover the pending deal between them."

The pending deal was then settled between them in the dining room, and the contract was signed on the dining-room table. Brush's daughter Natalie, who was a child then, remembered the long driveway edged with a double row of iris, the walls covered with tapestry, the draperies of heavily brocaded rose satin and velvet, the inlaid mahogany of the Adam period, the conservatory beyond the door past the dining-room table where a bit of baseball history was being charted.

The pre-dawn huddle was not the only piece of mystery in McGraw's switch from Baltimore. Years later his wife insisted that McGraw and Ban Johnson had worked it all out in advance with the collusion of owners in several other cities. The aim, she said, was to develop a healthy competition in a torn business. The "bitterness" between McGraw and Johnson was the window-dressing.

Still, her version did not enlighten people on the bitterness between the contending leagues, the franchise-jumping, the talent-robbing. And, while the degree of "collusion" may be disputed, the result was clear: McGraw and the Giants and the National League were turning a corner.

So, on July 16, McGraw jumped from Baltimore, switched leagues and took over "absolute control" of the New York Giants.

*   *   *

The day McGraw came to town the Giants were in Cincinnati, losing their third straight game to the Reds. Ban Johnson was in Baltimore, insisting that he had been expecting "this emergency" and was "fully able to meet it." McGraw was in Manhattan, reading headlines that said: "Latest Baseball Deal. Freedman Practically Buys Baltimore American League Team. Players To Join New York."

The next morning, July 17, McGraw made his first appearance at the palace, so to speak, and *The Times* noted the occasion with this headline: "McGraw At Polo Grounds. Andrew Freedman Gives The New Manager Power To Further Strengthen The Local Team."

Back in Baltimore, meanwhile, things were not so heady. The Orioles didn't even have enough players for their game against St. Louis. So the St. Louis players "took their positions on the diamond and went through the formality of playing the game while none of the Baltimore players appeared in uniform on the grounds, forfeiting the game." The headline there said bleakly: "No Baseball In Baltimore."

Having delivered this haymaker to Johnson, McGraw wasted no time on protocol with Freedman. He took the list of twenty-three men on the New York roster, struck nine names from the list and told the startled owner: "You can begin by releasing these." Freedman pointed out that the players had cost him $14,000. But McGraw, showing who was boss his first day on the job, replied, "If you keep them, they'll cost you more. I've brought real ball players with me and I'll get some more."

McGraw was particularly outraged to find that Mathewson had been alternated at first base by Manager Fogel and later at shortstop by Fogel's successor, Manager Smith, at Fogel's behest. So he advised Freedman that they might as well unload Fogel, too, and make Mathewson what he obviously was—a pitcher. Consequently, he released Fogel, kept Smith for a while as a second-baseman and, since he had nobody else to play there, took over at shortstop himself.

The standing of the top teams in the National League that afternoon was as follows:

	Won	Lost	Games Behind
Pittsburgh	54	15	—
Boston	37	31	16½
Brooklyn	41	35	16½

At the other end of the pecking order was New York: 22 victories, 50 defeats, 33½ games behind and incontestably last. "Of course," McGraw said, with a kind of patronizing concession to the facts, "the pennant is out of our reach as far as this year's playing season goes. But look out for us next year."

However, the arrival of the sharpshooters from Baltimore caused considerable excitement in New York right then and there, and an unusually large crowd was on hand at the Polo Grounds on July 19 when the famous old Orioles put on Giant uniforms for the first time and took the field.

"According to officials," reported *The Times,* "16,000 persons passed through the turnstiles" that Saturday afternoon. According to *The New York Evening World,* "John McGraw and his Baltimore recruits made their local debut before nearly 10,000 people." Whatever the true count, the customers were curious and a feeling of revival was taking hold. Nobody seemed too perturbed that the home team lost the game to Philadelphia, 4 to 3. In fact, a strange new note of patriotism crept into accounts of the occasion.

"New York's baseball team," *The Times* said, "played its first game at the Polo Grounds yesterday under the new management of John McGraw. The

Philadelphia nine were the opposing players. With the new management and the infusion of new blood the New Yorks played much better ball than they had been doing. They did not win, but the home players lost the game by only one run and *put up a good article of the game."*

Philadelphia	r	1b	po	a	e	New York	r	1b	po	a	e
Thomas, cf	1	0	1	0	0	Jones, lf	1	0	1	0	0
Barry, rf	0	0	1	0	0	McGraw, ss	1	1	1	2	0
Hulswith, ss	1	0	2	2	0	McGann, 1b	0	0	11	0	0
Dooin, c	1	1	4	1	0	Brodie, cf	0	2	2	0	0
Jennings, 1b	0	2	14	0	0	Lauder, 3b	0	0	3	2	0
Douglass, lf	0	1	0	0	0	Smith, 2b	0	1	2	2	0
Felix, 3b	0	0	1	4	3	Washburn, rf	1	1	3	0	0
Childs, 2b	0	0	4	1	0	Bresnahan, c	0	1	4	1	0
Iburg, p	1	1	0	6	0	McGinnity, p	0	0	0	0	1
						*Bowerman	0	0	0	0	0

*Batted for McGinnity in ninth inning.

Philadelphia..004   000   000—4
New York 100   000   110—3

Earned runs—Philadelphia, 3; New York, 1. Two-base hit—Brodie. Sacrifice hits—McGraw, McGinnity. Left on bases—Philadelphia, 4; New York, 8. Stolen base—Brodie. First base on balls—off Iburg, 3; off McGinnity, 2. First base on errors—Philadelphia, 1; New York, 2. Struck out—by Iburg, 2; by McGinnity, 4. Time of game—One hour and forty minutes. Umpire—Mr. Emslie.

Whatever that meant, it implied that McGraw already was on first base with the New York fans. In fact, he was on first base literally in two innings of the game with a single and a walk. He batted second in the lineup, with three of his Baltimore cronies stationed farther down the line—Brodie in centerfield batting fourth, Bresnahan catching and batting eighth, and Iron Joe McGinnity pitching and swinging ninth.

In the very first inning, they treated the customers to a flash of Oriole baseball. Jimmy Jones, the left-fielder, walked and McGraw promptly laid down a sacrifice bunt that advanced Jones to second base. It was McGraw's first time at bat as a member of the Giants, and his bunt was a hint of the run-scratching days ahead. When Brodie singled to centerfield, the Giants had a one-run lead and their long-suffering clientele had something to cheer about.

Unfortunately, Philadelphia scored four runs in the third inning. And even more unfortunately, the Giants left the bases loaded in the eighth inning after Brodie had doubled and McGraw singled. But the public was forgiving. If the Giants had lost a battle, they evidently stood a much better chance of winning a war.

"That the people of New York want to see good baseball," observed *The Times*, "and will liberally patronize the same was proved by the crowds that went to the Polo Grounds to see what their new team would do under the new regime. And they had nothing but encouragement for the home players. Although beaten, the crowd applauded the home team as it left the ground."

★   ★   ★

July 19, 1902: John McGraw's first day in the lineup of the New York Giants.

The game not only was the first for McGraw in New York but also the first for him anywhere in three weeks. His departure from Baltimore as a manager had been violent enough, but his departure as a player had been spectacular, and it added to the intrigue surrounding his debut in Manhattan.

His final sequence in an Orioles uniform had begun two months earlier, on May 24, when he was spiked at third base by an outfielder for Detroit named Dick Harley. His orange-and-black stocking was soaked with blood, but McGraw still put first things first and leaped for Harley's throat, and then they settled into a bruising round or two while a Saturday crowd of 4,000 went wild.

For five weeks, McGraw was on the sidelines because of the spike wound on his leg, not hitting again until June 25 and not playing third base again until June 28. Then, in his first game back, he immediately got embroiled in an argument with the umpire about a tag he either made or did not make during a rundown. Finally, he was ejected, refused to leave, was ejected again, and then was advised that the game was being suspended and the Orioles would lose by the forfeit score of 9 to 0. Ban Johnson thereupon suspended him indefinitely. But McGraw kept the argument raging in the public prints for two more weeks, then gave Johnson the back of his hand by defecting to New York.

"The McGraw-Baltimore incident," Johnson pronounced, "is closed. It took a long time for the patrons of baseball in Baltimore to learn McGraw's peculiar curves and angles, but they learned fast. The National League sent a good, kind angel in the form of Freedman's certified checks and the angels had wings enough to carry McGraw away. So Baltimore and the American League rejoice."

So McGraw caused rejoicing in two cities at the same time.

In the days following his first appearance in New York, he took the Giants to New Jersey for an exhibition game at the Orange Oval against the Orange Athletics. He left nothing to chance, even in an exhibition game, using Christy Mathewson to help nail down a 3 to 2 victory in 10 innings.

Then he took the Giants over to Brooklyn for two games against his old corporate cousins from Baltimore, the Trolley Dodgers, and stoked up a rivalry that would become one of the institutions of gamesmanship in the twentieth century. On Wednesday, July 23, the Giants beat the Dodgers, 4 to 1, before another good crowd of 7,000—their first victory as McGraw's men. Then, on Thursday, they swept the series by winning, 2 to 0, with Mathewson pitching a five-hit shutout and striking out 11 Dodgers. The fielding of the Giants was errorless, the press reported with some gushing, "and their base-running was first-class."

For the rest of the season, the Giants were the best last-place team in baseball. Before McGraw and the Oriole corps had arrived, they won 22 games and lost 50; afterwards, they won 26 and lost 38. McGraw, a broad-nosed, somewhat jug-eared whirlwind of energy both on and off the baseball field, appeared in 34 of the 64 games and, more significant, box-office business picked up as the season went along.

McGraw and his wife, meanwhile, moved into the Victoria Hotel at Broadway and Twenty-seventh Street, two blocks from the Giants' office in the St. James Building. Most of the theaters were clustered in that area then, with Thirty-fourth Street the drama center of town. And, although McGraw became an increasingly regular customer by night, he was a one-track-mind fanatic by day. He would stop in the front office bright and early each morning, then would head directly for the Polo Grounds, arriving by 10 o'clock most mornings even when the games did not begin until 4.

That in itself was an improvement in the team, which had usually been directed as a sideshow to something else. And almost immediately, the idea spread to the public that the Giants now were somebody's main event. By the new Sixth Avenue Elevated trains and even by Harlem River boats, they came out to see what the fuss was all about. Then, while waiters roamed the grandstand aisles carrying trays of ten-cent beer, they watched McGraw whip the Giants on to the attack, such as it was.

That winter, two more things happened that further shaped the pattern of New York baseball, with McGraw at center stage. First, the American League finally landed in town with a team that eventually became the counter-weight to the Giants in public favor. They were the Highlanders, so-called because their first president was Joseph Gordon and the Gordon Highlanders were then the best-known regiment in the British Army. Also, they played their games at Broadway and 165th Street, one of the highest points of land in Manhattan.

The Highlanders actually came from humbler stock than all that. They were financed by seven Democratic politicians led by Captain Bill Devery of the New York police and Frank Farrell, the poolroom king of Manhattan, who was basically a bookmaker with Tammany connections.

The second milestone involved the Giants themselves. Freedman's political grip already had been weakened the year before when his Tammany teammates were scattered in the reform election of Mayor Seth Low, with William Travers Jerome as the new district attorney and with Dick Croker coincidentally making one of his sudden extended trips to Europe. So, with his City Hall forces in retreat and his management already under long pressure from the other club owners in the National League, Freedman simply got out from under.

He formally sold the Giants to John Brush, the clothing man who had bought the Indianapolis team in 1888 and the Cincinnati team in 1889. The price was $200,000 and Brush got the money from two principal sources: The other National League owners, who were not saddened to see Freedman go, and the Fleischmann brothers, Julius and Max, the yeast kings, who took the bankrupt Cincinnati Reds off his hands.

Once the political threads had been sorted out, the baseball fabric quickly took shape. The Highlanders got to work under Manager Clark Griffith and within a couple of years began to be called the Yankees. And the Giants got to work under McGraw, who already was earning the fairly astronomical salary of $6,500 and who was about to put the Giants on the map with incredible speed.

McGraw held two aces—Mathewson and McGinnity—and he played them relentlessly. His favorite, probably for all time, was Mathewson—eight years younger than McGraw, a football and baseball player at Bucknell, a 6 foot 2 inch All-America type who neither drank nor smoked, who disdained playing baseball on Sundays and who had a photographic memory in baseball, checker and poker games.

Mathewson's wife Jane became Blanche McGraw's closest friend, and the two couples grew together like one family. They rented an apartment at Columbus Avenue and Eighty-fifth Street, a block from Central Park, on the elevated line to the Polo Grounds, and shared household expenses. The money, it soon developed, was plentiful, especially since the combination of McGraw and Mathewson almost immediately was worth a fortune to John Brush's baseball club.

After training in Savannah in the spring of 1903, the Giants opened the season in Brooklyn before 16,000 persons, then opened at home against Philadelphia before 18,000. In May they drew 31,500 for a game against Pittsburgh and in June hit 32,000 one afternoon. By now, Brush was giving McGraw free rein in running the club and was spending his own time trying to raise the capacity of his suddenly booming ball park. Even on the road, they began to pack them in, drawing 29,000 customers one day in Chicago alone.

On almost any afternoon, the public could be certain that McGraw would be playing one of his aces. Of the 139 games the Giants finished that season, Mathewson and McGinnity pitched in an even 100. More important, they won 61 of them—Mathewson 30 and McGinnity 31—and that was more than the whole club had won the year before. The team skyrocketed from eighth (and last) place in 1902 to second place in 1903.

But the best was yet to come. At the close of the 1903 season, McGraw started filling out the blank checks that Brush figuratively had granted him and started spending them literally. Second place was a big improvement over eighth but, as long as there was room at the top, McGraw's one-track baseball mind tortured him.

He bought Arthur Devlin, a young third-baseman, from the minor league club at Newark and Harry (Moose) McCormick, an outfielder and the leading hitter in the Eastern League, from Jersey City. Then he sent Jack Cronin and Charlie Babb to Brooklyn in exchange for Bill Dahlen, the shortstop who later became known as "Bad Bill" in tribute to his bellicose personality on the field. He was a man after McGraw's own heart: Fiery in the face of the enemy but, McGraw noted with delight, "an iceberg before big assemblages."

McGraw still felt he needed a hard-hitting outfielder, but nevertheless opened the season with two cheeky predictions: The Giants would play before *really* big crowds in 1904 after their impact of the year before, and they would complete their steep climb from the bottom to the top by winning the pennant—two seasons after finishing last.

He was right on both predictions. He even got the hard-hitting outfielder late in the season while the Giants were scuffling through a free-for-all pennant race with Cincinnati, Chicago and Pittsburgh. He bought Mike Donlin from Garry Herrmann, the Cincinnati owner, who had just become the chief of the new National Commission of baseball, which was set up in the winter of 1902-3 to keep the peace between the National and American Leagues. Herrmann, wearing his Cincinnati owner's hat, became fed up with Donlin's social life and the arguments it created with Herrmann. Still, Donlin was popular and he could hit. He could hit well enough to challenge Hans Wagner for the batting championship. Besides, his strutting manner earned him the nickname "Turkey Mike" and the admiration of that other strutter, John McGraw.

The crowds came early that season. On the opening day in April, Charlie Ebbets ferried McGraw and his entourage to Brooklyn for the game in two gasoline-driven cars he had rented. They paraded down Fifth Avenue and across the Brooklyn Bridge to the ball park, where the public already was raising the roof. The festivities included civic speeches, band concerts, welcoming rallies, the works. The game didn't start until everything had quieted down, well after 4 o'clock, and then the Giants knocked off the Dodgers for the first of Mathewson's 33 victories and the first of the team's 106.

From that day until late September, McGraw played in only five games at third base. But he took up his stance in the coaching box at third base when the Giants were at bat, and was a hellcat. He insulted rivals, baited umpires and stoked up the fans. At the end of the summer, the Giants swept into first place over Chicago and Cincinnati, with Pittsburgh fourth after three years of dominating the league.

So the season ended with two of the symbols of the next thirty years: The victory and the victory party. It was the first of either for the Giants, and they made the most of both. They pitched a rollicking bash at Erlanger's Theater, another symbol of the days ahead, and McGraw cemented an alliance with the stage world and its heroes that lasted a lifetime. Brush paid $5,000 for the first box for the occasion, and it seemed that everybody in the public life of Manhattan beat a path to Broadway and Forty-fifth Street that night. Tod Sloan, the jockey and racetrack crony of McGraw, was the master of ceremonies.

Actors like Louis Mann cascaded diamond-studded gifts on the new tigers of New York. Harry Stevens, who had started a catering empire with 100 pounds of peanuts a generation earlier, presented diamond cuff links to the man who had brought the pennant to Broadway.

Then McGraw, at the peak of his popularity, played out his role like a prima donna. With Brush's approval, he refused to let his Giants play in the World Series against the American League champions, the Boston Red Sox. Brush was still peeved because the American League had put its foot in the door in New York with the Highlanders. McGraw was still peeved on all fronts with Ban Johnson, who had after all compared him to Benedict Arnold. Besides, said McGraw with sweeping condescension, Boston was representing "a minor league."

The "minor league" presumably had ended its war with the "major league" two winters before. The Red Sox even had won the first modern World Series the year before by defeating the Pittsburgh Pirates in October of 1903. But now, with the biggest drawing cards in either league and with New York gathering at their feet after years of baseball drought, McGraw stalked off in that autocratic, maddening, calculated way that stirred the mob wherever he went.

Some people thought his barb actually was aimed at the Highlanders more than at the Red Sox. They had finished second in the American League race, a feat almost as remarkable as the Giants' finishing first in the National. They had heroes too, like Jack Chesbro, the spitball pitcher who won 41 games that season and then lost the key game against Boston by throwing a wild pitch over his catcher's head. Chesbro's widow conducted a campaign years later to have the record of that pitch reversed, to label it a passed ball, thereby putting the misplay on the catcher for not handling it, even though everybody agreed it had sailed far over his head.

Whatever name it went by, it was a pitch that nobody caught and that led to the Highlanders' downfall and Boston's victory. But for Brush and McGraw, it was a close call. If the Highlanders had won the pennant, they would have had a real monster on their hands—an all-New York World Series. That would be great later on, and it did happen seventeen years later. But now, just as the Giants were capturing the public fancy, they could again give the backs of their hands in one sweep to the Red Sox, the Highlanders, Ban Johnson and the "bush" league all of them represented—and they did it with exaggerated scorn.

With these ripples widening behind them, the Giants then created a spectacular splash in 1905. They won 105 games, lost 48 and lived up to all the love or hate they aroused every place McGraw took them. His contract contained a clause forbidding foul language or rowdyism, but he broke it as joyously as he broke the conventions of public manners everywhere across the country.

Once he offered to fight everybody in the Cincinnati ball park. Once he threw a ball at an umpire in Pittsburgh. And during the Pirates' first series at the Polo Grounds in 1905, he touched off a fight against his strongest rivals and bitterest enemies. He did that by baiting the Pittsburgh pitcher, Mike Lynch of Brown University, as Lynch passed him at the third-base coaching box no later than the first inning. The Pittsburgh manager, Fred Clarke, retaliated by threatening to fight McGraw. Both teams girded for the fight, and then McGraw was banished by the umpire. An inning later, Mathewson ran onto the field with fists cocked and was banished, too. The crowd of 18,000 howled, and other crowds kept howling for the rest of the season.

Shortly after, the Pittsburgh owner, Barney Dreyfuss, petitioned the president of the league, Harry Pulliam, in formal, legal language as follows: "Steps should be taken to protect visitors to the Polo Grounds from insults from the said John J. McGraw."

"What sort of times have we fallen on," McGraw roared back in a statement to the newspapers, "when the president of the league behaves in a way to indicate he can't forget his former role as the paid secretary to Dreyfuss at both Louisville and Pittsburgh. We might as well be in Russia."

Pulliam, wishing that everybody would just disappear, called a meeting of the league's board of directors for June 1 in Boston to "try" McGraw. But McGraw took the offensive well in advance. He telephoned Pulliam and simply bawled him out. Pulliam responded with a $150 fine and a 15-day suspension. Then all hell really broke loose. *The Evening World* in New York circulated a petition and got 12,000 fans to sign it, swearing fealty to McGraw. Brush leaped to his manager's defense. McGraw accused Dreyfuss of not picking up markers he had given to bookmakers. And when the "trial" finally was convened, the directors quelled the riot, exonerated McGraw, scolded Dreyfuss and somehow even praised Pulliam for his "handling" of the situation.

Pressing their advantage, McGraw and Brush then demanded to know about that fine and suspension. Pulliam replied that they stood. So McGraw and Brush marched to the Superior Court in Boston, where the Giants happened to be playing, and gleefully obtained an injunction restraining Pulliam from enforcing his own edict. That afternoon McGraw was back in uniform, having hoodwinked an owner, a board of directors and a whole league. He was insufferable, and the crowds ate it all up.

"In those days," he recalled with satisfaction, "it was not unusual for the papers to announce that 'the rowdy Giants, accompanied by representatives of the yellow press, got in town this morning.' We used to stay in the old Monongahela Hotel in Pittsburgh and from there drove in open carriages to the ball park, which was in Allegheny City across the river.

"To reach the bridge, we had to pass by the public market place. If we escaped a shower of small stones and trash outside the park, we were sure to get it as we passed the market. Understand, we dressed at the hotel then, not at the ball park. If the fans started razzing, we would razz right back.

"One day we were greeted with a shower of old vegetables—potatoes, onions, tomatoes, even cantaloupes. That whole club had the skylarking spirit of college boys, and I was just as bad as any of them. On the field, though, they thought like men of affairs. Always they were on a hair edge, ready to get into a row if anybody pulled the trigger."

To make certain that the trigger was pulled often enough to maintain the war of nerves, he and Brush would send telegrams to the next city on the team's itinerary, asking the chief of police for "protection" when the Giants arrived. The newspapers there would duly report the request, and the Giants could always be certain of appearing before large, hostile crowds—large being the key word.

They even began to tweak Pulliam and Dreyfuss for their Keystone Comedy attempt to discipline McGraw by "trial" of the league directors. The players began to swear out mock "affidavits" to protest umpires' rulings, and would solemnly mail them to Pulliam's office. They would read like this:

"Being duly sworn, John Jones deposes as follows, to wit: I am a resident of the City of New York and my occupation or profession is the playing of baseball for a team known as the New York Giants. My special occupation in the pursuit of said profession is the playing of a position known as second base and one requiring a certain amount of physical dexterity and mental acumen. On the 7th day of July, 1905, while engaged with the said Giants in a game of baseball with an opposing team known as the Pittsburgh Pirates, I was stationed at second base and was in position to see clearly a certain play made at third base by one Ritchie, an opposing player, it being part of his professional skill to slide into said third base, sack or cushion so as to avoid being touched with a ball in the hands of one Arthur Devlin, known as a third-baseman. Your deponent further saith," and so on ad nauseum.

Every player on the club would swear one out and sign it, then all the affidavits would be mailed in bulk to Pulliam. After a while, he used to see them being dumped on his desk and would say wearily, "Oh, it's some more of those damned Giant affidavits."

"In making protests," observed McGraw innocently, "I am sure our club had the smallest percentage of victories of any club in the world."

On the field, though, they had the largest percentage of victories. On October 1 they swept past Pittsburgh into the National League pennant for the second straight year and, having ascertained that the American League would be represented by Connie Mack's Philadelphia Athletics, graciously consented to extend the malarkey into the World Series.

Chapter

Well, Eddie,
Let's Be on Our Way

Three persons crossed the tumultuous path of John McGraw in 1905, and they were destined to influence his life on and off baseball fields for the next generation. They were Eddie Brannick, a twelve-year-old boy in knickers, who became his great confidant; Bill Klem, a rookie umpire, who became his great antagonist; and Connie Mack, the son of a Civil War wheelwright, who became his rival as manager of the Philadelphia Athletics in the World Series that October.

All three were drawn into the vortex that McGraw was creating along Broadway in 1905 because his New York Giants were winning their second straight National League pennant—and consenting to confront the "bush" American League for the first time in the series.

Brannick was a West Side kid of extraordinary talent for making himself useful in a world of adults. He was born over a saloon on West Forty-eighth Street and was raised on the fringes of Hell's Kitchen near Tenth Avenue and Thirty-first Street. He became involved with the Giants by helping his uncle install a mechanical scoreboard in the old Madison Square Garden. The Giants were so popular that summer as they swept to the pennant that their owner, John T. Brush, rented the Garden so that their fans could follow the team on the road.

Eddie showed such skill at manipulating the board and posting the scores each inning that Brush hired him as an office boy. With his new responsibilities, he would clip newspaper reports of the Giants' games, file them and otherwise help keep track of McGraw and his Polo Grounds heroes.

Half a century later, Eddie Brannick recalled his first meeting with
McGraw, who in three whirling years in New York had already acquired a
sizable reputation as an impresario, a genius, a brawler, a sport and an ogre.
Brush was crippled and somewhat of an invalid, and he customarily dispatched people like Eddie on missions and errands around town. One day in
1905, not long after he had hired the energetic little boy in knickers, he summoned Brannick to his suite in the Imperial Hotel at Broadway and Thirty-
first Street and told him to go find Mr. McGraw.

"I went downstairs," Eddie remembered, "and found him at the bar. I
went up to him and said: 'Mr. McGraw.' He said, 'What's your name, son?' I
said Ed Brannick. He said, 'What is it, Eddie?' And I said, 'Mr. Brush wants to
see you upstairs.' And he replied, 'Well, Eddie, let's be on our way.'"

And they were, for the next three decades. Brannick later became secretary of the New York Giants and the San Francisco Giants and was never far
from the blunt, thickset man he unerringly had found at the Imperial bar that
day. He planned McGraw's road trips, housed his players, shared his wiles,
administered his campaigns. He became known as "Mr. McGraw's boy," and
wherever the Giants went, Mr. McGraw's boy went with them.

"He was a great calculator," Eddie Brannick recalled 65 baseball seasons
later. "He was good at upsetting a town.

"Everything he did was calculated to draw people into the park. He would
make a statement insulting someone in St. Louis when the team was in Cincinnati. Or he would insult an owner like Barney Dreyfuss at Pittsburgh. Or Ban
Johnson and the American League. Even when he went on the stage, he would
do a stand-up monologue and answer questions from the audience, and he
would always be baiting them and stirring them up.

"But he really had a dual personality. He was a study in human nature. He
was tough with tough people and warm with soft ones. He might detest a
player—say, like Charley Herzog—but he still would fight to buy him back
from another club. When I got to be the traveling secretary of the club, he told
me there were no stars on this team. Nobody, Christy Mathewson included,
gets an upper berth on a Pullman or a lower berth out of any favoritism.
They're all ball players."

McGraw also taught Eddie Brannick another fact of life with the Giants:
While there might be no stars on the team there was only one boss—only one.
The point was delivered one summer afternoon after McGraw had noticed that
baseballs were disappearing from the ball bag in the dugout. He spoke to
Brush, who then started sending Brannick uptown on the afternoons when the
team played at home. Eddie would sit on the bench as the ball boy and keep
track of the merchandise.

One afternoon Eddie arrived later than the appointed hour of one o'clock
and was berated by the manager. "Mr. Brush sent me to the bank," Eddie
explained, invoking the biggest name on the horizon. He was startled when
McGraw replied in even, firm, unbending tones:

"I don't care about the office, the wastebasket, the bank, Brush or anything. Get here on time."

"I knew then," Eddie Brannick said, "who was running the ball club."

It didn't take Bill Klem long to learn who was running the ball club, either, after he had joined the National League umpiring staff in 1905 just as the Giants were reaching their peak of popularity.

On the afternoon when Klem first appeared at the Polo Grounds, a delegation of high school students from his home at Lakewood, New Jersey, asked McGraw's permission to bestow a gift on the new umpire. It was a ball-and-strike indicator, and the ceremony was to be conducted appropriately at home plate. McGraw courteously agreed, as the home-team manager, and even went so far as to shake Klem's hand and wish him well in his profession.

Then the game started and three innings later he abandoned his courtly manner in order to fly into a towering rage at Klem after a close play that had gone against the home team. Klem, showing early signs of his autocratic bearing and his conviction that he ruled with divine right, calmly threw McGraw out of the game.

They fought after that for the rest of McGraw's life. In private, McGraw conceded that Klem was the best umpire he ever saw. In private, Klem granted that McGraw was a "champion" among managers. But in public, they were at each other's throats, hurling insults, challenges and even dire accusations for almost thirty years after that sunny, gracious ceremony in the Polo Grounds.

So, both Klem and Brannick were established in the wild world of Mr. McGraw in 1905 when Connie Mack arrived. He was Cornelius McGillicuddy by proper name, born during the Civil War on December 22, 1862, in East Brookfield, Massachusetts, a boom town that mass-produced shoes for the Union troops. He was already ten years old when McGraw was born in 1873 and he was already working in a cotton mill twelve hours a day.

"It didn't seem so bad," he said later. "Most of the kids in our part of town had to go to work early. Besides, we got an hour for lunch and spent much of it playing town ball. A large ring was formed for two batsmen and they had to hit the ball out of the ring to be safe and stay at bat, or else take their place in the field."

Later he grew to 6 feet 1 inch, an incredibly erect and spare man of only 150 pounds with a high voice and high stiff collars. He scandalized his neighbors by playing ball on Sunday and he scandalized his mother by playing ball at all.

"You'll never get anywhere drinking and fighting," she warned, reflecting the prevailing view that ball players were a boisterous lot on the ragged edge of Victorian society. Mack tended to agree with her, especially after he turned professional in 1884 for $90 a month and moonlighted with the New York Metropolitans, whose players drank big five-cent schooners of beer in public saloons, to his discomfort.

"There is room for gentlemen in any profession," he said later after he had become a manager, "and baseball is my profession. We face the possibility of a charge that we are timid, but I always will insist as long as I am manager of the club that my boys be gentlemen. They may kid back and forth, but I will not tolerate profanity, obscene language or personal insults from my bench."

This pious outlook did not prevent Mack from engineering little tricks on his opponents, like freezing baseballs in the front-office icebox to congeal the life out of them. Nor did it prevent him from listening in respectful silence to lectures on the evils of drinking when they were delivered by Ban Johnson, a two-fisted drinker himself.

"Once a ball player gets drunk in public," Johnson said, while comparing notes with Mack on the dangers of drink, "it isn't long before the entire town knows about it. He will make an error on the field and everyone will say, 'Oh, yes, he was drunk again last night.' "

A tower of sobriety in a landscape of joyous tippling, Mack nevertheless commanded the admiration of the baseball crowd as he grew older and more important. By 1895, during the heyday of McGraw's Baltimore Orioles, he was the manager at Milwaukee and, he recalled, "I signed players, made the trades, arranged our railroad transportation, found hotels for the players and paid all the bills."

During the Spanish-American War, he would instruct the team's bus driver to head for the ball park by way of the newspaper offices. The latest bulletins from the combat zones were posted outside and Mack's players, like everybody else, wanted to keep up with the news. "There were bigger crowds in front of those bulletin boards," he noted, "than we had at our ball park."

Once the war was past, though, Mack and Johnson and McGraw all converged on collision courses. While McGraw was skipping to the National League in New York, Johnson was bestowing the Philadelphia franchise in the American League on Mack. And Mack, in turn, offered the public two sizable attractions. One was the 25-cent price of admission. The other was the chance to see new heroes like Rube Waddell, who became Mack's greatest pitcher and one of McGraw's greatest tormentors.

Waddell was a huge left-hander with an unpredictably blithe spirit who came from the Pennsylvania coal town of Punxsutawney. The first time Mack called him on the telephone to lure him to Philadelphia, Waddell said with innocent but colossal impertinence, "Who the hell are you?" When he found out, he signed with Mack's team and became a legend. Once he pitched 17 innings against the Chicago White Sox, helped win his own game by hitting a triple, struck out the last Chicago batters and then did a series of handsprings from the mound to the bench. Then he went back and won the second game of the doubleheader, 1 to 0.

He was just as carefree in his approach to money, too. So much so that at his peak Mack paid him $2,200 in one-dollar bills—to make the bankroll last longer.

On top of these attractions, Mack also had one of the two new baseball parks in the American League. Boston had the other, and it was used in the first World Series in 1903, in which Boston defeated Pittsburgh and gave the

American League its first memorable victory in competition. Mack's park was at Twenty-ninth Street and Columbia Avenue in the section of Philadelphia known as Brewerytown, an area permeated with the aroma of hops and yeast that Mack himself scorned. And it was there on October 9, 1905, that Mack and McGraw finally collided in the World Series.

The match was played in a torrent of public passion on both sides. For one thing, this was the first "official" World Series, the 1903 playoff having been a kind of challenge round between Boston and Pittsburgh. It brought into conflict two of the biggest cities in the country. Moreover, they were close enough for hordes of rooters to commute each day to the stadiums like mobs following the contending armies near Bull Run. And finally, it matched two of the titans of baseball's new high command, Mack and McGraw.

The Athletics won the American League title that year without a .300 hitter, which was rare enough. Their leading batter, in fact, was Harry Davis at .284, though he also led the league in home runs—with eight. To make matters even more bleak, Waddell injured his left shoulder a month before the series and was finished for the year.

Characteristically enough, Waddell hurt himself during a prank. He had "declared war" on straw skimmers and got into a fuss with Andy Coakley, who was wearing one at the railroad station in Providence. Waddell, during the scuffling, tripped over a suitcase, fell on his shoulder and wrenched himself right out of the approaching World Series. Waddell used to amuse everybody by his antics—donning a barkeep's apron and serving beer to a full house, diving off ferryboats or chasing fire engines during ball games. But this time Mack was not amused.

The Giants, on the other hand, rode into the series in high spirits. Mathewson and McGinnity gave them the best one-two combination in pitching, and Mathewson already was developing a reputation as a marvel on the mound.

"To me," observed McGraw, "he was pretty much the perfect type of pitching machine. He had the stature and strength, and he had tremendous speed. There never was another pitcher like Mathewson."

Mathewson also had noticed the ability of batters to "read" a curveball that broke outward with heavy spin. So he tried to develop a pitch that would veer inward, and came up with his fade-away curve, a forerunner of the screwball. He also had a sense of pace, threw as few balls as possible and went through entire seasons averaging one base on balls a game.

"In my opinion," McGraw said, firing a psychological shot even before the first pitch was thrown, "the Giants of 1905 can do anything the champion Orioles of 1893, 1894 and 1895 did—and have a shade on them besides."

To make sure that the effect was not lost on people, he sent his troops into action on the opening afternoon of the series in startling new uniforms. Starkly black flannels, with white piping, white boxy caps and stockings, and an immense "NY" in white across the shirts. Even McGraw was impressed.

"I will never forget the thrill I got," he said, letting his emotions slip, "when the Giants suddenly trotted out from their dugout clad in uniforms of black flannel, trimmed with white. Hundreds of New York fans escorted us to Philadelphia, and the scenes in the lobbies of hotels were lively. Giant rooters were all over the place."

So were Philadelphia rooters. And they were rarely out of earshot of the grinding battle that opened in Columbia Park that afternoon as two cities braced for a baseball war that seemed to clamor above and beyond the normal noises of the day. The Philadelphia North American even erected a huge gong west of City Hall at Fifteenth and Market Streets, and pealed the news of the struggle across William Penn's city. One gong for a two-base hit, two gongs for a three-base hit, three gongs for a home run—by the Athletics.

Then the series opened, and the mammoth gong tolled only five times in a week—each time for a two-bagger only—as the Giants and Athletics threw some of the strongest pitching in baseball history against each other.

The series opened in Philadelphia because Ben Shibe won the coin toss. It was as simple as that. Shibe was a onetime horse-car driver who made baseballs in his spare time, hiring the neighborhood women to hand-sew the covers. Now he owned the Athletics and when Garry Herrmann, the chief of baseball's National Commission, tossed a 50-cent piece into the air, Shibe called it. The series would start in Shibe's park, then switch to the Polo Grounds, then back until somebody had won four games.

For the opener, an immense crowd of 17,955 persons spilled across ropes that had been strung along the outer limits of the outfield. They milled, thronged, popped out onto the grass, hooted, cheered and roared. They also saw a bristling duel between those old college rivals, Eddie Plank of Gettysburg and Mathewson of Bucknell. The Giants, in their black-knight uniforms, made 10 hits off Plank. The Athletics, in their regular white uniforms, got only four off Mathewson, though three were bell-pealing doubles into the roped-off crowd behind the outfielders. The Giants scored twice in the fifth inning and once in the ninth, stole four bases and won, 3 to 0.

The next afternoon, the caravan migrated en masse 90 miles north to the Polo Grounds, and this time 24,992 demons paid their way in. They saw Iron Man McGinnity and Red Ames (in the ninth inning) hold Philadelphia to six hits. But they also saw Chief Bender hold New York to four. The Giants, to McGraw's horror, made two errors that led to runs in the only two innings that produced runs. But they were Philadelphia runs, and this time the Athletics won by the same score, 3 to 0.

Nobody knew it at the time, but they were the last runs, and the only runs, that Mack's team would score during the entire series. It rained on the third day, so the National Commissioners ruled that the third game would be held over in Philadelphia with the next two in New York—to give the Giants a Saturday date at home. Then, pitching with two days of rest, Mathewson stopped the Athletics on four hits and defeated the straw-skimmered Coakley, 9 to 0. The Athletics made five errors, the Giants stole five bases, and the Market Street gong was silent.

They flocked back to New York again, crowding the hotels and jamming Broadway with baseball arguments, bets and hoopla. Then in the fourth game McGinnity gave up five hits to Philadelphia, Plank gave up four to New York, but the Giants scored on two errors and won the game, 1 to 0. One of the errors was made at third base by Lave Cross, the captain of the team, and when the series ended he was promptly retired by the mild-mannered Mr. Mack.

Now McGraw had a lead of three games to one, and wasted no time on mercy. He wheeled in his ace, Mathewson, and before 24,187 customers in the Polo Grounds the great Matty outpitched Bender, 2 to 0. He gave six hits, Bender five. The winning run was coaxed home on two walks, a bunt and a fly ball.

New York reacted as though Teddy Roosevelt had just charged up Broadway on a white horse waving a sabre and shouting, "Follow me." The city erupted into an orgy of celebration and of lionizing the Giants, from Eddie Brannick in his plain knickers to John McGraw in his black baseball knickers with the white trim. They were the world champions after five games of incredible pitching—three years after McGraw had arrived in town to find the team in last place with Mathewson playing first base.

The five games drew 91,723 admissions for a gate of $68,436.81. Many people cheerfully paid fifty cents each day and more cheerfully stood and watched each day. The Giants, the new demigods of Broadway, collected $1,142 apiece for winning and the Athletics collected $823 apiece for losing—with Shibe contributing his share to fatten his players' purses.

Mathewson had pitched three complete games in six days. He had allowed 14 hits, one walk and no runs in 27 innings. He had struck out 18 batters. He was, as McGraw had raved, "pretty much the perfect type of pitching machine."

When Connie Mack led his boys home, they were greeted like conquering heroes, too. Six Philadelphia newspapers staged a tremendous baseball parade for both them and the Giants. Amateur and semi-pro teams from Pennsylvania, New Jersey and Delaware marched the length of Broad Street with bands playing and fireworks lighting the sky. Open carriages transported the players of both clubs through the streets, and then to a great banquet that celebrated the first formal World Series in baseball history, and in some ways the most unusual.

Huge caricatures of the players were carted along Broad Street, too, and an elephant from the Philadelphia zoo plodded along in circus fashion to symbolize Mack's White Elephants, the Athletics. At the height of the madness, a white sheet was draped over the elephant in order to perfect the symbol. They had wanted to whitewash him to make the day absolutely memorable, but the people at the zoo had drawn the line there.

★   ★   ★

It had been a year to remember, all right. By winning two pennants in 1904 and 1905 and a World Series in the latter year, the Giants had awakened

New York's zest for baseball with a clatter. McGraw became a household figure as the little king who had browbeaten a league president and numerous umpires, owners and rivals. A man who had cowed the enemy, and to top it all, a man who had beaten Ban Johnson's social-climbing American League.

The Highlanders were finishing sixth that year as New York's entry in the American League while McGraw's Giants were sweeping majestically to the top of the hill. So McGraw became a titan along Broadway, the crony of writers, jockeys, fighters and actors. Baseball was the dominant sport, and he was the dominant figure in baseball. Tennis and golf had not yet reached the point where great masses of people could appreciate or even afford them. Football was chiefly an Ivy League test among Harvard, Yale and Princeton. There was no radio or television. So baseball reigned as the national game on a stage uncluttered with distractions.

At times the action on the stage might be focused in one place, like the Polo Grounds; one set of rooms, like the Lambs, or even one room, like Diamond Dan O'Rourke's place at 156 Park Row. The cast of characters was small enough and celebrated enough, wherever the action moved. McGraw might be seen taking up his station for the evening at Diamond Dan's bar opposite a life-sized portrait of Jim Jeffries, the heavyweight champion. The portrait had been done two years before by Charlie Rose, an itinerant artist who made unusual drawings with ordinary schoolroom chalk and burnt match heads. He had done this particular piece for free beers and a free meal, and it was often gazed upon by the manager of the Giants along with people like Stanley Ketchel, Bob Fitzsimmons, the young politician Al Smith and Jeffries himself.

Diamond Dan's looked pretty much the same in 1905 as it had looked during the eighteen-eighties. The same mirrors and jockey silks and ornate old chandeliers with gas fixtures. Even the ghosts of the famous old Bowery heroes were revived in O'Rourke's conversations with the great men of McGraw's circle—people like Hicks the Pirate and Carrie Nation, who was not exactly a hero, though she reportedly liked O'Rourke so much that she customarily passed up Diamond Dan's place whenever she swept through the Bowery on her hatchet raids.

For the players, though, this after-hours world of gracious socializing and gracious drinking was sealed off—especially since McGraw himself took a stern view of mixing business with pleasure. Besides, he fought a constant war against bootlegging in the ball park itself.

Dan Whelan, who later became a banker and rose to president of the Guaranty Title and Mortgage Company, remembered how he used to lug cans of beer to Rube Marquard, Bugs Raymond and other ball players. They were big tins that cost ten cents but they used to console the players during the long hot hours of practice that McGraw scheduled before the games began late in the afternoon. Young Dan was a "stile boy." He watched the turnstiles and made certain that they turned only once for each customer. The turnstiles were free-spinning things then and if a customer pushed too hard they might click off any number of phantom admissions. The ticket-takers were required to produce one ticket stub for each click—or pay the difference out of pocket. So they hired the young Dan Whelan for seventy-five cents a day to regulate the clicks.

Eventually, Dan expanded his activities into beer-running errands for the ball players. At least, he did until one sunny day when he was lugging a tin of beer into the Polo Grounds and suddenly encountered John J. McGraw.

"What have you there, sonny?" McGraw asked pleasantly.

"Something to drink, sir," Danny replied.

McGraw opened the lid, sniffed the aroma, confiscated the tin and ordered Danny from the park. The next year on opening day he spotted the boy again, wagged his finger and said: "No more of that, right?" Danny said, "Okay," and that particular bootlegging route at least was shut down for good.

McGraw wasn't motivated so much by piety, or even hypocrisy. He just wanted sober, hungry players on the field when the afternoon's war began. And he also wanted to refine as far as possible the primitive conditions that still made professional baseball a kind of jungle with pay.

The players generally were paid peanuts then, rarely more than $2,400 a year. They ate in beaneries and lived in fourth-rate hotels. McGraw went a long way toward upgrading their status, or at least their image. He forbade the Giants to wear turtleneck sweaters or caps on trains, he began booking them into Pullmans and into good hotels, and he rode herd on them off the field as relentlessly as he stirred them up on the field.

When Ty Cobb broke in as a rookie in 1905, the regulars immediately hazed him by nailing his shoes to the floor in the accepted clubhouse prank. "I was just a mild-mannered Sunday School boy," he later told Arthur Daley of *The New York Times,* giving himself a shade the better of it. "But those oldtimers turned me into a snarling wildcat."

When Hans Wagner broke into the big leagues his manager, Fred Clarke, asked him: "Why don't you take batting practice?" Wagner said: "The regulars won't let me into the batting cage." Clarke replied: "Make them. You're big enough. Force your way in." Wagner forced his way in and later won eight National League batting championships.

One day a batter for the Giants hit a home run over the fence against Pittsburgh and, as he trotted past shortstop, Wagner mumbled: "Nice hit." The Giant replied: "Go to hell."

"I liked that remark," Wagner said later. "He was the first major leaguer ever to speak to me."

"When I was breaking in," Casey Stengel recalled, "you'd come to camp with a letter of recommendation from someone. Then you'd say to yourself, 'I think I'll go up to the batting cage and hit.' But some regular would challenge you and say, 'Whoa, there. Who are you and who sent you?' So you'd whip out your card and show it to him. If he thought your recommendation was okay, he'd step aside and let you hit—maybe as much as three times."

Paul Krichell, later a high-ranking scout for the Yankees, observed: "And do you know how you learned to correct your mistakes? Someone would call you a dumb so-and-so."

Cobb remembered that his greatest battles probably were fought with his own teammates while he was trying to win meager acceptance as a rookie. He signed for $1,800 a season, stayed in $10-a-week hotels, carried a pancake-styled Spalding baseball mitt and even walked to his first game with the Detroit Tigers at Bennett Field (capacity 8,500). The field, he recalled, was "like a cow pasture." They gave it the once-over with a rake every week, and the outfield was a marsh.

The players waited in line for the one shower that was available in the chicken-coop clubhouse. Their uniforms were seldom laundered. The gloves had no net-like webbing, nobody wore sunglasses, the outfield was often criss-crossed by cinder paths, rookies got the upper berths when traveling, pitchers doctored the baseballs until they were brown with licorice or slippery elm. On festive occasions the players might even queue up to use the bathtub reserved for Manager Hughey Jennings.

Even with all these hardships, though, the oldtimers guarded their jobs violently. They ostracized rookies who might snatch their livelihood, they forced Cobb to room by himself, the other outfielders sometimes declined to back him up on balls hit into his area and they picked fist fights as often as possible. The prevailing view, he was told, was "We're going to run Cobb off this club." One Detroit regular died fifteen years later, Cobb said, without ever having shaken his hand.

He had been with the Tigers one season when he developed an infected wound from persistent sliding while stealing bases. He went to the hospital for extended treatment, he said, and paid his own bill. He recalled that the owner of the team, Frank Navin, "visited me just once while I was invalided, and kept both hands in his pockets."

The Giants, meanwhile, were celebrities after their success in the 1905 World Series and, as such, encountered more of the rough-and-tumble treatment than ever. There were rewards, of course. They built a sizable following of stage actors, who tended to rise late each day, make it to the Polo Grounds by gametime at 4 o'clock and still get back downtown for the evening's performance. McGraw opened a billiard parlor at Herald Square near the theater district with Jack Doyle, the sporting oddsmaker, and Tod Sloan, the jockey, who meanwhile was courting Julia Sanderson, the actress. Mike Donlin of the Giants married Mabel Hite, the leading lady. And McGraw and John Brush spent more of their evenings at the Lambs, where many of their stage allies congregated and where Brush even lived for years.

In 1905 McGraw and his wife moved to the Washington Inn at 155th Street and Amsterdam Avenue, as did Roger Bresnahan and his wife and Hal Chase of the Highlanders. The Inn was not far from the Polo Grounds, and so McGraw settled down there astride both his worlds of the theater and the diamond.

Then it was the spring of 1906 and, after training at Memphis, McGraw brought his team home and pulled out all the promotional stops to prolong the magic. He dressed the team in those severe, dramatic black uniforms that had made such an impact at the series and had the shirt fronts embroidered with "World Champions." He decreed that the players should be transported to games in open carriages, four Giants to a carriage. Then the season opened and the magic went out of the marriage.

Mathewson contracted diphtheria. Donlin broke his leg sliding. Bresnahan was struck on the head by a pitched ball. The Chicago Cubs under Frank Chance won 116 games with players like Wildfire Frank Schulte, Johnny Kling and Mordecai "Three-Fingered" Brown, while exaggerated legends arose over the double-play combination of Joe Tinker, Johnny Evers and Chance. The Cubs one day bombed the Giants, 19 to 0, for the worst defeat McGraw absorbed in 30 years as a manager. And finally they ended the Giants' reign in the National League by winning the pennant, with New York next by a nose over Pittsburgh.

People had tried to work up a "second World Series" between the Giants and Philadelphia in the spring exhibition season of 1905. But because of the difficulties plaguing the Giants it was put over until 1907, and then it was staged with even more belligerency than the series itself.

In the opening game, on March 27, McGinnity outpitched Jack Coombs, 4 to 3. The Athletics evidently had found a way to score against that Giant pitching, but had not yet found a way to score enough. The next day, with Eddie Plank pitching for Connie Mack, an argument broke out when Bresnahan charged that Plank had committed a balk. McGraw loudly supported Bresnahan and they became so boisterous that the umpire, Charlie Zimmer, asked the New Orleans police to throw them out of the park. So McGraw removed his whole team from the field and Zimmer declared the game forfeited to Philadelphia.

The next day, McGraw announced that he wouldn't play at all if Zimmer umpired. So the game again was forfeited. Still, to appease the crowd that had been drawn by the raucous publicity of a "return match" between the World Series rivals, an unofficial game was played anyway with a New Orleans umpire making the calls. The game deteriorated into a comedy as the Athletics overwhelmed the Giants, 7 to 0, and McGraw thereupon forfeited the rest of the "spring training exhibition series."

Later, in the hotel lobby, McGraw insulted John Shibe of the Athletics' ruling family, touching off another round of catcalls on all sides. The local newspapers berated the Giants as "New York brawlers" and "hoodlums," and contrasted them to the better-behaved men of Mack, who observed in Philadelphian understatement: "McGraw was a firebrand then."

When the season started, the Giants again found themselves fighting a losing match against Chance's Chicago Cubs, who won 107 games and the pennant. The Giants slid to fourth place, but had the perverse satisfaction of seeing Mack's team suffer a moment of raging ordeal as the American League pennant race went down the home stretch.

The ordeal occurred on September 30 during a wild doubleheader in

Philadelphia between the Athletics and the Detroit Tigers, who had been dead-locked for first place with one week to go before Detroit won the opening game of the series. Trolley cars deposited thousands of fans at the ball park for the Monday doubleheader, and hundreds scaled the walls after the gates had been shut. The Athletics grabbed a 7-to-1 lead in the first game, with Rube Waddell pitching and Eddie Plank held in reserve for the second game.

But Detroit, with Ty Cobb raising the roof, rallied with four runs off Waddell in the seventh inning. And in the ninth, trailing now by 8 to 6, they tied the score with two more runs. Cobb, twenty years old and fighting for the batting title, hit a two-run home run over the rightfield fence and Connie Mack literally fell off the bench. Mack got up, though, and forthwith waved Plank into the game—letting the chips fall where they may in the second game—and they fought on into extra innings.

Then in the fourteenth inning, Harry Davis poled one into the crowd in left-center for a ground-rule double. Sam Crawford, playing centerfield for Detroit, ran to the edge of the roped-off mob as a Philadelphia policeman, sitting on a soft-drink box, jumped up and lunged for the ball. Or, as some people later contended, he had merely tried to get out of the way of it. Any-way, the umpire at home plate, Silk O'Loughlin, said he had seen nobody interfere with Crawford. But the umpire at first base, Tom Connolly, said that *he* had seen interference, all right. So O'Loughlin ruled Davis out and Philadel-phia exploded.

Monte Cross of the Athletics and Claude Rossman of the Tigers got into a fist fight. Players on both sides yelled that it was already too dark to see what the hell had been happening. One player wrestled the ball away from Umpire Connolly, called him "you Irish immigrant" and heaved it over the grand-stand. And the outraged Connie Mack began rounding up affidavits from policemen and fans testifying that nobody had interfered with anybody on Davis' expunged two-bagger.

The game finally ended in a 9-to-9 tie, but the Athletics had wasted a golden opportunity to hold a six-run lead and win. Mack, normally a serene man, kept up his feud with O'Loughlin for the rest of their lives. He also sold Waddell at the end of the season because the great, eccentric pitcher had lost the lead (only to have Waddell come back the next season with the St. Louis Browns and beat the Athletics, 5 to 2, before 28,000 customers and later that year strike out 16 of his former teammates in a second appearance).

The Tigers went on to win the pennant. So that October, both Mack and McGraw sat back in frustration and watched while Chicago played Detroit in the World Series. The Cubs won it, four games to none, with one tie.

As maddening as 1907 had been for Mack, 1908 proved to be totally frightening for McGraw, who lost a pennant almost one year to the day, in a manner just as galling.

The Giants took their troubles to the tiny town of Marlin, Texas, in the spring of 1908. For the next ten years they would train there along the Brazos River, walking along the railroad tracks to the ball park, eating cans of food shipped down by Harry Stevens, enjoying fish-fries on the banks of the stream and creating a home away from home not far from the Gulf of Mexico. But when they went north for the baseball season, the placid days of spring training were always replaced by the screaming reality of the pennant races. And one of their most screaming realities came on September 23 of 1908, with the Giants and Cubs tied in the ninth inning, 1 to 1, and the pennant at stake.

There were two outs and the Giants had Moose McCormick on third base and Fred Merkle on first base. Al Bridwell, a young shortstop who had come from Boston that year in a massive housecleaning trade by McGraw, lined a single to center field. McCormick trotted home from third base with the winning run as the Polo Grounds crowd swarmed onto the field and the players headed for the clubhouse. But the Chicago second-baseman, Johnny Evers, disappeared into the fans swirling across the grass, reappeared with a ball and stepped on second base, triggering one of the historic mixups in baseball history.

Evers insisted for years afterwards that he had called for the ball after Bridwell's single, that it had been thrown to him from center field through the crowd, that Merkle had gone only part-way from first to second while McCormick was scoring and that Merkle had been forced out at second base—nullifying the winning run. The Giants insisted forevermore that Joe McGinnity had actually retrieved the ball and had flung it joyously into the crowd.

The newspaper writers had already flashed the final score by telegraph: 2 to 1, Giants. But Evers kept screaming at the base umpire, who ignored him and ran into the umpires' room. So Evers pursued the home-plate umpire, Hank O'Day, who at 10 o'clock that night finally ruled that Merkle was out.

"If Merkle was out," roared McGraw, "the game was a tie and O'Day should have cleared the field and resumed the game. If not, we won the game and they can't take it away from us."

But they did "take it away from us." Pulliam, the league president, whom McGraw had baited and humiliated so gleefully three seasons earlier, pronounced the game a tie. If it was needed to decide the pennant, it would be replayed. And sure enough, it was needed to decide the pennant after the Giants and Cubs ended the season a week later in a mathematical dead heat.

The pennant was settled in one playoff game, and it was played at the Polo Grounds because the Giants won the toss of the coin—but that was the only thing they won. A howling mob besieged the ball park that afternoon, smashed through part of the rightfield fence and overran the stadium until city firemen turned streams of water on them. Then the fans pelted the Chicago players with cushions and bottles. But through all the debris, the teams managed to play the game and, when Joe Tinker hit a three-bagger off Mathewson to launch a four-run third inning, the Cubs won the game and the pennant, 4 to 2.

Merkle had lost fifteen pounds worrying about his "boner" in the tied game, and though he recovered his poise and went on to become a fine first-baseman, he was branded. The scorn he suffered was so constant that McGraw, having recovered his own poise, went to his defense.

"It is criminal," McGraw said, "to say that Merkle is stupid and to blame the loss of the pennant on him. In the first place, he is one of the smartest and best players on this ball club. In the second place, he didn't cost us the pennant. We lost a dozen games we should have won.

"Besides," he added, taking aim at Pulliam, "we were robbed of it, and you can't say Merkle did that."

If he forgave Merkle, though, McGraw never forgave Pulliam. Their relations had always been tempestuous, and soon they became tragic. Pulliam was re-elected president of the league, though the Giants cast the only vote against him. Then in February of 1909, he was granted a leave of absence from his desk "for reasons of illness." He stayed away from baseball that spring and early summer, and in July, while at the New York Athletic Club, shot himself in the head. He died at the age of forty.

McGraw, en route from Boston to Chicago, did not attend the funeral. Nor did Brush, who was ill himself and not feeling up to it. The subtleties of proper behavior, the ordinary graces of business life, even the facade of courtesy or the rules of war—none of these manners of conduct softened the bitterness of the raging feuds of the day.

Nor did the bonds of friendship intrude when McGraw set about the task of revamping his baseball team. He did it with the same no-holds-barred stubbornness that marked so many of his relationships. Even his old friend Bresnahan was not spared. A formidable, versatile catcher who also could pitch and play third base and the outfield, and who ran the bases well—even Bresnahan was cut loose before the 1909 season. He was traded to St. Louis, where he became manager, in exchange for three players.

The newcomers were George Schlei, who came by way of Cincinnati in a three-city swap; Jack Murray, one of the better outfielders in the league, and Bugs Raymond, a two-fisted drinker who also was a pitcher with considerable stuff. Raymond became an immediate problem because of the former talent, but was tolerated because of the latter. McGraw tried to shorten his social radius by sending his pay checks to Mrs. Raymond. He forbade the bartenders in the training town of Marlin to serve him a drink—ever. He even had him shadowed from the Polo Grounds to the Braddock Hotel on Eighth Avenue and 126th Street, where many of the Giants lived during the season.

The battery of Mathewson and Bresnahan was broken up as a result of these trading maneuvers and the character of the great teams of 1904 and 1905 was fundamentally changed. But sentiment was no match for the main idea: to win. And gradually the team began to win again.

In 1909, the Giants ran third behind Pittsburgh and Chicago, then began to edge up. In 1910, they ran second behind Chicago. In 1911, they reached the top again and were joined there by their old rivals, the Philadelphia Athletics, who a year earlier had finally overcome three years of domination by the Detroit Tigers.

Before Mack and McGraw were able to resume their memorable battles of

1905, though, Philadelphia had to endure more trouble at the hands of Ty Cobb. It was as though Mack and McGraw suffered outrageous trials in alternate years before earning the right to outrage each other. McGraw was still boiling over the Merkle episode when Mack went through one last ordeal with Cobb at the close of the 1909 season.

The Tigers, who had succeeded the Chicago White Sox as American League champions in 1907 and 1908, led the Athletics by four games in September that year. Cobb was in the midst of what was to become a nine-year stretch as the No. 1 hitter in the league. He had started it in 1907 with an average of .350 and would hit .324, then .377, then .385, then .420, then .410, then .390, then .368 and then .369 in consecutive seasons during this remarkable decade. Tris Speaker finally wrested the title from him in 1916 by hitting .386, but Cobb returned for three more years after that as champion by an incredible streak of consistency with averages of .383, .382 and finally .384.

So in 1909, when Detroit arrived in Philadelphia for the climactic series, Cobb was the strongest batter and the biggest target around. The Athletics had to sweep all four games to tie for the lead, and they almost did.

The series was played before riotous crowds that totaled 120,000, featuring a huge outpouring of 35,409 for the third game. On the opening day, September 16, Eddie Plank pitched Philadelphia to a 2 to 1 victory. The next day, Detroit evened the series as seven different Tigers stole seven bases. But Mack's team took the third game, 2 to 0, behind Chief Bender and the fourth game, 4 to 3, behind Plank.

The wildest action, naturally enough, centered on Cobb, who was accorded a welcome befitting an armed enemy. Not one to flinch, he crashed into two hometown heroes on the baselines, Jack Barry and "Home Run" Baker, spiking both and splitting their uniforms. The crowds went mad, bombarding Cobb with catcalls, vegetables and missiles of all kinds, and even with letters and telephone calls threatening his life. Several wrote letters promising to shoot him if he showed up at the park. His manager, Hughey Jennings, who had been McGraw's partner fifteen years earlier on the Baltimore Orioles, called Mack for police protection. So after that Cobb was convoyed to the park with a motorcycle platoon of policemen, and a solid line of bluecoats stood in the outfield between him and the angry mob that overflowed the foul lines and pressed against the ropes in right field.

The Tigers, who left town with their health and a lead of two games, clung to both and won the pennant two weeks later. But the following year, the Philadelphia players showed their loyalty for Mr. Mack as Cobb and the Tigers slipped back to third place. They chipped in and bought Mack his first automobile, which chugged up to home plate for the presentation ceremony. The Athletics, finally out from under Detroit's three-year domination, won the pennant and the World Series, and the stage was cleared again for their reunion in 1911 with McGraw and the Giants.

The stage was cleared in New York, too. The Giants finally had got out from under the Chicago Cubs and Pittsburgh Pirates, who had monopolized the National League since 1905, with Chicago winning four out of five pennants.

McGraw fought one rearguard action, though, before resuming things with Mack. In 1910, his irritating neighbors in New York, the Highlanders, had prospered enough to finish second to Philadelphia. Public pressure forced a city series, and the Giants agreed. They won the series, four games to two, with one tie. Mathewson, who had long since recovered from his siege of diphtheria, pitched three of the victories and saved the fourth.

So McGraw, after five years of rebuilding, was primed again. He had bought and traded players freely with John Brush's money and his own designs. He had paid the unheard-of price of $11,000 for a pitcher named Rube Marquard, who thereby came from the Indianapolis team of the American Association with the nickname "the $11,000 beauty"—or, for a time, "the $11,000 lemon." He had established a new infield of Merkle, Herzog, Larry Doyle and Art Fletcher, who had caught his fancy as a rookie by insulting him on the field one day. Chief Meyers, the California Indian, succeeded Bresnahan as the catcher and Fred Snodgrass and Josh Devore joined the outfield, with Mathewson and Marquard the ranking pitchers.

He had afflictions, like Raymond—who was angrily sent to the bullpen one day but who took the ball instead and kept walking, out of the bullpen, out of the ball park, until he reached the Eighth Avenue gin mills, where he promptly traded the ball for a few shots of "third-rail whiskey."

But on balance he had a winning combination again as 1911 started. He was well-fortified off the field, too. Henry Fabian, who had nudged him from Cedar Rapids to Baltimore a generation before, now was his groundskeeper at the Polo Grounds. Fabian still thought of him as a rookie, apparently, because he counseled him and even second-guessed him scandalously, but McGraw didn't seem to mind. Dan Brouthers, the old Oriole, became a watchman at the stadium. Amos Rusie, the famous pitcher of the nineties, worked the turnstiles. Bill Dahlen eventually helped run the park, Mickey Welch was on the gate, and Charles "Silver" King, a pitcher back in the eighties, became a sweeper.

His empire also included the constant claque of actors and athletes, like George M. Cohan, Charles B. Dillingham, Louis Mann and James J. Corbett. He cooled off at racetracks like Belmont, Jamaica, Empire City and Latonia, and he spent evenings at the Waldorf bar or getting his bets down at ringside.

He was king of the hill, and he was about to reclaim the hill. And whenever he ventured outside his own domain, he could be sure that his reception would be loud, turbulent and menacing. To know him was to love him or, just as likely, to hate him.

"His very walk across the field in a hostile town," wrote Grantland Rice, "is a challenge to the multitude."

Chapter

Honey Fitz

In April of 1911, a municipal tragedy of sorts befell New York City. The wooden grandstand at the Polo Grounds burned. The fire occurred early in the morning, so nobody was injured. But the central tragedy, it seemed at the time, was that they had just started a grand comeback after five years of pursuing teams like the Chicago Cubs and Pittsburgh Pirates, and now suddenly they were homeless.

Still, people were not easily defeated in those days, either on or off the baseball field. The owner of the Giants was John T. Brush, and after accepting an offer of temporary co-occupancy with the New York Highlanders of the American League, he drove uptown to survey the damage.

Brush was an unusually determined man. He had been born in upstate New York in 1845, had been orphaned by the time he was four years old, had become a clothing salesman in Boston, Troy and Indianapolis, had enlisted in the First New York Artillery in the Civil War, and later had drifted into a career as a baseball executive and owner. He provided the mood and the bankroll for John McGraw to build his baseball empire.

John Brush also suffered from rheumatism and locomotor ataxia, and as a result he surveyed the empire from a wheelchair. But he still displayed a runaway flair for the sideshows of life.

"My father," recalled his daughter, Natalie Brush de Gendron, "was definitely stage-struck. He married an actress and joined the Lambs club. Almost every actor in New York had a pass to the Polo Grounds and the big stars had boxes. There was some method, of course, in his generosity. The public was well-advised that, every afternoon when there was no matinee, Julia Sanderson, DeWolfe Hopper, Donald Brian, Frank Craven, William Collier, David Warfield and many others could be seen at the Polo Grounds.

"The passes were another distinctive feature of the era. They were made for my father by Lambert Brothers, the jeweler. They were different each year. One year, a pack of playing cards with an autographed picture of an actor on each card. Another year, a penknife with a magnified peep-hole picture of the Polo Grounds in the handle."

When the Polo Grounds pavilion in left field burned that April, the owner of the Giants drove through a bereaved Broadway to his ruined ball park. "He sat in his wheelchair among the ruins of the old stand," his daughter said, "so ill that almost any other man would have taken the insurance and quit."

Instead, he turned to his wife, a former actress, and said: "Elsie, I want to build a concrete stand, the finest that can be constructed. It will mean economy for a time. Are you willing to stand by me?"

Elsie was, and the next day Brush started work on plans for the third baseball stadium of concrete and steel. Philadelphia and Pittsburgh had taken the first steps out of the wooden-grandstand period three years before, and now New York would get Brush Stadium. Mrs. de Gendron remembered two things about the architectural marvel, besides her father's soaring ideas for it. One was the series of coats-of-arms that he had inscribed around the summit of the grandstand, for each city in the National League. The cost of painting all this ornamental work every year, she noted, was very high. The second thing she remembered was that the Stonehams, who took control of the club during the next decade, "promptly tore it all off."

In any event, the Giants shared the Highlanders' field until their own was shored up again, while Brush pressed ahead with his plans for the concrete stadium, which was sufficiently rebuilt for occupancy by late June. And by autumn they had already stormed back to the top of the league and were confronting their old rivals, the Philadelphia Athletics, in the World Series. They got there by overtaking the Pirates on September 1 and then sprinting far ahead of the pack to win the pennant by 7½ games.

The series was played with appropriate ballyhoo, as it had been in 1905, when every game was a shutout and the Giants had won four out of five. Cartoonists and writers converged on the Polo Grounds. Mathewson, McGraw, Rube Marquard and Chief Meyers "wrote" daily reports on the games for the New York press. Then Connie Mack, Eddie Collins, Chief Bender and other celebrities "wrote" rebuttals for the Philadelphia press. John Brush dressed his team in the famous black uniforms of 1905 with the white trim. The Lambs turned out en masse for McGraw, though George M. Cohan caused a fuss by betting on Philadelphia and was promptly denounced by McGraw and his allies for treason.

The newspapers were carried away by it all, too. They glowed over the crowds of 50,000 or so that filled the new stadium, which caused some eyebrow-raising in the locker rooms. The players, who were being paid for the series on the basis of the attendance, had been advised that the "official" gate for the opening game was 38,281. Suspecting that they were being short-changed, the players dispatched a delegation to the owners to find out exactly how many customers had paid their way in. The delegation, headed by Chief Meyers, came streaming back in retreat, though, when the lords of the game berated them for having questioned the integrity of the good old national pastime.

Then the series opened, and Christy Mathewson outpitched Chief Bender, 2 to 1. Mathewson was six years older than he had been in 1905, which may have accounted for the fact that Philadelphia finally scored a run off him. Then, there being no Sunday baseball in the East, the teams sat out the next day, rode down to Philadelphia and resumed the series in Shibe Park on Monday. Frank Baker hit a home run off Rube Marquard and the Athletics won, 3 to 1, behind Eddie Plank.

Mathewson's ghost-writer thereupon chided Marquard in his "review" of the game for having pitched the ball where Baker could hit it. The Athletics pinned the clipping to their bulletin board and treated themselves to a literary chuckle. Then they went out the next afternoon and treated themselves to the unthinkable—they not only scored off Mathewson but scored three times for a 3-to-2 victory while Jack Coombs muzzled the Giants on three hits. As if that weren't enough, they won it in eleven innings after Baker had hit a home run off Mathewson in the ninth inning to tie the game. And this time Marquard's ghost-writer chided *Mathewson* for having pitched the ball where Baker could hit it.

The baseball war, to say nothing of the literary war, then was interrupted for six long days by an October monsoon. It rained almost steadily from October 17 to October 23, and when the rain stopped everybody tried to dry out the field by burning cans of gasoline around the grass. When they finally revived the series on the 24th, McGraw immediately threw Mathewson against the Athletics again. But the A's evidently were better rested than the great right-hander. They raked him for three doubles in a row in the fourth inning (including one by the irrepressible Baker) and got 10 hits in seven innings before McGraw relieved him.

The score was 4 to 2, Philadelphia, and now the Giants trooped back to their new concrete stadium trailing by three games to one, with only one more defeat between them and an unhappy ending. They won a reprieve, though, when they entered the last half of the ninth inning on the short end of a 3-to-1 score, and with two outs rallied for two runs to tie the game.

The roar from the crowd rolled across Coogan's Bluff for 10 minutes, and it rose to a shattering level in the last half of the tenth inning when the Giants scored again to win the game. Eddie Plank was pitching for Connie Mack by then, having replaced Jack Coombs, who had strained his leg muscles way back in the sixth inning but who had insisted somewhat expensively on sticking it out.

Then Larry Doyle opened the tenth with a double, and beat the throw to third base on a bunt by Fred Snodgrass. One out later, Merkle sent Danny Murphy to the right-field wall at the foul line for his long fly ball. Murphy hesitated, considered letting the ball drop foul, then caught it just fair. Doyle, meanwhile, had tagged up at third and barreled into home plate with a fallaway slide right out of McGraw's Baltimore Orioles' repertoire. The only trouble was that he fell away from the plate and never touched it.

Bill Klem stood in his Solomon blue uniform behind the plate and watched in amazement, and said later that if any of the Philadelphia players had tagged Doyle before he left the field, he would have been out. Somehow, none of them ever did, and McGraw—taking the lapse without asking too many questions—still later complimented Mack and his captain, Harry Davis, on their "prudence and good sportsmanship."

The next day, though, the lapses were on the other foot, so to speak. Philadelphia got seven runs on seven hits in the seventh inning, while the Giants generally collapsed and McGraw sizzled. Merkle dropped a throw on a bunt, Marquard threw a wild pitch, Meyers declined to chase it and the Athletics won the game and the series by the unholy score of 13 to 2. Baker, who had batted .375 and hit two home runs, became a national hero as "Home Run" Baker. The Athletics, having avenged their World Series defeat of 1905, returned home as lions. George M. Cohan, who had scored a betting coup, returned to the grille room at the Lambs with money in his pockets but with the uncomfortable feeling that McGraw and his circle were staring at the back of his head.

The next month, McGraw left his disappointment behind in the chilly city and hied the Giants off to Cuba for some exhibition games. It was his first visit there in twenty-one years, when he had been a seventeen-year-old country boy on tour with Al Lawson's American All-Stars. He was startled to find that he was still *el mono amarillo* to the sporting public in Havana. His players, after losing two games to the Havana Reds, were even more startled when *el mono amarillo* ordered them out for morning practice.

They recovered their manager's affections, though, when Mathewson stopped the Havana Almendares on Thanksgiving Day, 2 to 0. And everything returned to normal that night when McGraw celebrated far and wide and high, and got into a cafe brawl that wound up in court. But this was a city of passions that he admired, and for the rest of his life he and Blanche McGraw spent anywhere from a couple of weeks to a couple of months most winters in the favorite island haunt of *el mono amarillo*.

In 1912, the Giants broke from the starting gate, took first place by May 15 and stayed there. It was a running, fighting team with Merkle and Meyers supplying most of the punch. It was joined by George Burns, a young outfielder from Utica of the New York State League, whom McGraw promptly told to sit on the bench near him and listen. Burns did, for the whole season, and then a year later took over left field—for nine seasons.

The Giants also were joined by the man the King of Sweden had described as "the greatest athlete in the world," Jim Thorpe. That was during the summer of 1912, when Thorpe had climbed from the Carlisle Indian School to world renown in the Olympic Games. And later, when Thorpe was stripped of his medals because he had played a few professional baseball games at Carlisle, McGraw hurried to sign him for the Giants. He wasn't sure Thorpe could play baseball, but he was very sure that people would pay to find out.

He was right. People did pay, and they kept paying as the Giants racked up 103 victories against 48 defeats. In the American League, meanwhile, the Boston Red Sox were racking up 105 against 47 defeats under Jake Garland Stahl, a first-baseman who could hit as well as manage the team and who also worked in the off-season as a banker in Chicago.

These were the Red Sox who had won the pennant in 1904, but who had missed the chance to play in a World Series because McGraw refused to meet the representative of a "bush" league. They had not won since then, but now they returned with muscles eight years later. They beat out Connie Mack's "greatest team"—his famous $100,000 infield and his great pitching staff, which had been strengthened by the signing of Herb Pennock, an eighteen-year-old Philadelphian who lived a manorial life as the "Squire of Kennett Square," who rode to hounds and who became one of the game's premier pitchers.

These were Red Sox of Smoky Joe Wood, who won 34 games and lost only 5; Hugh Bedient, a rookie who won 20; Bucky O'Brien, a spitball expert, and Sea Lion Charley Hall. Plus a distinguished outfield of Duffy Lewis, Tris Speaker and Harry Hooper. They also had a new home in Fenway Park that year, and one of the most riotous traveling claques in America. And they had a civic entourage led by Mayor John F. Fitzgerald himself, an incredibly energetic figure in a stovepipe hat who went where the Red Sox went, regaling them with tenor solos, and who five years later became the grandfather of John F. Kennedy.

"The World Series," recalled Frederick G. Lieb, the baseball writer and historian, who saw his first series in 1910, "had developed from a post-season event—of concern largely to the interested cities—to something like the great national spectacle that it is today. The country virtually shut up shop to await the result. The queue of fans started at the ticket windows to the Polo Grounds at Eighth Avenue and 157th Street, extended south on Eighth Avenue to 145th Street, where the police turned the line westward to Broadway. It was a line stretching from the Polo Grounds over a mile distant.

"Many started this long vigil the night before, and after standing in line ten hours and upward, they were rewarded by hearing the heart-rending cry: 'All sold out. No more seats or standing room for sale.' "

The fury was increased by people like Horace Fogel, the owner of the Philadelphia Phillies, who finished fifth in an eight-team league but who nonetheless took it hard. The race, he charged, had been "fixed" for McGraw's team to win. The collusion, he protested to the league's new president, Thomas J. Lynch, included umpires and Thomas J. Lynch (who wasted no time denouncing Fogel for his buckshot accusations).

The newspapers did their part, too. For days before the series, they ran pictures and stories comparing the teams position by position. They even ran personalized comparisons by writers like Hugh Fullerton, who had amazed people in 1906 by correctly predicting the outcome of each game between the Chicago Cubs and the Chicago White Sox. Fullerton was on the staff of the Chicago *Tribune* then, and even his own city editor hesitated to print his forecast that the White Sox, the original "hitless wonders" of baseball, would upset their crosstown rivals. They did, and Fullerton emerged as a seer with mystic vision.

His mystic vision seemed even more potent when he correctly called the next three World Series, and by 1912 his analyses were being published in papers like *The New York Times* under headlines that advised: "Hugh Fullerton Favors Gardner over Herzog," in the match-up between the rival third-basemen. *The Times* also ran letters from irate readers denouncing Fullerton's mystic vision at great length, to wit:

"I cannot too strongly object to that part of Mr. Fullerton's article in today's *Times* which says, 'If there is trouble during this coming series, which is extremely probable, it will come from efforts to cut Charlie Wagner, for already I have heard that the Giants' campaign is to make Wagner keep away from the bag.' All fair-minded fans will agree that such a statement is wholly uncalled-for."

Momentous events outside the sports pages seemed to fade in the face of such clamor, too. Less than six months earlier, the White Star liner *Titanic* had been wrecked by an iceberg during her maiden voyage from Southampton to New York with a loss of more than 1,500 lives. China became a republic that year and elected its first president. Captain Robert F. Scott and four companions reached the South Pole, only to perish on the return to civilization. Teddy Roosevelt, saying "I feel like a bull moose," broke away from the Republican party and fought both President Taft and Woodrow Wilson for the White House. Lieutenant Charles Becker of the New York Police Department was going on trial for complicity in the murder of Herman Rosenthal, a gambler who had accused Becker of being his silent partner. Rosenthal then was gunned down at 2 o'clock one morning as he left the Hotel Metropole by four trigger men with appropriately incriminating names—"Gyp the Blood" Horowitz, "Lefty Louie" Rosenberg, "Whitey" Lewis and "Dago Frank" Cirosici. A citizen noticed the license number of the getaway car, the plot was foiled (a little late) and District Attorney Charles S. Whitman rode to political fame by lining up an array of witnesses that included "Billiard Ball" Jack Rose, "Bridgey" Webber and other midtown creatures.

And, as the World Series crowded these events from the top of the front page, an immense naval armada of 123 ships approached New York on a visit. *The New York Times,* maintaining its perspective in this kaleidoscope of history, declared in an editorial on the morning of October 7:

"This is to be a week of notable incidents. As the third from the last week of the most bewildering Presidential campaign of recent memory, it should be full of political excitement. The greatest naval pageant in the history of this country will begin at the city's gates. A criminal trial of larger significance than any in late years will begin.

"Yet, who will doubt that public interest will center on none of these, but on the games of baseball at our Polo Grounds and in Boston?"

Mayor Fitzgerald of Boston was not one of those who might doubt the truth of such a statement. Turning aside from the cares of City Hall business, he threw himself joyously into the Red Sox pilgrimage to New York. He paused for a semi-pro game on the eve of the series that was held to raise money to buy a car for Manager Stahl, but that succeeded chiefly in clawing up the turf of Fenway Park. Then he paused to read a telegram from Mayor William Gaynor of New York, inviting him to share the municipal box at the Polo Grounds the next day "to witness the defeat of the Red Sox by the Giants."

Honey Fitz dashed off the following reply: "It will give me pleasure to be your guest as the Red Sox begin their onward march to the world championship and to congratulate you upon the fact that your city, the greatest in the country and possessing the best ball team in the National League, is to have the distinguished honor of adding to the glory of the best city in the world and to the laurels of the finest ball team ever organized."

Then the Mayor put on his stovepipe hat and joined the Red Sox, who were reported to be "polishing their arms for the clash." And with the boisterous mob of marching attendants known at the Royal Rooters, and with two brass bands, they all clambered aboard four special trains carrying more than a thousand Bostonians to New York for the big show.

They announced that they had "unlimited money to bet on the Red Sox," and they began to show it as soon as the cavalcade checked into the Bretton Hall Hotel at Broadway and Eighty-sixth Street. They roamed the lobbies of hotels, they swept through bars and restaurants, they looked blankly when a New Yorker in one taproom shouted: "I am ready to pay $100 right now for a pair of tickets to tomorrow's game."

William Pink, a wholesale liquor dealer from Boston who was in charge of the Royal Rooters invasion, said there was $100,000 in Sox money aboard the caravan and, he complained, it was going begging along Broadway. Scores of women added to the din with megaphones. The secretary of the Red Sox, Robert McRoy, howled that the mails had been tampered with and forgery committed by fans trying to claim tickets meant for others.

When the Boston crowd swept into Grand Central that day, it was 6 p.m. and the evening rush hour was well under way. They immediately created one of the greatest traffic jams in New York's memory. But the best, or possibly the worst, was yet to come.

That night, the sky over Manhattan was lit with a torchlight parade down Broadway in which they demonstrated their loud solidarity behind the Red Sox, to say nothing of their loud harmony behind Honey Fitz.

Marching diagonally across the busy island, the Royal Rooters and their allies touched off a rollicking celebration in anticipation of a victory in McGraw's own backyard. They serenaded the enemy along the sidewalks with numbers like "Tessie" and "When I Get You Alone Tonight," and every couple of blocks the procession would stop while Honey Fitz himself lifted his Irish tenor in solo salutes to the finest ball club in the world, the Red Sox.

"If the air around Times Square was surcharged with suspense of the approaching contest," reported *The Times* on page 1, "there was no word to describe the cumulative excitement in the atmosphere around the Polo Grounds, where the general admission line began to form at 9 o'clock last night."

The grandstand for the opening game was black with derby hats and 36,000 persons crammed inside the gates when the Royal Rooters marched onto the field of combat. They entered from the Eighth Avenue side with a 30-piece band, 300 parading fans and a ringleader known as "Nuf Ced" McGreevy. They crossed and recrossed the diamond like storm troopers until they finally were herded to their block of seats so that the game could begin. But through it all, they roared cheers and songs that clashed and crashed against the catcalls of the unorganized New York fans. One of their war songs, a paean to the Red Sox heroes, was put maliciously to the tune of "Tammany" and went:

> *Carrigan, Carrigan,*
> *Speaker, Lewis, Wood and Stahl.*
> *Bradley, Engle, Pape and Hall.*
> *Wagner, Gardner, Hooper, too.*
> *Hit them! Hit them! Hit them! Hit them!*
> *Do, boys, do.*

Immense crowds clogged Times Square to the south and followed the game on an electric scoreboard that had been hoisted on the north facade of the Times Building, and the press reported: "There have been vast crowds in Times Square before, but never one as large as that which congregated there yesterday."

The scoreboard was 16 feet long by 7 feet high, and was operated by direct wire from the ball park to *The Times,* where an operator flashed the play-by-play information to the board itself. Separate tables on the board showed the balls and strikes, the number of outs and so on, while lights depicted the base-runners as they worked their way toward home plate. The crowd gathered an hour before Jeff Tesreau's first pitch, and traffic was diverted from the Square by battalions of policemen.

Honey Fitz, meanwhile, commanded the stage of bedlam uptown in the Polo Grounds. Sensationally decked in his black silk hat and a gleaming white collar, he posed for pictures during the game with a police commissioner, a governor, several mayors and an admiral. He also kept up a running stream of encouragement for the Red Sox, who scored one run in the sixth inning when Josh Devore crossed in front of Fred Snodgrass, causing him to muff Speaker's line drive for a triple. Then they scored three more in the seventh and won the game, 4 to 3, while the Royal Rooters tore the place apart.

The next afternoon in Boston, Honey Fitz made a couple of speeches, presented the new car to Manager Stahl, presented another one to Tris Speaker, then took the first ride in it, and then presented a silver bat to "Heinie" Wagner. One astonished New York fan said: "If Barnum had lived in the same town with the Mayor, P.T. would have had a look-in."

The two brass bands struck up long before the game itself started, and kept blaring for eleven long innings as the Red Sox tore into the great Mathewson for three runs in the first inning. Mathewson had been held out of the opener, to the dismay of many New York fans, because McGraw had a hunch that Tesreau might surprise the Red Sox in the opener and then Mathewson would take over in Boston. But his hunch wore thin, and the Giants committed five errors behind Mathewson. Herzog gave Speaker the hip as Speaker rounded third base and a fight broke out, and the teams were still deadlocked when the game was called after eleven innings, 6 to 6.

The National Commission hurried into executive session and decided that the tie should be replayed in Boston the next day before everybody got aboard the night-owl express and returned to New York. So the Giants, the Red Sox and the Royal Rooters went at it again, with Rube Marquard outpitching Bucky O'Brien for McGraw, 2 to 1. But the game ended in even more monumental confusion as a heavy mist seeped into the ball park from the sea and blanketed the players like ghosts at sundown. Just then Forrest Cady hit a line drive toward the right-field corner with two Red Sox on base in the last half of the dark ninth inning. Josh Devore apparently made a running catch and kept on running right into the Giants' clubhouse. But many of the Boston faithful left the park thinking the ball had whistled past Devore for a 3-to-2 Red Sox victory. And it took a lot of loud hassling to prevent a full-scale riot in Kenmore Square that night.

In the Polo Grounds the next day, it was cloudy but not misty and everybody, including McGraw, had a clear view as Joe Wood again outpitched Tesreau, 3 to 1, and now Boston moved ahead, two games to one. Twenty-four hours later, on Columbus Day, a crowd of 34,683 in Fenway Park watched the rookie Hugh Bedient defeat Mathewson, 2 to 1, and now Boston stood one game from winning it all.

However, life was not that simple. Back in the Polo Grounds the next afternoon, the Giants rose up against the tide and scored five runs in the first inning on two infield singles, two outfield singles, a pair of doubles, a balk, a wild throw and, as the *coup de grâce* by McGraw, a double steal. It was a good inning's work, and it stood up under Marquard's pitching for a 5-to-2 victory, sending the World Series commuters back to Boston for the sixth complete game on October 15.

It was another memorable afternoon in Fenway Park, and if Paul Revere had come riding through the park during that tumultuous time, he might have gone unnoticed. President Taft was aboard the yacht "Mayflower" off Newport, and he inquired how the ball game was going. So the details were supplied through naval wireless at Torpedo Station—running details, as the

Giants and the Red Sox and their disciples raged at one another for four hours.

The scene was properly unhinged when the Royal Rooters marched onto the field singing their favorite campaign song, "Tessie," while the brass bands clanged and the crowd went wild. Then they started to clear the field for the game only to find their special section in the grandstand already pre-empted by Fenway fans. Back across the field in protest went the Royal Rooters en masse, as Smoky Joe Wood went to the mound to pitch for Boston. But the Rooters were trapped on the diamond without seats, and they weren't about to give up that easily. For 30 minutes they stormed about the field, fighting off waves of policemen on foot and on horses, until they were driven back toward the outfield fence. Finally, they charged the bleacher fence like the light brigade, knocked it down and flooded into the crowd, brass bands trumpeting away and havoc breaking out while Joe Wood stood by waiting to pitch.

There was also plenty of havoc during the game, which the Giants won with six runs in the first inning, 11 to 4. And, after the game, there was more when the Royal Rooters wreaked their vengeance on a team, a stadium and a town they felt had let them down.

The Giants, who had been on the short end of the series by three games to one, now were all even with their tormentors as the final game approached on Wednesday, October 16. It was played in Fenway Park, because the Red Sox had won the toss of the coin for the deciding match. But McGraw felt certain that was all they would win. He had Mathewson ready to pitch and what were the odds that his champion would go winless three times in one seven-game series?

Whatever the odds might be, Mathewson found himself in a desperate duel with rookie Bedient, who was making his second start of the series. New York scored one run in the third, and almost scored another in the sixth when Larry Doyle hit a rousing drive to the temporary bleachers in right-center that Hooper somehow caught.

In the seventh, the Giants' lead disappeared when Manager Stahl looped a two-bagger among three of the New York fielders in short left and a pinch-hitter, Olaf Henriksen, lined one of Mathewson's fadeaway pitches off the bag at third base for another double. Nobody scored in the eighth or ninth, as Joe Wood pitched for Boston in relief against Mathewson. But in the top of the tenth, Red Jack Murray doubled, Merkle singled and the Giants suddenly were ahead again, 2 to 1.

McGraw now was only three outs from taking the whole series, and he had Christy Mathewson pitching for those three outs. Then the first Boston batter in the bottom of the tenth, Clyde Engle, lifted a soft fly toward Fred Snodgrass in center. Snodgrass moved ten feet, raised his glove, seemed to catch the ball—and then let it trickle to the grass. Engle wound up on second base.

Then Hooper lashed a wicked line drive to center and, ironically, Snodgrass made a tremendous catch. But Mathewson walked Steve Yerkes, and then was pitching to Boston's best hitter, Tris Speaker. Again, McGraw seemed to be in good shape when Speaker raised a foul ball alongside first base. But again fate was outrageous. Meyers, the catcher, and Merkle, the first-baseman, played Alphonse and Gaston and let it drop. Then Speaker lined a single to right, tying the game.

McGraw played a final, long, forlorn card. With Yerkes on third base and Speaker on first, he ordered Mathewson to walk Duffy Lewis, filling the bases and giving the Giants a possible force-out at any one of them. But there was still only one out and Larry Gardner followed with a long fly to right field that scored Yerkes with the run that ended the struggle in another cascade of noise, shouts, cheers and tears.

As the game ended and the crowd swirled onto the field, McGraw ran over and shook Stahl's hand. As he did, he was tripped from behind by a rambunctious young man, at whom he promptly took a roundhouse swing.

The Giants, beaten by four games to three with one eleven-inning tie, streamed back to New York. The Red Sox, who had hung from a cliff and survived, lived through one more uproarious day before the tumult died down. The next day, from Fenway Park to Faneuil Hall, the streets echoed with cheers as Boston greeted the new world champions. Each of the Red Sox also got $4,028 plus an extra day's pay, because the final game had been played one day after the regular contracts expired. The management almost passed out the money then and there, but realized that $80,000 was a lot of cash for the players to be lugging around during the celebrating, and postponed the payday 24 hours.

"Mayor Fitzgerald, clad in his greatcoat in which he romped so joyously about the Polo Grounds," reported *The Times'* man in Boston, "was at the ball grounds early to congratulate the players. There was a tremendous rush of people at Faneuil Hall, where Mayor Fitzgerald and Speaker Walker of the Massachusetts House spoke."

Honey Fitz doffed his stovepipe toward the enemy, saying, "I am going to write to Muggsy McGraw—I believe that is what he's called—and tell him that any man like Matty who can give this team such a run must be the best in the world."

Then, doffing his stovepipe toward the home side, he promised silver cups to the Red Sox, extolled them in superlatives, and ended his speech with a plea for cheaper seats at the ball park.

Chapter

6

The Changing Of the Guard

On November 25, one month after the New York Giants lost the World Series of 1912, John McGraw's cup grew more bitter.

John Brush, who had staked him for ten years, was en route to California, hoping the climate would relieve his serious condition. In pain, he had watched the series from a wheelchair, and was now aboard his private railroad car, the "Oceanic," on the Chicago, Burlington and Quincy road. Two nurses, a valet and a railroad man were with him near the town of Louisiana, Missouri, northwest of St. Louis, when he died.

The owners of the other clubs in the National League, who, more often than not, had been at one another's throats, joined to mourn him as a pioneer who had taken the lead in settling the anarchy in baseball at the turn of the century. McGraw headed for the funeral in Indianapolis and said, "He was as tender as a dear girl. As I look back over it, it appears to me like a revelation of what man can endure. The lower portions of his limbs suffered intensely. Yet that head of his never suffered. He was there at all times when it came to the transaction of the great big business in life. This is a great battle, this battle of life. What a wonderful, what a beautiful, character was John Brush."

Control of the Giants now passed to Mrs. Brush and her daughters. A son-in-law by a first marriage, Harry N. Hempstead, became president. He was a shy man who had spent most of his adult life in Brush's clothing business in Indianapolis, and he tended to leave the baseball end of the Giants to the secretary of the club, John B. Foster. For McGraw, though, the front office seemed a little less cheery.

★   ★   ★

In June of 1913, the Giants started to move upward and were on top by July, winning their third straight pennant and their fifth in ten years. And for the third time, they faced their old rivals, the Philadelphia Athletics. Each team had taken one World Series, and this would be the deciding one, and the last, between the two most celebrated managers in the game. A fortune teller sat in the Philadelphia dugout before the series and told Connie Mack, "All signs are favorable."

They were, too. In the opening game, Marquard was overpowered by Bender, Baker, Eddie Collins and the rest of Mack's strong club, 6 to 4. Baker, living up to his nickname, even hit a two-run home run, an echo of his shots of 1911.

In the second game, Mathewson and Plank renewed a pitching rivalry that had started even before the great shutouts of 1905. With the game scoreless, Philadelphia put runners on second and third in the bottom half of the ninth inning and somehow failed to score. One runner was thrown out at the plate, another was run down on the bases and Mathewson finally threw out Eddie Murphy for the third out in an inning of unusual pitching. Then in the tenth, New York scored three times and Mathewson was a winner again, 3 to 0.

But that was the end of the trail. Philadelphia won the next three games and the series, with Plank pitching a two-hitter in the final one and beating Mathewson, 3 to 1. It was the end in more ways than one. Wilbert Robinson, who had been running the Diamond Cafe back in Baltimore for McGraw, had rejoined his old Oriole partner and now coached the Giants at first base while McGraw coached at third. But a fierce argument broke out between the longtime friends after Robbie sent a runner down to second base, only to see him thrown out. Robinson said McGraw had given the signal, McGraw said he hadn't, and the debate raged all day and all evening until McGraw ended the argument and a 20-year friendship by saying imperiously, "You're fired." Robinson later became manager of the Brooklyn Dodgers, and the teams became as bitter as their managers. But on that particular day in 1913, another fragment of the old order passed from McGraw's life.

One voice from the past that was heard at the World Series belonged to Albert G. Spalding, the baseball patriarch. He came east from his home in California, stopped off in Chicago to confer with Charles Comiskey, another of the old-timers, and then watched McGraw's boys lose their third straight series.

McGraw's boys also were watched by swarms of people from his current life along Broadway. The press, in fact, regularly listed celebrities at series games and even divided them into categories; for instance "the theatrical profession," which was represented that year by George M. Cohan, Samuel Harris, James J. Corbett, Miss Catherine Calvert, Miss Louise B. Johnson, Al Jolson, Wilson Mizner, Harry Bulger, Eddie Foy, DeWolfe Hopper, Jake Shubert, Lee Shubert, Willie Collier, Frank Fogarty, Billy Jerome, Gus Edwards, A. L. Erlanger, Marc Klaw, William A. Morris, Felix Isman, Paul Keith and William Hammerstein.

Even Connie Mack had become a public lion. His face beamed from newspaper advertisements during the series, a straw hat on his long, lean head, a smile on his face. "I drink Coca-Cola myself," Connie was saying in the ad, "and advise all the team to drink it. I think it is good for them." (It was cheap enough for them—five cents a glass.)

But Connie still wasn't in McGraw's league as a *social* lion. McGraw had even toured the vaudeville circuit for fifteen weeks the winter before, performing a stand-up monologue from material culled by Bozeman Bulger of *The New York Evening World* and using a stage technique implanted by his acting cronies at the Lambs.

Actors and celebrities were everywhere, even in the press box. A few years earlier, Hugh Fullerton arrived for a World Series game and found his seat taken by Louis Mann, the actor. Mann refused to leave, so Fullerton sat on his lap and covered the game that way.

One of the first by-lines carried over a sports story in *The New York Times* belonged to no less a celebrity than John L. Sullivan. He covered the fight between Jim Jeffries and Jack Johnson in Reno on July 4, 1910, and his lead paragraph read: "The fight of the century is over and a black man is the undisputed champion of the world." The managing editor of *The Times,* an Egyptologist, mathematician and all-around genius named Carr Van Anda, ran four pages on the fight and posted bulletins on the windows of the Times Building, drawing 30,000 sidewalk readers.

A few years later, the fight between Jack Dempsey and Georges Carpentier got banner headlines on page 1 and the by-line on the main story belonged to Irvin S. Cobb. And still later, Van Anda sent a Rhodes scholar named Elmer Davis to Shelby, Montana, to report the Dempsey-Tom Gibbons match, and Davis wound up with *three* by-lines.

It was an expanding world, and McGraw was about to expand his view of it. In fact, Spalding had come east during the World Series with precisely that in mind. He had taken a baseball team on a world tour in 1888, and now McGraw and Comiskey were asking his guidance in planning one for the Giants and Chicago White Sox in the winter of 1913-14.

Maybe they felt the passing of the seasons and of the old order the way John Barrymore did in a commentary on a book titled "The Broadway That Was." The actor described it this way: "Broadway has grown smugger. It has grown commonplace and garish. Everybody you see on the street is ready money. If you don't own an automobile, you don't belong on Broadway. It wasn't so in my time."

Whatever they felt, they decided to take their baseball teams across the continents and see something new. It would be their last chance for a long time. The nations of Europe were already flexing their muscles, and one winter later it would be too late for goodwill tours.

McGraw also was turning his back on those three straight World Series losses and on the passing of his patron, John Brush. So he threw himself into the tour details with exaggerated enthusiasm, recruiting players from other teams to flesh out his own. Even Bill Klem went along. They started in Cincinnati on October 18 and played their way west, raising money in Chicago, Missouri, Kansas, Oklahoma, Texas, California, Oregon and Vancouver.

They played in the snow in Springfield, Illinois, and in front of hundreds of Indians from the reservations near Sioux City, Iowa, who had come to cheer Chief Meyers and Jim Thorpe. Then, on November 19, the entourage of 50 players, officials and friends of McGraw left the eight-car special train and boarded the "Empress of Japan" to begin 23 rough days at sea. The tour took them to Yokohama, Kobe, Nagasaki, Shanghai, Hong Kong, Manila, Brisbane on New Year's Day of 1914, Colombo in January, through the Suez Canal to Cairo, Alexandria, Nice, Marseilles, Paris, Rome on February 8, London—and then home aboard a liner named the *Lusitania.*

"When I was a kid," McGraw said, explaining the motive for the trip in his somewhat pious public language, "I traveled with some teams whose members were very bad actors. After I joined the Baltimore team in 1891, there were more notorious bad actors on the club than on any team in the world. The old Orioles were champions of the world when it came to rough stuff. From the park to the nearest saloon, there was a beaten path that these players took as soon as they could get dressed.

"But in spite of the great improvement in the class of men who play the game, the bad name has clung to the sport, and lots of folks expect the professional ball player to be rough and are surprised when he talks English which can be understood."

So the tour, he said, was intended to be a "monument" to baseball. Six sets of newlyweds, including the Thorpes, were aboard to help cement the impression of propriety. And McGraw even dispatched a diary report of his adventures to *The New York Times.*

He told how "a great crowd" had turned out at Brisbane to see the Giants beat the White Sox. He reported "a most cordial reception in the Mikado's country" after a storm-tossed trip to Japan. He seemed surprised at a Japanese pitcher with good control, some "stuff" (but not enough) and "a pair of heavy, gold-rimmed spectacles." Jim Thorpe and his bride climbed into a rickshaw and their weight crushed it, spilling them to the ground. In Tokyo, a misunderstanding with a pair of policemen almost led to an old-fashioned fight until the Giants boarded a steamer for Nagasaki, while crowds of Japanese shouted "banzai! banzai!" at them.

"Someday," McGraw predicted, "the streets of Japan will have signs reading: Baseball today, Japan vs. United States. The Japs are great imitators. You'd be surprised to see how quickly they pick up the tricks of the game. The manner of throwing curveballs puzzles them, but they can run the bases and field the ball very well."

In London, after a brief comedy of protocol, in which the Giants switched hurriedly from high hats to bowlers and frock coats, they met the king.

"I am glad to meet you, Mr. McGraw," said George V. "Your game is very interesting and I would like to know more about it."

"We certainly hope that you will have a chance to see more of it," replied McGraw, bowing and retreating to his bench.

He played before 35,000 Englishmen that day, and also met the khedive of Egypt and the Pope of Rome before the expedition turned for home on February 28. They had gone from Cincinnati to Australia to the pyramids, and they came home on March 6, 1914, after 30,000 miles of trying to build McGraw's "monument" to baseball.

What baseball needed more than a monument, though, was some sanity. As they stepped ashore at 11 o'clock on a misty morning, the press noted, "the pier was as noisy as a suffragette meeting." It wasn't just that a delegation of baseball executives was on hand to greet them, including Ban Johnson and Charley Ebbets. Nor that the players stepped down the gangway with suntans and Bond Street clothes. Nor that newsreel companies struggled to photograph them all the way from the Quarantine Station to the Palace Theatre that evening. The big commotion that day was that the players stepped ashore into the middle of another baseball war. A rival group called the Federal League had reopened the era of talent raids, forcing the American and National Leagues to rush to claim their own stars before their clubs were picked clean. The Red Sox gave Tris Speaker the lordly sum of $37,000 for two years, a record salary, to keep him in Boston. Joe Tinker was offered $37,000 for three years by the Federals, who also offered McGraw $100,000 to jump from the National League.

The Federal League had little experience but a lot of cash. The bankrolls belonged to people like Harry Sinclair, the oil baron; Charles Weeghman, a Chicago restaurant man; Jil Gilmore, a coal and paper executive, and even Phil DeCatesby Ball, the "ice king of St. Louis." They wanted to share in the new, growing profits that were being stoked by the new, expanding stadiums and the stars who filled them with people. They picked off Tinker, then Hal Chase, Mordecai Brown, Chief Bender, Jack Quinn and Eddie Plank. Even Walter Johnson was tempted to jump, but backed off when the Washington Senators raised the ante at the last moment and kept him.

Ty Cobb, who had just signed another Detroit contract for $12,000, met with Sinclair in the Commodore Hotel in New York and got one of the most lavish offers of all. Sinclair, who later won the Kentucky Derby with the great colt Zev, and who later still went to jail after the Teapot Dome oil scandal, controlled $60,000,000. He offered Cobb a three-year deal for $100,000. If the league failed, Cobb remembered, the deal included a guarantee that Cobb would become the highest priced oil-lease man in the history of the Sinclair Company.

The league collected enough players to operate during 1914 and 1915, then lost out to World War I. Cobb, though, smartly used the league's pressure to win a 50 percent raise from Detroit and became the highest-paid player of his time.

But far more serious struggles hung over the Giants and White Sox as they returned home on the *Lusitania* in 1914. Lloyd George, the Chancellor of the Exchequer, observed that "people are tired of armies," and opened a "peace campaign." Woodrow Wilson foresaw a bright economic outlook with a downward revision of the tariff and the new income tax law. In New York, John Purroy Mitchel became Mayor and promised to end "waste" in the city. But the big thing, people noticed, was that the throngs in Times Square seemed quieter and more apprehensive.

The Giants had already opened their training base at Marlin, Texas, while McGraw and the nucleus of the team was abroad. They slipped back from the top again that year while the "miracle Braves" of Boston went from eighth place to the pennant and then the world championship. But a more important event for the Giants that season was the sale of the Highlanders, who by then were known as the Yankees, to two of McGraw's friends, Colonel Jacob Ruppert and Colonel Tillinghast l'Hommedieu Huston.

They were often seen at the Polo Grounds and once had inquired about the chances of buying the Giants. But McGraw had touted them on the Yankees, who even moved into the Polo Grounds as tenants because they needed a bigger park. They stayed until 1923, and by then were challenging McGraw for his grip on the New York public.

Before the Yankees became a problem in McGraw's world, though, there were numerous other things that caused that broad, blunt brow to furrow. For example, both McGraw and Connie Mack plunged from the top of baseball to the bottom at precisely the same time, in 1915. That was only two years after they had staged their third World Series, and their plunge was as spectacular as their ascent.

Age was one factor, and money was another. In Mack's case, he decided to unload his veteran pitchers in one salvo. So Bender, Plank and Coombs all were waived out of the league and released unconditionally, 24 months after they had outpitched McGraw's staff for the world title. Then the infield was jettisoned, in stages. Collins was sold to the Chicago White Sox for $50,000 and later Home Run Baker went to the Yankees for $37,500.

Mack came close to salvaging his whole situation for years to come. His friend Jack Dunn, the owner of the Baltimore club of the International League, was being crowded by the Federal League in his town. The Federals' team gave the city a "big league" feeling while it existed, and the city responded by ignoring Dunn's team. So Dunn tried to raise cash by selling players to friend Mack, especially two young pitchers he felt certain could "help" Philadelphia. They were Ernie Shore and Babe Ruth.

"No, Jack," Connie said, acknowledging the offer. "You keep those fellows and sell them to someone who can give you real money for them."

As a result of shrewd moves like these, the Athletics toppled from first place to last place in the American League in 1915. The Giants, meanwhile, fell from second place to eighth in the National—the only time in McGraw's days that they rode the bottom when he managed the full season. Rube Marquard, who had won 19 straight games in 1912, from opening day through July 3 without losing, was used up, and went to the Brooklyn Dodgers. Fred Merkle also was sold to Brooklyn and Larry Doyle to Chicago. And on July 20, 1916, even the great Mathewson switched uniforms. He went to Cincinnati as manager in a complex deal that involved four other players and that gave Mathewson a chance to make his debut in the dugout.

Among the players McGraw picked up in these and other deals were Benny Kauff, "the Ty Cobb of the Federal League," and Edd Roush, one of the great independent minds in the game. Benny made a splash by holding out for a $10,000 cut of his sale price from the Federal League to the Giants, and he got it. He then arrived in the Giants' training camp in a fur-collared overcoat and derby hat, with four trunks of clothes and $7,500 in his pockets. Roush, who later held out on McGraw for a whole season, twisted the lion's tail just as scandalously. After watching him for a few games in 1916, the manager scolded him for using a 48-ounce bat. "Too heavy for you," he snapped.

Roush, no shrinking violet, replied, "What kind of league is this where the manager can tell you what bat to use?"

"Where did you hit?" McGraw snarled.

"I hit .300 in every league I've been in," Roush said, "and I'll hit .300 in this one."

He did, too (although not in 1916), and finished his career with a .325 average and a plaque in the Hall of Fame not far from McGraw's.

During all this switching of talent, the Giants opened 1916 by losing eight straight games. Then McGraw began to move bodies around like chess pieces, and they suddenly won 17 straight—*on the road.* McGraw meanwhile was trading Mathewson to Cincinnati along with the talented but unblushing Roush, receiving in return Charlie Herzog and an outfielder named Wade Killefer. It was the second time around for Herzog, who disliked McGraw as heartily as McGraw disliked him. But they respected each other, and agreed that they would try to convert their mutual dislike into a mutual profit.

As for Mathewson, McGraw said simply, "He not only was the greatest pitcher I ever saw, but he is my friend. He could stay with the Giants as long as he wanted to. However, I'm convinced his pitching days are over, and he is ambitious to become a manager, and I have helped him to gratify that ambition."

Mathewson had helped McGraw to gratify a few of his ambitions, too. He not only pitched those three shutouts in the World Series of 1905, but won 30 games a season four times and won 20 games for twelve straight seasons. He did all this with outstanding speed and outstanding stuff, and his control was uncommon. Grover Hartley, one of his catchers, contended that Mathewson could throw any pitch consistently into an area the size of a grapefruit.

Another switch brought Heinie Zimmerman from Chicago, a good-looking, husky New Yorker from the Bronx who made a solid debut with the Giants by striding up to the hotel desk in St. Louis and asking, "Any mail for the Great Zim?"

Having completed this series of housecleaning exercises, the Giants still trailed the Dodgers, Phillies and Braves all summer. Then, on September 7 in the Polo Grounds, they beat Brooklyn and kept on winning for 26 straight games. They still finished the season fourth, despite those two streaks of 17 games and 26, as the Dodgers sneaked into the pennant by a fraction over Philadelphia. It had been a rough year. Matty had gone, injuries had slowed the team, Brooklyn of all rivals had won the league title and on the final day of the season even McGraw left the bench, angrily intimating that his own players had quit on him against Wilbert Robinson's Dodgers. He immediately went to Cuba and sulked.

The following spring, with the war drawing closer to the United States, Harry Hempstead visited the club in Texas and gave McGraw a five-year contract. Then the Giants and Detroit Tigers barnstormed their way north through Oklahoma and Kansas, fighting each other with fists all the way to Kansas City, where they finally split and went home. Herzog and Cobb even fought it out in a hotel room in Dallas after a riot on the field, and Cobb shouted at McGraw at the height of the feud, "If you were a younger man, I'd kill you."

On April 6, as the teams played in Manhattan, Kansas, just before breaking off their series, they read on the bulletin board of the town newspaper that Wilson had asked Congress to declare war. The baseball season began five days later, but for once the country was looking the other way.

The season had its moments, though. In June, McGraw took a swing at Bill Byron, the "singing umpire," who had a habit of humming snatches of songs between pitches. Then he was fined $500 and suspended sixteen days by the president of the league, John K. Tener, whom he promptly insulted as a tool of the Philadelphia Phillies.

Finally, after a remarkable comeback from last place in two years, the Giants won the pennant—only to lose a rip-roaring World Series to a good Chicago White Sox team in five games. The series was marked by lots of fights and one more legend: Heinie Zimmerman, playing third base, chased Eddie Collins all the way across home plate with the ball when the Giants' catcher and pitcher left the plate unguarded. It was the last game of the series, and Zimmerman took a solid chorus of unjust jeers for his supposed "boner." To which the Great Zim replied with total accuracy: "Who the hell was I going to throw the ball to? Klem?"

McGraw, still suffering through a crotchety time, proved less than gracious in defeat. As he left the field, Pants Rowland, the Chicago manager, ran past and said, "Mr. McGraw, I'm sorry you had to be the one to lose." McGraw looked up and snarled, "Get away from me, you damned busher."

The big show, though, was happening someplace else. The newspapers now were running columns of names of "Men Enrolled in the National Army," along with the number of those "needed to fill the quota." About 20,000 draftees paraded along Fifth Avenue. The American Army organized its first camouflage company, and appealed for volunteers to learn "the art of military concealment, to spread the magic veil of invisibility—*camoufleur* is to the modern soldier what the handiest bush was to the American Indian."

Songsheets of "Slide, Kelly, Slide" and "Our National Game" took on a patriotic fervor. The Washington Senators became "the Statesmen." Sarah Bernhardt, appearing in "L'Aiglon" at the age of seventy-two, said the great hope of her life was "to be in Paris when victory is won and France is restored." Colonel Theodore Roosevelt turned war columnist for *The Kansas City Star,* and the paper announced that his dispatches would make Kansas City "the centre of a momentous discussion of events of transcendent importance."

The baseball season was halted on September 1 that year, 1918, while the newspapers ran big cartoons showing Uncle Sam chopping away at a huge pile of "essential work" and calling to a bunch of kids playing ball: "Here, Sonny, come over and help me with the job for a while."

Mathewson resigned at Cincinnati to take a commission in chemical warfare. Harvard Eddie Grant was killed three weeks before the armistice. Players joined up in droves, and the big crowds skipped the ball parks in droves. The Giants played before a record low attendance of 256,000.

Harry Hempstead now was looking for a chance to sell the stock in the club, which he voted for the heirs of his father-in-law, John Brush. The war was ending, but a whole new time was beginning. McGraw discussed the sale with Harry Sinclair, the oil king and Federal League angel. Then George M. Cohan and Sam Harris talked about buying the stock. But at the last minute, it went to a curb-market broker named Charles A. Stoneham. He was unknown in baseball circles, but had been, as he said, "a Giant fan all my life and an admirer of Mr. McGraw." He also owned a small stable of horses and had political ties to Al Smith and other Tammany chiefs, which seemed to be the *sine qua non* of New York Giant baseball.

Stoneham paid a million dollars for 1,300 shares and became president, succeeding Hempstead. McGraw bought 70 shares for about $50,000 and became vice president as well as manager. His friend, Magistrate Francis X. McQuade, also took 70 shares and became treasurer.

It was January 14, 1919. The war was over. The Seventy-seventh Division was headed home for a gigantic welcoming parade from Washington Square to 110th Street. Mail was being flown by air, and New York was forming an air police squadron of 150 wartime pilots headed by the vice chairman of the Mayor's Traffic Committee. Nobody, including the Mayor, knew exactly what it would do. Brigadier General Douglas MacArthur was appointed commandant at West Point. In four months, Sunday baseball would come to New York and 35,000 patrons would turn out at the Polo Grounds and 25,000 at Ebbets Field on the same Sunday to "celebrate the death of a blue law." *The Ladies' Home Journal,* reveling in the end of Federal restrictions on paper, announced that it was immediately going to 184 pages with color pictures of the war, and articles like "How I Wrote The 'Battle Hymn of The Republic,' " by Julia Ward Howe.

But it was still a frosty day in January when the Giants were sold, and the rush of personal and public events was swirling. Mrs. McGraw recalled that late that January evening, seventeen years after they had arrived in New York, she and Mr. McGraw took a long hansom ride through Central Park across the snow.

1890: Not yet seventeen, John Joseph McGraw becomes a professional baseball player for Olean of the New York-Pennsylvania League. With the country boy playing third base, Olean loses its first six games.

The Baltimore Orioles of the Gay
Nineties, the grandest baseball
team in the land. Down front, Willie
Keeler (right) and the boy wonder,
John McGraw. The mustaches in
the center of the first row belong to
Ned Hanlon, the manager of the
team, and Wilbert Robinson, the
catcher who became the longtime
friend and confidant of McGraw as
their careers grew.

Don't let the fancy clothes fool you.
By 1899, McGraw was the manager
and chief perpetrator of "Oriole
baseball," a blazing bag of tricks.

"And so," Blanche McGraw remembered, "we went to New York and the Giants." That was in 1902, and when John McGraw was photographed two years later guarding the bag with that resolute look, he already was celebrated as manager of the Giants.

1907: "Stoutly knit, as game as a pit-bird," Gene Fowler recalled, and "he was very much in earnest when socking time was declared."

John T. Brush, the owner of the Giants, also was the owner of that great motorcar and that great manager.

Wilbert Robinson (left) and Christy Mathewson were the brightest gems in McGraw's crown.

When Bill Klem talked, even McGraw listened. Klem began his career as an umpire in the National League in 1905, the year the Giants won their first World Series. In his first appearance at the Polo Grounds, he was baited by McGraw and promptly heaved him out of the game. In private, McGraw said Klem was the best umpire he had ever seen. Klem said McGraw was a "champion" among managers. But in public, they were at each other's throats.

In his first twenty-three full seasons as master of the Giants, they won the pennant ten times and ran second nine times, and Mr. McGraw left nothing to chance.

Bert Niehoff (left), who had a relatively short career of six summers in the big leagues, and Ray Schalk (right), an 18-year man who made the Hall of Fame, both closed their careers playing for the master.

Yankee Manager Miller Huggins (left) was bedeviled by John McGraw. Their teams first met in 1921 in the first of three consecutive World Series that became the Battle of Broadway. At stake: the mind and money of New York.

The look says it all: "The main idea is to win." And McGraw aimed to win whether he was performing at the Polo Grounds against the Boston Red Sox and their Royal Rooters, with Honey Fitz leading the parade in stovepipe hat and beaver coat, or performing downtown in the lounge at the Lambs. Wherever he was performing, he was regally dressed and regally immovable.

Allison   Wallace   Van Leon

Julger   Cain   Lane   Stoneham   Brown   Corhem   Warner   Gould   Heydler   Trumbull   O'Brien   Lieb   Bihler

Wedge   Walsh   O'Neill   Kieran   'Daniel'   McGraw   McGechan   Robinson   Roberts

July 15, 1927: With a fine sense of history, and a fine array of hats, baseball writers and officials surround Mr. McGraw at a Silver Jubilee luncheon in New York to remember the day he took charge of the Giants, twenty-five years earlier.

And a year later, at Braves Field in Boston, he was still swinging—hitting ground balls to the infield in pregame practice.

1922: The young giant visiting the old Giant during the World Series is the heavyweight champion himself, Jack Dempsey.

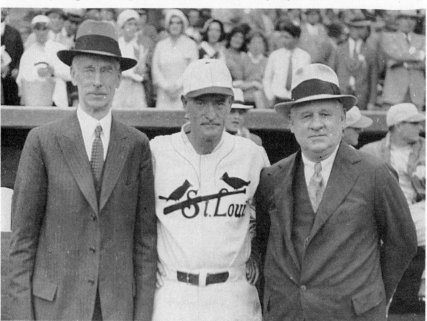

1930: The old Giant visits World Series combatants Connie Mack (left) of the Philadelphia A's and Gabby Street of the St. Louis Cardinals.

Eddie Collins spent a quarter of a century in the big leagues in a career that paralleled McGraw's. And, from two-tone shoes to straw hat, the master of the Giants extends his hand and his compliments.

The final act: On June 3, 1932, he went home and told Blanche McGraw: "I have quit."

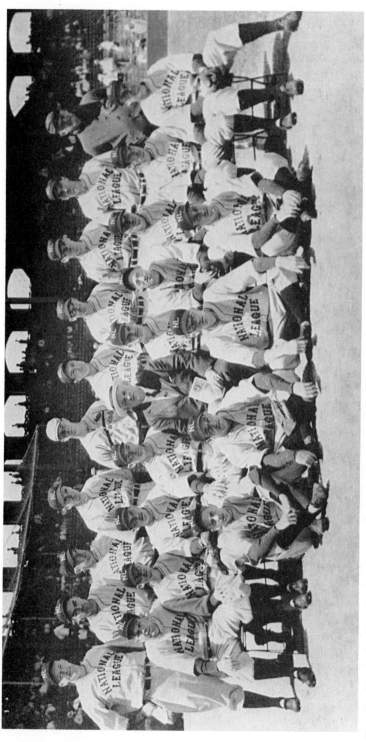

The final curtain: Mr. McGraw returns on July 6, 1933, as manager of the National League team in baseball's first All-Star Game. In the back row in Comiskey Park, Chicago, third and fourth from the left, Frank Frisch and Carl Hubbell keep the faith.

Chapter

Father
Of the Brainmeter

In the spring of 1921, the United States was spiraling happily into the decade of wonderful nonsense.

The boys were finally back from Over There, the "reparations problem" was left to grayer heads like Lloyd George, and the great tide of Prohibition was causing public inconvenience only in the new "rum courts," which were doing a landslide business in bootleg cases.

It was a time of suffragettes, heroes, heavyweights and hoopla; of Suzanne Lenglen, in flowing white dress, socking a backhand on the courts at Cannes; of Mary Garden, the "directrix" of the Chicago Opera Company, burrowing through papers on her desk in the midst of "the New York season"; of Man O' War making his final appearance on the course of the Kentucky Association at Lexington.

Ethel and John Barrymore were appearing at the Empire Theatre in Michael Strange's new play, "Clair de Lune." Ziegfeld offered Marilynn Miller and Leon Errol at the New Amsterdam in "Sally." Jackie Coogan was "Peck's Bad Boy" at the Brooklyn Strand.

The Lyric was unfolding "the world's greatest motion picture, 'The Queen of Sheba,' the most sensational and thrilling spectacle ever shown on the screen." (Its chariot scene, commented the critic of the New York *Evening Telegram,* was "the last word in thrills.") And at the Capitol, D. W. Griffith was opening his revival of "The Birth of a Nation," modestly described as being "to the screen what Hamlet is to drama, Faust to opera, Mikado to comic opera." All that plus an orchestra of *80* pieces in the pit.

In its gentler moments, American society might applaud "Madame Curie's genius," attend Sunday afternoon tea dances at roadside places like the Pelham Heath Inn, or warm to rotogravure photographs of Billie Burke as Mrs. Florenz Ziegfeld walking with her daughter Patricia at Palm Beach.

In its frenzied moments, which seemed more numerous, it might rail at the Bolshevik threat in Russia, issue ultimatums on occupying the Ruhr Valley, or rush to get cash down on the Dempsey-Carpentier fight.

Getting there was at least half the fun, and was not only faster than ever but more splendid. By air from Paris to Brussels to Amsterdam, for instance: Leave Paris at 11 a.m., arrive in Amsterdam at 3:30 p.m.—"thus, the journey consumes only 4½ hours, one-third of the time formerly required by railway."

Overland, the going was even sportier. A 1920 Chandler, "a chummy roadster," went for $1,275. A 1917 Amesbury Berlin sedan—"with Westinghouse shock absorbers, bumper, two spare shoes and other extras; just overhauled, painted and re-upholstered"—could be viewed "on inspection by appointment."

It was a time of idols and sometimes idols stacked on other idols. Douglas Fairbanks posed with Jack Dempsey perched comfortably on his right shoulder, and insisted cheerfully that it was "just as easy as holding up the Woolworth Building."

A time of "McGrawmen," who shared America's biggest ball yard with the homeless Yankees and their new hero, Babe Ruth. Of great expectations: For tenants like the Yankees, whose final payment of $400,000 on an even bigger stadium was made by Colonel Jacob Ruppert and the magnificently named Captain Tillinghast l'Hommedieu Huston. A time when a "little country estate" of four acres in Dobbs Ferry, 12 rooms, 4 baths, could be had for $175 a month (unfurnished).

It was a time when a war-weary public snapped up almost any pronouncement from the actors who paraded across this busy stage, and treated itself to a roller coaster of emotional responses.

People were impressed when Marshal Foch announced grandly that Napoleon himself had been the Allies' "teacher" in 1918. They were not dismayed that Napoleon had failed to teach the Allies how to collect for the lesson— eight-column headlines told almost every day of the Allies' frustration in forcing reparations from the Germans, despite warnings by Prime Minister George, Premier Briand and President Harding that Napoleon's pupils would march again if Berlin failed to reply in six days.

In London, the House was taken aback when Lady Astor "delivered another of her Friday afternoon sermonettes to the enlivenment of an otherwise dull sitting of Commons." Her theme: The duty of parents toward their children. A chorus of masculine "ohs" greeted her feminine assault on "rotters."

New York was elated when Madame Curie arrived from Paris and announced that radium could cure even the most deep-seated cancers. Two days later, it was deflated when her secretary announced that Madame Curie had meant only that radium could cure *some* types of cancer.

The public conscience was appeased when John D. Rockefeller Jr. contributed one million dollars "to the starving children of Central Europe." And it was exalted when he helped to dramatize China's "wretched harvest" by eating a luncheon of dried corn and tanbark from a bowl.

It was further redeemed when Henry Ford began to grow wheat on thousands of acres adjoining his estate at Dearborn, Michigan, ground it into flour and sold it to his workers for $7.80 a barrel instead of the $10 that retail stores commanded. Henry Ford, the press reported soberly, "has turned miller for the benefit of his employes."

Broadway listened gravely when Tex Rickard, the boxing impresario, disclosed that he had received formal "assurances" that Georges Carpentier would head for America aboard the S.S. *Savote* for the big fight on Boyle's Thirty Acres in Jersey City. And it swayed with anticipation at reports that the Frenchman had thereupon set sail "with dozens of sportsmen from England and the Continent intent on witnessing the battle, in which Carpentier will attempt to wrest the world's heavyweight championship from Dempsey."

From the ridiculous, the public could soar splendidly to the sublime. Professor Michael I. Pupin of Columbia declared in a lecture that great advances in nuclear studies showed that the electron of 1921 was not the "final unit" in the structure of the atom. (He was right.) Then it could plunge back to the ridiculous. Carpentier, getting more newspaper space than Professor Pupin, reported that "Dempsey is made to order for me." (He was wrong.) Dempsey's mother, winning bigger headlines than either the professor or Carpentier, predicted staunchly that Jack would win. (She was right.)

Still, none of the pronouncements or issues in that spring of 1921 equaled —in public fervor or identification—the controversies that suddenly swirled around two of the most celebrated figures of the day.

They were John J. McGraw, the most famous manager in baseball, and Thomas A. Edison, the wizard of Menlo Park. They were as different as two men could be. So were their causes célèbres. And so were the responses of a passionate public.

McGraw's case challenged the public's capacity to drink, Edison's challenged the public's capacity to think, and therefore—interrupting the flow of wonderful nonsense—was not nearly so open and shut.

McGraw marched before the bar of public justice first. On February 7, he was brought to trial in the Federal district court in New York City before the distinguished Judge Learned Hand. The charge: "having in his possession a bottle of whiskey at the Lambs," the theatrical haven in midtown Manhattan where the manager of the New York Giants spent many long evenings with the heroes of the Broadway stage replaying the afternoon's feats of his ball players at the Polo Grounds.

Having a bottle of whiskey in one's possession at the Lambs was considered neither unusual nor illegal by most persons, the Volstead Act notwithstanding. In fact, it would have been considered unusual if McGraw or any of his circle had spent an evening at the Lambs without a bottle of whiskey. But this particular bottle landed the renowned manager into Learned Hand's courtroom because it had been followed by a fight and a mysterious accident.

The fight had taken place in the grill room of the club six months earlier, on August 8, 1920. The principals were McGraw and William Boyd, the actor, who had been the leading man for Ethel Barrymore, Maude Adams and other prima donnas of the stage. McGraw, a veteran of numberless brawls on the diamond from his earliest days with the Baltimore Orioles in the nineties, said later that Boyd had objected to his language in the presence of the cleaning women at a late hour of a Sunday night, or Monday morning. And so McGraw had simply hit Boyd over the head with a water carafe.

The mysterious accident took place a short time later after McGraw had taken a taxi to his apartment on the northwest corner of Broadway and 109th Street. He was accompanied by John C. Slavin, the musical comedy actor, and Winfield Liggett, who lived at the Lambs. What happened as they poured each other out of the cab was never clear. But Slavin was found unconscious on the sidewalk later with a fractured jaw, and when detectives rang McGraw's bell, the manager roused himself from sleep and answered the door with a some-what battered face and a decidedly black eye.

The chief Prohibition agent in New York, James S. Shevlin, responded to the news with a swift sword. He pressed for a Federal indictment against McGraw for "willfully possessing a bottle of whiskey" in violation of the Volstead Act, and he got it. The Lambs, caught in the act of serving drinks in the grill room, promptly expelled McGraw in righteous indignation. William J. Fallon, the famous criminal lawyer, just as promptly leaped to the defense, took over as McGraw's counsel and clamored for a grand jury investigation to clear the name of the Little Napoleon of New York.

McGraw's defense had one bad moment before the case was called to trial. A month after the fight, the manager received a visit from Wilton Lackaye, another actor-friend and member of the Lambs. He went to McGraw's home "to give him some friendly advice" and came out with a broken ankle.

Despite setbacks like this, though, Fallon managed to win a one-month postponement when the trial opened in New York on February 7. Everybody realized that one month later McGraw would be in spring training with his Giants, thereby making another postponement inevitable. But in 1921 neither James S. Shevlin, Learned Hand nor the Volstead Act were likely to come between New York and the Giants as they prepared for another baseball sea-son.

As a lull settled over the case, a distraction was immediately presented from a laboratory in Orange, New Jersey, by Edison—who was every bit as combative in the public eye as McGraw, but not nearly so lucky in his choice of causes.

Three days after McGraw was granted his postponement, the inventor heralded the approach of his seventy-fourth birthday by expressing his ideas on mankind.

This had been a favorite pastime of Edison's for years. And while McGraw had been provoking people with his fists and tricks with baseball bats, Edison had been tweaking them with mental gymnastics for decades.

When he was twelve years old, he had been the most precocious railroad newsboy and candy butcher in the Midwest, a little hustler selling newspapers, apples, sandwiches, molasses and peanuts on the dawn run from Port Huron to Detroit.

When a stationmaster taught him telegraphy, he promptly invented an automatic repeater that relayed messages from one wire to another without the intervention of another operator.

When he decided to manufacture printing-telegraph equipment on his own, he opened workshops in Menlo Park and West Orange and revolutionized life in spasms of inventing that produced the megaphone, phonograph, motion picture camera, electric light and hundreds of other devices.

When he ended his long research on the electric light, he started the dynamos in his central station at 257 Pearl Street in downtown Manhattan, threw the switches at 3 p.m. on September 4, 1882, and declared majestically, "They will go on forever unless stopped by an earthquake."

When he began to offend educators with sweeping denunciations of formal schooling and college training, he touched off a running battle that irritated learned persons around the world. He once invited Professor John Dewey and some Columbia colleagues to the Edison Laboratory to view motion pictures as a teaching device. They shook their heads, and when one educator rashly asked how algebra could be taught on film, Edison replied that algebra was of little practical use and, besides, "I can hire mathematicians at $15 a week, but they can't hire me."

"I like the Montessori method," he said on another occasion. "It makes learning a pleasure. The present system casts the brain into a mold. What we need are men capable of doing work. I wouldn't give a penny for the ordinary college graduate, except those from institutes of technology. They aren't filled up with Latin, philosophy and all that ninny stuff. America needs practical, skilled engineers and industrial men. In three or four centuries, when the country is settled (sic) and commercialism is diminished, there will be time for literary men."

So Edison had long since established himself as a wizard at shocking the public when, in February of 1921, he crept into the news by offering his birthday views on the state of mankind.

He outdid himself, too, probably because he had been provoked by an interviewer who ventured to ask about reports that illness in his 74th year had undermined Edison's physical vitality. The white-haired inventor sprang from his chair at the suggestion, snapped to ramrod attention like a soldier, and challenged: "Do I look it?"

Without waiting for an answer, he thereupon launched into a formula for saving the United States: "Adopt Otto Kahn's plan for a tax of one-third of one percent on all sales and place Herbert Hoover in a position in the government where his great executive ability and experience can be utilized best." Besides, he said without transition, there was danger of war with Japan unless that country was given room to accommodate its increasing population. "But," he added quickly in a postscript, "I am absolutely opposed to letting them come over here."

Goaded royally now by the insinuations about his vitality, Edison stayed on the offensive for weeks. He was assured minimum competition from McGraw's celebrated trial, at least, when the trial was predictably postponed again on March 7. McGraw, explained the newspaper reports, "is at present with the Giants in their southern training center."

So the stage was Edison's, and he fired a shot heard 'round the world a few weeks later by revealing his latest invention—which was immediately dubbed the "brainmeter"—and declaring:

"Men who have gone through college I find to be amazingly ignorant. When I find that anyone fails to come up to the standard I set, I give him a week's pay and fire him."

The standard, he disclosed, was contained in an intelligence test he had drawn for job applicants and employees at his plant in West Orange. The results, he said, had "disappointed" him.

The next day, under headlines reporting that "Edison Condemns the Primary School," the battle was joined. "The trouble is," he insisted, "that boys' minds are atrophied before they reach college. I have never seen a boy who liked to go to school and I don't suppose I ever will unless they change the method of teaching."

But an intelligence test? Yes, he conceded a bit warily, he had indeed prepared the test himself and had administered it at his laboratory. It contained 163 questions, and only one of the 23 men who tackled it passed with a 100 percent, or "A" rating, in an hour and a half. They all looked "bright and well-dressed," he allowed, but the men who took more than two hours were classified in the "XYZ" group. And sure enough, he gave them a week's pay and fired them.

The cat now being out of the bag, the wizard of Menlo Park suddenly found himself besieged by disbelief, dismay and howls of protest. It was as though his disk phonograph had gone haywire and was amplifying a screeching babble. The United States Army had stirred interest in intelligence tests in 1917 by administering a million and a half of them to soldiers. But now, four years later, he had stirred an overnight clamor by administering his own home-made tests to prove a home-made theory.

Moreover, although a few of the questions were leaked out by disgruntled test-takers, he shrouded the rest in silence. But people were amazed at the leaked samples. On what day of the week was the Battle of Waterloo fought? Where is Mount Ararat? What is fiat money? Who is Brand Whitlock?

"We hope," editorialized *The New York Times,* cutting through the din, "that Mr. Thomas A. Edison will not despair of the Republic altogether because so many college graduates flunked in the examinations by which he tests the efficiency and intelligence of young men who aspire to high places in his shops and factories. There are eight-score questions on this list. It is not to be wondered at that they are not all answered.

"Besides, is Mr. Edison's questionnaire really a conclusive test? 'What is copra?' Was any man ever kinder to his mother because he knew what copra is? 'What is zinc?' Does Mr. Edison himself know what zinc is? Dante, one of the most learned men of his time, could have answered only one of six to test general knowledge. 'How did Cleopatra die?' John Milton no better. Even Henry Ford would be stumped by some of these questions. 'Where is Magdalena Bay?' How can anybody answer that question?"

It was May now, and while Edison was suddenly impaled on the hook of public protest, John McGraw was suddenly off the hook.

"The defendant," said *The Times* on May 3, reporting the manager's twice-postponed trial, "came into court on crutches due to a sprained ankle which he received while practicing at the Polo Grounds on Sunday. On motion of William J. Fallon, McGraw's counsel, the indictment was dismissed because it failed to specify where the defendant was when the alleged liquor was in his possession. Then McGraw was arraigned on an information which charged him with having the liquor in his possession at the Lambs Club on Aug. 8. He pleaded not guilty."

The prosecution, giving it the old college try, called an assistant district attorney, Albert B. Unger, as a witness. He testified that he had talked with McGraw on August 14 and that McGraw had said he indeed had had a bottle of whiskey at the Lambs. However, Fallon pounced on the witness with a stream of questions designed to show that McGraw had also said he had given all his money to two scrubwomen and therefore couldn't have bought a bottle of whiskey, even if he had wanted one.

The assistant district attorney, now on the defensive, didn't remember that part of the conversation exactly. But he did recall McGraw's saying that he had cashed a check in the grill room at the time. And that statement proved to be the Volstead Act's last time at bat in the case.

McGraw hobbled to the witness chair and testified in his own behalf—to the admiring stares of jury and audience alike—that he had been entirely without money that evening. He might have cashed a check, but if so he had not cashed one in the grill room.

The jury kept Judge Hand and McGraw—on his crutches—waiting exactly five minutes. Not guilty.

Fresh from this triumph, the public resumed its pursuit of the wizard of Menlo Park, who had neither William J. Fallon nor a sprained ankle to temper the opposition.

Jack Dempsey announced that he was studying French to understand what Carpentier might say in the ring, and New York boggled. The New York Athletic Club voted to permit women to smoke, and New York glowed (even though the vote was close, 187 to 134). Carpentier solemnly visited Teddy Roosevelt's grave on a pilgrimage to Long Island, and Oyster Bay was touched. Dempsey was reported stricken with spring fever, and Broadway swooned. But

Edison pontificated, and the United States was rubbed the wrong way.

When the headmaster of the Buckley School said no well-read man could fail to answer 80 percent of Edison's questions, he was rebutted by "victims" of the test who argued that only "a walking encyclopedia could answer the questionnaire."

"Edison Questions Stir Up A Storm," headlined the press. "Not a Tom Edison test, but a Tom Foolery test," complained one letter to the editor. And so it went.

The inventor, now afflicted with a cold (which aroused no such compassion as McGraw's sprained ankle), refused to answer an inquiry for a copy of his test. His secretary, H. W. Meadowcroft, said the questions were being kept secret because future applicants might crib the answers.

Still, 141 questions were mailed to *The New York Times* on May 11 by Charles Hansen, an unsuccessful candidate for a job at Edison's laboratory. No person taking the test was allowed to copy the questions, the paper noted, but Mr. Hansen had *memorized* them, a feat that impressed Edison less than the fact that he nonetheless had flunked, anyway. Mr. Hansen said they were "silly."

Across the country, the "brainmeter" or "ignorometer" became a a parlor craze. A reporter for the Chicago *Tribune* bearded twenty-five students at the University of Chicago and gave them a sample test. He picked sixteen men and nine women at random. On the first question (Where do you get shellac from?), seven gave the wrong answer, eight the right answer and the rest didn't know. On "what is a monsoon?" the tally was four right and twenty-one wrong. The first six who were asked "Where do dried prunes come from?" didn't know. And *no one* got the answer to "Where do domestic sardines come from?"

Two students thought cork was imported from Ireland. Nobody knew the voltage in a streetcar or which states produced phosphates or where the condor was found. One coed said that castiron was called "pig" because "it's unrefined."

The next day, editorial writers sprang to her defense as a heroine of repartee. It would be a mistake, said *The New York Times,* to mark her wrong on the pig-iron answer. It demonstrated "a quick mind, a sense of humor, the ability to hide ignorance and get along without specific knowledge."

"Edison's Questions Still Puzzle City" roared the headlines, and "College Men Pore Over Tomes and Maps."

In New York, "much perturbation" was reported among college graduates and students. In one university, the members of a literary club spent hours inspecting the map of West Virginia trying to find the exact boundaries.

In one book-publishing house, an editor gave himself a rating of 90 on a set of "leaked" questions. But "the glory of his performance was dimmed," it was noted, when he was discovered to be a lexicographer and a bit of a ringer.

On the Lexington Avenue subway, two young women became so engrossed in "What is the longest railroad in the world?" that they missed their station in downtown Manhattan and rode all the way to Brooklyn, presumably making the Lexington Avenue subway the world's longest railroad for them.

In Boston, the great Albert Einstein arrived at South Station en route to Harvard. He had just received an honorary degree from Princeton and was about to get another from Harvard. But the only thing the throng at the station wanted to talk about was the Edison brainmeter. "What is the speed of sound?" the physicist was asked. And through an English-speaking secretary he replied that he couldn't say offhand.

Finally, on May 13, *The Times* cracked the case wide open. In headlines, it proclaimed: "Here Is Edison's 4-Column Sheaf of Knowledge. His Most Famous Questions Answered by the Book, the Specialist and the Man in the Street." And, in a crossline and subhead, "Something Nobody Knows. That Is, Who Invented Printing?"

As for that last jab, *The Times* delved into arguments about printing and recited the history of Korean, Japanese and Gutenberg printing. But, wasting no time on side issues, it declared that "advocates of specialization hold that the ability to achieve a high mark in the tests is a sign of a misspent youth," and then proceeded to shake the skeletons from Edison's closet.

It listed 146 questions that had been "remembered" by various applicants for jobs and gave answers by experts, "some of which may be subject to correction and controversy."

No. 1 on the list was: "What countries bound France?" The answer rendered by the panel of experts: "Spain, the tiny independent state of Andorra in the Pyrenees, Monaco, Italy, Switzerland, Germany, Luxembourg and Belgium." And if that didn't discourage job-seekers at the Edison laboratory, nothing would.

No. 2. "What city and country produce the finest china?" Answer: "Some say Limoges, France; some say Dresden, Germany; some say Copenhagen, Denmark."

No. 3. Where is the River Volga? In Russia.

No. 5. What country consumed the most tea before the war? Russia.

No. 6. What city leads the United States in making laundry machines? Chicago.

No. 74. Where are condors found? In the Andes.

For those who stumbled on Cleopatra, the experts reported that she had been Queen of Egypt and (with colossal delicacy) a "contemporary" of Julius Caesar and Mark Antony who had committed suicide by causing an asp to bite her.

For the 25 pioneers at the University of Chicago, they disclosed that domestic sardines came from Maine and California.

For Albert Einstein, they noted that the speed of sound was about 1,091 feet a second in dry air at freezing; about 4,680 feet a second in water; and 11,463 feet a second through an iron bar 3,000 feet long.

As for Magdalena Bay, three were located—in lower California, in Spitzbergen and in Colombia. And as for "in what part of the world does it never rain?"—the United States Weather Bureau replied that nobody was ever in one place long enough to say, but that natives of the Sahara Desert had expressed amazement when told that water *ever* fell from the sky. Let the wizard of Menlo Park chew that one over!

However, if anybody thought that the inventor of the disk phonograph would be shattered by the pirating of his intelligence test, they underestimated him. The next day, Edison sat down and dashed off a new questionnaire. His ever-present secretary, Mr. Meadowcroft, reported that Mr. Edison had been "following" the controversy and had decided at once to draw up a completely new set of questions to preserve the integrity of his job-testing.

"Mr. Edison," said Meadowcroft, rising to the occasion, "is a man of extremely varied reading. He does not seem to forget anything."

Each week, he said, the inventor received 40 or 60 pounds of periodicals at his home, kept 62 on file, and also read three books every seven days. His field of reading extended, Meadowcroft added, from *The Police Gazette* to *The Journal of Experimental Medicine*—and included *The New York Times.*

But, in spite of this insight into the habits of the father of the brainmeter, the tide had turned against him.

Professor William Shepher of Columbia supported the formation of a National Women's Club in a speech at the university's Faculty Club, but said in a bon mot that "we will not make membership dependent on Mr. Edison's *300* questions."

The Times, in another editorial, said that the list of questions (sticking to 163) showed that the Freudian belief that nobody ever forgets anything was true only in a special Freudian sense. And if Edison took a test of similar questions he, too, would be "convicted" of ignorance.

A youth in Holyoke, Massachusetts, appeared at the police station and said he had written the answers to the Edison test in a book that now was worth millions. He wanted police protection. "The police," the press reported, "believe he has become temporarily demented as a result of studying the Edison test."

A professor of educational psychology at Teachers College in Columbia, Dr. E. L. Thorndike, said the test was only one-tenth effective anyway. "I wouldn't take an engineer," Dr. Thorndike said, "and cross-examine him on what he knows about Amy Lowell."

At Harvard, now receiving his second honorary degree of the week, Einstein said under pressure that, yes, he thought a college education was a good thing. And under heavier pressure from the mob at Edison's heels, he said he had "heard of" Edison—as the inventor of the phonograph.

"More Slams At Edison," the headlines cried. And as May turned into June, the sniping turned into a sweeping offensive. The brainmeter and its founder became the chief topics, mostly the chief targets, at college commencements, and even Lloyd George, the reparations problem and Georges Carpentier took back seats.

Edison got in one or two licks, but they were not haymakers.

He piqued the commencement speakers by declaring that numerous college professors still didn't know where Korea was, or the chief ingredients of white paint, or what voltage was used in streetcars.

Some people suggested in his behalf that perhaps he had been putting them all on, in a kind of gigantic tongue-in-cheek bit of mischief. After all, they noted, one of his favorite questions was "If you were desirous of obtaining an order from a manufacturer with a jealous wife, and you saw him with a chorus girl, what would you do?"

He also said, on another occasion, that he really didn't care if a man knew the location of Timbuktu. But he did care "if he ever knew any of these things and doesn't know them now."

Whereupon, flexing his mental muscles for the last time in the great debate, the old wizard rattled off the answers to a long series of questions in all fields—and scored 95 percent.

At the Haverford College graduation, some doubts about the public "victory" over the old man's arrogance also were expressed by Dr. John Alexander MacIntosh, professor of philosophy, religion and ethics at the McCormick Theological Seminary in Chicago. He told the Haverford graduates that "this is a serious charge, coming from a scientific man," and suggested that the colleges prove Edison wrong.

At the Johns Hopkins commencement, the president of the school, Dr. Frank J. Goodnow, told the graduating class that "a man of eminence in the world of practical affairs" had caused a furor by questioning the purposes of education. "If you have learned in your courses how to work," Dr. Goodnow said, sounding vaguely like Edison, "your education may be regarded as completed—so far as you can complete it in any institution."

Even Sears, Roebuck and Co. inadvertently cast a shadow over the controversy. It advertised the Encyclopaedia Britannica for $1 down and "the balance in small monthly payments"—29 volumes, 44 million words, printed on the famous India paper. "It answers questions like: How shall America readjust her industrial conditions? Is the present League of Nations likely to succeed? Is the fall of the Bolshevist regime in Russia imminent? Will Germany fulfill her treaty obligations?"

If the Britannica had supplied the correct answer to the last two or three of those questions, it would have been a bargain at twice the price. But the decade of wonderful nonsense rolled on, certain that "yes" was just as good an answer as "no," and impatient with any questions that ruffled the public's feathers.

It was much happier with provocateurs like McGraw, who was leading his Giants that summer to the heady glory of a National League pennant—the first of four straight. And it cheered when McGraw, exonerated in *his* moment of trial, retaliated against his critics at the Lambs Club by retracting the free passes given to members the next time they appeared at the Polo Grounds press gate. Three years later he was to be vindicated completely. He was readmitted to the Lambs after 300 members had signed a petition of forgiveness.

Edison, though, emerged from his part in the battles of 1921 with far less redemption. Still, he managed to give his pursuers a touching moment as the din reached a peak and then subsided.

On the same afternoon that Dr. Goodnow was cautioning the Johns Hopkins class about its future, *The New York Times* provided a final, poignant glimpse of the embroiled wizard. In a brief story headlined "Edison In The Box," it reported from West Orange that "Thomas A. Edison took part in his first baseball game today."

The inventor, who had been hearing impaired since childhood and who once said that "the happiest time of my life was when I was twelve years old," pitched five balls in a game between the Disk Record Department and the Laboratory staff of the Edison plant—all of whom presumably had passed his maligned intelligence test.

After winding up, Edison pitched the first ball, "which the batter avoided by ducking." The second, third and fourth pitches also went astray, but the fifth ball finally was pitched near enough to the plate to produce a foul.

Then the seventy-four-year-old genius retired to the sidelines.

"I was always too busy a boy to indulge in baseball," said the Father of the Brainmeter a little sadly.

Chapter

8

The Battle
Of Broadway

An important—and foreboding—thing happened in 1921 to John McGraw, the manager of the New York Giants. Babe Ruth hit 59 home runs. Not only that, but he hit most of them in McGraw's own ball park, the Polo Grounds, where McGraw had reigned for twenty years while the Giants galloped across baseball like Sheridan's horsemen.

Ruth's feat was important because the country was still convalescing in 1921 from the Black Sox baseball scandal, and badly needed a bracer. Ruth became that bracer, hitting more home runs than any man in history, and restoring the glamour to the dominant pastime on the American scene.

As far as McGraw was concerned, however, all this had the tinge of a mixed blessing. The reason was that Ruth's glamour began casting a shadow over the empire McGraw had built in New York since the day he had left the Baltimore Orioles at the turn of the century and became the baron of baseball. Worse, Ruth began casting his shadow across McGraw's own backyard, the Polo Grounds, which the Giants still shared with the homeless Yankees. And that was the foreboding part of the development.

Ruth wasted no time exalting baseball, enriching the Yankees and irritating McGraw. He hit 54 home runs in 1920, the first season he appeared in a Yankee uniform in New York, then made it to 59 a year later. (McGraw's first-baseman, Long George Kelly, unwittingly drew attention to the phenomenon by leading the National League with 23.)

Moreover, the Yankees' attendance had stood at 619,164 the year before they ransomed Ruth from the Boston Red Sox and it immediately skyrocketed to 1,289,422 when he began driving home runs over the fences in McGraw's stadium. That was double, and McGraw's irritation became triple—especially since the third-place Yankees in the American League outdrew the second-place Giants in the National League by more than 350,000 admissions.

"The Yankees," he raged to Charles Stoneham, the owner of the Giants, "will have to build a park in Queens or some other out-of-the-way place. Let them go away and wither on the vine."

The Yankees, however, had no intention of withering on the vines of Queens or any other place. On February 5, 1921, they announced instead that they had bought 10 acres of land in the Bronx between 157th and 161st Street, from River Avenue to Doughty Avenue. They bought it from the estate of William Waldorf Astor and noted that "the running time from Forty-second Street by subway will be about 16 minutes."

Moreover, exuded the Yankee drumbeaters, the stadium planned for the site would be an oval like the Yale Bowl and would be made "impenetrable to all human eyes, save those of aviators, by towering embattlements."

To McGraw, though, the worst architectural feature of all was the fact that the new Yankee Stadium would rise just across the Harlem River from his Polo Grounds, where it would not exactly be impenetrable to all human eyes. It was as though Ziegfeld had opened a theater next door to Belasco, and had promptly installed the Barnum & Bailey Circus for an indefinite run.

The confrontation of McGraw and Ruth, however, grew even more glaring farther downtown—along Broadway, the center of McGraw's world of actors, athletes, touts, Tammany tigers, con men, chorus girls, boxers and bootleggers. They collided at the crossroads of Manhattan Island, and it was there in 1921 that Ruth and the Yankees intruded at the height of McGraw's spell over the sporting life of New York.

They could not have chosen a busier stage, nor a gaudier one. Broadway was twirling into the passionate time known later as the Roaring Twenties, and nowhere did the Twenties roar louder than in McGraw's great old ball yard uptown and in his great old play yard downtown.

"The vandals sacking Rome," observed Gene Fowler, "were ten times as kindly as the spendthrift hordes on Broadway. The Wall Street delirium was reaching the pink-elephant stage. Chambermaids and counter-hoppers had the J. P. Morgan complex. America had the swelled head, and the brand of tourists that went to Europe became ambassadors of ill-will. The World War killed nearly everything that was old Broadway. Prohibition, the mock-turtle soup of purists, provided the *coup de grâce.*"

McGraw's circle of friends in this hippodrome atmosphere included the great and the small of the theater, the courts, the political clubs, the prize ring, the racetrack and the underworld, all somehow intertwined on Broadway as the demigods of public life.

The interlocking nature of this midtown society was perhaps best illustrated by McGraw's good friend and lawyer, William J. Fallon, who displayed the same genius in defending McGraw that he displayed on behalf of his other clients. They ranged from Arnold Rothstein, the tycoon gambler who some-times bet $10,000 on license numbers of trucks or Cadillacs (having taken the precaution of arraying fleets of vehicles in the side streets), to Admiral Dot, the 38-inch circus performer who chucked it all one day when the Ringling Bros. train was nearing New York and instead opened a bar in White Plains. There the Admiral would hold court every day and would regale the sporting crowd by repeating, to prove almost any point, "I sat on the Queen's lap."

Fallon's clientele also included Danny Arnstein, who was accused of ar-ranging a $5,000,000 heist of stock certificates and whose wife, Fanny Brice, the actress, developed such a regard for Fallon's talents that she named a son for the great mouthpiece.

He and McGraw also had cronies like Louis Mann, the actor, who was always a bit headstrong and conceited and who enjoyed crashing into the press-box seats in the Polo Grounds to the consternation of the displaced writ-ers. Mann even tangled once, for laughs, with Gentleman Jim Corbett in a dressing room at the Palace. They mauled each other joyously for 10 minutes before Mann, now getting the short end of the action, implored the massive former heavyweight champion, "For God's sake, Jim, let's quit before we kill each other."

The rollicking crowd also included Eddie Foy, the vaudevillian, who lived with his wife and seven children in New Rochelle, not far from McGraw's home in Pelham, Fallon's office in White Plains and Admiral Dot's thriving bar. "We both were friends of McGraw," Fallon recalled, in reciting the beau-ties of the good old days. "And we were ardent rooters for the Giants."

The only trouble, though, was that Fallon and Foy couldn't discuss the Giants' latest triumph above the uproar of the Foy children. Eddie Jr. would be removing handfuls of stuffing from a davenport to make wigs and false beards. Irving would be sawing the leg off a table. Charlie would be chipping porcelain from the kitchen sink. And Bryan would be driving nails through a screen door, while their doting father would shout, "Bryan, drive them nails *clear in.* Don't let 'em stick out to catch people's pants. And Irving, you're not going to leave the table that way, are you? Saw the other leg so they'll be even. A lamp's liable to fall off it, or something."

Fallon and McGraw not only moved in this jumping world of actors and the inevitable retinue of bookmakers and Broadway characters; they even became part of the cast on occasion. McGraw had toured the theater circuit 15 years earlier as a stand-up monologuist and was a regular at the Lambs, and Fallon was renowned as the prima donna of the courtroom with the voice, wit and presence of a professional.

The lawyer, who could recite movingly from Tennyson and Byron (but who preferred to do so principally to move beautiful actresses), once bet a colleague during a tedious case that he could remember the names and occupa-tions of all sixty prospective jurors. He won the bet, and later the case.

Another time, at the height of a sensitive trial marked by one of Fallon's outrages—he had impugned the judge for his instructions to the jury—Fallon airily told the newspaper reporters at the end of the session, "I think it was a shame I had to miss that doubleheader at the Polo Grounds today. The Reds beat the Giants twice, and we needed those games."

On another occasion, a judge recoiled when he detected liquor on Fallon's breath during a huddle before the bench and asked the lawyer if he had been drinking. The judge was a celebrated teetotaler, but Fallon charmed him by replying, "If Your Honor's sense of justice is as good as his sense of smell, my client need have no worry in this court."

His place astride the sporting, theatrical and political worlds was so fixed that his law firm became known as The Broadway and Forty-second Street Bar Association. He defended Arnold Rothstein in the preliminaries to the Black Sox scandal, and extricated Rothstein from any involvement. He pulled out of the Arnstein stock-theft case after an argument, and Arnstein wound up in jail. He even defended a bootlegger accused of making a $30,000-a-day profit, and lost. But his performances were the talk of the town.

In one of his most fabled defenses, he argued a case before Judge Learned Hand, the distinguished jurist who had presided over McGraw's whiskey-bottle trial. This time, in June of 1923, Fallon himself was implicated in an expose of bucket-shop operations that had sprung up during the stock market craze. His client was the firm of Fuller & McGee, which failed to the tune of $4,000,000 of apparently nonexistent securities on the Consolidated Stock Exchange (whose president, William H. Silkworth, later went to prison).

The celebrities in the case included Thomas F. Foley, the longtime Tammany boss and political patron of Alfred E. Smith, and Charles Stoneham, the principal owner of the New York Giants. The testimony disclosed that Foley had induced Stoneham to lend $147,500 to Fuller & McGee in an effort to prevent the firm from going bankrupt. Stoneham was left holding the bag, and got only $10,000 back.

Fallon, drawing on his publicized talent for courtroom wizardry, tried at great length to weave an innocent web around this chain of events. But he overplayed the part so grossly that time that Judge Hand, after listening in astonishment for a long time, finally issued a one-word commentary from the bench: "Preposterous."

Four years later, in April of 1927, while he was defending McGraw in a minor civil matter, Fallon collapsed in court. Two days later, at home, the lawyer (who had celebrated his acquittal from a jury-tampering charge on one occasion by going to a ball game at the Polo Grounds) told his wife: "Do you think for a minute I'm going to lie here when I can go see the baseball game?"

He tried to get out of bed, and fell dead on the floor. He was forty-one years old. At his funeral, the church and the street outside were thronged by legions of Broadway heroes, divas and characters—the people from the mixed-up world of the Roaring Twenties. They came to view him in a mahogany coffin bought by his old friend John McGraw.

    ★   ★   ★

The splendor of their world was reflected in rich, wide-open prose that was invoked by contemporaries to describe it. On May 2, 1921, the day Fallon had gotten McGraw off the hook in Learned Hand's court on the whiskey charge, Alexander Woollcott depicted an Actors Equity review for *The New York Times*. He termed it a "show of strength" at the Metropolitan Opera House, and portrayed it in these words:

"Here, for instance, was John Barrymore, a pallid, rose-clad Romeo, looking unutterably romantic to the last as the ruthless elevator withdrew him from sight. Here was Laurette Taylor, all loveliness as Ophelia, and Lionel Atwill, looking twice as melancholy and several times as Danish as the usual Hamlet. Here was Chrystal Herne, allowed just a moment to suggest how enchanting a Viola she might be, and Jane Cowl as the Shrew glaring defiance at the amiable Petruchio of John Drew.

"Here was Doris Keane playing Portia to the evil-looking Shylock of George Arliss, and here was Genevieve Tobin, a most delicate Ariel, dancing before the Prospero of Frank Bacon. There was no fairer vision than that which Peggy Wood presented as Imogen—an hour of 'Cymbeline' after two years of 'Buddies.'

"It was, in a sense, a night of reunions, for here was Lillian Russell resplendent as Queen Katherine and such old favorites as James T. Powers and Rose Coghlan to show that the Equity was no mere enthusiasm of the youngsters. But between these oldtimers and such stars of tomorrow as the Duncan sisters, the audience was all affable impartiality. When these frivolous newcomers did their turn there was wild applause. For their stage-setting they use a three-legged stool. Florence Moore brought it on for them. Herbert Corthell carried it off. The mind of the onlooking manager must have reeled at so idyllic a spectacle of cooperation."

In the sports field, the sense of intimacy and camaraderie was just as strong, and so was the prose created to report it.

When McGraw conveniently sprained his ankle just before his climactic appearance in court on crutches, the incident was described with heroic overtones like this:

"The stocky manager of the Giants pulled a Frank Frisch while he was batting them out in the practice before the battle. It was slippery around the plate despite the energetic efforts of the Fabianites to erase the moisture. McGraw slipped and strained his ankle. He had it massaged and bandaged and stuck to the bench thereafter."

The account did not report that his ankle had been bandaged by William Fallon, though some suspicious souls might not have been surprised if it had. Nor did it report that after McGraw's acquittal a few days later, he indeed stuck to the bench—rarely appearing in his old spot on the third-base coaching line, in what was perhaps a long-range fit of pique over his public letdown by his embarrassed drinking companions at the Lambs.

The Giants, in the midst of this exaggerated life, enjoyed the most flamboyant prose of all. Once, when they crossed into Brooklyn to play the

Dodgers, a 30-minute trip by taxi, bus or subway, their tribulations were described in *The Times* as "arduous and fruitless explorations in a region that makes the old stomping grounds of Stanley and Livingstone seem like Maiden Lane by comparison."

Another time, the Giants were able to "vanquish" the Boston Braves, 9 to 4, and to evoke these literary flourishes:

"Quite a lot of excitement in the stands betokened the appearance of one George Kelly, now back at home after a brief banishment to wildest Brooklyn. Kelly couldn't see much use in fooling around when action was needed, so he accepted the first offering of Fillingim. He not only accepted it, he took it right to the bosom of his cudgel. The leather-clad projectile soared in among such of the populace as had chosen the upper section of the right-field stands as their temporary habitation, and the procession across the plate began."

In naked language, Kelly hit a home run. But phrasing it so nakedly would fit neither the style nor the mood of the day. The point was well understood by Casey Stengel, who had traveled the same path as McGraw from the country to the city and who regarded the City—New York—and its Giants as the end of the rainbow. He had the vocabulary to go with the feeling, too, as he demonstrated in July of that summer when he got word in Philadelphia that the Giants had just bought him and Johnny Rawlings from the Phillies.

Stengel was almost thirty-one years old then, and suffered from a strained back, a gimpy knee and the assorted miseries of life with a last-place team. But he was so enthralled by the prospect of suddenly being transported to the Giants that he immediately double-checked the report of his sale to make certain that it was not simply a clubhouse prank. Having secured that emotional flank, so to speak, he presented himself before the Philadelphia manager, Bill Donovan, to say good-by. Donovan told him that he could settle his affairs that night and leave the next day to join the Giants in Boston. But Casey's reaction was that heaven could not wait.

"Leave tomorrow?" he said later. "Boys, I was leaving right now. I caught the 6:14 from North Philadephia for New York and the midnight out of New York for Boston. Rawlings waited over until the next day, but I wasn't taking any chances on the deal being called off."

Stengel had played for six seasons in Brooklyn, four of them under Wilbert Robinson, but this was New York. And when the Giants returned there from Boston a few days later, he appeared for the first time in the Polo Grounds in Giant uniform, surveyed the splendor of the scene and said to himself, "Wake up, muscles! We're in New York now."

However, it wasn't just the power of words that marked the rise of the Giants in 1921. McGraw also had the knack of making the right trade of talent, and the money to go with it. Besides getting Stengel and Rawlings from Philadelphia, he bought Emil (Irish) Meusel from the Phillies in a separate exchange for Curtis Walker, a center fielder, and Butch Henline, a third-string catcher, and lots of cash.

Then he switched Frank Frisch from second base to third, installed Rawlings at second, put Meusel in left field, George Burns in center and Ross Youngs in right. He had Kelly on first base, Dave Bancroft at shortstop, Frank Snyder and Earl Smith catching, and a pitching staff led by Art Nehf, Phil Douglas, Jesse Barnes and Fred Toney. In reserve he had Stengel and a young outfielder named Bill Cunningham, whom he had bought from Seattle.

Still, even after all this maneuvering, it required a kind of master stroke for the Giants to inspire superlatives of literary style from the people who kept track of their adventures. The problem was that the Pittsburgh Pirates held a lead of 7½ games in the National League late in August, with barely a month of the season left. The critical moment came on August 24, when Pittsburgh arrived in New York for a five-game series.

"It was a breeze for Pittsburgh," Stengel recalled later. "Charlie Grimm strummed the ukelele in the dugout while Rabbit Maranville and Cotton Tierney sang songs without a care in the world."

McGraw, watching from the home dugout, goaded his team with two short, snarling sentences. "Look at those clowns," he said. "No one ever had a softer touch than you fellows have."

Still, the Giants were losing, 3 to 0, in the seventh inning of the opening game. Babe Adams was pitching serenely for Pittsburgh, until the Giants suddenly filled the bases with Kelly batting. The count rose to three balls and no strikes.

"I almost don't bother to look," Stengel said, "because I know McGraw will flash the sign to take the next pitch. But I nearly fell off the bench. McGraw is giving him the sign to hit, and Kelly hits a grand-slam home run.

"It bugs me, though. I can't figure it out. It worked, but why should Mac go against the percentages? So after the game, I ask him.

" 'I'll tell you why,' shouts McGraw, giving it to me good. 'Kelly couldn't hit Adams' curveball if he stood at the plate all day. But on this one pitch Adams has to come in with his fastball. And since it would be the only fastball Kelly would get all day, I let him hit it.' "

When Kelly swaggered over to congratulate McGraw after the game, displaying a fine bit of magnaminity, he found the manager washing his hands at a sink in the locker room. His bravado as strong as ever, McGraw looked up and replied, "If my brains hold out, we might even win this pennant."

His brains did, and the Giants did. They swept on toward first place while Pittsburgh lost all five games in New York, then they swept into first place while Pittsburgh crossed into Stanley and Livingstone country and lost three more to the Brooklyn Dodgers.

When the season ended, McGraw stood at the top of the National League, where he would be standing on closing day for four straight years. And Ruth and the Yankees stood at the top of the American League, where they would be standing for three straight years. Somehow, the irresistible force of Ruth had met the immovable object of McGraw, and none of the script writers in the grill room of the Lambs would have had the cheek to plot such a match in precisely that way, that time or that city.

The World Series opened on October 5 and proved just as improbable. It was the first played under the jurisdiction and the bushy brows of Kenesaw Mountain Landis, the Federal Judge named for a Civil War battle, who had been called into the office as the Commissioner of Baseball to clean away the debris of the debacle of 1919—and who did so, with the grip of a tyrant wound firmly around the bat of Babe Ruth. It was also the last series played on the basis of five victories in nine games. It was the first for the Yankees on any basis, and it was the first played entirely in the Polo Grounds, where tenant and landlord were approaching the end of their strained joint occupancy.

With all this at stake, McGraw lived through a couple of absolutely miserable days before getting a grip on things. The Yankees got off to a rousing start the first time they went to bat when Ruth singled and drove across the first run. It was enough, as Carl Mays—another of the Yankees' prizes from the bankrupt Boston Red Sox—protected the lead that his former Boston teammate had provided. He allowed the Giants only five hits, four of which were made by young Frisch. To add insult to injury, Mike McNally stole home on the Giants, and in 98 fast minutes the Yankees racked up a 3-to-0 victory.

The next day McGraw changed his catchers but not his luck. Bob Meusel stole home this time while Earl Smith, the Giants' catcher, watched and McGraw stewed. Smith had a clubhouse reputation as a talker, but he came out second best in a talk with McGraw after the game and also was relieved of $200 by Landis for an inflammatory speech he had made at home plate after Meusel had scored. The Giants, meanwhile, made only two hits off Waite Hoyt and for the second straight day lost by the score of 3 to 0.

In the third game, the Yankees just kept rolling along. They scored four runs off Toney in the third inning, and now the Giants were two games and four runs down and still hadn't scored a run of their own in the series. Besides, no team in the previous 17 years of World Series history had spotted a rival two games and survived.

However, McGraw's "brains" rallied, with the help of three bases on balls by Bob Shawkey, the Yankee pitcher, and the Giants made one of their remarkable comebacks. They scored four runs in the home half of the third inning, then eight more in the seventh inning for a World Series record, and stormed along to win, 13 to 5.

McGraw felt better now. And he felt even better when the Giants evened things by winning the fourth game, 4 to 2, despite Ruth's first home run in a World Series—his first of 15 during the next dozen years.

The next day the Yankees went back ahead with a 3-to-1 victory, and Ruth made even bigger news. He beat out a bunt. However, he also developed an abscess on his left elbow and, except for one appearance as a pinch-hitter, his series was finished. So, for all practical purposes, were the Yankees. Without their champion, they did not win another game as the Giants tied the series, 8 to 5; went ahead, 2 to 1, and won it all, 1 to 0.

McGraw, who had lost four series in a row since 1905, treated himself to one of those rare moments of unmixed delight in the last inning of the last game. First, his nemesis Ruth pinch-hit for Wally Pipp and grounded out. Then Aaron Ward walked and Home Run Baker lined a pitch toward right field. But Johnny Rawlings, the boy second-baseman whom McGraw had bought from Philadelphia four months earlier, lunged for the ball, knocked it down on the rim of the outfield grass and, still on his knees, threw out Baker at first base. Ward had rounded second and was en route to third, but Kelly, the first-baseman, relayed Rawlings' throw across the infield to Frisch, who ended the series by tagging Ward at third base while McGraw's cup runneth over.

It ran over far into the night, in fact, in a typically roaring celebration in the Giants' suite at the Waldorf. They had won the pennant at the eleventh hour, had won the series at the eleventh hour and were headed for four straight seasons of unmatched prosperity. But for McGraw, there was only one victory worth crowing about.

"I signaled every pitch to Ruth," he said, savoring every boast from his first encounter with the big man. "In fact, I gave the sign for practically every ball our pitchers threw. They preferred that I do. It was no secret. You could see Snyder or Smith turn and look at the bench before signaling the pitcher. We pitched only nine curves and three fastballs to Ruth during the entire series. All the rest were slowballs, and of the twelve of those, eleven set him on his ear."

McGraw's sense of wellbeing was even strengthened by three incidents during the series that bedeviled the Yankees in a kind of comic-opera fashion.

The first involved a pair of actors, the sort who tagged along at all baseball extravaganzas and especially the World Series. One of them was working on press arrangements with Frederick G. Lieb, the baseball writer. He, in turn, introduced the second, and between them they dropped a small bombshell behind the scenes after the fourth game. The Giants won the game, 4 to 2, after the Yankee pitcher, Mays, had worked five hitless innings, then had given up a single in the sixth and a single in the seventh. But then Mays suddenly collapsed under the three Giant runs in the eighth.

The bombshell was an insistent accusation by the second actor that Mays' collapse had not been accidental. They were forthwith taken to the Martinique Hotel to the suite of the Yankees' co-owner, Colonel Huston (who had overtaken his partner Colonel Ruppert in military rank since they had embarked on their baseball caper). Huston in turn paraded the delegation before Judge Landis, who had been sleeping but who had a hair-trigger memory of the 1919 scandal and who could be aroused fast by any intimations of hanky-panky.

Landis immediately hired a private detective to shadow Mays for the rest of the series. But nothing incriminating was unearthed. In fact, three days later both Mays and the private eye watched in dismay as Mays lost a 2-to-1 thriller to the Giants because his second-baseman fumbled a ground ball.

The second incident concerned Ruth, and was more visible and more violent. The huge left-hander had struck out eight times in five games, had retired with the abscess on his left elbow and then had been outraged to read in Joe Vila's column in the New York *Sun* that he had been lying down on the job after all. Not being one to sulk in silence, Ruth made straight for the press box at the Polo Grounds, which was then at ground level behind home plate, and bearded his critic through the wire screen that protected the writers from foul balls. He became so thunderous and menacing that Vila finally picked up his typewriter and held it in front of his face like a Roman legionnaire's shield, while the Giants and Yankees on the field watched the "sick" man storm in amazement.

Finally, Ruth became involved with the commissioner himself, and demonstrated that while McGraw might be one to dwell on triumphs, Ruth was not one to brood about defeats. Ruth had signed for a baseball barnstorming tour and that was the issue. Landis said no, Ruth said yes. So Babe embarked on the trip as soon as the series ended, while McGraw was still chortling over the outcome of Round One of the Battle of Broadway. Ruth didn't even wait to collect his loser's share of $3,510 of the series revenue, which Landis finally impounded anyway.

He also was suspended for 39 days at the beginning of the next season, and did not play until May 20. To complete the rout, he thereupon suffered through his worst slump as a player.

Yet he stalked Fallon's famous client like an albatross. And there he was the following autumn at the Polo Grounds, flexing his muscles for another Yankee-Giant World Series and for Round Two of his troubled time with John McGraw.

Chapter

9

The Cheers Could Be Heard Throughout the Land

The art of skywriting was probably born in May of 1922, when Major John C. Savage, a pilot in the Royal Air Force, flew over Epsom Downs and traced a wind-blown message in smoke that read: "The Daily Mail."

Major Savage might have caused a commotion merely by flying over the course without leaving any message, since airplanes were less common than racehorses and since even motorcars were often greeted by cries of "Get a horse." But when Savage left a message behind his biplane, he blazed a trail of advertising and hoopla that fitted neatly into the sky-high mood of the day.

His art form, naturally, was bound to gravitate toward the most responsive audience of all, and it did. The Skywriting Corporation of America purchased the rights to the technique, and in October unveiled it at a time and place calculated to create a sensation. The company dispatched a single plane over the northern tip of Manhattan Island, where the pilot performed 270-degree turns, loops and chandelles over a crowd of 36,514 persons who were watching the World Series in the Polo Grounds.

The throng, which included the two ranking rivals of the moment in public life, Babe Ruth and John McGraw, looked up as the plane sputtered overhead and read: "Hello USA. Call Vanderbilt 7200."

For the next five hours, Vanderbilt 7200 was the most overworked telephone number in town. It belonged to the Vanderbilt Hotel, where the Skywriting Corporation of America had its headquarters, and during those five hours the hotel switchboard was engulfed with calls from a public that got its greatest kicks from buying low, selling high, drinking bootleg and living fast—

or from idolizing the people who did.

It was a time when people worshipped heroes, and when heroes later looked back and agreed that there had been no better time to be worshipped. Even failure often had a heroic tone. "In 1922," recalled Gene Sarazen, the golfer, "I was a 5-to-1 favorite to win the British Open. But I'm not a good mudder, and it was raining and I took an 85 at St. Andrews in Scotland and failed even to qualify." He paused, drew a breath and added with deep-down pleasure: "It was raining so hard they wouldn't let the ships out of the Navy Yard."

Even women were breaking into the news in extraordinary ways, and not just by taking up the cudgels of the suffragettes.

In New Brunswick, New Jersey, for example, no name was more famous than that of Mrs. Eleanor R. Mills. She was a singer in the choir of a church, or at least had been a singer in the choir of a church. But she and her pastor, the Rev. Edward W. Hall, became international celebrities when they were killed "by robbers or blackmailers." Their status as celebrities was assured a few days later when it was reported from New Brunswick that authorities had begun investigating rumors that Mr. Hall had been in the habit of receiving letters from Mrs. Mills and "placing them in a small box in the study of his church." That seemed to rule out robbers, and the public perked up.

In Atlanta, at the other end of the scale of notoriety, an eighty-seven-year-old woman named Mrs. W. H. Felton was appointed to the United States Senate by Governor Thomas W. Hardwick. She was to fill the vacancy created by the death of Thomas E. Watson and would thereby become the first woman in the Senate, which until then had prided itself on being the world's greatest deliberative male body. Governor Hardwick, rationalizing his choice, declared that "she is wise, even beyond her years." He apparently failed to recognize that no woman—not even one eighty-seven years old—would necessarily appreciate that particular argument.

To make the situation more farfetched, Congress was in recess until the next January and a special election was to be held in a month to fill the seat anyway. So Mrs. Felton would never actually sit. But the "pay and perquisites" of the office were to be hers for a month or so, and the public looked up as enthralled as when Major Savage buzzed Epsom Downs.

However, it remained for a considerably more obscure woman to cause what the New York press termed "a sensation," and she did it without skywriters, governors or blackmailers. She did it by appearing outside the bleacher gate at the Polo Grounds twenty-four hours before the World Series was to begin, and before Vanderbilt 7200 became the most popular number in town. She was fifth in line behind four bewildered men, she was identified as Mrs. Carrie Lentz of West 141st Street and, the press duly reported, "she will root for the Yankees."

"Truly," said *The New York Times,* frankly impressed, "baseball is the national game. From east and west, from north and south, the fans are gathering to see two New York teams battle in the blue-ribbon event of the diamond, the World Series."

In addition to Mrs. Carrie Lentz of West 141st Street, two governors, four former governors, two mayors and swarms of deputies like A. B. Lasker, head of the United States Shipping Board, were among those observed and reported at the home of the New York Giants as the series opened on October 4.

"J. P. Morgan is a boxholder," the press noted with public spirit, "as are also Harry F. Sinclair, Harry Payne Whitney, Finley J. Shepard and Charles H. Sabin." In a box near the dugout, Mary Roberts Rinehart entertained a group of friends. George M. Cohan, Louis Mann and Jack Dempsey took bows, and when General John J. Pershing made an unexpected appearance the crowd rose and cheered, as it did for Al Smith and the old brown derby.

Christy Mathewson, the old sensation of the Giants, who no longer was a combatant, got headlines just for attending. So did Babe Ruth, the new sensation of the Yankees, just for striking out twice. It was even noted with something approaching civic pride that Lord Louis Mountbatten and his bride had planned to attend but at the last minute had decided to view the polo matches at Meadowbrook, worse luck for *them.*

Major Savage was there, too, so to speak, and Casey Stengel glanced up during batting practice and thought he had seen a Yankee "spy" watching. "Yankee secret service," he told Earl Smith, the Giants' catcher, who was batting at the time with no thought that it was possible to hide anything from anybody in that busy scene.

Indeed, a big bold-faced advertisement in the newspapers that day guaranteed that nothing would be hidden from a public that had grown hungry all summer for a rematch between the champion Giants and the challenging Yankees. They were renewing their feud this day before the biggest of sports crowds, the 36,514 on the inside of the stadium and thousands on the outside who for the first time would hear a series game described by radio.

"Hear the crowd roar at the World Series games with Radiola," the public was exhorted. "Grantland Rice, famous sports editor of the New York *Tribune,* will describe every game personally, play by play, direct from the Polo Grounds. His story, word by word, as each exciting play is made by the Yankees or Giants will be *broadcasted* from famous Radio Corporation-Westinghouse Station WJZ."

This was no time to wrangle over past participles, nor even over price. "There's an R.C.A. set for every home and every purse. As low as $25. Prepare for the big event by buying your R.C.A. set from your nearest dealer and ask him for the Radiola Score Sheet." And a footnote advised the dealers not to stand in the path of history, either, urging them to "cut this out and paste in your window."

The irony of it all was that with a little bad luck the Giants and Yankees themselves might have wound up in the radio audience on the momentous occasion instead of on the field.

The Yankees had suffered until May 20 because of Ruth's suspension by Commissioner Landis. Then, when he was finally permitted to play, they suffered because he had lost much of the touch that had made him the blockbuster of 1921. He batted only .315, while George Sisler of the St. Louis Browns was rising to the astronomical level of .420. Worse, after three straight years of leading the major leagues in home runs, Ruth slipped while Ken Williams of St. Louis was hitting 39.

Still, St. Louis somehow could not capitalize on all this statistical success at bat and finished second in the American League while Ruth and the Yankees won their second pennant in a row.

Meanwhile the Giants were suffering, too. They had neither the Yankees' pitching nor St. Louis' hitting, and had nobody close to Rogers Hornsby of the Cardinals, who led the National League with a batting average of .401 plus 42 home runs and 152 runs batted in.

McGraw, however, had taken the precaution of fortifying the Giants against such inequities. During the winter he had trotted out one of his favorite weapons, the trade. He pried Heinie Groh from Cincinnati after several frustrated attempts, then put Groh at third base and sent Frank Frisch back to second. The trade cost him only George Burns and Mike Gonzales. McGraw had long admired Burns as the "perfect" outfielder, but now Burns was rather old as perfect outfielders went; Gonzales was merely a perfect bullpen catcher.

Next, McGraw got Jimmy O'Connell from San Francisco for something the Giants always could come up with—money. O'Connell was twenty-one years old, a graduate of Santa Clara University and a .337 hitter all in one, and he could play the outfield or first base. The price was $75,000, a record for a minor leaguer.

Then McGraw cashed in another of his well-known assets—the tout tip. Having worked, wheeled and dealed across the baseball landscape for thirty years, he now enjoyed the most far-flung scout-and-tout system in the game, and it forthwith produced two of his brightest properties of the future.

First, Kid Elberfeld, the manager at Little Rock in the Southern Association (and a longtime sufferer of pranks engineered by Casey Stengel), tipped him off to a young infielder from Arkansas named Travis Jackson. Then Tom Watkins, the owner of the Memphis club and an old friend, led him to Bill Terry—who not only would become the anchor of the team for a decade but also would become McGraw's successor as manager.

While McGraw was grateful for the help, he immediately sensed that the help would eventually cost him considerable serenity. Terry, who was then a pitcher, enraged McGraw at the outset by his indifference. Moreover, it was an indifference born of outside strength: a good job that he already held with Standard Oil. McGraw, who always liked his rookies hungry, was further enraged when he offered Terry the chance to go straight to New York and Terry calmly lit a long cigar and replied, "For how much?"

When McGraw seemed incredulous, Terry drove the point home in language that made it unmistakable that McGraw had crossed into a new generation that would soon replace his own. "Excuse me if I don't fall all over myself," Terry said, trying to be reasonable but managing only to sound patronizing, "but the Giants don't mean anything to me unless you can make it worth my while."

While McGraw was letting that bit of heresy sink in, Terry ended the conversation by saying, "If you want to make me an offer, you can reach me in care of the Standard Oil Company."

For McGraw, who was now forty-nine, this was a completely new challenge. And since it could not be countered by a smart rousing punch in the nose, it was an unsettling challenge. It offered none of the good, clean antagonism of a brawl—like the one touched off that summer by Columbia George Smith of Philadelphia, who hit Ralph Shinners of the Giants on the head with a baseball. When Philadelphia came back to town the next time around, McGraw and Shinners both piled into Smith and everybody had a great time until the police broke it up. But Bill Terry was something else.

However, a more immediate challenge was posed by Branch Rickey and his heavy-hitting St. Louis Cardinals, who fought the Giants for the league lead all summer. So McGraw responded with the old trump card. He bought Hughie McQuillan from the Boston Braves, giving the Giants something the Cardinals could respect—a first-class pitcher. The Cardinals, who were a lot leaner in the bankroll than the Giants, also could resent the way the Giants had acquired their first-class pitcher, and they did. They accused the Giants of buying the pennant for $100,000 and bemoaned the fact that they were "in no position to compete with them financially."

The incident even escalated into the kind of intrigue that Landis had been hired to dispel. One of McGraw's pitchers, Phil Douglas, wrote a note on Giants' stationery to Leslie Mann, an outfielder for the Cardinals, suggesting that if St. Louis made it worth his while, Douglas would "go fishing" for the rest of the season. Douglas by now was famous for wandering and was the bane of McGraw's life. He was an awesome drinker, and when McGraw put private detectives on his trail he amused himself by playing cat and mouse with them. Once he even took a four-day "vacation" from the team. But when he came back from that "fishing" expedition and McGraw lashed him verbally and unmercifully, Douglas sulked, then apparently wrote the note to St. Louis and finally was banished from baseball by Landis.

McGraw had other problems, too. McQuillan teamed with Jess Barnes after he joined the club and their shenanigans led McGraw to label them "Gallagher and Shean." And Earl Smith, the talkative catcher, irritated him so persistently that the manager finally complained bitterly: "He's an anarchist, he has no respect for law and order."

Still, McGraw gradually adjusted to his tormentors and his patched-up team began to mesh. He was also surrounded by the comfort of his private life, his home in Pelham, his Broadway cronies, his evenings on Travers Island at the summer oasis of the New York Athletic Club. On September 25, the Giants pulled clear of Cincinnati and St. Louis, clinched the pennant and nine days later stood in the Polo Grounds as the curtain rose on Round Two of the Battle of Broadway.

Broadway itself approached the rematch with caution, something it rarely did in such matters of passion. So did Wall Street, which was absolutely certain that oil and rail stocks were skyrocketing but not so certain that McGraw could induce a slump in Yankee hitters like Ruth. "Wall Street," reported *The Times,* "was particularly quiet yesterday before the start of the series. Fewer wagers were reported than ever before on the eve of the autumn classic."

One fairly sizable bet was reported through the brokerage houses, which treated such transactions the way they treated risks on the market: $3,500 to $2,500 on the Yankees. Tex Rickard, the major domo of boxing, leaned toward the Yankees. Devereux Milburn, the captain of the "Big Four" of the Meadowbrook polo team, took time out before riding for Lord Louis Mountbatten and said, "The Yankees, of course." Willie Hoppe, the billiard king, rode with the billiard proprietor McGraw and said, "I have a hunch the Giants will win."

Then the show was on, and in the sixth inning of the opening game the Yankees struck first, as they had done in the opening game of the 1921 series.

With one out, Whitey Witt hit a three-bagger, then tried to score when Joe Dugan bounced a grounder to shortstop, Dave Bancroft. But Bancroft threw the ball home and intercepted Witt, who was trapped between third base and home but who managed one thing before being tagged out: He hopped back and forth long enough to allow Dugan to reach second base. Dugan then scored from second when Ruth followed with a single to right.

It was the second straight year that Ruth had got in the first lick against McGraw by driving across the first run. But for the second straight year McGraw was destined to have the last laugh. It was the only run produced by Ruth in the entire series.

The Yankees scored again in the seventh, and now it was 2 to 0 with Bullet Joe Bush stifling the Giants all the way. But in the home half of the eighth, McGraw's trades came home to roost. Bancroft singled, Groh singled, Frisch singled and the bases were loaded with Giants and nobody out. Then Irish Meusel, late of the Philadelphia club, singled over Bush's head and drove home Bancroft and Groh, late of the Cincinnati club. Miller Huggins rushed in Waite Hoyt to do the pitching, and Hoyt stopped the hitting but not the scoring. Youngs lifted a fly to Witt, and Frisch ran home with the winning run.

While these developments thrilled the crowd of 36,514 inside the Giants' park, they absolutely captivated a huge audience beyond the stadium that huddled before loudspeakers.

"Radio for the first time," reported *The Times,* "carried the opening game of the World Series, play by play, direct from the Polo Grounds to great crowds throughout the eastern section of the country. Through the broadcasting station WJZ at Newark, New Jersey, Grantland Rice, a sports writer, related his story of the game direct to an invisible audience, estimated to be five million, while WGY at Schenectady and WBZ at Springfield, Massachusetts, relayed every play of the contest.

"In place of the scoreboards and megaphones of the past, amplifiers connected to radio instruments gave all the details and sidelights to thousands of enthusiasts unable to get into the Polo Grounds. Not only could the voice of the official radio observer be heard, but the voice of the umpire on the field announcing the batteries for the day mingled with the voice of a boy selling ice cream cones.

"The clamor of the 40,000 baseball fans inside the Polo Grounds made radio listeners feel as if they were in the grandstand. The cheers which greeted Babe Ruth when he stepped to the plate could be heard throughout the land. And as he struck the ball, the shouts that followed indicated whether the Babe had fanned or got a hit even before the radio announcer could tell what had happened."

Like immense magnets now, Ruth and McGraw were attracting national emotions to the rivalry at 157th Street and Eighth Avenue, and they were polarizing attention far beyond the old pastures of Coogan's estate. They were at the right place at the right time, and radio promised that an "observer" would be there with them every day to report their struggles.

"At 1:45 each day," the public was assured, "Grantland Rice will speak into a transmitter which will actuate the radio apparatus in Newark and carry the game play by play to the radio audience. The broadcasting will be done on a wave length of 360 meters."

Even Lord Louis Mountbatten, Grand Admiral of the Fleet, illustrious cousin of the Prince of Wales and uncle to an empire, could not be indifferent to that. Turning aside from the polo matches, he headed for McGraw's ball park the next day and confessed that "wireless" was indeed his hobby, too.

Page 1 gave way to the occasion too, as well it might, since most of the denizens of politics and finance had joined the rush uptown anyway. (Short notice was even accorded the most bizarre of other news, including the adventure of a furrier who was standing at the window of his shop on the third floor of 557 Fifth Avenue contemplating the scene below when an arrow flew through the window and struck him lightly in the chest. He was amazed, since no Iroquois had been reported in the area for a very long time. And he was even more amazed the following day when Douglas Fairbanks appeared at his door in person and said apologetically that he and some friends had been "fooling around" with a bow and arrow on the roof of the Ritz-Carlton and one might have got away.)

So all eyes and ears were on the Polo Grounds on October 5 when the second game got under way, and the biggest fuss of all developed before the biggest and most distinguished group of onlookers and listeners.

In the first inning, Groh and Frisch singled for McGraw and then Irish Meusel hit a ball into the left-field bleachers. But the Yankees got one run back in the bottom of the first, then another in the fourth when Aaron Ward hit one *over* the left-field bleachers, and in the eighth inning Ruth and Bob Meusel doubled to tie the score.

In the midst of the tumult, Lord Louis Mountbatten sat behind first base enthralled. He ate six ice cream cones and two bags of peanuts, drank four bottles of soda pop and rooted for Babe Ruth until he was hoarse. Lady

Mountbatten, one of the reigning beauties of Europe, resplendent in brown, watched through a tortoise-shell lorgnette. When Ruth appeared alongside the Yankee dugout, she leaned over and shouted, "Atta boy, Babe." When the umpire called a strike on Wally Pipp, Her Ladyship was heard to grumble, "Rotten." His Lordship said it was the greatest game he had ever seen.

It was the greatest game a lot of people had ever seen, and when it was unexpectedly ended with the score still tied, 3 to 3, it turned into the greatest mob scene a lot of people had ever seen.

The Yankees, the home team this time because their new stadium across the river was still unfinished, had just gone down in order in the tenth inning. Ruth fouled out, Pipp grounded out and Meusel lifted a high foul ball to the catcher near the screen behind home plate. It was 4:40 p.m. and the sun was still shining. But suddenly the home-plate umpire, George Hildebrand, wheeled around, swept his face mask through a wide circle with his hand and announced, "Game called on account of darkness."

Judge Landis, erect, dignified, crusty, had just been introduced to Mountbatten and his bride in the box of Colonel Ruppert, the owner of the Yankees. For a moment, the crowd did not quite grasp what Hildebrand meant. But then the players began running from the field and the enormity of the decision swept across the rows and aisles. And suddenly, thousands stood and raged and poured from the stands, making straight for Landis and his visitors like tribesmen in the Sahara besieging a British outpost.

Landis, standing upright in the box, his white hair shaking like a mane, tried to restore order. But he had no chance of reasoning with the mob and his voice was overpowered by boos, catcalls and shouts of "crook" and "robber." Some fans even implied that it was all a plot by the owners to prolong the series for more money. Somebody even had the intemperance to yell, in a reference to the sordid series of 1919, "Where are the White Sox?"

A police escort finally was marshaled to surround Landis and escort him and his wife from the park through the howling crowd. Mountbatten, startled by the violent ending of "the greatest game ever," turned to the beleaguered commissioner and observed, in splendid understatement: "My goodness, Judge, but they are giving you the bird."

Landis made a brave effort to turn the tables on his critics. He realized that he was the target because Hildebrand had walked over to his box in the tenth inning and the fans then assumed that Landis had ordered the game stopped. "I may not be the smartest person in the United States," he said later, "but at least I can tell day from night." Whereupon, to get the mob off his back, he announced that all the money from the game would be turned over to a charity for disabled soldiers.

The series was resumed the next day and everybody promptly forgot about Landis—except the club owners, who grumbled about his beau geste with *their* money, and except for dozens of organized charities, who promptly deluged him with requests for a piece of the $120,554 giveaway of the day before. He was even more harassed by petitioners than was President Harding, who was besieged in Washington that day by suffragettes demanding that he call a special session of Congress so that eighty-seven-year-old Mrs. Felton down in Georgia might actually sit in her new Senate seat.

The irony, noted Lieb, the baseball historian, was that both Landis and Hildebrand had taken a bad rap. The culprit actually was Bill Klem, the Old Man Mose of umpires, who had gone to Hildebrand near the end of the tenth inning and said, "It's light now, but will it be light by the time both teams complete their next turns at bat?" Klem was officiating in his tenth World Series and had convinced most people, including Hildebrand, that he could do no wrong.

As things turned out, that one tie was as close as the Yankees were to come to staging a palace revolution in 1922 on McGraw's home grounds.

The Giants made it two in a row on the four-hit, 3-to-0 pitching of Jack Scott, "a baseball derelict picked up by McGraw for the price of a uniform." The price really had been a uniform and $50 cash, which McGraw had anted up to stake the pitcher to one last fling in the major leagues. Scott, a big winner at Boston in 1921, had been traded to Cincinnati and then discovered that his arm was lame. He was even told by doctors that he could never pitch again. But he asked McGraw for a chance, worked out alone at the Polo Grounds while the Giants were on the road and now was shutting out the Yankees' power hitters in the World Series.

Not only that, but he opened the third inning with a single that launched a rally for the Giants' first two runs of the afternoon. After that McGraw's day grew steadily brighter. He even came face to face with Ruth after the game and prevailed. Ruth had been nicked by a pitched ball, had retaliated by barreling into the stumpy Heinie Groh, had spent the rest of the afternoon exchanging insults with the Giants' bench and, spoiling for a fight, finally stormed into the Giants' clubhouse with Bob Meusel after the game.

Just as the players on both sides were taking off coats and rolling up sleeves, McGraw came into the clubhouse with his old Baltimore crony and coach, Hughey Jennings, and ordered Ruth and Meusel to "get out and stay out." And they did.

Outside the locker room, the crowd was so thick that McGraw had difficulty forcing his way into his own inner sanctum. He and Judge Francis X. McQuade finally made it with the help of two policemen who ran interference through the cheering crowd while the press marveled at "the gray-haired, rotund figure, a true leader, who was the center of this spontaneous outburst."

Downtown, even bigger crowds gathered despite the sloppy weather and the dry comforts offered inside by the new World Series marvel of radio. They clustered around wooden scoreboards that posted the action of the game, pitch by pitch, in City Hall Park and at Broadway and Chambers Street. And the most persistent cry of the afternoon on the street corners of Manhattan wherever such crowds gathered was: "Put that umbrella down."

It was still raining the next day as the Yankees tried to get back into business. In fact, a steady downpour fell from the fourth inning on. But the game went on and another of McGraw's investments paid off. McQuillan, the $100,000 purchase from Boston, survived both the rain and the heaviest Yankee hitting of the series and the Giants won for the third time, 4 to 3.

It was becoming hard for the Yankees to escape the feeling that somehow the gods were allowing McGraw his finest hour.

The first time they batted, Witt and Dugan hit clean, hard singles. Then Ruth hit the longest shot of the series, a 450-foot drive to the deepest corner of center field. Normally, Stengel would have been playing there trying to patrol the wide open spaces on a pair of gnarled, bowed, aching legs. But McGraw had substituted young Bill Cunningham in center field this day. And Stengel was watching alongside McGraw in the dugout as Cunningham raced back, ran around the monument that stood like a headstone near the farthest wall and made an acrobatic catch in the narrow alley between the slab and the bleachers.

But the gods were not done toying with the Yankees. Pipp went to bat after the uproar had subsided and followed with a single—only to be thrown out trying to stretch it into a double.

By contrast, when the Giants batted in the fifth, everything came up roses. McQuillan hit a ball to Dugan at third base, and it bounced off Dugan's glove for a double. Bancroft hit one squarely to Ward at second base, and at the last moment it bounced over Ward's head for a single. Groh hit one back to the pitcher's mound, and Carl Mays knocked it down, but Groh was safe with a single. Then came a sacrifice, an infield out and a single, and the Giants had four runs and the game.

The next day was Sunday, October 8, and 38,551 persons packed the Polo Grounds—the biggest crowd that had ever seen a World Series game in New York. They watched the Yankees build a lead of 3 to 2, then they saw the Giants go to bat in the eighth inning, then they saw the furies break loose.

With one out, Groh singled and Frisch doubled. Irish Meusel hit a ball to shortstop, where Everett Scott grabbed it and threw home to cut down Groh for the second out. Now Huggins resorted to grand strategy. He ordered the Yankee pitcher, Joe Bush, to give an intentional base on balls to Ross Youngs, a left-handed hitter, and to pitch instead to George Kelly, a right-hander.

Bush did as he had been told. But he was mortified and while pitching the four balls to Youngs, he simultaneously was pitching insults at Huggins in the dugout. Finally, with the bases loaded and the right-hander now at bat, he pitched to Kelly—who lined the first ball solidly over Bush's head into center field for a two-run single.

The final score was 5 to 3, giving the Giants a four-game sweep of the series with only the 10-inning tie to break the continuity. After the game, Lieb rode downtown in a taxicab with Colonel Huston, the co-owner of the Yankees, who just sat and stared at the floor all the way to the Commodore Hotel. They went to the bar and then Huston could restrain his anger no more. He let out a wild war whoop, swung his right hand across the bar, sent drinks and glasses flying and shouted, "Miller Huggins has managed his last Yankee ball game."

Before the day was over, though, he tangled on that point with his partner, Ruppert, who argued just as vehemently that he could not fire a manager
who had just won two straight pennants. The dispute crystallized a number of
other differences between the two colonels, and before the winter was over
Ruppert bought out Huston's half-interest and became the sole owner of the
Yankees.

Back at the ball park, the second great riot of the World Series was sweeping over the Polo Grounds. But this time, instead of aiming insults at Landis,
the mob was aiming wild adulation at McGraw.

He had given the old generation of Giants two straight victories over the
new generation of Yankees. He had given the old National League two straight
over the new American League for the first time in 13 years. He had given the
old crowd of Broadway two straight over the new crowd of Broadway, and the
new crowd was about to retreat from the Polo Grounds forever into its own
temple across the river. The old had prevailed over the new, and had even
muzzled Babe Ruth with two hits in 17 times at bat for an average of .118.

When it was over, McGraw was besieged by thousands of shouting, scrambling fans from the stands, and the cheers could be heard throughout the land,
amplified and relayed from Manhattan to Newark to Springfield to Schenectady on a wave length of 360 meters.

They chased McGraw from his dugout, they pursued him across the field
toward his clubhouse, they patted him, jostled him, shook his hand. One fan
even kissed him. And an aged woman broke through the crowd somehow and
said, "I can go home now. I've seen the greatest manager in baseball."

"Every fan within hailing distance," reported *The New York Times,* "wanted a chance to slap the Little Napoleon on the back, to shake his hand or at
least to yell his admiration at close quarters. McGraw, for the time being, was
the hero of heroes. Men climbed on each other's shoulders trying to get near
enough to tell him what a wonderful manager he was. They leaped and danced
and yelled themselves blue in the face. The bleacherites were all waiting. They
made no rush for the exits. They remained where they were to cheer McGraw.

"Behind these latest triumphs of the Giants, the directing genius of John
McGraw shone more brilliantly than ever before. There is none to dispute his
right to the title of greatest manager in baseball history. Not one whit discouraged by the collapse of his team in 1915, when it completed the season in
eighth place, McGraw started the task of rebuilding his machine, and just two
years later led his players to another National League championship.

"His record stands alone and unchallenged. He is the outstanding figure
among all the managers in the history of the game."

Chapter

10

The Ruth Is Mighty And Shall Prevail

On a warm spring day in May of 1923, a young member of a jury left the Federal court in lower Manhattan and began strolling up Broadway. Court had just been recessed for lunch, but he decided to skip lunch and thereby accomplish two things: He would save 50 cents out of his jury allowance of $3 a day, and he would spend the lunch hour looking into something that had caught his eye.

His name was Graham McNamee. He turned into the building at 195 Broadway, glanced at the sign that read "Radio Station WEAF," rode the elevator to the little two-room studio on the fourth floor and stepped out into a new life.

McNamee had been born in Washington, D.C., on July 10, 1889, but had been brought up in the Northwest because his father was a lawyer for the Union Pacific Railroad. His life as a boy at the turn of the century was relaxed enough, but was somewhat bedeviled by his mother's insistence that he play the piano while the other kids on the block were out playing baseball.

He did as he was told, and at the age of eighteen even went his mother one better by taking voice lessons to go with the piano lessons. Then he packed off to New York looking for fame and fortune, and made his professional debut as a baritone at Aeolian Hall in 1921 while somebody else's son accompanied him on the piano.

"He sang," wrote the critic of the New York *Sun*, "with a justness, a care and style." Later, by the time McNamee was singing 150 times in one recital season, he would evoke notices like this one in *The New York Times:*

"Anyone who sings the air 'O Ruddier Than The Cherry' from Handel's 'Acis and Galatea' with such admirably flexible command over the 'divisions,' with such finished phrasing and such excellent enunciation as McNamee showed, is doing a difficult thing very well indeed."

Now it was 1923, and McNamee was getting hungry to try that excellent enunciation on something more rewarding than "O Ruddier Than The Cherry." So he presented himself to Sam Ross, the program director for WEAF, a sideshow subsidiary of the American Telephone and Telegraph Company, and was permitted to spend his lunch hour looking over the shoulders of a few of the pioneers of commercial radio. Before he returned to the jury box that afternoon, he had been hired to join the little troupe as a jack of all trades—at $30 a week.

Three months later, McNamee got his first big assignment as the baritone of the microphone. He sat at the ringside while Harry Greb was winning the world's middleweight championship from Johnny Wilson, and described it—blow by blow, elbow by elbow—with the old "finished phrasing" and "admirably flexible command" that had drawn compliments on the recital stage.

Then it was September, and one day Sam Ross called McNamee in and rewarded him with another assignment, one that would test his vocal powers more than Handel or Harry Greb and that ironically would lead him back to baseball after all those piano lessons. He was to broadcast the 1923 World Series, Round Three of the Battle of Broadway, the third straight between the Yankees and the Giants, the first in Yankee Stadium, the greatest in gate receipts, and the last confrontation between the titans of New York sporting life, John McGraw and Babe Ruth.

It was just four months since McNamee had left the jury room, skipped lunch and looked in on the primitive wonders of radio. Now he was being handed a saucer-shaped microphone, an engineer, a seat in the open, no precedents and the job of describing one of the great spectacles of the day.

He was surrounded by the biggest crowds in baseball history: 62,000 in the new Yankee Stadium and 46,000 in the old, enlarged Polo Grounds across the Harlem River. By telephone lines, his perch was also connected with crowds in crossroads and cities along the Eastern Seaboard. Stations like WJZ in New York, WMAF in South Dartmouth, Massachusetts, and WCAP in Washington, D.C., the press reported, "will also radiate the contests simultaneously with WEAF, as they will be connected by special land wires to microphones controlled by that station."

The stakes were awesome for baseball and so was the challenge for radio, which had had little experience in portraying human drama, real or imagined. On October 10, the day the 20th and most tumultuous World Series began, *The New York Times* framed this particular drama in soap-opera cadences on page 1:

"Will McGraw stop the greatest hitter in baseball? Will Ruth redeem his failure of 1922 and step forward as the outstanding star of the Yankees?

"Among the baseball men crowding the restaurants of New York the feeling was that McGraw, the master mind of the Giants, might again perform a baseball miracle and produce from his indifferent collection of twirlers the necessary skill and strength to hold the Yankees safe. In the background of all the discussions was this same figure, McGraw. In sum and substance, he is the Giants. If Ruth is the big figure among the players, McGraw towers high among the managers, and on his generalship, shrewdness and strategy the cause of the Giants seems to rest."

The challenge confronting McNamee and the small staff at 195 Broadway was framed more starkly. It was reflected in the WEAF program listings for that day, a prosaic lineup with one shattering innovation:

> 11 a.m.—Playing the Health Game, by Clara Tebutt.
> 11:20 a.m.—Writing for the Movies, by Mrs. Frances Patterson.
> 11:50 a.m.—Market reports.
> 1:30 p.m.—World Series, play by play.

Two and a half hours later, at 4 p.m., leaving little time for a slow game or even extra innings, and none for the locker-room critiques of later years, WEAF promised to return to its home studio for "Milton F. Rehg, baritone, with piano and soprano." That was a switch. Now McNamee was being *followed* by a baritone recital. However, WJZ showed a far greater sense of caution—either that or a far greater lack of programming. It gave the ball game until 5:30 to clear the airwaves, then snapped back to reality with "Closing Report of the New York State Department of Farms."

Radio's wariness in approaching its great hour was well-founded. Only ten years before, the earliest experiments in transmitting sports events from arena to studio had been pretty much of a university laboratory affair. Pioneers at the University of Minnesota had attempted to radio football games by using a spark transmitter and telegraph signals. And even as late as 1922, Texas A&M was experimenting in a play-by-play account of its Thanksgiving Day game against Texas.

The most aggressive sports broadcasting, though, was being performed by avant-gardists at KDKA in Pittsburgh and a few other cities. In April of 1921, capitalizing on the postwar frenzy in sports, KDKA carried a description of the Johnny Ray-Johnny Dundee fight. And on July 2, a milestone was passed by WJY, sister station to WJZ, at the Dempsey-Carpentier fight in the wooden bowl at Boyle's Thirty Acres in Jersey City.

All over town, crystal sets and one-tube receivers picked up the action from ringside. The reporter was Major Andrew White, with somebody named David Sarnoff at his elbow. Still, "remotes" were almost unheard of, so White's account of the fight was transmitted by wire to the studio, where it was reconstructed by another announcer, J. O. Smith. And it was Smith's voice that actually was heard by an audience estimated at 300,000 persons.

By the time the World Series rolled around in 1921, KDKA was in full operation. It already had broken out of the staid pattern of reciting baseball scores at fixed intervals and now was broadcasting them as soon as runs were scored. It took a little ingenuity and a lot of nickels to accomplish this. A staff member of KDKA was stationed in the top row of the bleachers at Forbes Field in Pittsburgh, and as each inning ended he wrote the results on a piece of paper. Then he leaned over and dropped the message outside the fence to an accomplice, who ran to the nearest coin telephone and called in the score to the studio announcer.

The series that October was the first between the Yankees and Giants, and a public event of the front rank. So the boys at KDKA installed a wire between New York and Pittsburgh, and Grantland Rice used it to report sporadic details of the action. In Manhattan, meanwhile, the plays were being telephoned from the Polo Grounds to the WJZ studio, where an announcer named Thomas H. Cowan sat at a microphone and recreated a game he never saw.

By 1922, the need for middlemen and nickels began to fade, and Rice made his pioneering—and largely unremembered—direct broadcast from the Polo Grounds to WJZ. And the following May, a Harvard baseball game was carried live over WNAC in Boston, just about the time McNamee was getting off the elevator and asking Sam Ross' permission to see what was going on inside the studio on Broadway.

The word was out now, and the radio early-birds began filling the air with the assorted sounds of the Roaring Twenties with the rapture of bright, bold children working mechanical marvels with a Christmas gift.

A precise, pontifical newspaperman named H. V. Kaltenborn had already broken ground in public affairs by discussing the coal strike of 1922 and offering an editoral analysis over WVP at the Fort Wood Signal Corps. A year later, he turned up at WEAF like McNamee and began broadcasting a weekly news report. Kaltenborn, who was an editor of *The Brooklyn Daily Eagle,* had an intellectual range almost as broad as McNamee's vocal range. In no time he was covering topics of the day like Lloyd George, conditions in the Rhineland and the old devil Prohibition.

On New Year's Day, WGY in Schenectady described the inauguration of Al Smith as Governor from nearby Albany. On August 2, within thirty minutes after the *Associated Press* had flashed word of President Harding's death, John Daggett was on the air at KHJ, Los Angeles, with a memorial broadcast— twenty minutes of extemporaneous talk over "suitable piano music" supplied by Claire Forbes Crane.

But sports and stunts rolled up the heaviest yardage. The following year, WJZ began carrying baseball scores *every fifteen minutes* every afternoon, and WGN regaled Chicago for seven hours with a nonstop description of the Indianapolis Speedway Classic as the racing cars whipped past the microphone at close to 100 miles an hour. By 1925 all home baseball games—not just the scores—were being carried by WMAQ, Chicago, and KHJ, Los Angeles, which wasn't even in the major leagues.

In 1926, radio really scaled the heights. In Pittsburgh, WJAS carried a two-way interview between an announcer and a lady flagpole-sitter on top of the Fort Pitt Hotel. In Cleveland, WTAM rigged up a three-way talk between the roof of the Allerton Hotel, the Goodyear plant in Akron and the crew of a dirigible bouncing around overhead. In Philadelphia, WCAU kept its feet on the ground but established one of the most enduring institutions of the century, the Amateur Hour.

Not all the performers who approached the microphone in a sound-proofed studio were convinced that there were people out there. John McCormack, the renowned tenor, winced when he arrived for his first studio concert and said fretfully: "My, oh my. This is dead. I can never sing here." Lucrezia Bori, arriving for *her* first studio recital, cringed, too. "Why, I can't even hear myself or tell what I'm doing," she mourned. "Does it sound that way outside?"

But McNamee plunged ahead, sensing as Grantland Rice had the year before that the cheers from the ball park could indeed be heard throughout the land.

He even learned immediately that the people out there considered him part of the action, not just a witness on the fringe of it. He made news when it rained during the 1923 series and his suit became soaked. He got letters from amused listeners when he dropped a thermos of coffee and soaked his suit again. He received 1,700 letters after the series, and two years later, following the 1925 series, was astounded when he received 50,000 letters.

He became a celebrity among celebrities at historic events like the 1924 Republican National Convention in Cleveland, which he broadcast *alone,* and at which he introduced Calvin Coolidge on the air and even teased a few words from the silent New Englander.

McNamee did it all with an enthusiastic, cultivated delivery and a towering sense of adventure. He conversed with his audience from ringside or convention hall to parlor and den. After the National Broadcasting Company was organized in 1926, he conversed with parlors and dens from coast to coast. He always opened his broadcasts with "Good afternoon, ladies and gentlemen of the radio audience," and he always closed with "Good night, all."

In between those greetings, he observed and interpreted sights like an informal, informed, chatty emissary. When Jack Sharkey fought Max Schmeling on June 12, 1930, at the height of McNamee's career, a low blow ended the fight suddenly at the end of Round Four. At least, a low blow by Sharkey at the end of Round Four gave the fight—and Sharkey's heavyweight title—to Schmeling either at the end of Round Four or the beginning of Round Five, when Schmeling could not answer the bell. Joe Humphreys, the celebrated ring announcer, then clarified the confusion by declaring that the fight was considered finished when the round was finished, not later. And McNamee, grasping the cash significance of such a ruling, leaned toward his microphone and reported exuberantly:

"Well, that clears that up. In other words, any of you boys who happen to have a dollar or so on this case, the knockout, according to Joe Humphreys, the demon announcer, the knockout took place in the fourth round, not the fifth."

The essence of it all, McNamee noted as he sat down to his debut at the World Series of 1923, was this:

"You must make each of your listeners, though miles away from the spot, feel that he or she too is there with you in that press stand, watching the pop bottles thrown in the air; Gloria Swanson arriving in her new ermine coat; McGraw in his dugout, apparently motionless, but giving signals all the time."

In any event, McNamee found himself and his ad lib theories at the right place at the right time, five months after his walk up Broadway. He was seated with a record crowd of 55,307 persons in the new, white Yankee Stadium in the Bronx and a record gate of $181,912 was in the till.

His medium of communicating all this was new but, like skywriting at the series the year before, was capturing the soaring imagination of an imaginative public. Downtown, the American Radio Exposition had opened on the eve of the series at Grand Central Palace and more than 100 manufacturers were displaying radio sets—from simple crystal types to "super-receivers" devised by the Radio Club of America and Edwin H. Armstrong, the inventor of the regenerative circuit.

Many of the leading manufacturers exhibited radio sets placed inside cabinets, like phonograph consoles. One set was fixed in the base of a table lamp. Another maker displayed a window shade within which flexible wires had been woven to serve as an antenna to "intercept" radio signals. On the floor of the exposition, an elaborate loudspeaking apparatus amplified concerts for the entertainment of the shoppers, and a couple of days later the voice of Graham McNamee was heard portraying the frenzy at Yankee Stadium.

The frenzy was growing to a fine pitch, too. The Yankees, the newest power in American life, had just bulldozed their way to a third straight league championship. They had drawn more than a million customers to their showcase park. Their excitable, proud owner, Jacob Ruppert, was in full control after buying out his partner, Tillinghast l'Hommedieu Huston, who had been so outraged by the loss of the 1922 series.

Their manager, Miller Huggins, was breathing easier and directing the team with new sureness now that he had been rescued from Huston's kibitzing. Herb Pennock, the last of the superstars bought from bankrupt Boston, fortified the best pitching staff in baseball. Babe Ruth had made a crashing comeback from his slump of the season before. The Yankees breezed home by 16 games.

The Giants, by contrast, were one of the oldest powers in American life. They had won nine National League pennants since McGraw's arrival twenty-one years before. They had outmaneuvered the Yankees in their first struggles, in 1921 and 1922. They and McGraw were now shooting for a record—three straight world championships.

They were, however, growing a little ragged around the edges and nothing showed it more than the rich, young, muscular, confident Yankees in their gleaming, modern stadium across the river. The Giants, said *The Times*, were "a collection of misfits." But they were a collection led by McGraw, who could impart "the unquenchable never-say-die fighting qualities to his men."

McGraw, moreover, had already imparted some other unquenchable qualities to his men. His friends across the country kept touting him and Stoneham kept staking him, so he kept patching together a team with new imports of talent.

When his shortstop, Dave Bancroft, became ill with pneumonia and needed understudy help in almost 100 games, McGraw reached out to Little Rock and brought up Travis Jackson. When the pitching staff wavered, he paid 65,000 of Stoneham's dollars to buy Jack Bentley from Baltimore of the International League, as he had paid 75,000 of Stoneham's dollars the year before to buy Jimmy O'Connell from San Francisco of the Pacific Coast League.

Even with these dollars and these new players at his fingertips, though, McGraw's sense of security was increasingly shaken by the irreverence of the new breed—not only of other people's employees like Ruth, but even his own, like Bentley.

He had been horrified by Bill Terry's insouciance in 1922; now in 1923 he was appalled when Bentley refused to report to the Giants, demanding a piece of his own sale price. Bentley boldly pointed out that he could pitch, hit, play the infield and outfield, and had been the home-run king of his league as well as the best all-around performer. He had a powerful argument, but McGraw was too overwhelmed to listen. So Bentley thereupon went home to Maryland while McGraw fumed in New York. Though Bentley finally reported and even helped McGraw win the pennant, he was a constant reminder that the Old Guard would soon be in full retreat.

Despite the irritations, McGraw's team beat off the Pittsburgh Pirates and Cincinnati Reds, won its third straight pennant and stood on the ledge of McGraw's dream of winning three straight World Series. Moreover, the dream might be realized in a ball park constructed specifically for Ruth's dimensions, and that would sweeten the whole thing. For McGraw by now hated the Yankees—not just as intruders into his world, but as potential heirs to it. Even his relations with his old friend Ruppert became strained. He petulantly refused to let his players dress for the series in Ruppert's resplendent stadium, ordering them instead to change into their baseball suits in the Polo Grounds and take fleets of taxicabs over the Central Bridge across the Harlem to the Yankees' park, like French soldiers massing in cabs to the barricades outside Paris a half-dozen years or so before.

His peevishness erupted into a hassle even before the series started when Ruppert asked permission to use the rookie Lou Gehrig at first base instead of the veteran Wally Pipp, who had broken several ribs during September. Gehrig had been summoned from Hartford, Connecticut, as Pipp's successor and hit .423 in 13 late games. However, he had reported well after the roster deadline of September 1 and was not eligible for the World Series. Ruppert, citing precedents, asked for an emergency waiver of the rule, and Commissioner Landis replied: "It's all right with me, but McGraw must give his consent."

McGraw, giving no quarter, said: "The rule is there, and if the Yankees have an injury to a regular, it's their hard luck." So the Yankee trainer, Doc Woods, bandaged and bundled Pipp, who thereupon played an outstanding series despite McGraw.

The only worries facing the Yankees, in fact, were injuries to Pipp, Meusel and Ruth. But as the great day arrived, they were not about to ease McGraw's temper by groveling. In their final workout, Meusel bombed the ball without flinching, Ruth reported he was in fine fettle despite a stiff ankle, and Pipp hit and cavorted like a healthy horse.

"Ruth," *The Times* observed, drawing the lines of battle, "win or lose, good or bad, is sure to attract more attention than any individual on either team. He was brimming over with the joy of living and playing the game. In this series, as in the two others, Ruth will be the figure in the foreground. The figure in the background will be that of John J. McGraw.

"This squat, gray-haired genius of the diamond, who is seeking his third straight world's championship to crown his managerial career, was at the Polo Grounds early yesterday afternoon. Derby hat pulled low over his eyes, he strolled about among his players, rarely speaking unless spoken to, unsmiling, intent. 'Will you name the two from which you expect to make your selection of a starting pitcher?' he was asked. 'I won't have the slightest idea who will pitch until tomorrow,' he replied. That ended the interview."

The whole city was bracing for the struggle. Thousands lined up to pay $1.10 for a bleacher seat, $3.30 for the upper stand, $5.50 for the lower stand and $6.60 for the boxes. And everybody stood up to be counted as though war had descended on the boroughs and now was the hour to swear allegiance. Somehow, everybody saw the duel in terms of two men, McGraw and Ruth.

John A. Heydler, president of the National League, sensed the long-range implications of the Yankees but stayed true-blue, even though the long-range implications of McGraw in his own league could be just as frightening. "McGraw's personality and his indomitable character," Heydler said grandly, "still play a vital part, a more important part probably, than ever was played by a manager in a World Series."

Ban Johnson, president of the American League, not giving his old nemesis McGraw any the best of it, said warily: "It is quite unfortunate that the Yankees should be seriously handicapped by the crippling of three of their star players. Could the Yankees meet the *enemy* with their full strength, there would be no doubt in American League circles as to the ultimate result."

"I like the Giants," declared Wilbert Robinson, a National Leaguer to the core, "for their smartness, hitting and team play."

"Pitching will decide," predicted Connie Mack, plainly divided against himself, "and I look for the Giants to hold up their end in this respect. McGraw has good pitchers, make no mistake about it. But so have the Yankees." Having thus analyzed the situation into clear confusion, he shrugged and concluded: "It's a tossup, and I can't honestly pick a winner."

Outside baseball, the loyalties were even more sharply etched and more stoutly proclaimed, especially along Broadway, the main axis of the McGraw-

Ruth rivalry.

"You know the old wheeze," said George M. Cohan. "New York will win the World Series. It is on my billboards, but honest to goodness I think the Giants will win it."

"Nothing to it," replied Leon Errol, "but the Yankees. The team has been going too good all year to be stopped now."

Walter Catlett said: "John McGraw and the Giants surely will win the series." But Fanny Brice said: "I pick the Yanks. Babe Ruth should be at his best and I believe that he will show that he can still (sic) make (sic) home runs."

Florenz Ziegfeld, one impresario to another, declared: "McGraw has demonstrated that he is the greatest manager in baseball and his team this year is as great as any he ever directed." But Marilynn Miller, one prima donna to another, said: "The Yankees will win, but I think it will be a hard-fought series. I am certain Ruth will be the big factor."

Willie Hoppe, one pool shark to another, observed that "McGraw has taught the Giants the winning habit." Honest John Kelly chose the Giants because, in all honesty, "they are at their best in a big series, and with McGraw doing the directing the Giants are sure to win." Charlie Chaplin, who said nothing in films, said: "The Giants look good to me. I expect to be here for the series and to attend the celebration for the Giants."

McGraw himself picked his Giants. Huggins himself "leaned to" his Yankees. "Sporting men" favored the Giants to make it three straight. Only Judge Landis, with Olympian detachment, had no opinion—or, at least expressed no opinion. "On that subject," he declared, "the Baseball Commissioner is not permitted to think."

On balance, the sentiment along Broadway was on the Giants. But as the series opened, it developed that most of the cash along Wall Street was on the Yankees. The books quoted 11 to 10, Yankees. One brokerage house reported Yankee money of $17,000 against Giant money of $15,000. J. S. Fried & Co., which handled risks of all kinds, put $4,400 against $4,000—on the Yankees. G. B. de Chadenedes & Co. at 20 Broad Street announced the biggest public bet in town—$23,000 against $20,000, Yankees.

Then there they were on October 10 before a packed house in Yankee Stadium. Ziegfeld, Cohan, Chaplin, Broadway, Wall Street. McGraw springing a surprise by pitching John Watson. Huggins going with the boy wonder, Waite Hoyt. And Graham McNamee leaning into one of Sam Ross' WEAF microphones and saying smartly: "Good afternoon, ladies and gentlemen of the radio audience."

For the third straight year, the Yankees struck first, and for the third straight year Ruth did the early striking for them. He scored the first run in the Yankees' first time at bat behind a double by Bob Meusel, neither of whom seemed to McGraw to be too hobbled by injuries as they ran around the bases. Two more Yankees scored in the second inning, and Fanny Brice's team had three more runs than Willie Hoppe's.

The Giants hadn't lost a World Series game to the Yankees since their first bash in 1921. They won the last three games that time, then all four the next October, and they had shown remarkable powers of revival each time. They revived this time, too, shortly before Rosy Ryan relieved Watson in the third inning.

Then they pounced on Hoyt, who had not allowed even one earned run in 27 innings in 1921 but who could not stand the prosperity of a three-run lead in 1923. Kelly opened the third with a single, Gowdy walked, Bentley (the outrageous holdout who could pitch, hit, play first and catch fly balls) pinch-hit for Watson—and singled. That loaded the bases, and they were promptly unloaded after a forceout grounder by Bancroft and a triple by Groh. Finally, Frisch singled, and now it was 4 to 3, Willie Hoppe.

In the seventh, the Yankees tied the game, though, when Bush singled and Dugan tripled. And they almost untied it when Ruth rocked a line drive behind first base. But Long George Kelly dived for the ball, clutched it on the bounce and made a great throw home to intercept Dugan.

That kept the score tied at 4 to 4 until the first half of the ninth, when Stengel—who was thirty-three years old and couldn't run fast—fooled the defense, which overshifted toward right field. Casey lined a clean "single" to the left side over the shortstop's head, and started galloping around the bases as the ball skidded to the deepest part of left-center field in the Yankees' immense new stadium with Witt and Meusel chasing it in the wide-open spaces.

"It was Casey at the Bat all over again," reported *The Times* in a page 1 report of "the greatest game of baseball ever played between championship teams." This time, though, "the great Casey did not strike out. With one leg injured and the other not as young and spry as it used to be, Casey ran the race of his life. Out at the fences, Witt was gathering the ball in. He turned and flung it to Meusel, and Meusel turned and threw it to the plate.

By now Stengel was rounding third, badly winded, but still going strong. It was a race between man and ball, but the man won, for Casey slid into the plate and up on one knee in a single motion. Then he waved a hand in a comical gesture that seemed to say, 'Well, there you are,' and the game was as good as over."

It was over, too, three Yankee outs later as Stengel fell into the dugout and sprawled on the bench alongside McGraw while young Bill Cunningham took his place in center field for the last half of the last inning. The final score was 5 to 4, giving the Giants eight straight victories (and one tie) over their upstart neighbors in their three-year feud, and putting them one-up in their final test.

But the die was cast, especially for any team that depended on Casey Stengel's bat to overpower Babe Ruth's bat. The crowd, like the Wall Street houses, already had begun treating Ruth with what the press called "respectful silence," in contrast to the booing that had accompanied his fall from the pedestal in 1922. He had regained his place in the public mind, and Stengel's dramatic inside-the-park home run was not likely to dislodge him.

"The fans did not plead for a home run when the great slugger took his place at bat," it was noted. "They had come to think of the Babe apparently no longer as merely a home-run hitter but as a star who was working for his team."

Nor could McGraw, endlessly flashing signals from his dugout, indefinitely stymie the strength of Ruth on the field. The press saluted the manager's "genius" high in its accounts of "the greatest game of baseball ever played," but it was Ruth who rated the headlines just for showing up. Prominent boxes were printed every day to describe "What Babe Ruth Did At Bat In The First World Series Game," and so on for six days. Each time the stage was precisely set to heighten the drama of the great man's time at bat:

"First inning: One out, one on base. One strike (called). Two strikes (swung). Hit to Groh and forced Dugan at second, reaching first safely. He scored from first on Meusel's double."

"Fifth inning: One out, none on base. Hit first ball pitched to left for a triple."

"When Ruth batted," confessed McNamee, "I was almost too engrossed to speak."

McGraw was engrossed, too, but not too engrossed to speak. Before the teams had crossed the river to the Polo Grounds for the second game, inflamed all over again by the adulation for Ruth in the face of the Giants' remarkable record against him, McGraw snapped: "Why shouldn't we pitch to Ruth? I've said it before, and I'll say it again, we pitch to better hitters than Ruth in the National League."

"Ere the sun had set on McGraw's rash and impetuous words," wrote Heywood Broun in the New York *Sun*, "the Babe had flashed across the sky fiery portents which should have been sufficient to strike terror and conviction into the hearts of all infidels. But John McGraw clung to his heresy with a courage worthy of a better cause.

"In the fourth inning, after lunging at a fastball with almost comic ferocity and ineptitude, the Bambino hit the next pitch over the stands in right. In the fifth, Ruth was up again and by this time Jack Bentley was pitching. Snyder the catcher sneaked a look at the little logician in the dugout. McGraw blinked twice, pulled up his trousers, and thrust the forefinger of his right hand into his left eye. Snyder knew that he meant: 'Try the Big Bozo on a slow curve around the knees, and don't forget to throw to first if you happen to drop the third strike.' Ruth promptly poled the slow curve around the knees into the right-field seats.

"For the first time since coming to New York, Babe achieved his full brilliance in a World Series game. Before this he has varied between pretty good and simply awful, and yesterday he was magnificent."

"Some fans," recalled *The New York Times* a generation later, "will doubtless remember the second game of the series of thirty years ago when the son of a Baltimore saloonkeeper, playing for the Yankees, hit two home runs and was robbed of a third by a Giants' outfielder who snared the ball just as it was sailing into the bleachers in back of the right-center field at the Polo Grounds. When the Yankees and Giants met on that October day in 1923, the American League champions had not been able to win a game from the Giants since October 10, 1921, and their prospects of drubbing Mr. McGraw's stalwarts seemed remote."

"The Ruth," wrote Broun, "is mighty and shall prevail."

He prevailed by a score of 4 to 2, and struck the first blows that were to shake McGraw's hold over a profession. He struck them in successive innings, too. And when Ward also hit a home run, all the Yankee runs had been pounded across by the awesome new weapon that was fast making McGraw's defensive style obsolete. Ruth's first shot even cleared the Polo Grounds roof and dropped into the parking lot on Manhattan Field outside, where a policeman stooped over, picked it up and examined it like some incredible fragment of a meteorite.

Even when Ruth made an out, McGraw winced. In his final turn at bat, in the ninth inning, there were two outs and a Yankee runner on second base. McGraw, wrote Broun, riding roughshod over the manager's rash boast at the start of the long afternoon, stood on the dugout step with "gritted teeth." He signaled his catcher, Snyder, "spelling out with the first three fingers of his right hand, 'The Old Guard dies but never surrenders,' which Snyder interpreted to mean, 'Pitch to the big bum if he hammers every ball in the park into the North River.' "

Ruth forthwith hammered a tremendous drive that almost became his third home run of the day. But it finally was caught by Stengel in front of the astounded fans in the center-field bleachers.

"Ruth showed that the Giant supremacy could be broken down," *The Times* observed, in a kind of social commentary on the issue of the day. "Leading the way himself, he showed that the Giants were not invincible, that their pitchers could be hit, and that John J. McGraw's strategy, while superb, was not invincible."

The Giants had one shot left before the tide swept in, and it was fired by gimpy old Casey Stengel. It was dramatic, all right, as his home run in the first game had been. And it was just as decisive.

It was fired before a record crowd of 62,430 in Yankee Stadium on Columbus Day, and for a while it appeared that all New York had taken off for the holiday and was storming the turnstiles of Ruppert's new park. When the gates were finally shut, the teams carried their one-to-one stalemate in games through six innings, and still they were stalemated. The Yankees scored no runs off Nehf, the Giants none off Sad Sam Jones—until Stengel popped one of Jones' pitches into the right-field seats in the seventh.

As he jogged around the bases before the howling mob, Stengel could not resist the temptation to rub it into the Yankees, the way a mischievous bad boy would rub it into the neighborhood bully, after beating him at his own game. As he jogged, he smartly thumbed his nose at the Yankee bench, sending Ruppert in rage hurrying over to Landis' field box demanding that Stengel be banished for public insults "to our patrons."

Landis, tempering justice with mercy and exasperation, fined Casey $50 in the interest of decorum but vetoed any harsher punishment on the ad hoc ground that "I guess Casey Stengel just can't help being Casey Stengel."

The score was 1 to 0, and the only thing the Giants lost on that noisy day was Stengel's fifty dollars. Moreover, they held the lead again in the series and they had seized it before the biggest gathering in baseball history. But Babe Ruth could not help being Babe Ruth, either, and the hour of rejoicing along Broadway was brief.

Back in the Polo Grounds the next day, where they had evened the series two days earlier, the Yankees evened it again—and with no ploys, gimmicks or maneuvers that could be foiled by McGraw's strategy. They simply bunched six runs in the second inning. Pipp singled, Ward singled and Schang bunted the ball back to the pitcher, Jack Scott, who fumbled it. Now the bases were filled, until Everett Scott singled to score two runs and to bring Rosy Ryan hustling in from the bullpen to try to restore order. But Shawkey flied deep to the outfield for another run, Witt doubled for yet another, and Dugan grounded to third, where Groh tagged Witt for the second out.

Now came the muscle part of the Yankee lineup: Ruth followed by Meusel. McGraw, whose choice of Ryan as a relief pitcher had just backfired, chose now to walk Ruth and pitch to Meusel, and that decision backfired, too. Meusel tripled, scoring both Dugan and Ruth, and the Yankees were out of sight. A home run by Ross Youngs in the ninth was as close as the Giants could come to matching that explosion. The Yankees won, 8 to 4, and gave the American League one of its best days since its feud with McGraw's league supposedly had ended twenty years before.

In the fifth game, on Sunday, October 14, the teams shuttled back to Yankee Stadium, where the Giants had won the first and third games. But the Yankees finally broke through before 62,817 persons, an even bigger crowd than the one that had packed the park on the holiday forty-eight hours earlier. Joe Bush pitched for the Yankees and enjoyed a leisurely afternoon. He coasted to an 8-to-1 victory, his first in a series since he was a twenty-year-old rookie in 1913 and had beaten the old spitball king Jeff Tesreau for Connie Mack's Athletics.

Bush's given name was Leslie, but he preferred the nom de combat of Bullet Joe. He allowed the Giants just three hits—a single, double and triple by Irish Meusel. The Yankees, meanwhile, made seven runs in the first two innings alone. They rocked Bentley for three runs in the first inning in this sequence, which was beginning to haunt the Giants: A single by Dugan, a walk to Ruth, a triple by Bob Meusel and a long, scoring fly by Pipp.

McGraw, like McNamee, by now had become so engrossed with Ruth that he was being killed by Meusel. In the second inning, riding too long with Bentley, he was further jolted when Bush singled, Witt walked and Dugan hit an inside-the-park home run. Trailing by six runs, the Giants finally pitched to Ruth, who hit a grounder behind first base to Kelly, who fumbled it. At long last, McGraw removed Bentley and brought in Scott, who promptly yielded another run on Meusel's single and Frisch's wild throw.

Bob Meusel now had done more damage to the Giants than his brother Irish Meusel had done to the Yankees. And worse, he was about to deliver the *coup de grâce* while the Giants were still being decoyed by the engrossing Ruth.

The fateful day was Monday, October 15, and they were all back in the Polo Grounds with the Yankees now leading, three games to two, and needing only one more to overthrow the dynasty on its own grounds. The Broadway crowd was there in force. George M. Cohan, the Giant rooter; Leon Errol, the Yankee rooter; Al Jolson, entering from the first-base side, circling behind home plate to his seat on the third-base side, all the while clasping his hands over his head like Jack Dempsey in the ring as the crowd shouted, "Hi, Al."

Outside the stadium, the descriptions broadcast by WEAF were being relayed to a widening audience. WJAR in Providence, Rhode Island, joined the World Series network, along with WGY in Schenectady, and the newspapers could easily see the day approaching when the noise would reverberate across the country.

"The system," noted *The Times*, "was recently reversed, and a Marine band concert in Washington was rendered before WCAP's microphone and forwarded by telephone lines to WEAF's apparatus at 195 Broadway, through which the music was also broadcast. The system works successfully, and it is anticipated that a chain of stations across the country will make it possible for San Francisco and Denver performers to speak or play before a microphone and have their words or music heard at New York and other cities.

"One engineer in England believes it will be possible one day to speak in London and have the words go into the air in every country in the world by means of a system of relay stations extending around the earth. Present development strengthens his prediction, and before many years pass a New York program may not only be rendered by artists in New York but also by a Guards Band playing in London, a jazz orchestra in Chicago, Hawaiian music from Honolulu and sounds from the Orient."

But on this day, the nucleus of the radio world was behind home plate on the grounds of the old Coogan farm, where McNamee was broadcasting the sights of the series with a rising sense of urgency.

One game from being eliminated, the Giants were scrambling to stay alive and were even pitching to Ruth—who promptly hit a home run in the first inning, his third of the series.

But Nehf allowed the Yankees only one other hit for the first seven innings, while the Giants came back to tie the game with one run in the bottom of the first, and to go ahead with single runs in the fourth, fifth and sixth. And now they led, 4 to 1, with the Yankees batting in the eighth—the less menacing lower half of the Yankee lineup, at that—and with Nehf apparently in control as he had been in the 1-to-0 game three days before.

Then with one out in the eighth, Schang and Scott hit singles, and McGraw stood in his dugout and began to watch his dream come a little undone.

Huggins, standing in his dugout, now went to his bench and a war of grand strategy broke out between the two old rivals who had ferried their troops across the river for six days like field marshals. Huggins called on two pinch-hitters in a row, Freddy Hofmann for Pennock and Joe Bush for Witt. Nehf walked them on eight straight, maddening pitches while McGraw wilted, pitch by pitch.

His lead now cut to 4 to 2, his world teetering, McGraw made his counter-move. He popped his head out of the dugout and motioned to his bullpen. The crowd roared almost hysterically, three Yankees leaned off the bases, Dugan stepped toward the plate—and Ruth moved into the on-deck circle, with Meusel behind him.

"Away went Nehf to the showers," McNamee recalled, his baseball idiom bristling. "Manager McGraw called in Rosy Ryan, a right-hander. But before he properly got under way, another pass was issued and another run scored.

"Then came the thrill of all time, all World Series and all sports. Babe Ruth stepped up to bat. One hit would mean victory for the Yanks, and for them the series. It was another Casey at the Bat, and the stands rocked with terrific excitement.

"John McGraw took the biggest chance of his historic life. He ordered Ryan to pitch to Ruth. The crowd faded into a blurred background. Cheering became silence. Ruth lashed out at the first ball. Ruth hurled his bat and weight against the second. Ruth spun at the third. Ruth shuffled back to the dugout, head hung low. A picture of dejection."

"The mighty Ruth," reported *The Times*, "was furious, the Yankee dugout shrouded in disappointment. The Giants, though, were wild with delight and their supporters staged impromptu war dances in the stands."

"Ruth was so anxious to hit," McGraw said, "that I knew he didn't have a chance. So I ordered Ryan to throw him three pitches right in the dirt."

But fate was about to play a cruel trick on the short, stocky manager of the Giants, just when he appeared to have trumped Huggins' ace. Huggins, in a new spasm of strategy, sent in two pinch-runners for his pinch-hitters to gain maximum mileage out of anything that might be hit by his next batter, Meusel —who three times before in the series had hurt the Giants immediately after Ruth had been safely walked or neutralized. Three Yankees were still on base, but they still trailed by two runs, and now Ryan boldly threw a strike past the tall, powerful Meusel.

Then Meusel hit a high bouncing ball right back through the middle, over the head of Ryan, who had replaced the best fielding pitcher in the National League. The ball skipped over second base into center field for a single, scoring two runs—the pinch-runners Huggins had just selected in his match of wits with McGraw.

However, the worst was yet to come. As the tying and go-ahead runs scored, Cunningham fielded the ball in center field and unloosed a mighty throw in the general direction of third base, trying to cut down Dugan, who represented a precious insurance run. But the throw bounced wildly past the base and Dugan sprinted the 90 extra feet home with the fifth Yankee run of the inning.

Sam Jones then stopped the shocked Giants in the eighth and ninth innings, and the final score was 6 to 4, giving the Yankees the series, four games to two, and tumult shook the old baseball park.

"But the biggest thrill," said McNamee, his emotions (but not his vocabulary) overwhelmed, "had passed when the great Babe fanned. Time's phantom flits into oblivion in moments like this. I was a dripping rag draped over the microphone when the 1923 diamond laurel finally graced the Yankee brow. The crowd was exhausted. So was I."

The Yankees exploded into uncontrolled celebrating in their clubhouse beneath the stands, where champagne flowed in little rivers across the floor. Ruth surrounded Meusel in a locked bear-hug and both fell in a wrestling embrace onto the training table. Clothes were joyously shredded, heads rubbed, cheers shrieked, until Ruth stormed like a mammoth bear to the center of the room and shouted for order. When some silence finally took hold, he pulled out a jeweler's box and announced:

"Boys, we've won the world championship and we owe a lot of that accomplishment to the guiding hand of Mr. Huggins. We want to present you with this ring in token of the esteem we hold you in."

Huggins, often harassed, insulted and persecuted by Ruth and his club-house cronies, was swept onto the shoulders of his troops, clutching his new diamond bauble as they tossed him perilously about, and another burst of cheering shook the room.

The Yankees had won their first world championship, and had arrived. They hit .293 collectively as a team, 90 points above their average the year before. Ward had hit .417, Ruth .368 with three home runs, Meusel .269 with eight runs batted in. It was the first million-dollar series, the first gate of 300,000, the first "network" broadcast of a series, the first time a player would pocket as much as $6,143 for winning or $4,112 for losing.

"All of the important radiophone stations in the country radiated the World Series," *The Times* said, "giving a running story of the games. This year radio furnished instantaneous reports to great crowds that formerly heard of baseball plays through megaphones on street corners or watched chalk marks reveal the story inning by inning on score boards. Hertzian waves carried the impact of the bats and ball, so the radio audience was aware of what had happened. So true did radio picture the games that listeners in Western New York reported in several instances the ball could be heard as it struck the catcher's glove, just as clearly as if the game had been staged in the local ball park."

Downtown in New York, printers in a dozen newspaper composing rooms were setting headlines that would blacken page 1 with the story of the rise of Yankee power. Eleanora Duse was having dinner before driving to the Metropolitan Opera House for a "gala performance," and the noise was deafening. Ruth Chatterton and Laura Hope Crews were rousing themselves for their appearance at Henry Miller's Theatre in "The Changelings," though Forty-third Street was still crowded with milling, shouting scoreboard-watchers from Times Square. Anna Pavlova and the Ballet Russe wondered about all the commotion as they wound up seven days at the Manhattan Opera House at Thirty-fourth Street and Eighth Avenue. Even the dancers in the fifth annual staging of George White's Scandals at the Globe chattered about the drama that had just unfolded uptown, as did the master of the Ziegfeld Follies troupe at the New Amsterdam, who had remained loyal to "the greatest manager in baseball."

At the Polo Grounds, paper still littered the field where Ruth had stood at home plate like the Colossus of Rhodes. Cheering, sulking, whooping, silent fans gathered in clusters and refused to leave. The noise from the Yankee clubhouse echoed across the darkening outfield.

"I just can't see that third World Series victory," said John McGraw, still standing in his baseball knickers and cap. "It just don't seem to be my good fortune. I guess that's one ambition I'll never have fulfilled."

The mob caught sight of Charlie Chaplin alongside the gloomy dugout of the Giants, the deposed champions of baseball. He was immediately besieged by hundreds of people, mostly young ones, who shouted to him to "Make a funny face for us, Charlie," and "Have you got your mustache with you?" and "Let's see your shoes."

Chaplin looked dapper and polished in his rich clothes, but now he grew bashful and mournful, like the waif tramp he portrayed with pathos on the silent screen.

"I'm sorry," he said, "that I had to see Mr. McGraw's players defeated."

Chapter

Ruffling
The Old Oriole

In the nineteen-twenties, observed Gene Fowler, "there were two 'Misters' on the New York public scene"—two men who were customarily, indisputably and almost invariably addressed as "Mr." They were Charles F. Murphy, the power behind the throne of Tammany Hall, and John J. McGraw, the kingpin of the New York Giants.

It was no accident that the public courtesy was bestowed, in a time of runaway public passion, on a pair of public tigers like Murphy and McGraw. They represented two of the enduring institutions of New York life. In fact, they controlled two of the enduring institutions of New York life, and the two institutions had been intertwined even before McGraw had been enticed to the city a generation earlier by the Tammany politicians who for years had called the pitches for the Giants.

Moreover, both institutions provided New York with the day-to-day outlets for the emotions of the twenties, which were rampant. Heroes, villains, idols, demons—all paraded across the stages of Tammany and the Giants, and all were dominated by *Mr.* Murphy and *Mr.* McGraw.

Indeed, their worlds overlapped so persistently that it became difficult to separate them. Political life blended into sporting life, which in turn faded into theatrical life, until all the characters—heroes and villains alike—became fused into a kind of common public life.

Sensationally typical of this Broadway bouillabaise was James John Walker, protégé of Murphy, confidant of McGraw and, starting on January 1, 1926, the 100th Mayor of New York.

Walker was born in Greenwich Village in 1881, when John L. Sullivan and Charles F. Murphy both were twenty-three years old and were headed upward in a gas-lit city whose elevated trains burned soft coal. Walker's ambition was to be a songwriter, and he developed carousing friendships with frontline show people like Jimmy Durante, Irving Berlin and George M. Cohan, to say nothing of Mose Grumble, the song-plugger who warbled from the infield of Madison Square Garden during the six-day bicycle races and from the grandstands of the Polo Grounds during the heyday of McGraw.

Walker, who was universally called "Jimmy" instead of "Mr. Walker," had in fact written a song that became unfortunately prophetic of his own public life and its twists of fortune. It was titled "Will You Love Me In December As You Do In May?" And while December was just around the corner for both Walker and McGraw, and other card-carrying members of their rollicking world, they still basked in the affection and ardor of May at midpoint in the Roaring Twenties.

Jimmy Walker presided over a city that by this time had grown to six million persons, though "presided" was not precisely the right word. He behaved more like the master of ceremonies. His office was his hat—a top hat or derby or stylish fedora, as the occasion demanded, which he was likely to wear or hang almost anywhere around town where the action might be the liveliest.

"Both Jim and his wife Allie were baseball fans," Fowler recalled. "They went as often as possible to see the Giants play. That baseball club always had been an intimate part of the city's life, even after Colonel Jacob Ruppert brought the great Babe Ruth to the Yankee team of the rival league."

On days when the baseball schedule was light, or when the City Hall schedule could be ignored for a while, Walker would often repair to an oasis known as Billy LaHiff's Tavern on West Forty-eighth Street, where he might join McGraw and other knights of public life like Damon Runyon, Heywood Broun, Westbrook Pegler, Walter Winchell, Ed Sullivan, Grantland Rice and Fowler, and discuss issues like the hit-and-run play or the outfield cutoff. Order would be maintained, if need be, by a husky bouncer and head-waiter named Toots Shor.

Or they might all descend on the old Madison Square Garden, which was moving to a new location uptown at Eighth Avenue and Forty-ninth Street, to listen gravely while the demon public-address announcer Joe Humphreys recited an elegaic poem titled "The Temple of Fistiana."

As one of his first "official" acts, Walker presided at ringside when the new Garden opened its doors late in 1925. Indeed, he hadn't even gone through the formality of being sworn into office yet, being merely the Mayor-elect. But he had long since become the symbol of the town's taste for the sporting life, and he had already become a legislative hero of sorts as the author of the bill in the State Assembly that permitted baseball on Sundays.

By then Joe Humphreys was as much of an institution in New York as Jimmy Walker and was just as steadfast a member of the McGraw circle. If Walker was the pride of New York, McGraw the titan of New York and

Graham McNamee the radio reporter of New York—Joe Humphreys was the voice of New York. He was a holdover from the early time when prizefights were staged on river barges, and until late in his career he spurned the use of a loudspeaker, regarding it as an abomination. Instead, standing grandly in the center of the Garden ring and speaking in a clear, pleasant tone that could easily be heard all over the arena, he enthralled the Mayor and his constituents by sonorous introductions of the evening's gladiators.

When Humphreys passed from this clamorous scene, his funeral service was conducted in the lobby of the Garden (a tribute also conferred upon George "Tex" Rickard, the promoter). He then was succeeded as "the voice" by Harry Balogh, a genius at delivering ad-lib remarks and extemporaneous speeches. Balogh probably reached a peak of achievement in filling time one night when he received an urgent appeal from the management to delay the proceedings. He thereupon launched into a meandering monologue about nothing in particular and ended it gloriously by intoning to the audience: "And in conclusion, may I extend to you my best wishes for a happy and enjoyable *Memorial Day.*"

Many times, if the Mayor had been working or drinking late, he could find happy release at almost any hour of the day or night at the Garden, where the six-day bike races were held relentlessly every December and March for a quarter of a century.

It was a scene to behold. Two-man teams whirled around for six days and nights while the crowd from Billy LaHiff's or Lindy's or even the Algonquin sat on the sidelines and forgot the cares of the world and its rocketing stock markets. Song-pluggers like the Mayor's friend, Mose Grumble, regularly filled the night air with new tunes while Frank Basile and his silver cornet band from Newark sat in the infield and serenaded the dawn patrol. And later, when the Garden felt the need for even more music to entertain the gang, the bicycle teams would be accompanied by immense ensembles from Harlem like the sixty-piece band of "Wen Talbot and his Madison Square Garden Syncopators."

It was a time of virtuoso performances, whether by McGraw's baseball club, Joe Humphreys or the Mayor himself.

On February 12, 1924, a few months after Babe Ruth and the Yankees had finally knocked a hole in the roof of McGraw's empire, a young symbol of the day named Paul Whiteman staged a milestone concert at Aeolian Hall, the city's sanctuary of classical music. Whiteman, who came to be known as "Pops" instead of "Mr. Whiteman," led his jazz band through a brisk scrimmage that featured "Limehouse Blues," "Alexander's Ragtime Band," "The Volga Boatman," four pieces composed for the occasion by Victor Herbert, and Gershwin's "Rhapsody in Blue," with Gershwin himself at the piano.

The audience included some pretty distinguished names not normally associated with concert jazz: Heifitz, Kreisler, Damrosch, Stokowski, Stravinsky, Rachmaninoff and even Mary Garden. The revolutionary evening, wrote Lawrence Gilman in the *Tribune,* was "an uproarious success."

Whiteman now became the jazz king of the twenties, and joined the other heroes of the era of wonderful nonsense. Once he received $10,000 for an evening of music at the Long Island estate of Clarence Mackay, the dean of the Postal Telegraph Company, who had transformed his acreage for the occasion into a likeness of the Versailles gardens. In 1925, Whiteman collected $680,000 for his work as a piper, and his recording of "Three O'Clock In The Morning" became a kind of theme song of the era and sold 3½ million copies.

But the thing that best typified Whiteman and his niche in the twenties was probably his lavish stunt of conducting his group of 46 musicians on the stage of the Hippodrome—all 300 pounds of him—from the back of a white horse.

At the other end of the scale, another virtuoso performer serenaded the smart set—an eleven-year-old violinist named Yehudi Menuhin, who played Beethoven's Violin Concerto at the Mecca Temple (later the City Center) in a pair of short velvet pants. The onward-and-upward mood was promoted by women, too, like Eleonora Sears, who made national headlines on December 14, 1925, by walking the forty-four miles from Providence to Boston in eleven hours and forty-five minutes when she was forty-five years old.

The few stray somber notes of the day were even being sounded by the titan types like the 240-pound foreign correspondent Frazier Hunt, the one-time cheerleader at the University of Illinois, who had written biographies of King Edward VIII and of Billy the Kid, who had shot craps with the Prince of Wales and who now was circling the world interviewing political upstarts named Benito Mussolini and Adolf Hitler.

But New York was a long way from Munich, and not even the shadow of Samuel Seabury had fallen yet across the happy tables of Jimmy Walker and his sporting cronies. True, some sober-sides were growing fretful about the spiraling stock market and some civic souls were complaining about the city's disappearing Mayor—who during his first two years in office rarely missed an important baseball game and who otherwise took seven vacations that totaled 143 days.

As for John McGraw, he tried to put aside the irritations of *his* day—the loss of the 1923 World Series to Babe Ruth and the marauding Yankees—by sailing for Europe in the fall with his old Baltimore Orioles teammate Hughey Jennings, now his deputy on the Giants.

Despite his vexations in the series, McGraw was the toast of the Continent. He was hounded by Americans in Paris and anywhere else he went, and he was wined and dined in the most elegant places. He returned the favors by posh little gestures of his own, like the dinner he threw one evening in London for the Marquis of Clydesdale, later the Duke of Hamilton—on whose estate fifteen years later an airplane was to land carrying Rudolph Hess, the No. 2 Nazi of Hitler's Reich. The Marquis was a student at Oxford in 1923, and was best known as the middleweight boxing champion of his school. He was brought to McGraw by Eddie Eagan, the Rhodes scholar and one of the original Yanks at Oxford, who then was the world's amateur boxing champion.

McGraw's only setback on the jaunt was his vocabulary. He knew only one word of French—"toujours"—and somehow he overworked it regardless of circumstances. Even when heading back home to tackle the problems awaiting him in New York, he would shake hands, wave, tip his derby and say affably: "Well, toujours, old boy, toujours."

Back home, he recovered his vocabulary sufficiently to explain to his New York public the necessity of tearing apart the Giant team that had just won three straight National League pennants. He traded his shortstop, Dave Bancroft, and two of his outfielders, Casey Stengel and Bill Cunningham, to the Boston Braves in exchange for an outfielder, Billy Southworth, and a pitcher, Joe Oeschger.

The trade, which was described in the newspapers as "the most sensational of recent baseball history," had been prompted by the first cracks that had begun to appear in McGraw's club. The cracks were induced by the arrival of Ruth's bat and the arrival of the Yankees as the crosstown enemies of McGraw. And, although his Giants had just won two of the last three World Series against the interlopers, their manager at the age of fifty could see the handwriting on the wall.

Recalling his promise to "rebuild the Giants from the bottom up," McGraw thereupon resorted to some complex vocabulary to explain the fear that had crept into his relations with the tough young Yankees. He couched his explanation in terms of piety, self-sacrifice and regard for his old hero Christy Mathewson, now the president of the Boston Club. He used almost every cliché in the book but "toujours, old boy, toujours."

"The New York club," he declared, "realizes that in giving up Mr. Bancroft it is losing the best shortstop in baseball without a doubt. We have several reasons for making the sacrifice, the three particular ones being as follows:

"For the good of baseball and with the desire to do something big for my old friend Matty, and finally to give to Bancroft the opportunity which is due him to become a big league manager.

"Matty is the only man in baseball who could get Bancroft away from me," he went on imperturbably, glossing over the bitter statements he had made after the Giants had lost the World Series to the effect that he would trade anybody on the club except Frankie Frisch, Ross Youngs and Travis Jackson. These were the Young Turks he was staking his chances on for a fourth straight pennant.

The peevishness extended into the spring of 1924, when McGraw was persuaded to establish the Giants' training camp in Sarasota. In the three-ring mood of the day, he was inveigled there by John Ringling, the circus man, who pitched his tents there each winter and who dominated the resort city on the Gulf coast of Florida.

However, a loud dispute broke out with the arrival of McGraw, who had never seen Sarasota and who was startled to find that his hotel was not big enough to house his ball club and its retinue of writers and followers. McGraw finally divided his players among several hotels, but grew increasingly vexed by the necessity of darting from one to another just to keep track of his athletes.

Then the local papers began inviting the Giants to leave. And in turn, stories from the New York papers were clipped to bulletin boards in downtown Sarasota, taking note of the Giants' complaints about life with the circus and containing friendly handwritten marginal comments like: "If you don't like our weather, keep your damned mouths shut."

When the season began, the thread of trouble that had begun with the Yankees and their new stadium kept right on unwinding. McGraw fortified his lineup by bringing up Bill Terry, the oil man who played first base, and Freddie Lindstrom, the eighteen-year-old Chicago boy who already had played third base professionally for two seasons at Toledo. Then they all tackled the legend that the Brooklyn Robins prospered in presidential election years, having won in 1916 and 1920 and having established a strong threat to the Giants in Calvin Coolidge's summer of 1924.

Sure enough, the teams challenged each other all summer and headed into the home stretch in a dead heat. Then the simple problem of outrunning his old partner Wilbert Robinson and the Brooklyn ball club was suddenly complicated by another scandal.

The shortstop for the Philadelphia Phillies, Heinie Sand, told his manager, Art Fletcher, that Jimmy O'Connell of the Giants had offered him $500 not to bear down on the Giants during a series in the Polo Grounds. Fletcher took his player to the National League president, John Heydler, who immediately took them both to Commissioner Landis, the enemy of corruption.

O'Connell, when he was confronted by Landis, openly confirmed the version related by Sand and added that he had been induced to make the suggestion in the first place by four other Giants, Cozy Dolan, Frank Frisch, George Kelly and Ross Youngs.

All this O'Connell told with a kind of innocent candor. But when his four teammates were summoned before Landis, they pulled the rug out from under him for all time. Landis, hurling his usual thunderbolts, banished O'Connell from baseball; similarly expelled Dolan, who testified "I don't remember"; cleared Frisch, Kelly and Youngs, who did remember, though not the way O'Connell remembered it, and commended Sand for having sounded the alarm.

McGraw simply exploded. For one thing, if five of his players were indeed implicated, his reputation would suffer a roundhouse at the height of his career. If not, then he was still outraged that his own league president, Heydler, a longtime antagonist, had not told him about the accusation before telling Landis. Finally, he regarded the outcome, especially in Dolan's case, as a travesty of justice.

McGraw even suggested that his old friend William Fallon, the sharp-shooting criminal lawyer and bon vivant, take up Dolan's case. But Fallon decided not to, because Dolan himself kept hoping childishly and forlornly that Landis would somehow reinstate him. There was one great regret in the situation, Fallon said later: not getting Landis on the witness stand in open court.

"I'd like to get Landis on the stand and have some fun with him," Fallon confided. "I was in his court one day when he was a judge and heard him sentence a bootlegger to two years, and I've never forgiven him for it."

McGraw's resentment was not soothed by the fact that Ban Johnson, the president of the American League and one of his most persistent critics, got an oar into the mess. Johnson suggested publicly that Landis disqualify the Giants like a racehorse that had swerved in the stretch and place the No. 2 team first. Barney Dreyfuss, the owner of the Pittsburgh Pirates, the No. 3 team, went even farther. He suggested that Landis cancel the World Series.

Nor was McGraw pacified by the fact that none of these barbed proposals was accepted. Nor by the fact that the Giants sweated out that dismal last week of the season by finishing 1½ games ahead of Brooklyn and 3 ahead of Pittsburgh. Nor by the fact that his chief scourges, the Yankees, were thwarted from a fourth straight pennant in the American League by the humble Washington Senators.

The Senators, who had trailed the Yankees by 23½ games the year before, led the world champions to the wire by 2 games, this time under the leadership of their "boy manager," Bucky Harris, who not only called the shots but also played second base. New York was dumbfounded by the result, but Washington was catapulted into a tizzy of excitement by a team that had finally won a pennant after 23 seasons of frustration in the American League and 12 in the National League at the end of the previous century.

Moreover, it would be the first World Series for the great Walter Johnson, the gentle giant with the stunning fastball whom Casey Stengel had said "could pitch for a second-division team." Which is pretty much what Johnson had done for 18 seasons. But now, at the age of thirty-six, he had dramatically, almost poignantly, made it. He had begun to show signs of the ravages of age, although winning 23 games, losing 7 and leading the league with the lowest earned-run average.

So, after three Octobers of sustained tension between the Yankees and Giants, New York suddenly was without an interborough World Series. McGraw had won two, Ruth and the Yankees had won one. But somehow the Yankees had driven a nail or two into the coffin, and McGraw missed them in the series the way a sailor misses an albatross that has been stalking his ship and then unaccountably vanishes. Besides, losing to the Yankees was one thing; losing to the inoffensive Washington Senators was unthinkable.

The series was the first played under Charles Ebbets' plan of two games in one city, then three in the next, instead of the daily switching of past years. So when the action began on October 4 in Griffith Stadium, Washington was certain of occupying center stage for two long-awaited days, and the drama exceeded the city's wildest expectations.

The proper presidential tinge was supplied by Calvin Coolidge and his wife, Grace, who was as vocal and emotional a baseball fan as her husband was silent and starched. They were dismayed in the opener when their team of destiny foiled Walter Johnson in the grand old manner, just when the patriarch with the overpowering speed seemed to realize a great ambition.

He pitched 12 long innings that afternoon and was rattled for 14 hits by the Giants, though he struck out 12 of them. For 11 innings, the only runs off Johnson were home runs by Terry and Kelly. But in the twelfth, two walks and an error by a teammate proved Johnson's undoing and he lost, 4 to 3. His pitching rival, Art Nehf, said later that he was proudest of the fact that as a batter he had made three hits off Johnson.

The next day the Senators evened the set, 4 to 3, behind the pitching of Tom Zachary and Fred Marberry, the relief expert deluxe. Jack Bentley allowed only six hits for New York, but two were home runs by Harris and Goose Goslin.

When the series shifted to New York for the third game, the Giants moved back on top by 6 to 4. The most notable event of the day was a home run by Rosy Ryan, making him the second pitcher in series history to hit one—and showing that now everybody was getting into the act introduced and perfected by Babe Ruth.

The next day the Senators tied the series again by winning 7 to 4, and then Johnson went to the mound in the fifth game and the whole country outside of the Giants' roster was probably rooting for him. However, he had less stuff than in the first game, striking out only three men and allowing 13 hits, including a home run by Bentley. The New York pitchers now were beginning to hit more home runs than the fulltime batters. However, Johnson was hurt more by four hits by the teen-ager Lindstrom, and he contributed to his own downfall by fumbling a sacrifice bunt in the eighth inning as the Giants rolled on, 6 to 2.

Back in the capital, the Senators now had lost twice with Johnson and faced the improbable chore of beating McGraw's money-players twice in a row. They trailed in games, three to two; one slip and they were finished. But history had been playing strange tricks on the Little Napoleon of New York lately, and he was about to suffer as maddeningly as he had suffered at the Yankees' hands the year before.

First, Washington got back into contention by winning the critical sixth game, 2 to 1. Then came the winner-take-all game, and the boy-manager Harris elected to joust with the ranking manager in baseball with his own best weapon—grand strategy.

Harris began his supposedly suicidal joust by deciding that somehow he had to maneuver Bill Terry out of McGraw's lineup, since Terry had been hitting .500 in the series. Terry batted left-handed, Kelly batted right-handed. It was as simple as that: If McGraw could be pressured into outfoxing himself in the choice of a first-baseman, Harris might eventually turn McGraw's best weapon against himself.

In pursuit of these long odds, and to the Giants' great amazement, Harris warmed up Curly Ogden, a right-handed pitcher of no great distinction. Ogden, though, was merely a decoy. He opened the game by striking out Lindstrom, then he walked Frisch, then he was withdrawn from the game and was replaced by a left-hander, George Mogridge. Now Harris was daring McGraw to counter his thrust by removing Terry for a right-handed hitter. But McGraw didn't fall for it that time, or the next time Terry batted, either. Terry was too hot a hitter to be superseded before a blow was struck.

The third time around, though, with time running out and the series at stake, McGraw lunged for the bait. He sent the right-handed Irish Meusel to bat for the left-handed Terry, looking for the shot that would decide the game and the series. But then Harris pulled the trap. Having maneuvered Terry out of the lineup, he relieved his left-handed pitcher with Marberry, a right-hander, and followed Marberry with the greatest right-hander of the generation, Johnson.

At that, the Giants still were leading, 3 to 1, going into the last half of the eighth inning and were only six outs from winning. But in the eighth, McGraw's ordeal suddenly grew intense. Harris, his grand strategy behind him, hit a grounder to third base that took a bad bounce over Lindstrom's head for a two-run single tying the score. In a lifetime of high-level tactics, he could hardly have punished the Giants more.

Then old Walter Johnson, pitching in the last hours of a remarkable career, rose to the occasion as the series stretched beyond the ninth inning of the seventh game into overtime. In the eleventh, with a Giant in scoring position, he struck out Frisch and Kelly, while McGraw and the outflanked Terry watched from the dugout. In the twelfth, too, Johnson kept the Giants at bay, and then came the home half of the twelfth and a capricious jab of fortune.

Muddy Ruel lifted a high pop foul behind home plate to start the trouble. It should have been the second out, but Gowdy, circling under the ball, got his foot stuck in his own discarded face mask, like a bear caught in a clamp trap. He tried to shake it loose, failed, then lunged as the ball dropped to the ground. Then Ruel compounded the irony by hitting a clean double to left field.

Next, Johnson batted for himself and bounced a grounder to shortstop. Travis Jackson fumbled it, and Johnson was safe at first while Ruel held second. Finally, Earl McNeely hit a grounder toward third base and, as Lindstrom stooped to pick it up, the ball suddenly took a high hop over his head the way Harris' ball had done in the eighth. Ruel scored from second and for the second year in a row McGraw's house came tumbling down.

Washington went wild with jubilation, as though it had just received word of a great naval victory on some distant sea. Coolidge issued a presidential declaration congratulating the new, unlikely world champions. New York froze in disbelief.

McGraw, feeling the pinch again, was dazed by a triple defeat: The O'Connell scandal, the loss of his second series in a row and the loss of the 12-inning seventh game by the quirks of landscaping in Griffith Stadium. He headed back to Manhattan rather wearily, but somehow managed to rally from the gloom long enough to gather the troops around him. Before leaving Washington, he instructed his players to wire their wives in New York to meet them at the Commodore, where he pitched a defeat party.

A kind of pall settled over the Giants that night, though. They had won many battles lately, but now were in danger of losing the war. Even their singing reflected an air of downfall. Instead of the roisterous old tunes of past celebrations, they followed Jimmy Flynn in singing war favorites like "Dear Old Pal of Mine." Somehow, the days of the empire were slipping past.

Even a post-season trip to Europe lacked the old zing. It was a repeat performance of the barnstorming of a decade earlier, with Charles Comiskey again heading the American League contingent and McGraw heading the Nationals. The Olympic Games had been held that summer in Paris, and Europe was still crowded with the heaviest touring since the war. The baseball travelers were inspected by George V, were "covered" for the London *Evening Standard* by George Bernard Shaw and were even appreciated by Sir Arthur Conan Doyle.

They played baseball in London, Manchester, Dublin, Paris and other places. They drew a throng of 20,000 to Stamford Bridge, including the King and his son, the Duke of York, who in the next decade would become George VI. Shaw, "reviewing" the performance for the *Evening Standard*, put a tongue in the Shavian cheek and wrote:

"I shall never forget that Mr. McGraw, in whom I at last discovered the real and most authentic Most Remarkable Man in America, shook hands with me. He even shook hands with the Duke. But though he was very nice to us, there is no denying that he played us both right off the stage."

Conan Doyle, in a letter to the editor of the London *Times*, asked sympathy for the ambassadors of baseball and ventured to predict: "I believe it would sweep this country as it has done in America." He was wrong, Watson.

In spite of the trappings of royalty, though, the caravan was beset by sloppy weather and revisions in the itinerary. Stengel, who had been traded to Boston the year before, made the trip with his old teammates and even brought along his bride, Edna Lawson, for a delayed honeymoon. Years later, on another visit to London, he recalled the lack of heraldry on both junkets.

"We played at Wimbledon," Casey said, "and the place was as deserted as the airport was tonight. The British are very consistent. They were just as calm about my arrival tonight as they were back in 1924. They showed extreme restraint on both occasions."

The British might have gone from restraint to absolute indifference if McGraw had revisited the tight little isle the following year. He was in a slump, personal and professional, and things just kept growing bleaker with a kind of perverse momentum.

For openers, he became ill in the spring of 1925 after the club had returned to New York from Florida. He left the team for the first time, and stayed away two weeks. One newspaper even suggested that he was planning to resign. As of April 7, he was only fifty-two years old.

Then the Giants failed to win the pennant for the first time in five years. They had won ten in the twenty-three years since McGraw had arrived in New York, but this time they trailed Pittsburgh at the finish and they were fated not to win another during the rest of McGraw's term.

Finally, McGraw suffered one of his bitterest sorrows while watching the World Series between Pittsburgh and Washington that October 7. He received word that his old favorite Christy Mathewson had died at his home at Saranac Lake in upstate New York. Mathewson, never really robust after the war, had left the Giants in 1921. He spent two years at the tuberculosis resort in Saranac, but improved enough to become the front man for a syndicate that controlled the Boston Braves and made him president. Then in the spring of 1925 his health deteriorated again, so he slipped away from baseball and retired with his wife to the mountain village of Saranac Lake.

When he got the jarring message, McGraw left the World Series, returned to New York and took his wife north to the Adirondacks. They had all been like affectionate relatives from the day in 1902 when McGraw had spotted Mathewson playing first base and had decided that he was a victim of atrocious miscasting. They had lived and prospered together after that as Mathewson bloomed into the pride of the pitching corps. And on October 10 the McGraws and Jane Mathewson made the long journey to the cemetery in Lewisburg, Pennsylvania, where Matty was buried.

For years, McGraw sat at a desk in his little office in the Polo Grounds with only two photographs hung on the wall behind. They were his pets, his prodigies: Mathewson and Ross Youngs. Now in the space of two years, both were gone. Youngs died on October 22, 1927, in San Antonio. And four months later McGraw lost Hughey Jennings, his playmate, deputy and confidant for thirty-five years going back to the rollicking days of the Baltimore Orioles.

To make matters even more depressing, McGraw derived little comfort from his relations with the generation of ball players who succeeded his old friends. They simply were too spirited, and in some cases too rebellious, to absorb steady dosages of the old heavy-handedness. Even team captains like Larry Doyle and Frank Frisch sulked, and Frisch was not appeased when Doyle told him that McGraw used to upbraid him in team meetings by taunts like: "Look at him, the miserable yellow thing, the captain of my ball club."

Frisch wasn't one to suffer in silence, and as the Giants spiraled downward toward the second division in 1926 for the first time in 11 seasons he decided he'd had enough whipping. One summer night he checked out of the Chase Hotel in St. Louis, where the Giants were housed for a series against the Cardinals, and took the train back to New York.

Many persons felt that Frisch eventually would be McGraw's choice as his successor. But now the temperamental young second-baseman and team captain was fed up with the old-time discipline and simply bolted. When he reached New York, Frisch said only that McGraw had hounded him. When McGraw reached New York, he had a short talk with Frisch that bore three results: He changed Frisch's status to *former* pride and joy, he never forgave Frisch for the insult of leaving the club, and he prepared to sack Frisch in order to maintain his iron grip on the rest of the Giants.

The team finished fifth, and three months later McGraw traded Frisch and Jimmy Ring to St. Louis for Rogers Hornsby. It was a blockbuster deal and a troublous one for both sides.

McGraw said he had been trying for several seasons to land Hornsby, the greatest right-handed hitter in the game, and had raised the ante to the point where the Giants were offering more money than any player in history had commanded. Hornsby, meanwhile, having completed a three-year contract at $30,000 a season, had taken the manager's job from Branch Rickey in midseason of 1925 and then was offered $50,000 that winter for another year as player-manager.

When he insisted on another three-year contract, Sam Breadon of the Cardinals telephoned McGraw and asked if he still wanted Hornsby. McGraw said yes, and backed the deal with Frisch, Ring and more of Stoneham's cash.

Breadon, trading one malcontent for another, immediately was engulfed in the full fury of fan resentment. He was besieged with letters and wires from St. Louis supporters who derided Frisch as trade bait and who raged at Breadon's choice of Bob O'Farrell as Hornsby's successor in the manager's chair. The Chamber of Commerce even adopted a resolution denouncing the swap, and other civic organizations threatened to boycott the club.

Hornsby promptly showed that he could vex people in two cities at once. Not that more vexation was what McGraw lacked in New York. He already was up to his elbows in manpower problems. Edd Roush, who had returned to the Giants from Cincinnati, now was holding out for more money, and McGraw was saying bravely that Roush be damned, he would get along with a center fielder named DeWitt (Bevo) LeBourveau. Then the great Rube Marquard, sent to Brooklyn thirteen years earlier, begged for a last chance and McGraw gave it to him. Then he discovered what he should have realized sooner—that Marquard was too old to help.

Finally, there was the new problem of Hornsby, who upon his arrival from St. Louis was named captain of the team and second in command. Except that Hornsby strutted as though he was really first in command.

It was bad enough that Hornsby began to poach on McGraw's executive preserve, but he also began to lord it over players of solid rank like Lindstrom, who finally told him that the Old Man wanted it done another way and, besides, "When you put that bat down, you're no bargain." After that Hornsby began to eat meals alone in spring training.

The straw that broke McGraw's back in all this, though, was even more bizarre. Hornsby still owned stock in the Cardinals, and Heydler, the president of the league, was saying that unless he disposed of it he couldn't play for New York. Moreover, Hornsby stunned Breadon by insisting on $116 a share for it, and when Breadon pointed out that he had paid only $45, Hornsby replied, "That was before I won the pennant for you."

Royally embroiled, and hating every minute of it, McGraw finally threatened to sue unless the league let Hornsby play. So the rest of the clubs, to restore some trace of peace, were pressured into chipping in to a special Hornsby stock fund. It would make up the difference between the purchase price and the sale price demanded by the investor who now complicated McGraw's already complicated life.

It was a bad time all around for McGraw. There was tension in the clubhouse and there was tension even in the front office, where the Hornsby problem and McGraw's growing peevishness had strained things with Stoneham. Then, to his lasting discomfort and expense, he became involved in the Florida land boom—and his tumble from serenity was complete.

The Florida land boom, like the Hornsby stock boom, reflected a basic fact of economic life in the twenties that was gathering runaway momentum: The sky was the limit. Or, in Jimmy Walker's breezy monetary philosophy, "There's more where this comes from."

By newspaper, radio and telephone, the public now was bombarded with word of the Great Opportunity at hand. Even by word of mouth and grasp of lapel. On Central Avenue in St. Petersburg, the boom was kept alive by swarms of speculators who bearded and buttonholed visitors from the north, and few targets were as inviting as well-paid, ill-informed ball players. Sometimes the buttonholers hired ball players to buttonhole other ball players for them, particularly instantly recognized types like Rube Marquard.

All roads seemed to lead to opportunity, whether on Wall Street or Biscayne Boulevard. The New York papers ran enormous 40-page automobile sections on Sundays. The Seaboard Air Line Railway offered two deluxe trains to Florida every day—the East Coast Limited and the West Coast Limited, with special direct service to West Palm Beach for those who were headed straight for their own place in the sun. The Admiral Line took longer, but still offered 48 hours of luxury aboard ships like the "H. F. Alexander" that made the magic run between New York and Miami every five days.

"Everybody," trumpeted the New York *Sun*, "is talking about Florida." The *Sun* bought advertising space in its rival papers in New York to spread word of its own coverage of Florida's news, declaring it more extensive than anybody else's. With a touch of pride one day, the *Sun* announced that it was publishing its fourth special section on the great land in three months' time.

The rest of the world could spin along in the rest of the news columns. In the New York *Evening Graphic*, former Mayor Hylan was writing "the whole truth" about his eight years in office preceding Walker's arrival, and at 2 cents daily and 5 cents Sundays the paper promised "amazing disclosures." In the *Journal-American*, one issue carried articles by Mussolini saying "there will be no strikes in Italy, the state will prevent them"; by Lloyd George finding "all Europe feverishly at work eager for peace"; by Kathleen Norris describing how "the herded millions contrive to live in New York," and by William Jennings Bryan revealing all in "his fascinating memoirs."

All that, plus signed humor by Ed Wynn, Stephen Leacock, George Ade and Montague Glass, "and a separate book of jokes and puzzles"—presumably to lighten the gloom cast by Hylan, Mussolini, Norris, Bryan and the others.

But New York was less interested in the herded millions than in the hellbent millions, and they seemed hellbent on striking it rich either in the stock market or the real estate market.

Florida was ready to oblige, too. While the city slickers were being bearded by speculators on Central Avenue outside the baseball camps, an even bigger pitch was being made to the folks back home. Full-page ads in the New York press were bought by the Florida Chamber of Commerce extolling the "health, wealth and opportunity" to be found under the citrus trees. New colonies like Olympia Beach-Picture City sang in big, black type: "I don't care what happens in Florida, our slice of it is safe." And for investors who wanted to share that slice of paradise, a cut-out coupon was attached to the ad with the pledge of instant information on the attractions of "Florida's Land Boom."

On Sunday, January 17, 1926, the *pièce de résistance* was offered in a full-page advertisement in *The Times*. The cherubic face of John McGraw shone out over a picture of a planned haven called Pennant Park on Sarasota Bay, with these warm words of assurance from the Little Napoleon of New York:

"I am building another winner in which *you* may share. Millions of Americans have come to associate my name with the building of winning combinations. I have worked with might and main to build great baseball teams for those whose interests I served. And I have had more than the usual amount of success—for which I thank those who have chosen to work with me.

"Today I am building something to last long after my ball teams are forgotten. I am building something to make the name of John J. McGraw stand for something permanently worthwhile. It is my hope that people in years to come will thank me for giving them the chance to find health, happiness and opportunity on the shores of matchless Sarasota Bay."

Warming to his task, the man who had found irritations on matchless Sarasota Bay two springs earlier now found great pleasures, and in fantastic prose he portrayed them:

"Here I am building a beautiful community, Pennant Park, to be enjoyed not by a few stockholders but by a thousand or two people who have confidence in me. Some will find health and pleasure here. Many will share in its recreational and social features. Many others will find unusual profits here. I believe that Pennant Park is the greatest winning combination I have ever managed.

"All who know baseball know how I took my New York Giants to city after city searching for an ideal place to train. Finally I came to Sarasota. I fell in love with the place."

Having thus glossed over a little white lie, he now played an ace card, proclaiming: "The principal thoroughfare will be a monument to my friend, the greatest pitcher of all time, Christy Mathewson."

The commercial delivered, the pitch ended with a price list ("first payment of $625 buys a $3,500 homesite, up to $1,250 for a $5,000 homesite"), then a printed form with the magic words "herewith my check" for so-many dollars, and finally a clinching invitation to "call personally or telephone John J. McGraw's New York Pennant Park office."

So many people called personally or telephoned John J. McGraw's office —and so few houses and thoroughfares were actually built on the idyllic site— that McGraw spent the next several years fighting off disgruntled investors, searching out their claims and eventually paying off their demands. His wife calculated later that, before he got out from under the fiasco, he spent $100,000 of his own money keeping the wolves at bay.

Life somehow had turned tortuous for the man who not so long ago had worried only about the number of fat pitches thrown to Babe Ruth.

★   ★   ★

For a few hours on the 19th of July, 1927, the curtain of gloom lifted, and the Polo Grounds basked for one afternoon in a flashback to the good old days of a couple of summers before.

All New York, in fact, cavorted in the calm before the storm that was gathering on the horizon—the Great Depression and the great wars of the next decade. On this particular, isolated afternoon, the only thing on the horizon was the trans-Atlantic liner *Leviathan*. It carried four pioneers to a hero-worshipping public in Manhattan: Richard E. Byrd, Clarence D. Chamberlain, Bernt Balchen and Bert Acosta. They were the first men to pilot an airplane from America to Germany, and this day they were coming home.

Graham McNamee and Milton Cross were there, describing the tumult on the sidewalks as New York roared one of its good old blaring welcomes. They described the tickertape and turbulence to an audience of millions with one thing in common: Their radio speakers were tuned to the same wave length, as when McNamee had reported the World Series along the Atlantic Coast four years earlier.

By now, radio had grown with startling speed, and much of the growth was hinged on sports. The year before the *Leviathan* steamed into the Upper Bay, the No. 1 drawing attraction for the industry was the Dempsey-Tunney fight; No. 2 was the inaugural program of the National Broadcasting Company; No. 3, the World Series, and No. 4, the Army-Navy Game. All outnumbered the inauguration of Calvin Coolidge two years before. The Dempsey-Sharkey fight in 1927 was even more spectacular. It was reported over 14,000 miles of wire line from Maine to Los Angeles to Jacksonville to Seattle, all tied to WEAF in New York with 300 radio and telephone engineers maintaining the largest network since the Lindbergh celebration in May. At the microphone for the fight was McNamee, giving it the old cultivated excitement for 30 million listeners.

This day in July, McNamee was there, too. And on the pier along the Hudson River to greet the four fliers stood Charles A. Lindbergh, and alongside him, Floyd Bennett. Now the six greatest aviators in America were grouped shaking hands on the one wooden West Side pier. Byrd remarked that now he was aiming for another horizon, the South Pole. Then they were all swept along in the private tide of Jimmy Walker, who led them on a merry round of civic celebrations in the finest traditions of the celebrating Walker administration. But the best, in Jimmy's eyes, was yet to come.

Promptly at 2 o'clock on this riotous afternoon, Walker and his official red-carpet, Grover Whalen, drove by the McAlpin Hotel in mid-Manhattan. They picked up Byrd and Chamberlain, who still were stunned by the pace, and behind a screaming motorcycle escort zoomed up Broadway to Central Park, then through the park to the Polo Grounds.

A crowd of 25,000 was waiting in the old ball park, and at the gate waited John McGraw with Charles Stoneham, John Heydler, Judge Emil Fuchs and other overlords of baseball. Commander Byrd was resplendent in his white dress Navy uniform, Chamberlain well-turned-out in a brown suit with a felt hat. As far as their eyes could see inside the stadium, festoons of bunting were hung with the colors of the United States, France and Germany.

Then Joe Humphreys, on a busman's holiday from his oratory at Madison Square Garden, marched to the infield grass and began to intone a roll-call of celebrities: Walker, Cohan, Eddie Cantor, Leon Erroll, Louis Mann, Bert Wheeler; and James J. Corbett, "the man who licked John L. Sullivan," and Hughey Jennings, limping on a cane.

They all came down onto the grass around home plate and surrounded those new heroes, Byrd and Chamberlain, and the old hero McGraw—for whom, as it turned out, the celebration was being staged in the first place. There was so much noise that Humphreys had to run over and interrupt Byrd and Chamberlain to get them to acknowledge their own introductions. Then, as the Fire Department Band paraded, wheeled, tooted and crashed, Joe introduced the guest of honor on this loud day in Walker's city—a "champion of champions," he said, using the public-address microphone that he so often spurned indoors.

He walked over to the manager of the Giants and held his right hand high, as he'd done in the ring so many times with the heavyweight champions. The actors from the Broadway shows played a comic game of baseball for their crony in the baseball knickers. A loving cup in solid silver was bestowed for ten pennants and three world titles. A silver platter was presented by the men of the Lambs. A silver cane from the ushers in the Polo Grounds. A silver cup from the city. A silver service from the players of the Giants, who then went out and lost to the Chicago Cubs, 8 to 5.

It was the silver anniversary of the July day 25 years before when he had first walked onto the grass there as manager of the ball club. In one huge box near the home dugout sat Giant heroes of past years. Nearby were thousands of injured war veterans and children from orphanages. Out on the field surrounding the short, blunt-faced man in the baseball flannels stood the new

Giants in their batting lineup for the day:

    REESE, 3B
    LINDSTROM, LF
    OTT, CF
    HORNSBY, 2B
    TERRY, 1b
    JACKSON, SS
    HARPER, RF
    TAYLOR, C
    FAY THOMAS, P.

McGraw cradled the immense loving cup in his stocky arms, looking only vaguely like the silver statuette of himself that crowned it—the one of McGraw as the old Baltimore Oriole. He walked into his dugout through the ovation and, one report said, "John McGraw heard himself called more nice names in one day than he has in any one of the last 25 years."

"To have captivated the public and impressed them with his fine personal qualities," *The Times* said in an editorial, "to have won the unanimous favor of baseball writers; to have saved the National League from Ban Johnson's drive in the first decade of the century; to have helped put baseball on a high level and never failed in compassion toward its failures—these are some of the achievements of John J. McGraw which make his silver jubilee an agreeable occasion for many who never think of attending a baseball game, but who recognize the importance of any professional sport which occupies so much of the leisure thought of the whole nation."

"The feathers on the head of the old Oriole are gray now," the editorial continued, "but the feathers on his back ruffle as belligerently as when, 25 years ago, he took over the management of the New York Giants."

Chapter

12

"I Have Quit"

Even before the nineteen-twenties turned the corner into the nineteen-thirties, a kind of ill temper began creeping over that careless, carefree time. People were probably too worried or even hungry to get much pleasure out of sights like Bill Robinson tap-dancing on the roof of the New York Giants' dugout during games at the Polo Grounds. Or Ethel Barrymore keeping meticulous track of the hits, runs and errors on her scorecard behind first base. Or Al Jolson making one of his ceremonial entrances into the grandstand before joining George M. Cohan in the box seats, where more actors flocked on summer afternoons than in Lindy's on summer nights.

It was no longer amusing for shadowy citizens like Arnold Rothstein to score staggering coups at the racetrack, as he did one day at Belmont Park when he collected something like $870,000 because a horse named Siderial ran faster than the others. Or at least less slowly.

Nor was it fashionable or feasible to serve the public passion for action—as it had been on the day that the American champion Zev beat the English champion Papyrus in a race that was followed by 23 observers for *The New York Times* in a spectacular example of mass coverage.

Then there was the night Mark Hellinger came into the office of the New York *Mirror* and, feeling unusually flush, offered his $4,000 Stutz Bearcat as the prize in a pool that he organized on the spot for the office boys. He charged each boy—including Harold Weissman, later the executive sports editor of the paper—a pool fee of $1 and collected a total of $14, which he pocketed. But then he drew stubs out of a hat to determine the winner, and one astounded kid drove away that night in a Stutz Bearcat.

Nor were there so many casual moments like the times when John McGraw used to leave Wrigley Field in Chicago and drive out to suburban

Hinsdale for an evening of dinner, drinks and gibes with Bill Veeck's father. Bill, who was not yet eleven years old, would sit and eavesdrop in wonder while the manager of the Giants spun yarns and exchanged friendly insults with his father, who was trying to get the Cubs out of a slump that had lasted since 1919.

The Cubs were fabulously inept in those days, as inept as the Giants were splendid. During one stretch ending in 1925, they finished seventh, fifth, fourth, fifth and eighth—in an eight-team league. "We could have beaten you even with our batboy in the lineup," McGraw said one evening after dinner.

The joshing stuck in Bill Veeck's mind, and twenty years later when he was running the St. Louis Browns he executed a variation on McGraw's theme. He sent a midget named Eddie Gaedel to bat one day and, he said later, "I'm sure that the idea started with McGraw's kidding remark to my father." Gaedel walked on four straight pitches and ended his career as he had started it, in phenomenal success.

The twenties were a time when WEAF, New York, would regale its radio listeners with all sorts of pleasant, informative, palatable program material that contained few of the harsh realities of Depression life of the thirties. On Thursday, January 7, 1926, for example, WEAF offered the following programs:

> 6:45 a.m.—Setting-up exercises.
> 11 a.m.—Myrtle Mason, contralto.
> 11:10 a.m.—Mayfair extension talk.
> 11:25 a.m.—Myrtle Mason, contralto.
> 11:30 a.m.—Columbia University cookery lecture.
> 12 Noon—Market and weather reports.
> 4 p.m.—Edwin Breen, baritone.
> 4:15 p.m.—"Can Personality Be Acquired?"
> (Dr. Kate Upson Clark).
> 6 p.m.—Waldorf-Astoria dinner music.
> 7 p.m.—Midweek hymn sing, New York
> Federation of Churches.
> 7:30 p.m.—Smith entertainers.
> 8 p.m.—The Larkinites.
> 8:30 p.m.—Hire's Harvesters.
> 9 p.m.—Clicquot Club Eskimos.
> 10 p.m.—Silvertown Orchestra.
> 11-12 Mid.—Lopez Orchestra.

The changing nature of things in the United States, and of the games its people played and the heroes they ogled, was probably foreshadowed in 1926 by a public imbroglio involving two of the giants of the era. They were Ty Cobb, then manager of the Detroit Tigers, and Tris Speaker, the manager of the Cleveland Indians. They were a pair of the towering figures of baseball during McGraw's years, and now as his generation began to lose its luster in the public eye his co-heroes began to lose some of their Olympian status, too.

In this case, Cobb and Speaker were the victims of unsupported insinuations. But it was a creeping sign of the times that two titans of the day could be assailed at all, to say nothing of losing their jobs as managers one month apart.

Along with Joe Wood, the old pitcher, they were accused of having arranged for Detroit to win a game against Cleveland in 1919—which was seven years earlier and also the year of the Black Sox scandal. The accuser was Hubert (Dutch) Leonard, another old-time pitcher, who was drawing a bead on two fabled outfielders at once.

His only mistake, though, was that Cobb and Speaker had built reputations as competitors who neither gave nor asked any mercy on the baseball field. In fact, on the day in question, the day when Detroit was supposed to have gained from their alleged arrangement, Cobb made only one hit in five times at bat. Speaker, on the other hand, hit two triples and a single and just missed a home run. Wood, who by 1926 was the baseball coach at Yale, hadn't even played that afternoon.

The reaction across the country was violent. The *Cleveland Press* headlined an editorial: "America Believes In Ty Cobb." Billy Evans, the umpire-columnist, wrote off Leonard tersely by saying: "As a pitcher, he was gutless." Will Rogers wrote in *his* column: "I want the world to know that I stand with Ty and Tris. I've known them 15 years. If they are crooked, it shouldn't have taken them 20 years of hard work to get enough to retire on. If they had been selling out all these years, I would have liked to have seen them play when they weren't selling."

Charles Evans Hughes was so outraged by the injustice of it all that he urged Cobb to sue the baseball establishment for defamation. Cobb, who was thirty-nine years old, was bitter enough to take the advice. But he finally had his day in court in another manner. He was absolved of any scheming, along with Speaker and Wood, and he was flooded with offers to play for other clubs. He even took parting shots at the baseball hierarchy, which he suspected of not having rallied round as vigorously as Will Rogers, Charles Evans Hughes and the editorial writers. For Cobb, the ultimate villains were Commissioner Landis, Ban Johnson, who resigned as president of the American League the following January, and Frank Navin, the owner of the Detroit club, whom Cobb berated as a man trying to "slide out from under my $50,000 contract."

At the height of the argument, the public became so gripped that a minister in Kansas City delivered a sermon proclaiming the Ten Commandments of baseball. They included: "Thou shalt not make a mountain out of a molehill of backyard gossip."

The trouble, though, went deeper. It sprang from the fact that Cobb, Speaker, McGraw and all the demons of the turn of the century had passed their zenith. There even were hints of this irreversible fact in the compliments still being paid to the Old Guard, as on July 19, 1927, when McGraw was feted for 25 years of success in New York and the National League's president, John Heydler, said:

"When John McGraw came to New York from Baltimore, the National League was tottering. It was close to bankruptcy. The fight being waged by the new American League threatened the very life of the old circuit. But McGraw saved the situation. He put New York back on the baseball map. He built the Giants into the most powerful machine in baseball."

Heydler's words were true enough, and they were pointed enough. But they represented a kind of parting salute to the era of the impresario who ran the whole show, the field marshal who gave genius and demanded obedience in return.

"Eventually," observed Tom Meany, the writer, "McGraw's genius defeated itself. It wasn't the changes in the game induced by the livelier ball and Babe Ruth's free swinging, but the players themselves. A new type of player was coming into the game, players with greater backgrounds and greater independence. The tongue-lashings of McGraw and his arbitrary, dictatorial manner of handling them was intolerable. They rebelled, wittingly or unwittingly. He wasn't the type to be the thinking man's manager."

The rebelling, which had been bad enough before McGraw traded Frank Frisch to St. Louis, took a turn for the worse after he got Rogers Hornsby *from* St. Louis. After suffering Hornsby's autocratic manner for just one season, McGraw unloaded his bête noire on the Boston Braves on January 10, 1928, even though Hornsby had hit .361 and had become a kind of violent favorite with the Polo Grounds crowds. In return he got Frank Hogan, a catcher with only one year of experience, and Jimmy Welsh, an undistinguished outfielder. But he spared himself further affronts to what was left of his old dignity and command.

Even if he had been inclined to absorb more slings and arrows, Charlie Stoneham was not. In fact, McGraw was wintering in Havana when the trade was announced in New York. Stoneham, it was recalled, had been confounded the year before when questioning Hornsby about a pinch-hitting decision made during McGraw's absence, and Hornsby had replied: "Are you trying to tell me how to run this ball club?"

Stoneham, who merely owned this ball club, was properly taken aback. And he was completely rubbed the wrong way when Hornsby added: "If you don't like the way I'm running the club, get somebody else to do it." Stoneham did.

When McGraw returned to New York a few days later, he continued the housecleaning. He traded Burleigh Grimes, who was holding out for more money despite a poor season in 1927. In exchange, he got Vic Aldridge, who had not had a particularly good year himself at Pittsburgh but who also was holding out. As in the Frisch-Hornsby deal, he and Barney Dreyfuss were exchanging malcontents in the continuing struggle to preserve their old unquestioned ways.

In the old days, high spirits and unruly tempers had flourished, too, but they had been tolerated only so long as they served McGraw's all-purpose dictum: "The main idea is to win."

Cobb, a rival member of the same school, went to bat 11,429 times during 24 years and hit .367. But, he said as though reciting an axiom, "If I was in a slump, I'd take special batting practice in the morning."

Steven Owen, later the coach of the football Giants, was a kind of neutral observer of this intense approach, and was both appalled and impressed. As a professional football player in the late twenties, he hired himself out to the Polo Grounds staff in the summertime to earn "eating money" and later told Arthur Daley that this is what he saw:

"I'd report every morning and I'd be working away long after the ball game was over. But I noticed something I never forgot. One day a Giant player was trapped off second base and he didn't maneuver too well in the rundown. So he was tagged out and John McGraw was furious.

"At 10 o'clock the next morning the entire Giant squad was out on the field for a special practice. The man who'd been picked off second ran until his tongue was hanging out. McGraw was teaching him how to take a lead and how to return safely to the base. Then he taught him how to dance back and forth in the rundown. While he was doing that, he also was polishing up the other Giants in how to make the pickoff and how to nail a base-runner in the quickest possible fashion in a rundown. Everybody was learning something and perfecting himself.

"Do you ever see anything like that today? Please keep in mind that McGraw held practice almost every day at 10 a.m. This, mind you, was for a 3:30 ball game."

They were like shock troops preparing for combat. Heinie Groh was so small at 5 feet 7 inches and 160 pounds that McGraw suggested he try a bat with a bigger hitting surface. So Groh kept using bats with bigger heads and skinnier handles. Finally, he exceeded his own fondest expectations, and McGraw's, by going to Spalding's in New York and burrowing himself into the basement workroom until he had whittled his own bat—the freak known as the "bottle bat."

When Al Moore joined the Giants late in 1926, he was assigned to left field by McGraw for defensive strength since he had a great reputation as a throwing outfielder. Then one day with the Giants on defense and a runner on second base, the batter singled to left field. Moore, living up to his reputation, threw a strike to the catcher, the ball carrying all the way on the fly, and the runner was out by yards. Moore was beaming as he trotted into the dugout, just in time to hear McGraw bellowing:

"Moore, you've just joined us. Otherwise that throw would have cost you fifty dollars. I thought I explained that I always want throws from the outfield to take one bounce in case a cutoff is necessary. You probably think you made a fine throw. You heard the fans cheering. Let me tell you something, young man. If I were to announce that tomorrow afternoon there'd be a throwing exhibition by Al Moore, how many fans do you think would show up? They come here to see the Giants win, not to see Al Moore exercise his arm."

Zach Taylor, who spent sixteen years as a big league outfielder, said he had learned more in half a season under the martinet of Manhattan than during the rest of his career. But as the twenties faded, the iron grip began to fade, too, in the imaginations of the new, educated young men who crossed McGraw's path. Some tried to accede, and did; others bucked him; still others, like Red Reeder of West Point, flirted with the possibility and then elected a lifetime in the Army, instead.

Reeder, a new graduate of the Military Academy, was a second lieutenant in 1928—a time when the Army welcomed resignations. He was approaching "an election of professions," he recalled later in his autobiography, and one of the professions was playing for the New York Giants. When he joined them in spring training at Augusta, Georgia, the manager asked how much leave he had and Reeder replied "a month and a half, sir."

"Good," McGraw said. "We can find out about you in that time. Can you hit?"

"Yes, sir," Reeder said.

"Against any pitcher in the game?"

"Yes, sir," Reeder said again, without flinching.

"That's the way you have to feel," McGraw commented, beaming as though he had discovered an old, reincarnated Baltimore Oriole.

Reeder then hit .413 in 13 exhibition games and was offered a contract for $5,000. Army pay then was $1,716 for a second lieutenant. He was amazed. But he still decided to skip a career under General McGraw and return to his first love, an Army career. It ended eighteen years later when he lost a leg on Omaha Beach during the invasion of Normandy.

Still, McGraw liked to think that he appealed to Reeder's type of thinking man, and in his own mind he did.

"The college boy," he said, "has at the start the very thing the less fortunate young man has to acquire. He steps right in with the advantage of mental training. With the same amount of natural common sense behind him, the college boy has a full two years' jump on the town-lot boy. The difference is simply this: The college boy, or anyone with even a partially trained mind, immediately tries to find his faults; the unschooled fellow usually tries to hide his.

"Some of our greatest stars have never been to college, but that does not mean that they were better off without such training. It means that they had brains enough to see the handicap and through persistence and determination overcome it. Men of this type are Hans Wagner, Tris Speaker, Napoleon Lajoie, Delahanty—oh, a lot of them. I might add that Hughey Jennings and myself also were of that type, but we were quick to see the need of what other young fellows had been given by their parents."

Yet, just before the 1922 World Series, McGraw primed his players—some of whom were college boys—with these words establishing the chain of mental command:

"All I ask of you is to forget about those odds. Those figures merely represent the opinions of sporting writers. Get out there and play baseball just as you have all season. I'll do the directing and if anything goes wrong I'll take the responsibility."

In moments of extreme crisis, as in pitching to Babe Ruth, he left even less to the imagination of his troops.

"Ruth," he said, "is a ball player of the freak type that is likely to bust up a game at any moment. Nobody could ever hit a ball as far as he, and it was my business to see that he didn't get hold of one. Under those circumstances the natural thing to do was to pitch him slow ones. It is difficult for a long hitter to brace himself against a ball that barely lobs over the plate.

"I signaled for every ball that was pitched to Ruth. I think ball players, as a rule, can do a more workmanlike job when they feel that someone else is taking the responsibility. Those who watched the games may have noticed the catcher invariably turned and looked at the bench. I gave him the sign, which he in turn gave the pitcher."

When this "summit" view succeeded extravagantly, as it often did, McGraw tended to disclaim—or, at least to localize—the full credit a bit pompously.

"There appears," he said after the World Series of 1922, "to have been a disposition on the part of sporting writers and the public to give me the entire credit for winning this last series. I wish sincerely that they had not done this. I did do all the directing, but directing and so-called generalship are of no value whatever if the players do not carry them out. They deserve the credit for delivering the punch. I merely pointed out the weak spots."

On another occasion he also went to considerable verbal lengths to attempt to define the relationship between brains on the bench and brawn on the ball field.

"Never in my life," he said, probably shading the truth, "have I blamed a ball player for failing in an effort to carry out instructions. But I also have made it a point to censure a player, even if he won the game, for failing to obey orders. If it were possible for a ball player always to carry out his instructions —even to making the play successfully—then we should have no baseball. Managers could simply sit down in the spring and figure it out with pencil and paper."

However, players could not unfailingly make the play—that was the essence of the game's intrigue. And that was one great reason behind his fanatic devotion to the springtime as the source of the mental discipline—and publicity—that he regarded as the cornerstones of the game.

"You cannot expect a man in New York with his nose in his high coat collar suddenly to get excited over baseball overnight," he said once, while reflecting on the totality of his preparations for a baseball season. "Also, the public as well as the smart manager expects his players to be fit and ready to play on opening day as in July. A game won in April counts as much as a game in September."

On the field, he saw the game as a duel of strategy between the contending managers, almost the way fleet admirals might regard great naval engagements as duels between the respective bridges. Once when he was asked how he liked the proposal to allow pinch-hitters for pitchers, who then could remain in the game, McGraw snorted:

"Ridiculous. If you want to substitute brawn for brain in baseball, go all the way and let a club play nine defensive players in the field and then have nine sluggers do all the hitting. The very essence of baseball strategy stems from such moves as the intentional pass by which one manager forces the other manager to decide whether to remove his pitcher for a hitter or let him stay."

By the late twenties, though, as he neared his sixtieth birthday, this tide of mental gamesmanship seemed to be turning against McGraw. Either his own players were becoming less manageable, or less subject to his steel-trap strategies, or his rival managers were becoming more adept at such things themselves. Even Bucky Harris, the "boy manager," had upstaged him tactically in the 1924 World Series by switching from a left-handed pitcher to two right-handers and thereby maneuvering McGraw's left-handed power out of the lineup.

Now it was 1928, and McGraw's slide from the top was being hastened by ironic things beyond the reach of that mental strength that had been his great weapon.

He had just traded the difficult Rogers Hornsby and Burleigh Grimes and was trying to re-establish his control of the situation when he was injured one afternoon in Chicago. The Giants had just lost a close game to the Cubs and McGraw, running for a taxicab outside Wrigley Field, was struck by another cab. He thought he had bruised his left leg. But when the team finally reached New York after a series in Pittsburgh, he found that he had broken it.

The broken leg was the least of the indignities he was to suffer that season. But before the trouble steepened, he enjoyed one windfall, one that rewarded his successors even more than himself. One of his "private eyes," Dick Kinsella, was in Houston that June as a delegate to the Democratic National Convention. So naturally, one afternoon he went out to the ball park to see Beaumont play Houston in the Texas League. Particularly he saw a left-handed pitcher named Carl Hubbell, who had been up twice for trials with the Detroit Tigers, had been sent back to Beaumont and finally had been released.

There were conflicting reports on Hubbell and his sidearm screwball, a pitch that resembled a fastball but that tailed off into a pronounced break—in the direction opposite the conventional curveball. Cobb, when he was manager at Detroit, reportedly had said that Hubbell would "throw his arm out with that screwball." Later, though, Cobb noted that Hubbell still had belonged to Detroit at the time of Cobb's uproarious departure as manager. Moreover, Cobb said, he had told Navin, to whom he was still speaking at the time, "never let Hubbell go."

Somehow, they let not only Hubbell but also Cobb go. And now on that summer afternoon in 1928, the absentee delegate Kinsella watched the left-hander pitch for Beaumont and headed straight for a telephone. McGraw answered the call in New York and agreed that Hubbell's style was no problem in itself. After all, McGraw said, reaching for his classic comparison, hadn't Mathewson's famous "fadeaway" been a right-hander's screwball, and hadn't he thrown it for a generation with no ill effects?

Kinsella forthwith skipped the rest of the National Convention and, while Al Smith was being nominated by the Democrats, he was busy signing Hubbell for the Giants. Then, when everybody was back in New York, the Giants and Hubbell put on a late-summer drive, passed the Cardinals and moved grandly into first place.

A lot of things had happened to McGraw since the days of wine and roses early in the twenties, and most of them had been bad. The Giants had slipped from four straight pennants into a series of frustrations that took them to second place, fifth and third. Grimes, whom he had traded to Pittsburgh, was now pitching well, consistently and perversely. Hornsby, whom he had traded to Boston, was now leading the league in hitting. But now the Giants had finally struggled to the top again, and the old dictator's revenge was at hand.

At least, on August 19 it was at hand. Then, three days later, the storm began gathering around him again. The Giants suddenly reversed direction, retreated into second place, then nosed over into a tailspin.

Bedeviled, and still hurting from his collision with the Chicago taxicab, McGraw began to lash them bitterly. Then even he realized the uselessness of it all, and he relented. Once he changed his tactics so completely that he sat in the clubhouse while one of the young pitchers worked, so that McGraw wouldn't unnerve him from the bench.

The gods, who had been leading McGraw on a merry chase, had one more trick up their sleeves. They permitted his new, gentler touch to succeed for a while, then delivered the knockout punch. The success came during September, when the Giants recovered their poise after he had relaxed the reins— though it was more an act of resignation than of relaxation. The knockout punch came on September 27, when the Giants, only half a game behind St. Louis in the last week of the season, played the Chicago Cubs.

It was a capricious punch, the kind that no lifetime of planning, no superior wit, no Tammany Hall connections could countermand. It was an umpire's decision, and at that late stage it cost McGraw the pennant. It was made by Bill Klem in the sixth inning with the Cubs leading, 3 to 2, and with Hubbell pitching against Art Nehf, the onetime Giant. The tying run came sprinting down the third-base line in the form of Andy Reese, but as Reese approached home plate he was grabbed in a kind of bear hug by Gabby Hartnett, the Chicago catcher, and physically detained until he was tagged out.

The explosion of protest from the Giants' dugout reached all the way to Heydler, the president of the league. At that, it did not have to reach far, because Heydler was watching the game from a box seat. He immediately enraged McGraw even more by calling for news photographs taken at the critical moment. Then, after studying the pictures, he ruled that Hartnett had not really interfered with Reese.

The Cubs won the game, the Cardinals won the pennant and McGraw never forgave Heydler or Klem, both of whom had long been guilty of numerous unforgivable decisions in his view. He even memorialized the black day by getting one of the photographs, framing it and hanging it in his office as a reminder of man's inhumanity to man.

"And so," observed *The New York Times,* "it was that John McGraw, eager to get back to the war of another World Series, sat on the bench and saw another season pass on with that ambition unfulfilled. It was the sort of day on which hopes are destroyed—a grim day, gray and gloomy."

It was worse than that. McGraw's critics were so imprudent to point out that Hornsby had hit .387 for Boston and Grimes had won 25 games for Pittsburgh, while Vic Aldridge, who had come to the Giants in the Grimes trade, ended the season in Jersey City. It had been a bad year for a man who once had owned the surest touch in baseball.

In 1929, which turned out to be a bad year for almost everybody, the second-guessing boomed while the Giants collapsed with the stock market. They finished third behind Chicago and Pittsburgh, and this time the critics noted that Frank O'Doul, whom McGraw traded to Philadelphia, led the league in hitting at an astronomical .398, which was 108 points higher than Fred Leach, whom McGraw had obtained as the "prize" in the trade. Hornsby, they pointed out, had been traded from Boston to Chicago, batted .380, was elected the most valuable player and led the Cubs to the pennant.

In 1930, the Giants were still stuck in third place while St. Louis won with Chicago second. The new Giants—Carl Hubbell, Bill Terry, Mel Ott and Freddie Fitzsimmons—performed well. But the old Giants were beleaguered. Even the front office was being shattered now by the ravages of the Depression and the family bickering that grows with hard times.

Francis McQuade, the longtime friend and confidant of McGraw, had been voted out by the board of directors as the club treasurer and Leon Bondy had been voted in. So McQuade sued Stoneham and McGraw, and the family bickering was being aired in the State Supreme Court.

McQaude contended in the suit that his troubles stemmed from his insistence that Stoneham repay loans made from the club's till. Stoneham denied this, and countercharged that the true troublemaker was McQuade, who in turn depicted the hierarchy as a bunch of brawlers in Havana and New York. The defense counsel, Arthur Garfield Hays, called McQuade a liar in his summation. The counsel for McQuade, Isaac N. Jacobson, replied: "All these men are of a type—all greedy, fighting men—and a rough element was in control of the club."

The trial judge refused to reinstate McQuade but ordered that he be paid $30,000 as three years' back pay. The club bucked the case higher and was upheld in the Court of Appeals. Everybody agreed that it was a royal mess.

In 1931, the Giants crawled up a notch to second place, but the royal mess continued and the Old Guard suffered the most. Attendance slipped steeply in New York as the Depression brought the Roaring Twenties to a stifling close.

Charles Comiskey, one of McGraw's oldest friends in baseball, died and left behind him a Chicago team that had never risen to the first division since 1920, a year after the Black Sox scandal of twelve years before.

Connie Mack, another of his old friends and rivals dating back to the eighteen-nineties, had won three straight pennants and his 1931 team even won 107 games out of 154. But the high price of success was bankrupting Mack in Philadelphia, and he began to sell his success piecemeal just to meet the payroll. Within a year he would peddle stars like Al Simmons, Mule Haas and Jimmy Dykes to Chicago for $150,000 and he would also calculate that he had thereby "saved" himself the bittersweet burden of Simmons' $33,000 salary. A year later he would sell Mickey Cochrane to Detroit for $100,000. At the same time he would send Lefty Grove, Max Bishop and Rube Walberg to Boston for $125,000 more, and ultimately the great Jimmy Foxx would go to Boston for $150,000.

"We had spent $700,000 to $800,000, renovating our park," Mack said. "Our payroll was terrific. We didn't have a man under $10,000. We operate in an industrial city where the Depression hit hard."

The Depression was hitting hard all over. By the time Franklin D. Roosevelt and Herbert Hoover began campaigning across the country in 1932, the country had lost 5,000 banks, 12 million jobs and 50 billion dollars in stocks. Even the irrepressible Jimmy Walker was fighting a rearguard action. When the money ran out, he was called on the carpet to answer 15 charges of "malfeasance, misfeasance and nonfeasance," which may have set a verbal record for judicial emphasis.

Jimmy was almost as nimble in defeat as he had been in victory. He refused to flinch under the righteous pursuit of Judge Samuel Seabury, who, Walker noted with a mixture of admiration and resentment, "could get a conviction of the Twelve Apostles." Still, Walker unloaded a few memorable bons mots, like the time Seabury asked if he remembered what had been said at a meeting three years before. Walker replied: "No, and I don't remember what I may have said at a meeting two weeks ago."

He resigned as Mayor, though, on August 10, 1932, and another of McGraw's cronies from the happy time bit the dust.

The Depression had one ironic effect on baseball fortunes. It forced some owners like Mack to sell high-salaried athletes because of the shortage of money. But it also prevented most other owners from buying the high-salaried athletes for the same reason.

The Giants had one such asset, Bill Terry. He had tied Chick Hafey for the National League batting title in 1931 (they finished in a dead heat at .349, though Hafey had a micrometer's edge of .0003). Now in 1932 Terry was complaining that he had been cut 40 percent in spite of his good season, and he was demanding that Stoneham pay him or trade him.

Stoneham was well aware that Terry had something to fall back on, which was something not even Stoneham had in those lean days—a job with Standard Oil. But having little to lose either way, he replied: "Terry has made trouble about signing every year since he was a rookie. Last year he was paid within $1,500 of what Hafey and Bottomley received together. We tried to trade him last year but no one wanted him because of the high salary he was commanding."

At the height of the cash crisis, McGraw stumbled from irritation to irritation, even during times of some sentiment. The Giants trained in Los Angeles that spring for the first time in twenty-five years, and a parade of oldtimers visited their old chief in his quarters at the Biltmore Hotel as well as the ball park. Chief Meyers, Fred Snodgrass, Mike Donlin—all showed up out of the palmier past.

Then on the way back to New York, the club agreed to play an exhibition game at Santa Cruz during a nine-day stop in the San Francisco area. The mayor declared a holiday, children were released from school, the Giants went sightseeing to the redwood forests, and then the public address announcer shattered the peace of the occasion by intoning before the game:

"There he is, ladies and gentlemen, the famous—Muggsy McGraw."

It was the nickname that had been hung on McGraw back in Baltimore in the nineties, and it was one that he had despised ever since because of its implication of brutishness. The reminder, on this otherwise serene spring day, drove him into a raging mood that was already black with problems.

When the season started, McGraw's mood was worsened by a kind of players' revolt led by Freddie Lindstrom. The players, sensing that McGraw's grip had been weakened by the accumulation of trouble, suspected that he now was relying on a secret agent to maintain control—"a snitch, a copper, a lousy stool pigeon," they said, in unmistakable language. The revolt did not subside until Lindstrom, the ringleader, had broken a bone in his left foot. But then, having lost their third-baseman, the Giants began to subside on the field, too.

The most serious challenge to McGraw's grip, however, was his health. He suffered from ptomaine poisoning, then from a recurrence of sinus trouble. He grew so fretful that one day in Cincinnati, though confined to his hotel room, he drove out to the ball park to give Bill Klem a piece of his mind for having forced the Giants to play through a downpour the day before.

In St. Louis a few days later, he roared at an umpire during the game and was chased from the bench. The next afternoon he renewed the battle, and this time dissolved into an uncontrollable rage.

When he received a telegram from Heydler advising him of a $150 fine, McGraw did not have to think back too far to his past confrontations with the league president. So, realizing that Heydler happened to be in St. Louis, too, he waited in ambush at the press gate the next day and unleashed a flood of insults when Heydler walked into the trap. While spectators watched in amazement, McGraw denounced Heydler and "those lousy, rotten umpires of yours," then killed two birds with one stone by giving prominent vocabulary to Bill Klem.

When he noticed the crowd staring, McGraw shouted to them to "get the hell out of here." Then, depleted, he wearily asked a sportswriter to "tell Bancroft to take the club" and he rode a taxi back to his hotel. Heydler, shaken, said: "I'm afraid that McGraw is a sick man." Bancroft, when he returned to the hotel after the game, found McGraw sitting silently in his room, the shades drawn.

Back in New York a few days later, his wife insisted that he see their doctor, which he grudgingly did before a Sunday doubleheader at the Polo Grounds. At a dinner gathering with friends after the games, the doctor took her aside and said simply: "Mrs. McGraw, your husband is a very sick man."

The following Friday, June 3, 1932, the Giants were at the Polo Grounds for a doubleheader with Philadelphia. It had been raining for two days and was raining again, and the "No Game" sign already had been hung outside. Down in Philadelphia, Lou Gehrig was hitting four home runs for the Yankees against the Athletics and was tying a record set by Bobby Lowe of the Boston Nationals in 1894, a big year for McGraw and the old Orioles. But something even more momentous was brewing back in the Polo Grounds, game or no game.

"I was told the Old Man wanted to see me in his office," recalled Bill Terry, who had settled his holdout for $18,000, a cut of $5,000 for the league's batting champion. "What made it so unforgettable was that he hadn't spoken to me in a long time.

"He was mad at me because I'd held out until after spring training had started, and he was still sizzling when the season began. Then one day we were playing the Dodgers when Val Picinich hit a home run off Larry Benton and Picinich couldn't hit hard enough to knock your hat off. We had a four-run lead, but we lost the game because Johnny Frederick bounced a scorching grounder off my chest.

"McGraw climbed all over me and blistered my ears. 'Don't blame me,' I said. 'Blame yourself. Anyone could have seen that Benton didn't have it today. If you'd done what you should have done, you'd have yanked him. I didn't lose the game. You did.' "

"McGraw was so mad," Terry continued, "that he didn't speak to me for weeks. It was a funny feeling to go through spring training without ever talking to your manager. Then the next conversation I had with him was in June, when I was told he wanted to see me in his office. I knocked and walked in."

McGraw's first words, Terry remembered, were: "Sit with your back to the door." His next words were: "How would you like to be the manager of this ball club?"

Terry, who was "almost floored," then heard McGraw's voice say: "I'm quitting. I want you to think it over for a few days before answering."

"No, no, Mr. McGraw," Terry said, making a remarkable recovery, "I'll take it right now."

When McGraw got home to the big house on Ely Avenue in Pelham Manor late that afternoon, his wife asked: "What are you doing home so early? Was the game called off again?"

"I quit," John McGraw said.

★   ★   ★

Neatly, but unfamiliarly, dressed in a brown suit with a white sailor straw hat squared on his head, McGraw stood in the National League dugout in Comiskey Park, Chicago. It was July 6, 1933, and 47,595 persons were watching baseball's first All-Star Game. McGraw, sixty years old, had been asked to mastermind the Nationals; Connie Mack, erect, white-haired and seventy, called the shots for the American League. They were the patriarchs of the game.

They watched as Babe Ruth hit a gigantic home run off Bill Hallahan of St. Louis and, wrote John Drebinger in *The New York Times,* "there was nothing the sagacious John J. McGraw could do about it."

The American League won the game, 4 to 2, with Mack and McGraw matching their ancient wiles for the first time since the World Series of 1913. When Tony Cuccinello struck out and Rick Ferrell caught the last strike, McGraw hopped out of the dugout and made his way to the other side's dressing room, where he congratulated Mack.

"Ruth?" he asked rhetorically, sorting out his unhappy memories of Ruth across the years. "He was marvelous. That old boy certainly came through when they needed him."

"The National League," wrote Drebinger, "is still trying to catch up to Babe Ruth. McGraw was looking through the dust of many baseball diamonds —the years when Christy Mathewson was one of his prides, the years of Frank Chance and Johnny Kling and other stars of the past."

The flags were flying around the perimeter of the stadium and the bands were playing, drowning out the noble platitudes that were uttered that afternoon about the glories of baseball history being unfolded in the first All-Star Game. Somebody, exhilarated by the music and supercharged by the hoopla, suggested that maybe McGraw would make a comeback after all.

"I'm through with it," he replied. "I have quit."

Chapter

13

Giants
In the Earth

It was September 29, 1957, and the sun was slanting across Manhattan when a man named John Drebinger sat in front of a portable typewriter in the press box at the Polo Grounds and wrote:

"As the clock atop the ancient, weather-beaten clubhouse in center field read 4:35 p.m., New York's oldest baseball institution came to an end.

"For this was the last game to be played in the historic Polo Grounds, the home of the Giants since 1881. When the Giants next swing into action to start the 1958 season, it will be in San Francisco nearly 3,000 miles away."

The Giants left Manhattan the way John McGraw had found them when he appeared half a century before—losing. They lost to the Pittsburgh Pirates that afternoon, 9 to 1, because they could make only six hits off a husky man named Bob Friend, who smoked cigars, pursued long-range careers as an economist and banker, and also pitched for Pittsburgh with an economist's indifference to the sentiments of the moment.

"The only flourish," Drebinger observed, "was supplied by the crowd of 11,606 fans, some of whom said farewell to the Polo Grounds with an outbreak of rowdy souvenir-collecting.

"It was a warm, sunny afternoon. The old boys in the stands, who before the game had been introduced at home plate amid generous cheers, were more than a mite puzzled. Even Coogan's Bluff in the background looked sad.

"But perhaps the most touching scene of all in the pre-game ceremonies came at the end when they called on the First Lady of the Polo Grounds, Mrs. John J. McGraw, the widow of the Little Napoleon, who still hasn't recovered from the shock of seeing her beloved Giants move elsewhere."

The manager of the Giants, twenty-five years after McGraw had suddenly retired, was a young infielder named Bill Rigney. He walked over to the front-row box where Blanche McGraw sat and handed her a bouquet of American Beauty roses.

"I still can't believe I'll never see the Polo Grounds again," she said. "New York can never be the same to me."

★　　★　　★

New York had stopped being the same for Blanche McGraw on February 25, 1934.

It had been a troublous two years since her husband arrived home in Pelham Manor that June evening and said: "I quit." He was ill and he was unsettled, and he spent most of the time in the 12-room house on Ely Avenue reading newspaper reports on a world that seemed ill and unsettled, too. The simple madness of the twenties had given way to the complicated madness of the thirties.

Even the underworld was losing its grip. In a seamy postscript to the brutally straightforward feuds of Prohibition, a woman named Alice Kenny Diamond was found one day in 1933 on the floor of her home on Ocean Avenue in Brooklyn. There was a bullet in her right temple. She had been appearing in Brooklyn speakeasies saying she was tired "of protecting a lot of mugs." Her husband, Jack Legs Diamond, had been shot to death in Albany eighteen months earlier by a lot of mugs. She was thirty-three years old.

On the streets of Europe the mugs were marching, too. Nazi deputies were ejected from the Diet, but several thousand supporters of National Socialism demonstrated outside on cobblestones that would soon echo the parading boots of Nazi divisions.

A formation of 25 Italian seaplanes headed for Chicago and its Century of Progress Exposition—at which McGraw was making his final public appearance as manager of the National League team in baseball's first All-Star Game. The air fleet was led by the bearded General Italo Balbo, and American newspapers chronicled the mass flight as it crossed the Atlantic and penetrated the continent to the Great Lakes.

They also chronicled news of a different sort from Washington. Air Reserve flying in the United States was being reduced from 21,000 hours to 8,500 hours, and Naval Reserve flying was being cut from 48 drills a year to 24. The reason was economy.

Economy was a problem, all right. Franklin Roosevelt, in office since March, spent much of his time trying to "steady" the dollar. He even conferred with a delegation of bankers on board the cruiser "Indianapolis" after a vacation on Campobello Island. The cruiser carried him down to Washington, where the bankers climbed aboard.

In the middle of the country, Henry A. Wallace was conferring with the corn and hog growers in Iowa. Back in Washington, new postal rates went into effect: 2 cents in local areas, say as far north of New York City as Pelham, where McGraw lived; 3 cents outside.

Just about the only encouraging news on the economic front came from South Carolina, where the bootleggers reported that the legalized sale of beer had had "no appreciable effect" on the sale of bootleg beer. The legal 3.2 beer apparently was just too weak for their customers' taste.

However, even the entertainment world, the longtime ally of the sporting world during McGraw's heyday, was losing some of its institutions. In Los Angeles, Mary Pickford disclosed that "the house of happiness" was unhappy. She and Douglas Fairbanks, married since 1920, were parting and were selling Pickfair, their half-million-dollar nest. In New York, Roscoe C. Arbuckle died on June 29, and his funeral in the Gold Room of the Funeral Church on Broadway at Sixty-sixth Street was attended by 1,000 persons. "The majority," reported the press, "were curious." But Fatty Arbuckle's pallbearers included some of the Old Guard, like Bert Wheeler, Bert Lahr, Leo Carillo and Gus Edwards.

In Hollywood, the Paramount studio was announcing plans for 65 films. They included Marlene Dietrich in "Song of Songs," Maurice Chevalier in "The Way To Love," the Marx Brothers in "Duck Soup" and Charles Laughton, Mary Boland, Charlie Ruggles and Alison Skipworth in "Alice In Wonderland."

But in Berlin, a world away, the Ministry of Popular Enlightenment and Propaganda—a title as incredible as its policies—announced a new film law. It excluded Jews from any function in the production of German movies. Two days later they were excluded from any public office as well.

On February 26 the following winter, the headline on page 1 of *The Times* read:

> John J. McGraw Is Dead At 60;
> Called Baseball's Greatest Figure.

Below these lines, the first paragraph said:

> John J. McGraw died yesterday in the New Rochelle Hospital. The "Little Napoleon" of the baseball diamond, who led the New York Giants through 30 successful years, passed away at 11:50 a.m. in his 61st year.

It was noted that McGraw had attended the annual dinner of the New York baseball writers on February 4, then the National League meeting two days later, at which the 1934 baseball schedule was adopted. He was still the vice president of the Giants, but the signals were being given by his sulky protégé, Memphis Bill Terry. After the league meeting, he went to the team's victory dinner in the evening and watched the Giants celebrate their pennant of 1933—Terry's first full season. He stayed only an hour.

Two weeks later he went into the hospital, and nine days after that "death resulted from an internal hemorrhage caused by uremia." The officials of Pelham Manor, just north of New York, realized that "many callers" would visit 620 Ely Avenue and sent a force of laborers to clear the snow away from the streets and sidewalks in front of the house. He was eulogized in St. Patrick's Cathedral and buried in Baltimore, where he had arrived from the sticks forty years before.

Then the big house became quiet, and Blanche McGraw spent the next twenty-five years reliving her memories, answering the mail and occasionally commuting to Seat 1-B, Box 19, at the old ball park.

She held passes to every baseball league in the country, but never showed one at the Polo Grounds. All the gate men knew her, and people would come over during games and shake hands, and about three or four times a week she got letters asking for his autograph "for my son." She would sit at a desk and cut his signature, "J. J. McGraw," from his old canceled checks, all of which she had saved.

She always wore two charm bracelets to the games. Tiepins, medals, watch fobs, mementoes from his forty years in a baseball suit. She even strung one set of them on his old watch chain. He had given her a small gold piece after a trip to the Orient in 1914 and it was initialed "KBA." She never knew what it meant until years later at a dinner when Giles Stedman of the United State Lines told her it stood for "Korean Baseball Association." She didn't know there had been a Korean Baseball Association in 1914.

"Will Rogers used to come quite often," she said once, remembering the days when the house was alive with people. "He'd call and say, 'Mac, when are you going to have chili?' He was very fond of chili. We had a chauffeur, Eddie James, who had been with us since he was sixteen. We brought him from San Antonio. Eddie could make fine chili, which Will liked.

"Judge Landis always came up for dinner when he was in town. There were a lot of actors—DeWolfe Hopper, Brandon Tynan, Louis Mann, Frank Belcher. Most of them just came home with John without his telling me. But if there were more than three, he'd call and ask if I had enough to eat. He wasn't much of a visitor to other people's homes, but he liked always to have other people come to our home."

In 1941, after the rooms in the house had been quiet for seven years, she moved into a third-floor apartment at 30 Fifth Avenue in Manhattan, not far from the hotel they had stopped at during the first summer in New York at the turn of the century.

Besides clipping his signatures off canceled checks, she spent a lot of time answering letters on a typewriter that wrote in script. Once she received a letter from Illinois addressed: "Mrs. John McGraw, widow of John McGraw, the best National League manager of All Time, New York, N.Y."

There were good moments and bad. In 1951 the Giants, under Leo Durocher, lost 12 of their first 14 games and spent the rest of the season stalking the Dodgers. They were 13½ games behind in August, but caught them as the season ended. Then they were behind again, 4 to 1, in the ninth inning of the third playoff game and made history with a four-run rally that ended the game, the chase and the season. And the rally itself ended when Bobby Thomson hit an inside fastball into the left-field seats for the most dramatic home run in baseball history.

Rube Walker was catching for Brooklyn that day, and years later he relived the shattering moment and said, "It was a fastball inside, and it wasn't even a strike. He fell off it and hit it out of the park. The *next* pitch would've been a breaking ball."

Then there was Mel Ott's departure, twenty-seven years after he had reported to McGraw as a sixteen-year-old child from Louisiana. He hit 511 home runs, scored 1,859 runs, batted in 1,860, got 1,708 bases on balls and made 1,071 extra-base-hits. He hit .304, led the league in home runs six times and was McGraw's pride and joy, as well as his link to the era of Willie Mays—and the San Francisco Giants.

Wherever the Giants were, and whoever they were, on April 7 each year they would conduct a silent little ritual to commemorate the passing of the era. On April 7, 1953, three months after Ott had retired from the game as the manager at Oakland, John Drebinger wrote:

"This being the birthday anniversary of the late John J. McGraw, the thinning ranks of the old guard drank their usual silent toast to the man who, though dead these last nineteen years, left an indelible mark upon the Giants.

"Were he still alive, the Little Napoleon would be just eighty, and one wonders what his reactions would be were he to see some of the present day's catch-penny 'innovations,' such as overloaded night schedules and murderous spring-training barnstorming expeditions. He was the master showman of his time, but his innovations were always sound and he had little truck with circus stunts.

"The only survivors of the McGraw regime with the Giants today were a few old writers, Coach Freddie Fitzsimmons, whom McGraw developed in the twenties, and of course Secretary Eddie Brannick, who was always 'McGraw's boy.' "

They were in Mobile, Alabama, that day on the way home from spring training. Then it was four years and five months later, and Drebinger was sitting at his typewriter recording "the end of New York's oldest baseball institution," while Bill Rigney was approaching Blanche McGraw with the bouquet of American Beauty roses.

★   ★   ★

High over the Polo Grounds, a foreign correspondent named Milton Bracker left the cares of the world and returned for a last visit to the rocky place he used to prowl about as a boy. Coogan's Bluff, he noted, is "an outcropping of mica schist that juts up through upper Harlem and lower Washington Heights high enough to loom over the ball park." The path along the bluff starts at 158th Street and Edgecombe Avenue and, he recalled:

"It is not the physical but the nostalgic quality of Coogan's Bluff that counts. Down through the heyday of John McGraw, particularly through the first Giant-Yankee World Series of 1921-22, the bluff was an improbably wonderful place for baseball fans—particularly those over sixty and under sixteen.

"In those days a grandstand seat cost only $1.10 and you could get into the bleachers for 50 cents. But who wanted to? Because all you had to do was amble along the bluff, find a ledge that suited your contours and you were at the game."

It was true, Bracker remembered, that you rarely got to see the battery and almost never got to see the right-fielder or first-baseman. But you always got to see the shortstop, the left-fielder and the center-fielder. You saw the second-baseman on plays near the base and the third-baseman on plays away from it.

"But, best of all," he said, "you could see the scoreboard. None of those measly latter-day boards on the facade between upper and lower decks. No, sir! For until 1923 the Giants had a magnificent big board atop the spacious bleachers in center that was easy to see from the rocks. The combination of the scoreboard, a clear view of second base and an average of four players was just like being at the game.

"One prize example. The date: October 13, 1921. The situation: One out in the eighth game of the series between the then-upstart Yankees and the still lordly Giants. The score: 1 to 0, Giants.

"Aaron Ward was on first. Frank (Home Run) Baker was batting against Art Nehf. Those on the bluff couldn't see any of these players but they knew exactly what was at stake. What happened then was something they could see—well, most of it—and they haven't forgotten it since.

"Baker ripped one to the right side. From the bluff, the second-baseman, Johnny Rawlings, was seen to dive to his own left and disappear from view. An incredulous roar welled up from the stands. Ward, sure the ball had gone through, rounded second and headed for third. (Right in front of every man and boy on the bluff!) Then he dived, too, for a long slide around third that found Frankie Frisch waiting for him with the game's final tag.

"It was the famous Rawlings-to-Kelly-to-Frisch double-play that gave the Giants the series, 5 games to 3, and gave everyone who saw it one of the big thrills of his baseball life."

Often, Milton Bracker remembered, you saw "the Babe chugging around, arms flexed at the elbows, close to his sides, as he trotted out another homer. You saw outfielders like George Burns and Bob Meusel, and a man named Stengel range deep for the long balls. When Bill Cunningham somersaulted after hauling down Ruth's first-inning drive in the fourth game of the 1922 series, it was another big moment on the property former Borough President James J. Coogan had willed to his family."

Later, when the Colonial Park housing project on the Harlem River Drive was completed, a total eclipse came down on the choicest vantages on the bluff. Officially, it wasn't even "Coogan's" any more. Now it belonged to the city as park land overlooking the Harlem River Drive.

"At Friday's game with the Milwaukee Braves," Bracker said, a little mournfully, "an oldtimer sat alone on a remembered rock and managed to see the left-fielders trot to position. The loudspeaker system, blaring out all over the valley, made plain who was at bat, without benefit of a scoreboard. But somehow the sound was incongruous—like the implacable vertical of the housing project and the grim letters '———KEE STADIUM' twinkling in the twilight across the river.

"An era had ended. But it was great while it lasted."

★   ★   ★

Down on the field, just out of sight of the oldtimer on the bluff, the old Giants were grouped around the new Giants in front of Blanche McGraw's front-row seat. Jack Doyle was there, eighty-six years old and the oldest Giant alive. He had even managed the club for a time in the nineties when McGraw was still playing third base for the Baltimore Orioles. Red Murray was there, too, with George Burns, Moose McCormick, Hans Lobert, Larry Doyle, Rosy Ryan and old Rube Marquard, the "$11,000 lemon" of 1908 who later pitched 19 victories without losing.

Then came the new ones: Willie Mays, Hal Schumacher, Carl Hubbell, Monte Irvin, Billy Jurges, Willard Marshall, Sid Gordon, George Kiddo Davis, Buddy Kerr, Babe Young and Sal Maglie, who by now had also pitched for the Dodgers and Yankees.

"They even had eighty-one-year-old George Levy on hand to take a bow," wrote John Drebinger, recording the moment for people who weren't lucky enough to be seated inside the Polo Grounds or on the bluff beyond. "In the pre-electronic age, it was George's stentorian voice that rang out to the far corners of the arena, 'The battereez for today's game.' He did it all with a simple megaphone and he had the antique device with him this time to give it a final whirl.

"It was here, where once stood the wooden horseshoe stand, with its carriage drive circling the outfield, that John J. McGraw moved on the scene in 1902. For thirty years the Little Napoleon was to blaze a trail that was to make the names *Giants* and *Polo Grounds* the most famous in baseball.

"It was here that Christy Mathewson and countless others attained legendary status with exploits that doubtless will live long after the Polo Grounds has vanished completely from the scene."

Then Blanche McGraw took the roses from Rigney and sat back sadly to watch the last game. It didn't matter that the park would survive a few more years and for two seasons would even serve as the temporary home of a team to be called the New York Mets. Nor that the Mayor of San Francisco, George Christopher, had sent her "a beautiful letter" saying he understood that she was disturbed about the Giants' leaving New York and promising her they would get a "great welcome" in San Francisco.

"That was nice of him, wasn't it?" she asked.

Then, nine innings later, the Pittsburgh shortstop, Dick Groat, glided in front of a grounder bounced to the left side of the infield by Dusty Rhodes and threw the ball to Frank Thomas at first base, and the New York Giants were out for the last time.

"An era had ended," wrote Arthur Daley, taking up the echo. "The gloom was so thick that not even nostalgia could save it.

"It is probably impossible for a modern fan to appreciate the hold that the Giants had on the populace in the days when McGraw dominated baseball. For close to thirty years they were the darlings of New York.

"Souvenir hunters swarmed about the place. They ripped up home plate and dug up chunks of the sacred sod where Christy Mathewson's feet had pressed. They dismantled the furniture and tore out the decorations. They assembled in front of the clubhouse and jeered Horace Stoneham, the owner of the ball club. Some just wandered about in disbelief."

When the tumult had faded and the mob had scattered, the shadows began creeping over the old grandstand and reached into the silent dugout where the stocky, squat man in the striped baseball knickers had stood for 30 seasons giving the signals, flashing the hit-and-run, calling the pitches to Babe Ruth.

The last person to leave the empty scene was Blanche McGraw. As she went down the steps, a slight, white-haired figure, she was crying and clutching the bouquet of flowers in her hands.

"It would have broken John's heart," she said.

"So New York will be left with its memories," *The New York Times* wrote. "There were giants in the earth in those days, the days of 15 league pennants, of five world championships, the days of Mr. McGraw."

Acknowledgments

The days of Mr. McGraw are revived here with the help of many persons who remembered, reported, studied and lived them.

Eddie Brannick, "Mr. McGraw's boy" of 1902, was at John McGraw's elbow for thirty years. He has helped house, feed, transport, pay and run the Giants for sixty-five years in New York and San Francisco, and his reflections are gratefully acknowledged.

Warm thanks also to Natalie Brush de Gendron, the daughter of McGraw's patron, John T. Brush, for her memories and mementoes. And to John B. Hempstead, the son of the late owner of the Giants, Harry Hempstead. And to Richard L. Tobin of the Saturday Review for his suggestions and advice.

Also, to Joseph Stevens Sr., whose family wined and dined the stadium crowds in the days of McGraw, as they do now; Casey Stengel and Edd Roush, who played for and against him; John Drebinger and Arthur Daley of *The New York Times;* Garry Schumacher of the Giants; Harold Weissman of the old New York *Daily Mirror* and the new New York Mets; Robert O. Fishel of the Yankees; Ed Weisman of the National Broadcasting Company, and a special salute to John F. Royal, one of the pioneers of NBC in the time when Graham McNamee was a rookie.

They all contributed nobly, as did my colleagues in the microfilm library and morgue of *The New York Times* and the library staff of the National Broadcasting Company.

—Joseph Durso

Appendix

JOHN JOSEPH McGRAW

Born at Truxton, New York, April 7, 1873.
Died at New Rochelle, New York, February 25, 1934.
Height, 5:7. Weight, 155 (as a player).
Batted left, threw right.

Record as a Player

YEARS	TEAM & LEAGUE	G.	AB.	R.	H.	AVG.
1891	Baltimore, A.A.	31	106	15	26	.245
1892-99	Baltimore, N.L.	802	3,048	818	1,036	.340
1900	St. Louis, N.L.	98	341	84	115	.337
1901-02	Baltimore, A.L.	93	293	87	99	.338
1902-06	New York, N.L.	58	131	15	31	.237
Major league total		1,082	3,919	1,019	1,307	.334

Career stolen bases—444.

A.A.—American Association
N.L.—National League
A.L.—American League

Record as a Manager

New York Giants

YEAR	FINISHED	WON	LOST	PCT.
1902	8 (last)	48	88	.353
— (Before he became manager:		22	50	.306)
— (After he became manager:		26	38	.406)
1903	2	84	55	.604
1904	1	106	47	.693
1905*	1	105	48	.686
1906	2	96	56	.632
1907	4	82	71	.536
1908	2 (tied)	98	56	.636
1909	3	92	61	.601
1910	2	91	63	.591
1911	1	99	54	.647
1912	1	103	48	.682
1913	1	101	51	.664
1914	2	84	70	.545
1915	8	69	83	.454
1916	4	86	66	.566
1917	1	98	56	.636
1918	2	71	53	.573
1919	2	87	53	.621
1920	2	86	68	.558
1921*	1	94	59	.614
1922*	1	93	61	.604
1923	1	95	58	.621
1924	1	93	60	.608
1925	2	86	66	.566
1926	5	74	77	.490
1927	3	92	62	.597
1928	2	93	61	.604
1929	3	84	67	.556
1930	3	87	67	.565
1931	2	87	65	.572
1932	6 (tied)	72	82	.468

(Retired June 3, 1932; succeeded by William H. Terry.)
*Won World Series.

TOTALS: Finished first 10 times, second 11 times, third 4 times, fourth 2 times, and fifth, sixth and eighth once each.

Elected to the Baseball Hall of Fame—1937.

On August 21, 1968, a baseball diamond was dedicated to Willie Mays at the housing project built on the site of the Polo Grounds in Manhattan. Mayor John V. Lindsay of New York said:

"There are many ways of measuring the greatness in the game of the Giant we honor today . . . by statistics . . . by the memory of those who have seen so many of them play. But you have measured him best here today by naming this new Polo Grounds diamond for him, when only 20 years ago it would have been named for Mathewson or Hubbell or Ott.

"This is, you know, a kind of hallowed ground we are standing on. Some of the greatest baseball players in all of history trod the sod here, on the site of these towering homes.

"And they were Giants—the New York Giants, who dominated baseball during the first quarter of the twentieth century. They were the Giants of John McGraw. . . ."

CASEY

*"Something of insanity
has gone out of the performance."*
—BROOKS ATKINSON.

Chapter

You Could
Look It Up

His name was Charles Dillon Stengel, but because he had been born in Kansas City, Missouri, he was the man from K.C.—*Casey.* But he also was called "Dutch," because his family was German; "the Professor," because of his Socratic manner of presiding over baseball dugouts; "the Swami," because, under mild promotional prompting, he affected exotic headgear and stared wildly into crystal balls, and "Doctor," simply because he had an uncertain memory for names and called everybody else "Doctor."

Branch Rickey, the "deacon" of major league baseball, called him "the perfect link between the team and the public."

It was a link he had started to establish as a 19-year-old outfielder in a place called Kankakee, Illinois, in a league called the Northern Association in 1910. That was four years before World War I, a decade before Babe Ruth became a Yankee, more than half a century before the first big league game was played indoors. The league folded in July.

Stengel thereupon squirreled a couple of Kankakee uniforms into a suitcase and moved over to Shelbyville, Kentucky, in the Blue Grass League. The franchise collapsed.

He packed again and moved to Maysville, Kentucky, where a stream skirted the outfield grass, and one day he drifted back for a fly ball, sloshed a few feet farther back and caught the ball while standing in the stream. The link was taking shape.

For the next 55 years, Casey Stengel grew old, rich and famous while the United States moved from William Howard Taft to John F. Kennedy and beyond, with talking pictures, the automobile and the Lunar Excursion Module revolutionizing life, and baseball expanding as a multimillion-dollar business into the West Coast, the Deep South, Central America and even Japan. He had been transported to his early baseball games in horse-drawn surreys and he wound up a regular traveler from Los Angeles to New York in Boeing 727 jetliners.

He owned oil wells in Texas, was vice president of a bank in California and controlled real estate that made him a millionaire. His face was heavily wrinkled, his ears were floppy, his voice was guttural, his endurance beyond belief. Like Mickey Mouse and Charles de Gaulle, he was a household figure of towering identification.

But for all his status, he was best known as a baseball man, earned his "source" money in baseball and for 55 years exerted his greatest influence on baseball players, fans and franchises.

He had been a player, coach or manager on 18 professional baseball teams. He had been traded four times as a left-handed outfielder in the major leagues. He had been dropped or relieved three times as a manager in the big leagues. He had even been paid twice for *not* managing.

He had retired at the age of 70, had returned at 71, and had been re-hired at 73 and 74. Then, as he turned 75, he fell and broke his left hip somewhere between Toots Shor's restaurant in Manhattan and a house in Whitestone, Queens, and had to watch on television from a room in Roosevelt Hospital while 39,288 persons in Shea Stadium sang "Happy Birthday, Dear Casey, Happy Birthday to You."

One year later, to the day, he limped into the Baseball Hall of Fame alongside Ted Williams, having completed the course from Kankakee to Cooperstown as a national figure, an average player, a controversial coach, a wheeler and dealer of minor league talent, a second-division manager of dismal teams, a first-division manager of the Olympian Yankees, a man criticized as an expert at *over*-managing wherever he managed—a mixture of Santa Claus and Jimmy Durante as he duck-walked out to home plate with his lineup card, wearing flannel pinstripes and No. 37 on the back of his uniform.

Was he the greatest baseball manager who ever lived? Was he the luckiest manager who ever lived? Was he simply a manager whose fortunes oscillated with the talent available? Was he a meddler, a tyrant in the dugout, a slave to the "book," a wizard, a patriarch, a Merlin, a charming old man or an "angry old man" with great press notices?

Whatever he was, when he signed his final contract as manager of the New York Mets on September 29, 1964, he received the following telegram from Rickey, then seven years younger than Winston Churchill and eight years older than Stengel—who was 74 years and two months old:

"You are exactly the right age to manage a major league baseball team in my book."

Later, sitting in his box seat between home plate and third base in Busch Stadium, St. Louis, Rickey leaned forward on a gnarled cherrywood cane, chewed on a cigar and watched the St. Louis Cardinals bat their way into a tie for first place in the National League.

Rickey had been born on a farm in Ohio 82 years earlier, once had pedaled a bicycle 18 miles each way to teach school and later had become a lawyer with three degrees, the creator of baseball's first farm system and the dominant figure in the major leagues in three cities. But what excited him now was that Casey Stengel—in his 75th year—had just signed a $100,000 contract to manage a baseball team. And he reacted as though he suddenly had put his finger on something constant in the sweep of a busy life.

"Exactly the right age," he said. "You know, it's a great waste for universities to force brilliant men to retire at 65, when they're at the peak of their ability. And baseball needs men like that, too—like Casey Stengel—who are so able, so alive, so articulate, so aroused.

"People in New York have spent a lot of time and effort trying to ferret out the reason for the Mets' astounding attendance," he said, peering out beneath strong, bushy eyebrows, his hands folded across the knob of the cherrywood cane. "You need look no farther than Casey Stengel. He is the perfect link between the team and the public."

The perfect link between the team and the public, at that moment, was landing in Milwaukee aboard a jet airliner from New York. In 72 hours, his team would arrive in Deacon Rickey's St. Louis and cause panic in much of the Midwest by reaching up from the league cellar to defeat the Cardinals twice at the climax of one of the great finishes in baseball history. He had the knack, it seemed, of living at the eye of the hurricane.

The Mets required one full page in their handbook that season to record his three-quarters of a century, but somehow managed to compress his vital statistics into these four lines of spectacular understatement:

> STENGEL, Charles Dillon. 'Casey.' Manager. Born July 30, 1890, at Kansas City, Mo. Height: 5 ft., 10 in. Weight: 175 pounds. Batted and threw lefthanded. Married and lives in Glendale, Calif. Former outfielder.

Before he had become a "former outfielder," though, Stengel had played baseball from 1910 to 1931 for four minor league teams, five major league teams and two more minor league teams. Then, as a manager, he lived through 25 seasons of almost abject frustration in both the major and minor leagues, finishing no higher than fifth in an eight-team league during one entire decade, before suddenly graduating to the New York Yankees as the 15th manager in their 46-year history of dominating the sport. He won 10 pennants in 12 years and finally, at the age of 72, wound up with the Mets where he had started—at the bottom of the ladder.

During the next four years, the Mets fielded a team that won 194 games, lost 452 and ran dead last in the National League each time. But they fielded a team that was cast in the precise image of the waddling old man who directed it, a team whose sins were pardoned by an adoring public, whose life was surrounded by legend—and could be understood only in terms of legend—and a team whose bank credit grew as indisputably as the lore.

In 1965, Casey Stengel's last year in a baseball uniform, 1,768,389 persons paid up to $3.50 each to watch the Old Man and his celebrated Youth of America in their new ball park on Flushing Bay, and 1,075,431 paid to see them on the road.

Only the Los Angeles Dodgers, en route to the world championship, and the Houston Astros, en route to great wealth under baseball's first roof, did better business at home, and with a World's Fair enlivening the Meadow next to the stadium, Stengel completed the "perfect link" to the public that had so enthralled Branch Rickey.

But Stengel's rapport with the American public went far beyond the box office.

"He's not a clown," his wife Edna said after 40 years of marriage. "He's one of the smartest men in baseball, in business, in anything he'd try."

He was a turn-of-the-century athlete, country boy and Broadway character rolled into one and, it was widely believed, was the model for Carey in Ring Lardner's *Alibi Ike*. He drove a taxicab as a husky, rather oldish teen-ager in Kansas City; played football and basketball as well as baseball in high school; turned to semi-pro baseball in 1910 to earn money for dental school; consternated his laboratory instructors by attempting to practice dentistry lefthanded; was paid 25 cents for pumping the organ in St. Mark's Episcopal Church in Kansas City, $1 a day for pitching with the Kansas City Red Sox, $135 a month for playing the outfield with Kankakee and, 55 years later, $100,000 a year for managing the New York Mets.

When he was poor, he was duly impressed by small wealth. "I found they'd pay me $135 a month for playing ball," he told the members of the Senate Antitrust and Monopoly Subcommittee on July 9, 1958, during hearings on baseball's business growth. "I thought it was amazing." But, he said later when private conversations got around to his personal fortune, "people are always talking about how much money I got; they never remember how much money I lost."

He earned all this to the loud accompaniment of theatrical antics both on and off the baseball field, until he was accused of carrying on in order to distract people from the less effectual performances of his teams. But even in his heyday as skipper of the lordly Yankees, he performed from a full repertoire of practical jokes, pantomime and anecdotes.

"He can talk all day and all night," John Lardner said, "on any kind of track, wet or dry."

His talent for outlandish behavior outraged owners like Barney Dreyfuss of the Pittsburgh Pirates, officials like Judge Emil Fuchs of the Boston Braves, commissioners like Kenesaw Mountain Landis and umpires like Bill Klem.

"Every time two owners got together with a fountain pen," observed Quentin Reynolds, "Casey Stengel was being sold or bought."

"I never played with the Cubs, Cards or Reds," Stengel acknowledged. "I guess that was because the owners of those clubs didn't own no fountain pens."

When he was installed as a one-man triumvirate—president, manager and outfielder—for the Braves' farm club at Worcester, Massachusetts, in the Eastern League in 1925, he fretted through his first assignment as an executive for one season. He even played in 100 of the team's 125 games and the team finished third. But at the end of the season he executed a monumental front-office triple play to escape. As manager, he released Stengel the player. As president, he fired Stengel the manager. And as Stengel, he resigned as president.

He once slid into a potted plant in the Sheraton-Cadillac Hotel in Detroit to demonstrate Ty Cobb's famous fallaway slide. But when he was criticized in 1918 for not sliding home during a close game when he was, according to his own judgment, a grossly underpaid member of the Pittsburgh Pirates, he replied: "With the salary I get here, I'm so hollow and starving that I'm liable to explode like a light bulb if I hit the ground too hard."

Putting him into the outfield was likely to become an adventure for both sides. When he returned to Ebbets Field in Brooklyn for the first time as a member of the Pirates, he was welcomed back with a rousing round of catcalls from the same fans who had applauded his tricks for his first five years in the major leagues. In reply, he marched to home plate, bowed with courtliness to the grandstand, doffed his cap, and out flew a sparrow.

When he took over right field for Montgomery of the Southern Association in the spring of 1912, he achieved a complicated variation of the fly-ball-in-a-stream routine that had helped launch his histrionic career two years earlier. He found a drainage hole in the outfield and simply disappeared from sight. A short time later he rose like Triton from the sea, drainage cover under his arm, just in time to grab a fly ball. His manager, Kid Elberfeld, was not amused.

When umpires pulled rank to thwart his tricks, he sometimes counterattacked with passive resistance. He would swoon in a mock faint and just lie down on the ground while they raged. He did this effectively one day against Beans Reardon, one of the National League's senior umpires, but Reardon trumped Stengel's ace by lying down alongside him.

"When I peeked outa one eye and saw Reardon on the ground, too," he recalled later, "I knew I was licked."

When another umpire rejected his suggestion that it was growing too dark to continue playing, Stengel goaded him by signaling his pitcher with a flashlight. When yet another umpire appeared to give him the worst of a series of decisions, he stripped off his uniform shirt on the field, held it out and said impudently: "You try to play on our side for a change."

When John J. McGraw, his idol as a manager, attempted to stifle him, Stengel rebelled somewhat more gently. McGraw hired a private detective to shadow Stengel and Irish Meusel, the two most celebrated hell-raisers on the New York Giants. So the two players simply split up, forcing McGraw's man to track one quarry and neglect the other. Stengel, with pretended petulance, then went to McGraw and complained: "If you want me followed, you'll have to get me a detective of my own."

Later, when he became a manager himself, Stengel looked back on his wayward years and said: "Now that I am a manager, I see the error of my youthful ways. If any player pulled that stuff on me now, I would probably fine his ears off."

Indeed, he was frequently accused of intolerance in the face of others' antics, though the degree of intolerance appeared to fluctuate with the degree of the culprit's success with ball, bat and glove.

When he was a new manager at Toledo in the American Association in the late nineteen-twenties, his players, like most other working adults in the country, became Wall Street buffs who played the soaring stock market and showed more frenzy over the stock averages than over their batting averages. The team dropped off from first place in 1927 to sixth in 1928 and plunged to eighth in 1929 just before the market plunged even deeper.

He called the team together one day at the height of the boom and said, with a tone of formality: "You fellows better start buying Pennsylvania Railroad and Baltimore & Ohio stock, because when we start shipping you out to the bushes next week those roads are going to get rich."

A quarter-century later, his New York Yankees eased into a game of Twenty Questions aboard a train en route from a catastrophic series against the meek Philadelphia Athletics. When he could stand the frivolity no longer, he poked his head around from the manager's front seat in the special car and growled: "I'll ask *you* a question. How many of you fellas think you're earning your salary?"

Still, he proved unregenerate himself no matter what rank he occupied. Arthur Daley wrote in *The New York Times:* "His humor is constant and ever-flowing, but most of it is strictly visual. You have to see him in action to appreciate him, an item which perpetually confounds those chroniclers who strive to capture his hilarious antics in print. He acts funny but he doesn't write funny because his violent pantomime and mimicry need a much broader stage than the confining limitations of type."

He displayed this bent on a sufficiently broad stage sometimes in situations that might have been perilous for a less-talented mimic. On a tour of the Pacific he once devoted an entire 20-minute "speech" at a rally to a violent pantomime of arm-waving, finger-pointing and head-shaking, clenching his fist and going through all the signs of an orator without actually saying anything, while the crowd roared.

He was not insensitive to the possibility of diplomatic or physical dangers, however, exhibiting a kind of Charlie Chaplin stoicism to the tightrope course he often plunged along.

In the spring of 1915, his third with Wilbert Robinson's Dodgers, a sports writer was driving across the trestle between Charles Ebbets' "beautiful Daytona" and the beach when his headlights caught the figure of a man leaning over the railing toward the water. He stopped, ran over and looked into the anguished face of Casey Stengel. "I'm sick," the young outfielder moaned, "and Uncle Robbie doesn't like me and I can't hit, and I'm deliberatin' whether to jump in."

When he became manager of the same Dodgers 20 seasons later, he slumped into a barber's chair after the team had fumbled away a doubleheader with flourishes, ordered a shave and cautioned the barber: "Don't cut my throat. I may want to do that later myself."

When he became manager of Oakland in the Pacific Coast League in 1946, he noted the geographical advantages of the area with appreciation. "Just like Brooklyn," he said, "wherever I go they throw in a bridge as part of the service. Every manager wants to jump off a bridge sooner or later, and it is very nice for an old man like me to know he don't have to walk 50 miles to find one."

He did not have to walk 50 miles to find an audience, either, for his nonstop, marathon, circuitous style of speaking that became known as "Stengelese."

It was a kind of rambling semi-doubletalk laced with ambiguous, assumed or unknown antecedents, a liberal use of "which" instead of "who" or "that," a roundabout narrative framed in great generalities and dangling modifiers, a lack of proper names for "that fella" or simply "the shortstop," plus flashes of incisiveness tacked onto the ends of sentences, like: "And, of course, they got Perranoski."

When a listener's interest appeared to wane, Stengel recaptured his attention by suddenly exclaiming, "Now, wait; let me ask you," etc. And he would then pose a question in the form of a lengthy monologue. Finally, when the central point was delivered, he would extend a finger, wink with exaggeration and ask: "Got it?" Strict followers of Stengelese always found a point at the end of the trail, though often an hour later; between the layers of dangling participles and fused phrases, a point lurked.

Sometimes the point was made rather quickly in a form of short, clipped, Stengelese, most frequently to summarize a baseball player's ability or idiosyncrasies or to define a situation starkly.

Of Jim Bunning, who had pitched successfully for both the Detroit Tigers of the American League and the Philadelphia Phillies of the National League, he said: "He must be good. He gets 'em out in both leagues."

Of Van Lingle Mungo, his impetuous pitcher with the Dodgers in the nineteen-thirties: "Mungo and I get along fine. I just tell him I won't stand for no nonsense—and then I duck."

Of Roger Maris, the aloof, arch power-hitter of the Yankees: "That Maris. You'd tell him something and he'd stare at you for a week before answering."

Of baseball itself and the nature of the game: "You got to get 27 outs to win."

Of the logic of the double play: "It gives you two twenty-sevenths of a ball game."

Of a pitcher who throws sinking balls that tend to be hit onto the ground into such double plays: "He throws grounders."

Of ball players and their occasional lack of hustle: "I ain't seen no one die on a ball field chasing flies. And the pitchers. I bet I lost six games fieldin' by a pitcher. He's got an eighteen-dollar glove, ain't he?"

Of Willie Mays, who played for the San Francisco Giants in windy Candlestick Park: "If a typhoon is blowing, he catches the ball."

Of a ball player with a problem: "That feller runs splendid but he needs help at the plate, which coming from the country chasing rabbits all winter give him strong legs, although he broke one falling out of a tree, which shows you can't tell, and when a curveball comes he waves at it and if pitchers don't throw curves you have no pitching staff, so how is a manager going to know whether to tell boys to fall out of trees and break legs so he can run fast even if he can't hit a curveball?"

Stengelese flowered, though, in even longer, fuller public utterances that reached Olympian heights in Congress, where a rambler of Stengel's range might be accused of carrying coal to Newcastle. When he testified in 1958 before the Senate's Antitrust and Monopoly Subcommittee, he took the members back in history and syntax as he reviewed the ramifications of Oliver Wendell Holmes' decision of 1922 that baseball was not a business subject to trust laws but was "a local exhibition."

"I had many years that I was not so successful as a ball player, as it is a game of skill," Stengel said, appearing as the manager of the Yankees and the patriarch of the national game. "And then I no doubt was discharged by baseball, in which I had to go back to the minor leagues as a manager and after being in the minor leagues as a manager I became a major league manager in several cities and was discharged, we call it 'discharged' because there is no question I had to leave."

But should there be a new law governing professional baseball's relations with its players?

"Well," the Professor replied into the microphone, "I would have to say at the present time that I think baseball has advanced in this respect for the player help. That is an amazing statement for me to make, because you can retire with an annuity at 50 and what organization in America allows you to retire at 50 and receive money?

"I want to further state that I am not a ball player, that is, put into that pension fund committee. At my age, and I have been in baseball, well, I will say that I am possibly the oldest man in baseball. I would say that when they start an annuity for ball players to better their conditions, it should have been done and I think it has been done."

Estes Kefauver, the tall Tennesseean who became a Presidential contender after staring down Frank Costello and other powerful starers in other Senate hearings, received the loudest laugh of the day when he cleared his throat and said: "Mr. Stengel, I'm not sure I made my question clear."

The feeling persisted, after performances like these, that Stengelese was at least 50 per cent "put on" and 50 per cent "personality." As a vice president and director of the Valley National Bank of Glendale, which he and his wife's family controlled, Casey was considered as clownish as a barracuda despite straight-faced monologues like this one during an exposition on his bank's branch at Toluca Lake:

"We're a national bank and this is what you call a subsiduary. That's correct. Our main office is over in Glendale and this is a subsiduary—a branch. You can't ask me to go downstairs and run an IBM machine without a college IBM course. And I'm not supposed to talk about the banking business at all, because gold is leaving the country.

"Now this is the board room. See over there on the chart—capital assets and all that. Now you ask me: if this is the board room, where is the board, and I say this ain't the day the board meets. Okay?

"Now, in there where it says 'escrows' is where they can take people in and talk about escrows so it won't be out in public."

Part of the anatomy of Stengelese consisted of certain understated adjectives, like "fairly" as in "fairly amazing," and certain rich or mid-Victorian words or usages that he dropped neatly among the "ain'ts" and "fellas," such as "commence" and "numerous" and "splendid."

When 1,400 banners were paraded around the perimeter of Shea Stadium in New York during the Mets' annual Banner Day contest, "numerous splendid" hand-made signs carried messages in short, pure Stengelese, including one that caught the essence of the Stengel philosophy toward his astonishingly forlorn ball club in the Professor's own metier: "Commence Bein' Amazin'."

Even the Stengel telephone had a touch of the legend. His home number in California for years carried the exchange "Citrus"; his office exchange, appropriately, "Popular." One day in January 1965, just before he began what turned into his final season as a manager, the phone rang in the bank and the vice president, who had been alerted for a call from this writer on the East Coast, answered.

"I feel fairly good, yes, sir," he boomed, his flair for understatement in mid-season form. "We've been going to all them big football games at Southern Cal. And now we're going ahead with our new bank building here in Glendale, and then there's a branch in North Hollywood that we're goin' to dig ground for, and if I had Berra and Spahn and some of those pitchers here I'd see that they'd dig in and I'd show 'em who's the boss—around the bank, anyway."

"Spahn and Berra the opening-day battery?" he asked, barely pausing to field a question. "Well, I tell you. You know the amazing fans we have in Shea Stadium, which have stormed us with mail from all over, and now we have a girls' group and a women's group. There's nobody in the world I've seen will buy more tickets, and more fans are going to show up on opening day whether the Dodgers show up or not. So maybe we'll fill the park anyway and let those boys play 'em another day."

The point being delivered was that Stengel the Banker never let Stengel the Manager indulge in non sequiturs in money matters. The Los Angeles

Dodgers, with Sandy Koufax, Don Drysdale, Maury Wills and many memories of the team's 68 years in Brooklyn, were scheduled to open the season three months later in New York. It was to be a one-day stand and a certain sellout, followed for two days by the Houston Astros, who were certain not to sell out the stadium. So behind the doubletalk lay the seeds of a plan to fill the Mets' coffers on those quieter days with Stengel's "money" combination of Yogi Berra and Warren Spahn, two of the game's ranking stars who had been signed by the Mets near the end of their careers.

"I think we have a number of spots open on the ball club," Stengel went on, having, as usual, all of his time-outs left. "We have numerous jobs which our men can fill on the pitching staff, in the outfield and in the infield, too. You could look it up, but very few players last more than five years, or maybe ten, and you'll find that the annuities are made out that way."

Did he know that his second-baseman, Ron Hunt, had returned his contract unsigned?

"Is that so?" he asked with interest. "Well, Mr. Hunt has given 100 per cent, and he'll probably have to be a second-baseman again this year. I have a proposition with Hunt that he'd have to beat out several outstanding players, and he did win the job against competition without ever being in Triple-A baseball."

Translation: Hunt resented suggestions that he shift to third base to make way for unproved players at second base, and he probably was right.

Edna Stengel added a postscript to the conversation, displaying some Stengel understatement herself, by saying: "We're kind of an active family, you know."

Stengel's entourage of baseball players and writers had watched one-half of the active family that season in cities from San Francisco to Philadelphia, as they traveled the country with their 74-year-old manager, watching him in action before the public around the clock.

In Milwaukee, we watched him rush onto the field when the Mets and the Braves got into a ninth-inning rumble one night. Some players said later that they were so surprised to stumble over "the Old Man" in the dust that they broke up laughing. Hours after, the Old Man was enthralling friends and writers by reenacting great team fights of two generations earlier.

In Pittsburgh one day, a family named Stengel sent a birth certificate into the dugout with the name David Casey Stengel written on it—their son, who had been born nine years earlier after Casey's Yankees had won their fifth straight championship. He bounced over to the dugout railing and held court with his namesake for 20 minutes.

In St. Louis, before a glittering mink-and-tails crowds on Robert Goulet's opening night in the ballroom of the Chase Hotel, Goulet eased into his first number, cruising around a raised dance floor murmuring a love song to the ringside tables. He turned left and ("Why not take all of me?") came face to face with the unmistakable features of Casey Stengel, who was sitting at the ringside, too. The singer did a double take, fell to one knee, stopped his show and, to deafening applause, introduced the manager of the Mets, who stood and croaked: "You know, I've got a way with the ladies myself." After that, Goulet sang and Stengel was besieged by dozens of stunningly gowned women, who thronged his table pleading for autographs, and it became the Robert Goulet and Casey Stengel show.

In Cincinnati, a radio interviewer asked about Washington's place in the national life and Casey said proudly that "people want to see three things there, don't they? The White House, the Washington Monument because Gabby Street once caught a ball dropped off it and the ball park—because in what other sport does the President throw out the first ball every year?"

In Houston, a man brought his skeptical son to the visiting team's dugout and said hesitantly: "I wonder if you remember me. I pitched against you when you broke in with Kankakee." The Mets had just traveled from the Coast, were sleepless and, as usual, somewhat hopeless, and they were showing signs of total collapse as a baseball team. But the old manager looked at the visitor and his son and said: "Sure, sure. The old fireball himself. Why, I was sure glad when you quit that league. Did you make me look bad. I never could hit you."

In San Francisco, a minister leaned over the visiting team's dugout, introduced himself and said he had pitched batting practice to Stengel in 1910 in Kankakee. The census listed Kankakee, Illinois, at 27,666, and that was half a century after Stengel and all of his visitors supposedly had crowded the little town, but he showed no flicker of disbelief this time, either. He turned in astonishment to a man standing near him in the dugout and, spanning the 54 turbulent years since Kankakee, said warmly: "You know, he helped me hit."

That was a depression, two world wars, three generations and a dozen leagues earlier. And now, Branch Rickey was saying on that mild September evening in 1964 just before Casey Stengel headed into his last season as the most splendidly flamboyant, influential and controversial figure in the game, "he is exactly the right age to manage a major league baseball team."

Chapter

Kankakee

Casey Stengel, the manager of the New York Yankees, winners of three straight American League pennants, was 62 years old in 1952 and Mickey Mantle was muscular, inexperienced and 20. Mantle had been signed to a professional contract by Tom Greenwade, a Yankee scout, on June 13, 1949, had been braced with a $1,000 bonus, had played one season at Independence, Kansas, one at Joplin, Missouri, then had taken the giant step to the major leagues.

Now he was being billed as the successor to Babe Ruth, Lou Gehrig and Joe DiMaggio—the premier New York Yankee players of the century. But he was at the stage when life seemed a constant torture of third strikes on offense and line drives on defense that caromed unpredictably off the low outfield fence in Yankee Stadium.

So now Mr. Stengel stood in right field alongside him, faced the wall, trapped an imaginary baseball as it rebounded, and wheeled as if to throw it in to one of the infielders. Mantle, it seemed to the Old Man, appeared reasonably bored, skeptical and unimpressed.

"He thinks," Stengel said later, diagnosing their relationship in a few words, "that I was born at the age of 62 and started managing immediately."

If so, Mantle had a faint point. Stengel probably did look, to a rookie outfielder two generations younger, as though he had been born at the age of 62 and had started managing immediately. He had had a kind of old, strong, eagle look about him even as a child, in an era that Mantle might read about but that might only confirm his suspicions that the Yankees' manager of 1952 was an anachronism, misplaced in time and miscast as an expert on the angle, carry and velocity of caroming baseballs.

Victoria had been Queen for 53 years on July 30, 1890, when Charles

Dillon Stengel was born to Louis E. and Jennie Jordan Stengel in Kansas City. Benjamin Harrison was President of a country that was slipping from the post-Civil War period into the so-called Gay Nineties, and Grover Cleveland, who had already served one term, was about to confound the statisticians of Presidential succession by returning for a second term four years later.

Louis Stengel's father had emigrated to the United States from Germany in 1851 at the age of 13, had settled in Rock Island, Illinois, married Katherine Kniphals and died in 1865 when Louis was 4. Rock Island was typical farm country, across the Mississippi River from Davenport, Iowa, which is where Louis Stengel found, courted and married Jennie Jordan. She was the daughter of John B. Jordan and the niece of a judge of the Iowa Supreme Court, John F. Dillon, who also served as counsel for railroad companies that had spread their tracks south and west from Chicago.

Louis and Jennie Stengel had moved from the Davenport-Rock Island area to Kansas City and had two children at that time—Louise, born in 1886, and Grant, born in 1887. Louis Stengel was a short, strong man who made a comfortable living as an agent for the Joseph Stiebel Insurance Company, which also owned a commercial street-sprinkling system. For a fee, a wagon with a wooden water tank pulled by horses would sprinkle the main street of town and the wealthier, more fastidious neighborhoods. The company persuaded Stengel to take over this part of its diversification. He did, and became a familiar figure riding behind the horses on the streets of Kansas City until the city commandeered the sprinkling itself in 1915 and he more or less retired.

"Charley," meanwhile, was living the unhurried life of any midwestern boy at the turn of the century. The family switched houses fairly frequently, his mother became locally renowned as a formidable cook, and in grammar school he had to undergo the usual transformation faced by thousands of other children with one of the outstanding social afflictions of the day: he was left-handed.

Being left-handed proved no affliction, though, when it came to the things that became his chief interest in life—games—as he moved through Woodland grade school and Kansas City Central High School, displaying a neat right hand for penmanship and an increasingly neat left hand for throwing baseballs, footballs and basketballs. He was the leading athlete in his class at Central High, halfback and captain on the football team, a member of the state championship basketball team, and the third-baseman, pitcher and captain of the baseball team, which also won the state championship.

Baseball steadily outgrew the other sports as a way of afternoon life, though. For one thing, it didn't cost much to come up with a ball or even a glove. For another, Kansas City was blessed with enough vacant lots to accommodate the teen-agers who were trying to copy the great Ty Cobb, who had reached the big leagues in Detroit in 1905 and, starting two years later, won nine American League batting championships in a row; or Hans Wagner, who led the National League in batting eight times between 1900 and 1911.

The ball yards were likely to have tremendous bumps and ruts, or even ravines, across the outfield, unlike Yankee Stadium a generation later, which, Stengel noted, had an outfield turf "like a pool table." But no matter. Nor did it matter that the customary way to get to a ball game, aside from a bicycle, was by horse-drawn surrey, the kind that carted the Armour packinghouse team around, including the teen-aged Stengel brothers, Charley and Grant.

Grant, who was three years older, had managed to get his brother a spot on the team. They played together until a day when the team was coming back from a game and Grant was scuffling with some of the other boys on the surrey, slipped, caught his foot in the brake and lost part of his heel. "He was a good outfielder, an accurate thrower and very bright on the bases," his brother recalled, but Grant's career in baseball was ended and Charley was on his own.

During his last two years in high school, "Dutch" Stengel—or Casey, as he was being called—traveled during summer vacations with the Kansas City Red Sox. They even got as far as Cheyenne, Wyoming, playing for $1 a day and fringe benefits like candy and snacks.

Then, in his junior year at City Central in 1909, he pitched the final game for the state championship against Joplin, a town that was to send Mantle to the major leagues 40 years later. He pitched 15 innings, won the game, 7-6, left high school the following year without actually graduating, walked into the front parlor of his home one spring day in 1910 holding a paper in his hand and said to Louis Stengel, "Hey, Pop, sign this, will you?"

"So I put down my paper and pipe and signed," his father said. "You never could change the boy's mind, even then. He had been working out with the Kansas City (professional) club, the manager liked his looks, though not as a pitcher, and thought he'd make quite an outfielder. But he needed his parents' consent to join the club."

Strictly speaking, joining the Kansas City Blues was a means to an end, though two years later the means grew into the end. The end was to collect enough money to stake Casey through dental school, and, having secured his financial flank, so to speak, and having earned enough high school credits even without a diploma, he enrolled in the Western Dental College in Kansas City aiming for a career in dentistry.

This became a part-time effort that lasted two winters and that finally foundered for three reasons, any one of which would have been adequate: He really wanted to become a full-time baseball player, no strings attached; left-handed dentists had a considerably more obscure future in Kansas City in 1910 than left-handed baseball players, and, as he acknowledged later, the college did not have the daring to turn him loose with a "weapon" in his hand.

In fact, he recalled, his first clinic patient was also his last. While still a student, he was entrusted (under supervision) with the task of extracting a tooth from "a guy who must've been nine feet tall and which was the strongest man around." Casey bent to his task without hesitation, but the harder he tugged the more impossible his task became. The patient, he noticed, seemed to be growing taller and taller as he yanked on the tooth. He just could not get

any leverage, had almost encircled the victim's head with his arm and extracted the patient almost completely from the chair, the tooth unmolested, when
his instructor came running up, halted the farce and cried: "You're left-handed, you're left-handed!"

"I did everything right," Casey reported, "except switchin' hands."

As things turned out, his debut as a professional ball player that summer
ran a gantlet of mishaps, too. They were typical of the primitive state of baseball economics then and untypical of the situation 40 years later when 16 clubs
would pursue a college boy with bids as high as $200,000 and nurse him pain-
stakingly toward the major leagues. Or, 50 years later, for that matter, when
the first draft of "free agents" was put into effect and more than 800 amateur
players were drafted, or claimed, by 20 major league clubs for future consideration and consignment.

For one thing, though he joined the Blues and even trained for his professional debut at Excelsior Springs, Missouri, he was relegated to a considerably
more obscure station when the season began: Kankakee of the Northern Association. He also abandoned his career as a left-handed pitcher, became an
outfielder for good and reported for work in the dim minor leagues in rural
Illinois.

"I found they'd pay me $135 a month for playing ball," he told the Ke-
fauver committee in his celebrated Senate appearance 48 years later. "I
thought that was amazing."

He was even more amazed, though, when the league collapsed from financial anemia midway through the season. He had appeared in 59 games, gone to
bat 203 times, made 51 hits (including one home run), batted .251, stolen the
respectable total of 16 bases and was owed a month's pay when the league went
bankrupt—"blew up," according to a footnote in an otherwise staid baseball
guide that chronicled his career 15 years later.

"The team didn't last the season," he said, "and I was out of work before I
had a job."

So, he packed his suitcase and moved down the road to Shelbyville, Kentucky, in a league with a picturesque name, the Blue Grass League, but with no
cash to speak of. This time, the Shelbyville franchise collapsed.

However, it staged a comeback of sorts a few days later by reviving itself in
a nearby town, Maysville, which, except for the stream flowing past the outfield, was on more solid footing.

Stengel also finally got a line in a record book that outlived the league. He
played in 69 games for Maysville in 1910, went to bat 233 times, made 52 hits,
including 10 two-baggers, 5 three-baggers and 2 home runs; scored 27 runs,
and finished his first season in the minor leagues with two franchises shot out
from under him and a batting average of .223.

That winter he was back in dental school, a comic-opera figure in a Prince
Albert frock coat, he said later; but a bright student trying to work out his
future in something more secure than the Blue Grass Baseball League. But too
many things were stirring to let a 20-year-old of his assertive nature become

secure and settled in a dentist's parlor in Kansas City.

Glen Curtiss had just won $10,000 from the New York *World* for making the first nonstop flight from Albany to New York City, 137 miles in 152 minutes. A dynamite explosion had rocked the Los Angeles *Times* building during a dispute between building contractors and structural ironworkers, killing 21 persons and touching off a legal hassle in which Clarence Darrow argued for the defense and Lincoln Steffens finally was enlisted as a conciliator. And Sir Robert Baden-Powell was transplanting his Boy Scouts from England to America, though more boys in Kansas City that year probably had their eyes on Ty Cobb, the "Peach" from Narrows, Georgia, who had signed a baseball contract for $500 and now, in his sixth season in the big leagues, was batting .385 with eight home runs.

When spring came in 1911, Stengel quietly said good-by to his instructors at Western Dental, appeared briefly on the roster—but not on the field—for his old Kansas City team, and then settled into the lineup of Aurora, Illinois, in the Wisconsin-Illinois League. This league survived, and he made the most of it: 121 games, 420 times at bat, 115 singles, 23 doubles, 6 triples, 4 home runs, and a batting average of .352.

Aurora was only a short run down the line from Chicago, and a rookie with a batting average of .352 was worth a look by the major league scouts, even in those days. So a scout from Brooklyn named Larry Sutton made the trip to watch Stengel play. When he left, Aurora had a check for $300, Brooklyn had first rights to Casey Stengel and Stengel had a contract to play eventually for Brooklyn, a team variously nicknamed the Superbas, the Bridegrooms and the Trolley Dodgers—but a major league team. Before another year was out, he would be standing in Washington Park, Brooklyn.

That winter he severed his last ties with the dental profession and, when spring arrived in 1912, he arrived at the Brooklyn farm club in Montgomery, Alabama, having leapfrogged all the way from the "low" minor leagues to the "high" ones and being now just a telegram away from the major leagues. He had played only one complete season, not counting the misadventures in Illinois and Kentucky in 1910, but he latched onto a regular job playing the outfield in the Southern League, which he did for 136 games. He was batting .290 for Montgomery that September when the telegram came. He had been called up by Brooklyn.

When Stengel arrived in the big leagues in September 1912, baseball had evolved from rounders and cricket in England to town ball in America, then into a gentleman's game called "base ball" and finally into a fairly roughneck sport.

Seven years earlier, when he was a 15-year-old starting through Kansas City Central High, the presidents of the two major leagues—Harry C. Pulliam of the National League and Byron Bancroft Johnson of the four-year-old American League—had organized a commission to search out the origins of the game.

Pulliam and Johnson outdid themselves in selecting the commission. They named Morgan G. Bulkeley, onetime Governor of Connecticut and first president of the National League; Arthur P. Gorman, former Senator from Maryland; A.G. Mills, third president of the National League; Nicholas E. Young, fourth president of the National League; Alfred J. Reach, second-baseman for the Philadelphia club in the first professional league, the National Association, in 1871, and later the head of a giant sporting goods company that produced, among other things, the baseballs used in the American League; George Wright, shortstop for the first professional club, the Cincinnati Red Stockings, and James E. Sullivan, president of the Amateur Athletic Union.

For three years they researched the subject, trying to distinguish between primitive forms like "one old cat"—or, phonetically, at least, "one o' cat," in which the batter had one or two swings at a ball of twine with a stick or paddle; and town ball, a more organized form of mayhem in which the whole town was invited to take part and each side grew frequently to a mob of 30 or more players.

One thing seemed constant: all the variations involved hitting a ball and trying to run to a base before a defending player could retrieve it.

The commission, having pursued witnesses and descendants of witnesses as far west as the Rockies, finally decided that these earlier forms had been developed into "base ball" by Abner Doubleday in the farmland around Cooperstown, New York, in 1839—just before he left home to enter West Point and 21 years before he gained considerably less fame as the captain of artillery at Fort Sumter, South Carolina, who fired the first shot for the Union in the exchange that escalated into the Civil War.

Several kinds of "base ball," though, were being played at about the same time Doubleday was laying out a diamond-shaped area with four bases at Cooperstown. In New York City, the Knickerbocker Baseball and Social Club was organized in 1845 and two or three times a week split into two teams for a game of ball, with the first team to score 21 runs winning the game.

Rules, though, were as numerous as the players sometimes had been in the old town ball matches, and they remained that way until one of the well-to-do sports of the Knickerbocker Club, Alexander Joy Cartwright Jr., headed a "committee" to draw up a set of rules. Cartwright had been playing ball for three years with other more or less wealthy young men on open land near Madison Avenue and Twenty-seventh Street, and he was already a superior ball player. He promptly performed a monumental job of standardizing rules that lasted: a diamond with bases 90 feet apart, nine men to a team, unchangeable batting orders, three outs to a side in each inning, and no throwing the ball at a base runner to put him out, like a clay pigeon.

Once this amount of order had been established, the game spread with a speed that might have astonished even the 20 major league clubs who, 120 years later, were paid $25,510,000 by television stations for the rights to broadcast games coast to coast. On June 19, 1846, the Knickerbockers played the first match of record, a four-inning contest umpired by Cartwright and won, 23-1, by a rival club, the New York Nine, and how the mighty had fallen. The game was played at Elysian Field in Hoboken, New Jersey, across the Hudson River from Manhattan, and the niceties were maintained with some difficulty by Cartwright, who established perhaps an even more revealing precedent by fining one of the players 6 cents for "cussing."

In 1849, the Knickerbockers appeared in the first baseball uniforms— long blue woolen trousers, white flannel shirts and straw hats. Cartwright himself was too preoccupied with another project to take part, having bought a covered wagon and headed west in the gold rush, and later growing into an imposing figure with white hair and a long beard by the time he died in Hawaii in 1892.

As usually happens when the boys leave home and take their banjos, songs and games with them, the game that Doubleday had helped start got its greatest momentum from the war that Doubleday had helped start. Union and Confederate soldiers alike played camp baseball games, sometimes against each other when prisoners of war were allowed a few hours' free time.

With this momentum, the Nationals of Washington, D.C., took baseball on its first road trips after the war, covering 2,400 miles in three weeks, which became par for the course even in chartered jetliners a century later. The Nationals were tough, and their scores tended to get out of hand. They won games by 113 to 26 and 88 to 12, and were subdued only when a teen-ager named Albert Goodwill Spalding outpitched them in Rockford, Illinois, 29 to 23.

The first professional team, the Red Stockings of Cincinnati, was formed in 1869 and immediately enjoyed a season to end all seasons. The Red Stockings traveled 12,000 miles, won 65 straight games and, more significantly, played before 200,000 persons, unfortunately including hordes of gamblers who began to follow baseball teams eagerly and make book openly in the grandstands.

Worse, for a few dollars, the new professional players could be tempted to jump to other clubs, which they began to do in droves. When the situation got out of hand, ten of the clubs met in New York in 1871 and organized the National Association of Professional Base Ball Players, a governing body that tried to keep house against long odds. The association also authorized the first "world's championship," a title bestowed on the team that finished the season with the highest playing percentage of games won and that thereupon was entitled to fly a "championship streamer," or pennant.

The Athletics of Philadelphia won the first such streamer, in 1871, then the Red Stockings of Boston the next four with unusual flourishes, including an excursion to Canada during the season. The Red Stockings met and defeated teams from Guelph, Toronto, Ottawa, London, Dundas and Montreal before recrossing the border to resume their "pennant race."

When the gambling and raiding of players continued to increase in spite of the association's surveillance and, more important, the gate receipts started to decrease, eight of the professional clubs banded in 1876 into the National League. Hulbert, who was president of the Chicago White Stockings, drew up a constitution along with Spalding, the teen-aged pitcher of the eighteen-sixties, who was to succeed him six years later as head of the club. The cities were Chicago, Boston, New York, Philadelphia, Hartford, St. Louis, Cincinnati and Louisville, in that order of admission. Bulkeley, who headed the Hartford team, also headed the league for one year, after which Hulbert took over and ran the league and the Chicago franchise simultaneously until he died in 1882.

The National League's outlook was fairly austere. No Sunday baseball was permitted, no beer was allowed in the grandstand and no ticket-scalping was countenanced. For all three reasons, dissent was sure to set in, and it did after just six years in the form of a rival league, the American Association, which berated the National League owners as fat cats who thrived on exorbitant admissions of 50 cents and saddled the public with intolerable restraints. The National League replied by deploring the corruptive influence of a "beer and whiskey" organization, a league that included teams in Baltimore and Louisville that were owned by breweries and distilleries and in St. Louis by Chris Von Der Ahe, a prosperous saloon-keeper, and that charged only 25 cents for a ball game.

The "beer and whiskey" issue, as it turned out, was an omen that survived many other aspects of the game, including legal spitballs and 46-ounce bats. Eighty-four years later, the New York chapter of the Baseball Writers Association of America, in their 1966 winter follies, satirized this aspect of ownership and of the sponsorship of television broadcasts by depicting four members of the New York Yankees as singing this lament, to the tune of "The Whiffenpoof Song":

> From the bar in Newark Airport
> To that joint in Lauderdale,
> We're accused of impropriety and sin,
> Even though the ones who pay us
> Make their dough from beer and ale
> We are punished if we sip a little gin.

The feuding of 1882 was not exactly dissipated, either, when the White Stockings of Chicago challenged the American Association's best team, the Reds of Cincinnati, to a "world series." The association had forbidden its teams to compete with the "rowdy" National League, but the Reds ignored the injunction, went through the motions of disbanding after the season, then revived themselves as an "independent" club—and promptly knocked off the Chicago team, 4 to 0, causing dancing in the streets of Cincinnati and consternation in the older league.

Chicago recovered its poise the next day, though, and tied the series by winning, 2 to 0. However, the clandestine match was halted when H.D. Denny McKnight, president of the association, threatened to expel the Cincinnati players if they continued. So, the first "world series" ended in a one-to-one tie.

This sort of skirmishing led, as skirmishing often does, to a treaty of sorts—the National agreement of 1882. The "agreement," the first code for professional baseball, tried to end the talent raids between clubs by declaring contracts off-limits to raiders and by assuring each club firm control over its players. However, as treaties often do, the agreement led to disagreement. Slavery, it was called by many players; and a new issue was created that was to hound baseball owners as long as contracts reserved such rights to the clubs.

As might be expected, a third force soon appeared on the scene to offer the disgruntled players an alternative: a new organization calling itself the Players League, which promptly challenged the original "major league," the National League, and its principal rival, the American Association.

Now the situation became chaotic. Most of the ranking players in both the National League and the American Association began crossing over to the new league in a mutiny against the National Agreement of 1882, and by 1890, the year Stengel was born, baseball was embroiled in a civil war of its own.

The Players League, however, survived only one season in spite of its ready-made issue. But before it collapsed, it weakened the American Association to the point of collapse, too. So frantic was the infighting that one entire team, the Brooklyn team, switched en masse in 1890 from the American Association to the National League. Worse, for the association, Brooklyn had won the championship the year before and, worse still, it made good its escape by promptly winning the championship of the National League.

The confusion lasted far into the autumn. Brooklyn, the renegade, met Louisville in a "world series" between the feuding leagues that started late, October 17, was delayed four days by rain and was finally deadlocked at three games apiece with one tie when everybody decided nothing had been settled and called it a season on October 28.

The association, though, had clearly begun to totter. So the National League maneuvered clear of the tangle by annexing a total of four of the association's clubs, expanding from 8 to 12 teams, and for the next 10 years at least it was not seriously challenged again—until the American League was formed in 1901 and the modern pattern of the game, hinged on two equal major leagues, took shape.

The American League was not exactly welcomed when it crowded its way into the act. It evolved from the strong Western League, whose president, Ban Johnson, announced in 1899 that his group would be known as the American League. Johnson then invaded the National League's pioneer city, Chicago, moved quickly into Milwaukee, Cleveland, Detroit, Washington, Boston, Baltimore and Philadelphia; staged a series of punishing raids on National League talent; subtracted Milwaukee and Baltimore, added New York and St. Louis, and by 1903 confronted—and won equal status with—the National League.

The newcomers cemented their grip in the first World Series between the leagues, too, a series played over a two-week period in 1903 with the Boston Pilgrims, or Puritans, as they were known, defeating the Pittsburgh Pirates of the National League in eight games.

The crowds in that historic series contributed almost as much action as the players. The Pirates' Exposition Park in Allegheny seated only 8,000 persons. Yet, twice that many were crammed into the stands and behind ropes that were stretched down the foul lines, hemming the infield and making the outfield a ground-rule hazard that came to be known as "triples paradise," and, in fact, 17 three-baggers were hit into the crowd in four days.

When the series shifted to Boston, the Pilgrim's park, which reportedly could seat 16,242 persons, bulged with 18,801 and fights broke out in the grandstand when squatters refused to move for late arrivals whose ticket stubs, however legitimate, simply led to blows.

Anyway, when the sound and fury faded, there were two major leagues. And when Stengel took the train from Montgomery to Brooklyn nine seasons later, the pattern was firmly set.

The Dodgers in those days were playing out their last season in Washington Park, a wooden bandbox typical of the antiquated ball yards that were just beginning to be replaced. Connie Mack had built the first "modern" stadium, Shibe Park in Philadelphia, a park that was three years old in 1912 and that seated 25,000 persons at a time when big league clubs often played to capacity crowds of 10,000.

Washington Park held 12,000 persons with lots of overhanging seats on nearby buildings and Stengel, getting his first glimpse of New York, recalled how the tempo rose inning by inning, with the players of both teams caught in the middle:

"It cost 10 cents for a can of beer to sit up on the fire escape, and they didn't get real insulting until the beer had begun to take effect—in about the fourth inning. It was like playing for Harvard against Yale."

The ball players who were thus egged on were largely a breed that was perfectly suited for rough-and-tumble. The dominant player in the game was Cobb, the hellcat for the Detroit Tigers, who wound up with the highest career batting average in the game, .367, and who was so tough that the manager of the St. Louis Browns advised his players before Detroit came to town to "keep him in a good humor." The dominant manager was John J. McGraw, whose New York Giants won 10 pennants after he had ended his career as third-baseman for the famed Baltimore Orioles of the nineties, a defensive star so grim that Connie Mack later recalled the "horror" of advancing as far as third base.

The players were hungry, too. Hans Wagner held out one year for $10,000, but salaries rarely exceeded $6,000 in Stengel's first years. The great Christy Mathewson earned no more than $6,000 until his later years. Hal Chase, who played first base and also managed the Yankees in 1912, was paid $6,000 for both jobs.

As a result, the players tangled not only with each other but with the fans and the executives of the game, too. When the Polo Grounds burned in April 1911, the Giants shared the Yankees' Highlander Park for four months while their own park was being rebuilt and fitted with an upper deck. The Yankees thereupon switched to the new Polo Grounds along with the Giants, and the clubs reversed their landlord-tenant roles. But when they did, the Giants found it too much of a strain to adjust from a park that seated 12,000 persons to one that seated 32,000.

The strain showed when newspapers announced that crowds as high as 50,000 were attending the World Series that fall in the new Polo Grounds. The Giant players, whose share of the series revenue was based on the gate receipts, were incredulous at what they sensed was a "short count." After all, if 50,000 persons actually had crammed into the park, the "official capacity" of 32,000 was pretty obsolete.

So they dispatched a delegation led by Chief Meyers, a California mission Indian, to carry a protest to the National Commission, which presided over baseball then. To their amazement, the commissioners ranted right back at them and issued stern reprimands to the players for casting aspersions on the integrity of the game.

On the playing field, order was maintained precariously. Frederick G. Lieb, the baseball writer and historian, saw his first big league game as a boy in 1904 and watched one umpire call balls and strikes and "work" the bases as well, stationing himself behind the pitcher's mound and roaming as the action warranted.

By 1912, two umpires were being assigned to games, one working behind home plate and one on the baselines. They wore blue uniforms, as the teams of four umpires later did (six at World Series games), but they held no pre-game meeting at home plate and they helped hustle the players through games that rarely lasted more than two hours.

The players themselves were a trifle more civilized in appearance, if not in temper, than they had been during the more violent nineties. John Titus, right fielder for the Philadelphia Phillies, sported a stubbly blond mustache early in the century. Jake Beckley of the St. Louis club even displayed a bit of a handle-bar, contrasted with the full-flower handlebars that Wilbert Robinson and John McGraw and their cronies had grown 10 years before. The decline of the mustachioed ball player had set in, though Wally Schang, the catcher for the Philadelphia Athletics, grew a mustache as late as 1914 before shaving it off under mild duress.

Stengel, who was described by an eyewitness as "petulant, perhaps, truculent, maybe even bellicose," as a player, underwent a somewhat understandable change of heart on the subject of flamboyant players in his later years as a manager. When Frenchie Bordagaray appeared in Brooklyn in 1934 with a substantial mustache, Stengel fumed.

"Every time you get on base," he said, "I have asked the catchers in this league to throw the ball at your mustache. If they happen to kill you, I will pay the funeral expense."

Bordagaray removed the offending mustache, but it was by no means likely that he would have done so if the incident had occurred in 1912. Life was considerably more casual then. On the road, for example, the teams traveled around the 16 cities in the major leagues in Pullman car expeditions—one car for the writers accompanying the team and perhaps a second-string pitcher or two, and two cars for the team's regulars. Promptly after a game on "getaway day," the train would pull out of town, taking 20 hours or more from New York to Chicago, with occasional obnoxious variations like the "Owl Train" that left New York for Boston at midnight.

The players whiled away the hours by endless hands of poker or hearts or, much less frequently, bridge. No dice-rolling was permitted aboard, however. Many players sported peaked caps, though McGraw insisted that his Giants wear hats. One disadvantage of the trains, Stengel noted, was that they gave managers like Uncle Robbie "time to get sore after we'd lose a series, and he'd call me over and give me hell."

In most overt matters of public morals, the baseball clubs hewed a straight line. The only cities that permitted Sunday baseball were Chicago, Cincinnati and St. Louis. In the nineteen-twenties, Cleveland and Detroit acceded, along with New York, which received authorization from the Legislature through a bill sponsored by State Senator James J. Walker. The last holdouts, Philadelphia and Pittsburgh, did not capitulate until ten years later, though not for the loftiest of motives. In Pittsburgh, Barney Dreyfuss had often pointed out that Sunday baseball was dangerous because it was likely to kill the Saturday gate.

On other days of the week, ball games did not start until 3:15 in the afternoon or later, a holdover from the eighteen-eighties, when a starting time of 4 o'clock gave members of the Stock Exchange and other businessmen time to make it to the park after work.

Public recognition was just beginning to be accorded to the game in high places, in ways that would almost be taken for granted later. William Howard Taft was from a baseball-oriented family; his half-brother, Charles P. Taft, owned the Chicago Cubs and Mrs. Charles P. Taft owned the National League ball park in Philadelphia. The President was known to go out to the ball game when he was spending vacations back home in Cincinnati. When he consented to throw out the "first ball" on opening day in 1910, he erected an institution that has amused, sometimes annoyed, Presidents since then.

One other institution that was revered with almost total enthusiasm in 1912 was hazing, ignoring or insulting the "busher," the boy from the bush leagues, the rookie, the rube.

On the day Stengel joined the Dodgers, he was greeted only by Zack Wheat, an Indian from Missouri who, like Stengel, had been "discovered" by Larry Sutton and routed to Brooklyn through the Southern Association three years before. The other players in the clubhouse ignored him. So, Stengel put his best foot forward to break the barrier; he begged into the crap game that was at full tilt in the locker room before the Dodgers took the field. He was rattling the dice for his first roll when he felt a heavy hand on his shoulder. He turned and looked into the steady eyes of Bad Bill Dahlen, who had played for 20 years as a shortstop, who had earned the nickname because he had been ejected from so many games by umpires and who was now the manager of the Brooklyn ball club.

"Are you a crap-shooter or a ball player?" Dahlen asked.

"I guess I'm a ball player," Stengel said.

"Then get out there and shag some flies," Dahlen thundered.

A short time later, Stengel was astonished when Dahlen called to him and said: "You start in right field for me today."

So, a few hours after he had arrived by train from Montgomery, suitcase in hand, he was standing in right field for the Dodgers. Then he was batting against Claude Hendrix, the best pitcher on the Pittsburgh Pirates, the best in the National League that season with 24 victories and 9 defeats, and a spitball artist of the front rank.

Stengel singled his first time up, then the second, third and fourth times up, and he had the comforting total of four-for-four in his first major league game when he went to bat a fifth time and found that the Pirates had just switched to a left-handed pitcher named Hank Robinson. So, to the amazement of Dahlen, Wheat and the rest of the Dodgers—to say nothing of Robinson and the rest of the Pirates—the rookie from Kankakee turned around at the plate and batted right-handed.

"It was probably the only time I ever batted right-handed in the league," he said. "And I'd built such a reputation by that time that he walked me."

Stengel got into 16 other games for the Dodgers that September before the season ended, but his gaudy debut had made him a marked man. "I broke in with four hits and the writers promptly decided they had seen the new Ty Cobb," he recalled. "It took me only a few days to correct that impression."

He went to bat 53 other times in that first month, made 14 other hits, including a double and a home run, batted in 12 runs and finished with a batting average of .316. On defense, though, he made four errors, averaging one for every nine fly balls that he caught. But his reputation as a "fresh busher" who had made a flamboyant, almost insulting, start was secure.

In fact, his reputation preceded him to Chicago, where the Dodgers played a series against the Cubs and where Stengel would have his first nose-to-nose confrontation with one of the lions of the game, Johnny Evers. Evers, who had weighed 95 pounds in his first season in professional baseball, had matured to 135 by 1912 and still resembled a small child in a Chicago Cubs uniform, except for the fact that he carried himself with such authority and tenacity that he became known as "The Crab." He also became known as the youngest member of baseball's most legendary trio: Joe Tinker, Johnny Evers and Frank Chance.

Joe Tinker was a third-baseman from Muscotah, Kansas, who also could play shortstop. Johnny Evers was a shortstop from Troy, New York, who also could play second base, and did for most of his 1,776 games in the major leagues. Frank Chance was a catcher from Fresno, California, who had played at the University of Washington before joining the Cubs in 1898, converting to a first-baseman in 1901 and becoming manager in 1905.

They made their first double play on September 15, 1902; helped to make Chicago dominant in baseball for a decade; were so temperamental that Evers and Tinker ignored each other off the field for two years; were so sought-after that Evers was offered—and refused—$30,000 in cash and $15,000 a year for five years to desert to the "outlaw" Federal League, choosing to remain with the Cubs, who then traded him to Boston; and were so cohesive on the playing field that they were voted into the Baseball Hall of Fame as a unit. They also moved Franklin P. Adams to these lines:

> These are the saddest of possible words,
>   Tinker to Evers to Chance.
> Trio of Bear Cubs and fleeter than birds,
>   Tinker to Evers to Chance.
> Thoughtlessly pricking our gonfalon bubble,
> Making a Giant hit into a double,
> Words that are weighty with nothing but trouble,
>   Tinker to Evers to Chance.

Now the great Evers was at second base for the Chicago club when Stengel and the Dodgers arrived in September 1912, and Casey later described the unequal relationship between a rookie and a regular under the least provoking of circumstances.

"It was rougher then," he said, looking back on his hazing days. "Now, when a pitcher happens to get a ball close to a hitter, the hitter comes back to the bench and says, 'I think he was throwing at me.' Boys, when I broke in, you just knew they were throwing at you. The first month I was in the league, I spent three weeks on my back at the plate."

On the day he met the Cubs for the first time, he conceded, "they had me pretty scared at first, since I was just a busher and they were a lot of famous ball players. Jimmy Archer was catching and the first time I went up to hit he said to me: 'So you're Stengel, eh?' "

" 'Yes,' I said, 'I'm Stengel.' "

Then, Casey recalled, the conversation grew pointed.

"I see you broke in pretty good," Archer said.

"Yeah, pretty good," Stengel replied. "Four for four and stole a couple of bases."

"Well," said Archer, squatting behind the plate with an air of expectation, "when you get on there, let me see you run."

"Not today, Mr. Archer," Casey said politely. "I know you."

"But the last time up," he recalled years later, "I got on with two out and I had to run, and this Archer threw me out from here to there. But I wasn't giving up easy, so I rode in feet first to try to knock Johnny Evers out of the way. He tagged me and then, while I was still lying on my back, he bellowed at me: 'You fresh busher. The next time you come into me like that I'll stick the ball down your throat.'

"Up to then I was scared, but now I was mad. So I jumped up and bellowed right back at him. 'That's the way I slid in the bushes and that's the way I'll slide up here,' I said. 'My name is Stengel, Evers. Take a good look at me, because I'll be up here a long while.' "

Chapter

King of
The Grumblers

The two greatest influences on Casey Stengel's life in baseball after he arrived in the major leagues in September 1912, were Wilbert Robinson and John J. McGraw. They had played side by side for the old roughhouse Baltimore Orioles in the eighteen-nineties, Robinson a barrel-sized catcher with an enormous handle-bar mustache curling out from behind his face mask, and McGraw a demon third-baseman with the imperious stance, stride and spirit of a Little Napoleon, which was his nickname during his 42-year career.

When Robinson joined the Orioles in 1890, the year Stengel was born, the team belonged to the American Association, which was then caught in a giant pincers between the established National League and an interloper, the Players League. The following year, McGraw joined the Orioles—not yet 18 years old and, at 5-foot-7, an inch below Robinson's maximum height.

One year later, the Orioles stepped over the corpse of the American Association, which had just collapsed along with the Players League; switched to the surviving National League, and began to create baseball legends.

Besides McGraw and Robinson, the short dynamos who once made 10 hits between them in a game in 1892, the Orioles included Hughie Jennings, a red-haired, freckled-faced shortstop who batted .357 in 663 games before becoming manager of the Detroit Tigers and chief keeper of Ty Cobb during his most hellbent years; Wee Willie Keeler, 5 feet 4½ inches tall, a left-handed infielder who became an outfielder, hit .393 in 642 games and, swinging the lightest bat in baseball, used to "hit 'em where they ain't"; Dan Brouthers, 10 inches taller than Keeler and a .348 lifetime hitter who had hit three home runs in a single game in 1886, when home runs were rare; and Joe Corbett, the brother of the heavyweight champion, Gentleman Jim Corbett, who would have felt comfortably at home among the team's roughnecks.

The Baltimore Orioles wasted no time organizing the National League to their liking. They won the championship in 1894, 1895 and 1896, and five of their eight regulars eventually were elected to the Baseball Hall of Fame, including McGraw and Robinson.

When the American League was formed in 1901, the National League reacted by regrouping, pulling in its horns to meet the competition and raiding of a new baseball war. It reduced its franchises from 12 to eight, with Baltimore among the victims, though most of the Oriole stars were switched over to the Brooklyn Club. That is, except for McGraw and Robinson. They moved instead to St. Louis, but reappeared a year later back in Baltimore, which by then had just been awarded a franchise in the new American League.

McGraw now became the manager of the Orioles and Robinson his chief deputy as well as the team's catcher. The understanding was that the Orioles' wanderings would be ended when the American League engineered one more shift: the Baltimore club would move to New York, with McGraw as manager and the Giants of the National League as their combined target.

But McGraw shortly sensed that the scheme was about to be altered without his knowledge or approval. So he abruptly engineered a spectacular shift of his own: He left the Orioles in July and switched himself to New York as manager of the Giants.

Until he died in February 1934, he was the impresario of New York Giant baseball, winning 10 pennants and establishing a record that would stand until Stengel himself won 10 as manager of the Yankees. However, McGraw's defection to New York broke up his act with Robinson, who stayed behind in Baltimore, then broke a finger in 1904—an occupational catastrophe for a catcher—left baseball and finally opened a cafe, with McGraw as his absentee partner.

In 1911, McGraw revived their partnership on the baseball field by inviting Robinson to work with him as a coach of the Giants, who had won the pennant in 1904 and 1905 and were headed for another. Robinson accepted, and he was once more side by side with his old crony as the Giants won in 1911 and again in 1912 and 1913, Robinson coaching at first base and McGraw at third.

Then, on one play in the 1913 World Series against the Philadelphia Athletics, their friendship was shattered. A Giant runner was thrown out while trying to steal second base, McGraw loudly blamed Robinson for concocting the play, argued bitterly with him all day and most of the night and finally uttered the magic words, "You're fired."

Robinson thereupon switched to Brooklyn, their teams became blood rivals, the two old Orioles rarely spoke to each other for the next 30 years and they died six months apart in 1934.

When Casey Stengel arrived in Brooklyn late in 1912, the Dodger-Giant rivalry was already in flower, though McGraw and Robinson were still together on the Giants. But the 1913 season was approaching, putting them all on a kind of collision course. Brooklyn was scheduled to open the season against New York, the Dodgers were moving into a new park—Ebbets Field—and Stengel, a veteran of 17 big league games, was packing for the great day.

He went south to his first major league training camp that winter, to Augusta, Georgia, where the Dodgers were preparing for the 154-game season in a series of exhibition games. Spring training games were played chiefly against minor league clubs in the region, since travel was difficult and teams within the same league were discouraged from playing one another, at least until the policy was changed in the mid-twenties.

The great spring-training boom was just beginning in Florida that year, with the Chicago Cubs pitching their camp in Tampa, in a beach area on the Gulf of Mexico that would have as many as eight teams in training at one time half a century later. The New York Yankees showed the greatest flair, training that spring in Bermuda, moving in 1914 to Houston, in 1915 to Savannah and in 1916 to Macon.

Stengel had two things going for him that spring in Augusta: he had a reputation as a clever runner and he played right field in an outfield that also included Hy Myers in center and Zack Wheat in left. Myers and Wheat had professional experience and suitably off-beat personalities, providing a buffer in both respects for the shenanigans that the rookie left-hander was about to hatch during 12 seasons in the National League.

Casey also had a "caddie," a right-handed hitter named Jimmy Johnston, who took over right field for him frequently when a left-hander was pitching against the Dodgers—the theory being that when a left-handed pitcher throws to a left-handed batter, or a right-hander to a right-handed batter, the pitcher has a commanding advantage since he delivers from the batter's blind side and his curving pitches break away.

It was a theory that Stengel used to considerable advantage—and considerable criticism—as a manager with the Yankees later, the criticism being that he adhered to the strategy slavishly. But it was not one that he invented, and it did not keep him on the sidelines when the Dodgers went north in April 1913, to open the season in their new ball park in an exhibition series against the Yankees the weekend before the regular season started.

It was a gala, and somewhat bizarre, weekend. Frank Chance, the old double-play partner of Joe Tinker and Johnny Evers, was making his debut as manager of the Yankees, Ebbets Field had 25,000 seats, double the capacity of Washington Park, but it also had an unfinished playing surface with grass on the infield only and a solid "skin" of frozen dirt in the outfield.

So, when the inaugural game got under way and Stengel drove a ball between the Yankee outfielders, it skidded past them on the frozen ground, shot like a rocket to the deepest corner of the park and ricocheted around while the 22-year-old rookie ran around the bases for the first home run hit in Ebbets Field.

When the regular season opened two days later, Stengel was in right field, Nap Rucker was the pitcher and 25,000 persons again were in the new grandstand. The Giants had McGraw strutting in the dugout as manager, Christy Mathewson and Rube Marquard pitching, and four fast outfielders—Josh Devore, Fred Snodgrass, Red Jack Murray and Beals Becker—who had been instrumental in setting a record number of 347 stolen bases for the team the season before. The Giants also had won two straight pennants and were about to win a third. But the Dodgers had an inning or two that day—as they were to have on other days in their rivalry with the more affluent Giants—and won the first regular game in Ebbets Field, 3 to 2.

Stengel played in 123 other games that season, his first full one in the league. He went to bat 438 times, made 88 singles, 16 doubles, 8 triples and 7 home runs, batted in 44 runs, caught 270 fly balls, threw out 16 base runners, made 12 errors and batted .272. And the team finished sixth.

"I was fairly good at times," he said later, reviewing his first days in the big leagues with a kind of objectivity. "But a lot of people seem to remember some of the stunts I pulled better than they do the ball games I helped win."

One of the people who remembered some of his stunts better than the games he helped to win was Robinson, who was then 50 years old and only a semi-reformed stuntman himself. He made his appearance in Ebbets Field at the start of the 1914 season as manager of the Dodgers and also now as the sworn enemy of McGraw, who was presiding over the Polo Grounds across the East River a few miles north.

Uncle Robbie was still a broad-shouldered little man with a barrel shape, but without the handlebar mustache of the old Baltimore Oriole era in the nineties. He was given to atrocious malapropisms, like Stengel a quarter-century later, such as "Lumbago" for "Lombardi." He still prided himself on his background as a catcher, too, and this was shortly to make him the principal victim of an incident that became increasingly typical of his Dodgers' pranks, which in turn became increasingly attributed to his right fielder.

Stengel, during Robinson's first year in Brooklyn, had completed his transition from ignored "busher" to acknowledged regular, and was in fact well along toward becoming a clubhouse ringleader. He played in two more games than in the season before, 126, and though he went to bat 26 fewer times he made 11 more hits, batted in 12 more runs and added 44 points to his batting average, bringing it to .316, the same figure he had reached during his 17-game break-in month and the highest figure he would reach for a full season during the next 10 years.

The Dodgers, who had ranked seventh two years earlier and sixth the previous year, crept to fifth place.

Then it was the spring of 1915 and the Dodgers were headed for the first division of the league for the first time in 13 years since Ned Hanlon, already notorious as the late manager of the old Baltimore rowdies, had made it to second place. But the owner of the Dodgers, Charles Ebbets, was already expressing forebodings about the state of the world and later would "retrench" to align his ball club with the international situation, which was marked that year by the sinking of the British liner Lusitania by torpedoes, with 128 Americans and a thousand other persons as victims.

The "big stick" had already given way to "dollar diplomacy," which in turn had yielded to "watchful waiting." But while others watched and waited, Robinson's Dodgers nested in Daytona Beach and one spring day there appeared Ruth Law, the pioneer woman flier, puttering over the ball field in a biplane with flat sail-like wings supported by rods and wires, and there were the Superbas looking up and remembering that Gabby Street had recently caught a baseball dropped from the Washington Monument, and wondering if you could catch one dropped from an airplane.

Wheat and Stengel and the other clubhouse regulars were among those considering the problem and, Stengel said later, "we had this here Jack Coombs, a very brilliant man which could figure out the velocity of a baseball, and he would even know when people said which weighed more, a ton of feathers or a ton of steel, and he could tell you."

The experiment being so irresistible, and Coombs' calculations being regarded as inconclusive, it was decided to test the velocity theory directly. The team's trainer would climb in behind Ruth Law, fly over the field and release the ball while the "gloves" on the team would try to catch it. In the excitement —or, Robinson long suspected, in the evil machinations of Casey Stengel—a grapefruit was substituted for the baseball, and soon the biplane was chugging over and everybody was looking up at it.

"Uncle Robbie had a belly out like this," Stengel recalled, "and he was warming up this pitcher on the sidelines—we didn't have six coaches in those days. And this *aviatorix*—it was the first one they had—she flew over and dropped it. And Uncle Robbie saw it coming and waved everybody away like an outfielder and said, 'I've got it, I've got it.' And the thing kept coming closer and getting bigger.

"Robbie got under the grapefruit, thinking it was a baseball, which hit him right on this pitcher's glove he put on, and you know, the insides of it flew all over, seeds on his face and uniform, and flipped him back right over on his back. He lay there, looking like a ghost. Everybody came running up and everybody commenced laughing, all except Robbie, who got burned up. And six months later, we didn't have that trainer."

Robinson's tribulations were only beginning. Stengel was now the ordained ringleader of a clubhouse clique known as "the Grumblers," with a deputy named "Jeff" Pfeffer, a pitcher who had earned his nickname because of a rowdy resemblance to Jim Jeffries, the heavyweight champion. Stengel was bold and even pugnacious himself, and he led the Grumblers through a series of barroom adventures in 1915 and 1916 that kept the team's front office in a chronic state of anxiety.

One Sunday night they had somehow been inveigled into a brawl in Coney Island, there being no Sunday baseball then and, supposedly, no Sunday brawling. Ebbets had joined the Dodgers in 1890, had later taken control in 1898, had still later sold tickets outside his own ball park and finally had sold 50 per cent of his stock in 1913 to Stephen and Edward McKeever in order to build Ebbets Field. He tended to keep a close, baleful eye on details, and so the day after the fight he summoned Stengel and asked in exasperation:

"What kind of hoodlums do we have on this club, anyway?"

Stengel, with an air of injured respectability, replied: "No, Mr. Ebbets, we only had four beers," and he held up four fingers to illustrate. ("But," remarked Uncle Robbie, after Stengel had got off the hook with this bit of piousness, "they were as big as pails.")

For years after, the Grumblers were taunted around the league by other players who held up four fingers in a silent, mocking salute to their sobriety.

"I was always in a lot of damn trouble," Stengel acknowledged, looking back on his misadventures. "We didn't have any Landis in those days, and players used to give even the umpires hell."

He illustrated, giving full credit to the Dodgers' pitcher, Leon Cadore.

"Cadore was my room-mate," he said, "and he was an exceedingly handsome man which was very good at card tricks; he could hand you the jack of diamonds. And he said to me one night, 'I bet I can control an umpire.' So one night on a Pullman coach, he was showing us these card tricks and he had Bill Klem there, riding with us, and he told Klem he'd give him the nine of spades. And I was standing behind Klem and slipped it under his collar, Cadore was shuffling the cards and dealing them and he suddenly says, 'Look under your collar, Mr. Klem.' And in front of all these ball players—which Mr. Klem didn't like.

"Anyway, it didn't stop there. We had concrete walls then and you could scuff the ball pretty good. But Cadore used to stop between pitches in the game and I was the right fielder, and he'd look out toward right as if he was shifting me around, but he was just saying to me: 'Don't miss this one. Watch.' And then he'd wave his arms at the catcher as though he didn't get the sign, waving with one hand while scuffin' up the ball with the other, he was so slick. Between pitches, with one hand.

"Then he'd pitch, and for five innings he'd call every pitch himself as he was thrown' it. 'Strike one' and 'Strike two,' and finally Klem came out and stood between home plate and first and yelled at him: 'You don't call them on me, Cadore, damn it. I'll call the pitches here—you're not dealing me those card tricks now—so cut it out.' "

Stengel was undeterred from his pranks by the fact that the 1915 season developed into a personal decline for him on the ball field. He played in 132 games, missing only 22 in spite of the "platoon system," but his batting average plummeted 79 points to .237. By contrast, Ty Cobb batted .369 that year, so any resemblance between the two that might have been encouraged by Casey's 4-for-4 performance the day he arrived had long since been adjusted.

The Dodgers, though, responding to Uncle Robbie's insistent ambition to overtake McGraw and the Giants, advanced from fifth place to third. They now had crept almost imperceptibly from seventh place in 1911 to sixth two years later, when Stengel joined them; then fifth the next season, when Robinson joined them, and finally third in 1915.

They may have been gaining reputations as the foremost rascals in baseball, but they were winning games in a steady, almost mathematical, progression, too. They won only 58 and lost 95 at their low point in 1912, then won 65 the following year, then 75 and now 85.

Then it was 1916, and Wilbert Robinson was about to have his revenge on McGraw. How he accomplished this was a little vague, since the defending champion Philadelphia Phillies had another fine team led by Alex the Great, Grover Cleveland Alexander, the hard-drinking, hard-throwing Nebraskan who had won 28 games in his first season—more than any rookie in the twentieth century—and who won 30 or more games for three straight years, starting in 1915.

Boston and New York stayed near the top of the league, too, and the Giants even won 26 games in a row as the four clubs struggled through September. But the Dodgers won 94 games, lost 60 and ended the season in first place by 2½ games over the Phillies, with Boston third and the Giants fourth. McGraw angrily left the stadium during the final Giant-Dodger doubleheader, grousing: "I want no part of this," while his old crony Robinson accused him of trying to dilute the taste of Brooklyn's first World Series since 1900.

The Dodgers were actually not a particularly formidable team. Not as formidable, say, as they were after hours, when the Grumblers rode high. Robinson managed a team composed mainly of discards from other teams: Coombs from the Philadelphia Athletics of the American League; Mike Mowrey, the third-baseman, from Pittsburgh; Ivan Olson, the shortstop, from Cleveland; Larry Cheney, a pitcher, from Chicago, and Rube Marquard, Chief Meyers and Fred Merkle from the unloved Giants. The president of the National League, John K. Tener, surveyed the situation and remarked: "I never saw a club go into a series so willing to settle for the loser's end."

Still, the Dodgers had three of the most colorful outfielders in the game in Wheat, Hy Myers and Stengel, and Stengel had just redeemed himself somewhat during the season by adding 42 points to his batting average—making up half of the decline that had set in the season before. He finished at .279, with 8 home runs—only four below the leaders of both leagues—and 8 triples, 27 doubles and 53 runs batted in.

When the World Series opened in Boston on October 7, the feeling lingered that the Dodgers were slightly miscast. The feeling was intensified as the Red Sox, who had won the American League pennant for the second straight year, hit Marquard freely and took a 6-to-1 lead.

World Series games started at 3 o'clock then and often ended in semidarkness on chilly October afternoons. And, as the shadows began to fall and many in the crowd of 36,117 persons began to leave, the Dodgers, in their unpredictable way, came to life.

Jake Daubert, the team's captain, first-baseman and batting champion of the league two straight years, started the trouble by getting a base on balls.

"Charles Stengel," who was listed in semi-formality in the official record as the right fielder, hit a single. A walk to George Cutshaw loaded the bases, and then a Boston error, another walk and an infield single gave the Dodgers four runs. But they were stopped there when Everett Scott made a fine play at shortstop to cheat Daubert of a hit, while Charles Stengel knelt in the chalk circle in front of the dugout waiting to bat next.

The next time he batted was in the following game, two days later, and the Red Sox pitcher was the 21-year-old strong boy from Baltimore, Babe Ruth. Stengel was to meet Ruth in a World Series seven years later, after Ruth had ended his career as a left-handed pitcher who won 94 games, lost 46 and compiled a winning percentage of .671 that was almost as unassailable in its way as his lifetime batting average of .342 and the 714 home runs he hit as a left-handed batter.

Now, in the 1916 World Series, he was about to start a string of pitching 13 scoreless innings, adding 16 more two years later for a record of 29. He never lost a World Series game as a pitcher and, having won 23 games in the regular season that year, he wasn't about to lose the second game of the series against Robinson's Dodgers. In a drawn-out struggle that lasted 14 innings and that ended in the dark, Ruth outpitched Sherry Smith, 2 to 1. Smith had one consolation: at bat, the great Ruth got no hits in five times up, which was no small accomplishment. But now the Dodgers trailed, two games to none, and the series was slipping from their reach.

In fact, except for the third game, which the Dodgers won, 4 to 3, the series slipped from their reach without interruption. Boston won the fourth game, 6 to 2, and the fifth game, 4 to 1, and the only exceptional developments were Casey Stengel's batting average of .364 (four singles in eleven times at bat), making him No. 1 on the frustrated Brooklyn club, and two financial crises.

The first crisis arose when the series shifted from Boston to Brooklyn, and Ebbets quietly raised the prices of a grandstand seat from $3 to $5, and only 21,000 persons appeared. Exactly twice as many had paid to see the last game in Boston, and 20,000 persons had been left milling around outside the park.

Crisis No. 2 arose when the Brooklyn players met after the series and decided how their shares of the players' pool were to be divided. They promptly made a decision that was as unpopular as Ebbets' price scale. They allotted nothing to the coaches, locker-room staff and other attendants, but instead pocketed $2,834 each, a record share for a losing team in a World Series. The Red Sox players were each $3,910 richer, but everybody aimed their darts at the ungenerous Dodgers—from the president of the league, who had been critical, on down to the writers, who had been skeptical, and the fans, who had paid $5 apiece in Ebbets' grandstand caper and who now got their money's worth of comeback by berating his players for their "greed."

Their revenge became complete the following season, when the Dodgers made a spectacular plunge from first place to seventh, while two shadows began to fall across the club. One was the shadow of McGraw, whose Giants rebounded in 1917 as convincingly as the Dodgers declined. The other was the shadow of the war, which had begun to reach to the United States during the World Series the previous fall, when German U-boats roamed the near-Atlantic in packs and began picking off ships near Nantucket while the Dodgers struggled with the Red Sox in Boston.

So impressed was Ebbets by the approaching menaces of the war that he began to retrench even before his team went into the tailspin of 1917. The axe fell on Stengel, for one thing. Despite his mild heroics as the team's regular right fielder, batting leader in the World Series and foremost after-hours personality, his salary was cut by $2,600—almost the amount of his World Series bonus. In fact, he did not agree to the terms of his contract until March 28, just in time to join the Brooklyn-Red Sox Special as it left Hot Springs, Arkansas, at 1 o'clock in the afternoon, headed for Memphis and the next stop on the "World Series train," where it arrived eight hours later. And nine days later, the United States entered the war and Stengel entered his final season in Brooklyn.

If he thought that his relations with Ebbets had grown a bit strained, however, he was in for an even greater shock at the end of the season. It was a full season: 150 games and 549 times at bat, the fullest of his six seasons in Brooklyn. But it had depressions. Though he made 141 hits, his batting average slipped 22 points to .257, the Dodgers won 24 fewer games than the year before and only one club fared worse—Pittsburgh. And it was to Pittsburgh and to Barney Dreyfuss that Stengel was traded in January 1918.

The trade sent Stengel and George Cutshaw, the Brooklyn second-baseman, to Pittsburgh for Chuck Ward, an infielder, and two pitchers, Burleigh Grimes and Al Mamaux. It involved Casey in one of those riches-to-rags switches that he seemed addicted to throughout his 55 years in baseball. The riches had materialized in the Dodgers' grand march to the World Series; the rags now appeared even before he climbed into a Pittsburgh uniform for the first time. He immediately became embroiled with Dreyfuss in a long hassle over salary, did not sign his contract until just before the season opened and went out to right field with strong advance billing as the bête noire of Pittsburgh baseball.

First, though, a little score was to be settled with the faithful in Brooklyn, who had reacted in rage at the tight fists of the Grumblers and their clubhouse cronies. Stengel was still known variously as "Casey" or "Dutch" by most of the players, including his new teammates, though Bill McKechnie and a few others still preferred "Charley." But, by any name, he was undismayed when the Pirates paid their first call on Brooklyn in 1918 and in the last half of the first inning he trotted out to right field while the crowd whistled and hooted and called after him with the mixed affection and derision that followed him around the National League for 14 seasons.

The next inning, when he went to bat for the first time in Brooklyn in a Pittsburgh uniform, the catcalls reached a peak. In complete courtliness, he advanced to home plate, bowed deeply toward the grandstand, removed his cap—and out flew a sparrow. He had given them the bird.

Where did the bird come from? Tracking down any of his comic-opera plots could become as complex as trying to follow and solve Harry Houdini's sleight-of-hand, especially when Casey's own testimony was heard. Later he laughed and said that when he had taken his post in right field during the first inning, he had found the bird lying on the grass as though stunned, so he slipped it under his cap. Another time he acknowledged a little help from the bullpen, where, he said, "One of my buddies, Cadore, had found the bird and slipped it to me over the bullpen railing."

Wherever he acquired his menagerie on that occasion, and his elaborate changes of costume on others, Dreyfuss was no more amused than Kid Elberfeld had been over his disappearing act down the drainage-hole five years before. But Dreyfuss' trials were mercifully short. Stengel played in only 39 games with the Pirates before finding temporary refuge somewhere else, the Brooklyn Navy Yard, to be exact. But to reach that haven back in his old stomping grounds, he required an incident and a cause.

The incident arose the day after he had outraged the umpires by removing his Pittsburgh uniform shirt, offering it to one and suggesting impudently, "You try playing on our side for a while."

For this irreverence, he was fined $50 by the president of the National League, with the towering approval of his harassed owner, Dreyfuss. But the next day, Stengel found the "cause" that would deliver him from both the fine and Dreyfuss.

"I went down and enlisted in the Navy," he said. "I beat the league out of fifty bucks, but it wound up costing me seven hundred fifty in pay. They put me to work in the Navy Yard in Brooklyn, not far from the ball park; I was supposed to paint ships, they found out I could paint. But then one day this lieutenant commander walked in and said, 'You're the manager of the ball team.' "

So, for the rest of 1918, Barney's Bad Boy survived in a no-man's-land between the Western Front and Pittsburgh. He was safe from Dreyfuss, at least, and that was something. Then, turning his Machiavellian talents toward the job at hand, he contrived to win ball games with psychological twists that the Navy might have found useful in tactical situations.

"I used to board them ships," he said, "as soon as they got in, and make a date for a game the next day. I found if they'd been on land too long, we couldn't beat them."

He suffered one setback in brinkmanship—at the hands of a child—and it was recorded in magnificently exaggerated straight-faced language on September 1 by *The New York Times:*

> The astute police have been requested by Casey Stengel, one-time outfielder with the Brooklyn and Pittsburgh National League baseball teams, but now a toiler in a shipyard, to find the boy and the $50 which disappeared simultaneously yesterday from that part of Prospect Park where Mr. Stengel was practising baseball.

Stengel is captain of a shipyard nine, which is to play another shipyard nine today. He led his men into Prospect Park yesterday for a little necessary practice.

In the old days the man at the clubhouse used to look after Stengel's bankroll and bibelots. In the park yesterday, no other repository being available, he left his coat and wallet with a boy from the sidelines, who stepped forward and offered himself as custodian.

There the matter rests. There was $50 in the money sack. Boy and money were missing when the practice hour ended, and although Stengel has made all the traditional motions of informing the police, his expectation of ever glimpsing his cash again is exceedingly small.

He never did. But 48 years later, when he was reminded of an "incident" during his Navy days of 1918, he laughed and said without hesitation, but with a trace of admiration: "The kid and the fifty bucks. He was just a little kid on a bicycle, and when practice ended I can still see him riding away on that bike with my fifty."

The armistice of November 1918 meant no particular armistice between Stengel, who was now 28 and saucier than ever, and Dreyfuss, who was fully driven to the only way out for a sensitive soul who owns a bugbear. He sold him. Stengel actually had returned to Pittsburgh from his semi-comic Navy hitch in outstanding fettle. He raised his batting average 47 points to .293, hit 4 home runs, 10 triples, 10 doubles and 70 singles in 89 games and much to his relief—and Dreyfuss'—he was traded to Philadelphia in August of 1919 in a straight swap for another, though vastly more inhibited, outfielder named George Whitted.

"I was glad to get away from Pittsburgh," he confessed, "if for no other reason than that I wouldn't have to listen to a loud-mouthed guy in the right-field stand who used to holler at me every day: 'Hey, Casey. How's Big Bess?' "

And who was Big Bess? he was asked.

"I never found out," he said innocently.

However, life in Philadelphia was no joy, either. After six years of moving onward and upward with the Dodgers, he now was retreating steadily downhill—from the World Series in 1916, to seventh place with Brooklyn, fourth with Pittsburgh and now last with Philadelphia. Worse, the Phillies were a tattered bunch of miscast ball players who performed in a bandbox ball park while their manager watched and suffered. For six years, the Phillies ran either last or next to last in an eight-team league before rising to a tie for sixth place; but then they lapsed back to last place for three more years, as though caught in the act of something unethical.

"At that," Stengel recalled, "playing right field for the Phillies was the softest job in baseball. I had the wall behind me, the second baseman in front of me, the foul line on my left and Cy Williams on my right. The only time I had a chance to catch the ball was when it was hit right at me."

People who watched ball games in Philadelphia in 1920 and 1921 confirmed the stationary nature of playing right field for the Phillies, and more. Irish Meusel, the left fielder, was afflicted with a sore arm and couldn't throw; Stengel, the right fielder, was beginning to feel his legs growing unsteady at the age of 30, and couldn't run. That left Williams, the center fielder, who could do both, and so wherever Stengel and Meusel played, as they did together on the Giants a short time later, the cry was raised: "Hey, Cy, you take it."

The closing days of 1920, though, veered from mild nonsense of this sort to a more serious matter. The World Series of 1919 had been played between the heavily favored Chicago White Sox and the Cincinnati Reds, descendants of the first professional baseball club, who had finally made it to their first National League pennant. To considerable surprise, but with no great suspicion as yet, gamblers were seen openly, almost desperately, trying to get money down on the underdog Reds in the lobbies of Cincinnati hotels on the day the series opened.

The Reds immediately won the first two games. Chicago won the next, but Cincinnati won two more and took a 4-to-1 lead in games, five victories being required that year (and the next two) under a change in the 4-out-of-7 rule that had been initiated, ironically, to improve the financial return to the players in the series.

The White Sox rallied to win two more games, but were demolished in the final game, 10 to 5. With even greater irony, the White Sox players survived the rumors that began to circulate and became embroiled in a lively pennant race against the Yankees and Cleveland Indians with one week left in the following season before evidence was finally submitted to a grand jury in Chicago that the series had been fixed. Eight of the Chicago players were indicted.

The fact that one of them, Joe Jackson, had hit .375 while presumably living up to his part in the fix was only one of the farfetched developments that surrounded the case. Arnold Rothstein, foremost of the big bettors, testified in court that he had been offered a chance to underwrite the scheme but had declined the invitation. The grand jury's findings, including three confessions from ball players, were stolen from the District Attorney's office in Chicago. The White Sox, now being referred to as the Black Sox, still finished second to the Indians and ahead of the Yankees, although eight of their players were indicted in the waning hours of the season.

It wasn't until August 2, 1921, however, that a jury in Cook County reached a verdict—not guilty of criminal conspiracy. But a Federal judge, Kenesaw Mountain Landis, had been installed as the first Commissioner of Baseball on November 12, 1920, replacing the National Commission—one of whose members, Garry Herrmann, had simultaneously been president of the Cincinnati Reds and, as such, had found it difficult to accept the suspicion that his underdog ball club had won a tainted World Series.

Landis, who had been appointed to the Federal bench by Theodore Roosevelt and who was named for the Civil War battle at Kennesaw Mountain where his father had lost a leg, disregarded the jury's finding. He immediately issued a statement that said with remarkable idiom:

"Regardless of the verdict of juries, no player that throws a ball game, no player that entertains proposals or promises to throw a game, no player that sits in a conference with a bunch of crooked players and gamblers where the ways and means of throwing games are discussed, and does not promptly tell his club about it, will ever again play professional baseball."

None of the eight ever did. Judge Landis, though, required an accomplice to move baseball out from under the cloud, and by considerable luck he found one in Babe Ruth, who had pitched for the Boston Red Sox in the 1916 World Series against the Dodgers and who now was being sold to the New York Yankees for $525,000 in cash—$400,000 of which was considered a loan to help bail the Boston club owner, Harry Frazee, out of the financial narrows.

Ruth was worth the half-million to the Yankees' owner, Jacob Ruppert, and inestimably more to Landis because he had already displayed a great flair that had recaptured the public's interest in baseball: he hit home runs.

Stengel, who had been chafing with the Phillies during this strained period, had suffered a certain slowing down as an outfielder but none that was apparent as a clubhouse comic.

His talent for theatrics reached a zenith of sorts one spring afternoon in 1920 when the Phillies stopped in Fort Wayne, Indiana, for an exhibition game against the local team. At game time, Stengel was observed neither at the team's hotel nor at the ball park, and the Phillies, who had ranked eighth and last the season before, took the field without him but with a constant torrent of heckling from one corner of the grandstand. The heckling became louder and louder, and in the second inning was traced to a farmer type, dressed in country clothes, complete to bandana handkerchief and straw hat.

"You're a bunch of city dudes," he yelled to the Phillies, "and you're a bad apology for ball players."

One of the Philadelphia players sauntered over to the grandstand, looked toward the big-voiced heckler and said: "I guess you could play better."

"You bet I could," the hick shot back.

"Well," he was told, "come out and try."

So he came out and tried, and to the amazement of everybody—except the Phillies, who were in on the prank, and Casey Stengel, who had produced, directed and starred in it—the "rube" whacked the ball over the fence for a home run.

The "unknown marvel" of Fort Wayne actually played one of his better seasons with the Phillies, though it was one of his least happy ones. In 1920, he recovered from his detour in the Navy, played in 129 games, the most since 1917; batted in 50 runs and hit .292, with 90 singles, 25 doubles, 6 triples and 9 home runs, the most he hit in 14 seasons in the major leagues.

In 1921, however, the Phillies were securely in last place and Casey, who was 31 now, was suffering from a strained back. He was showing signs of becoming prone to knee and back injuries, in fact, and played in only 42 games the entire season. One day in July, it was raining hard in Philadelphia, the game had been postponed and the Phillies were back in the clubhouse changing into their street clothes. Jim Hagen, secretary of the club, went up to Stengel and handed him a note.

"Things had been pretty hot in the clubhouse that summer," Casey recalled, "and as I had been dressing next to Donovan, I had my locker moved into a little room off the dressing room where I couldn't hear old Bill rave. One day one of the players told him I was dressing in the little room after a game and he hadn't noticed it, I guess, so he said: 'He is, eh? Well, he'll be dressing farther away than that pretty soon.' I said to myself, 'Oh, oh, he's going to send me to Kalamazoo.'"

So when Hagen handed him the note, Casey guessed that he had had it. To his surprise, the note advised him that he and Johnny Rawlings had been traded to the lordly Giants for $75,000. Having grown suspicious of pranks in his long, distinguished career as a prankster, Stengel quietly placed a long-distance call to New York to confirm the "trade." It was no gag.

With a well-developed sense of the moment, and with great relief at putting Philadelphia behind him, he went to his locker and put on a clean Phillies uniform. Then he trotted out the runway onto the muddy field, looked up into the wet sky, put his head down and charged toward first base.

He reached the bag in a spectacular slide through the mud that sent water cascading into the air, then headed for second base, sliding in with another torrent of mud. At third base, he did the same, and at home plate he outdid himself, churning water and dirt high in the air and completing a flamboyant farewell to Philadelphia before 20,000 empty seats.

In the clubhouse, Donovan said simply: "You can settle your affairs around here tonight and leave tomorrow to join the Giants in Boston."

Casey's reaction, he said later, was: "Leave tomorrow? Boys, I was leaving right now. I caught the 6:14 from North Philadelphia for New York and the midnight out of New York for Boston. Rawlings waited over until the next day, but I wasn't taking any chances on the deal being called off."

From Boston, the Giants returned to New York, where Stengel appeared for the first time in a Giant uniform. He had played six seasons in Brooklyn under Uncle Robbie; but this was New York, and he was playing for Robbie's nemesis, John Joseph McGraw. He looked over the Polo Grounds when he arrived and said to himself: "Wake up, muscles! We're in New York now."

His muscles didn't actually have too much waking up to do that first half-season in New York. McGraw already had more muscles than he needed: Long George Kelley at first base; Rawlings, the expatriate from Philadelphia, at second; the talented youngster, Frankie Frisch, at third; Dave Bancroft at shortstop; Irish Meusel in left field; Georgie Burns in center, and Ross Youngs in right. Frank Snyder and Earl Smith were the catchers, while Art Nehf, Phil Douglas, Jesse Barnes and Fred Toney did most of the pitching.

Stengel mostly watched, but he watched a great show. The Phillies had been doomed tail-enders; the Giants were perennial contenders. They were 7½ games behind Pittsburgh on August 24, but in one spectacular series won five straight games from the Pirates and narrowed the gap to 2½ games. They closed it completely in September and won the pennant by four games.

An even more intriguing situation developed in the World Series, the first for the Giants since 1917 and the first for Stengel since Brooklyn's one year in the sun in 1916. The American League in 1921 was being treated to a spectacle that appealed to Judge Landis in his first year as commissioner following the Black Sox scandal and that thrilled the public to an extraordinary degree.

With Babe Ruth completing his transformation from a superior pitcher to a home-run hitter of record proportions, Yankee attendance leaped from 619,164 in 1919 to 1,289,422 the following year, and was keeping pace in 1921 as Ruth slugged the far-fetched total of 59 home runs.

Even in the hands of Frank "Home-Run" Baker, the home run had been a rare sight; in 1911, Baker won the American League leadership as a power hitter with 11 home runs. He hit 10 the next year and jumped all the way to 12 the year after that. When Ruth, in 1919, hit 29 for Boston, he surpassed all of the home-run hitters in the game, and in his first season with the Yankees, with Baker as a teammate, he hit 54 while Fred Williams of Philadelphia led the National League with 15.

The Yankees had finished third the year before, but now they outdistanced the defending champions, the Cleveland Indians, and won the first pennant in Yankee history—a history that would see them reaching the pinnacle of success in baseball by winning 29 pennants in the next 45 years.

The World Series, being the first between New York's two principal teams, was spiced by the fact that the Giants were the Yankees' landlord in the Polo Grounds, since Yankee Stadium was still two years away. It was also the last of the 5-out-of-9 series, and the Yankees got off to a fine start by winning the first two games by identical scores of 3 to 0, and winning the first game in exactly one hour and 38 minutes. The Giants, in fact, did not score a run until the third inning of the third game. But they scored four then and went on to win the game, 13 to 5.

No team had ever spotted an opponent two games in the 17 previous World Series and survived, let alone a club led by Babe Ruth. But somehow the Giants survived. They won the fourth game, 4 to 2, despite Ruth's first home run in a World Series, but lost the fifth, 3 to 1. Now the Yankees lost Ruth because of an abscess on his left elbow, and McGraw was never one to miss an opportunity like that. The Giants swept three straight games, 8 to 5, then 2 to 1, and finally 1 to 0.

Stengel took no part in the series, the first one that the Giants had won in 16 years, but he took part in the division of the spoils; $5,265 worth. And his muscles had already followed his call to wake up. He had hit .284 that first season in New York, then went fairly wild in 1922 by raising his average 84 points to the highest in his career: .368, with seven home runs and 48 runs batted in, though he appeared in only 84 games out of 154 with the well-stocked Giants.

"I never hit that high before," he said, "and I thought to myself, that's amazing. But I woke up on the last day of the season and found that Hornsby was leading the league 33 points higher."

Rogers Hornsby, whom Casey called the toughest right-handed batter he had seen, indeed was leading the league with an average of .401, so Casey was eclipsed in his finest hour. And worse, in the American League, George Sisler hit .420. The following year, Stengel outreached himself again, batting .339 in 75 games, but Hornsby again led the league with .384 while Harry Heilmann of Detroit hit .403 to lead both leagues.

Being part of McGraw's traveling circus, though, helped to make up for little frustrations like these. The Giants won the pennant again in 1922, with Cincinnati second and Pittsburgh and St. Louis tied for third. In the American League, the Yankees won over St. Louis, Detroit and Cleveland in that order.

Judge Landis decided that the series had wearied the public when forced to a decision in five games out of nine, so he restored the 4-out-of-7 rule. But it still proved dismally long for the Yankees. Ruth was finishing a relatively poor year in which he hit only .315 and had been ineligible to play until May 20 because he had gone barnstorming after the 1921 series against Landis' orders.

In the series, Ruth hit .118, while Stengel went to bat five times, got two singles and wound up batting .400. The Giants, meanwhile, swept all four games, though the Yankees salvaged a tie in the second game, with the umpires causing a storm of insults when the game was halted "because of darkness" with the score 3 to 3 in the 10th inning and the clock pointing to 4:40 p.m. in fairly broad daylight.

One of the high spots for Stengel came off the field, when Ruth and Bob Meusel barged into the Giants' locker room in fighting mood after the third game looking for Rawlings, the second baseman who had waited overnight in Philadelphia while Stengel high-tailed it to New York. The Giants were removing their coats to accept the challenge when McGraw entered the room and ordered Ruth and Meusel out.

Another high spot came in the next game, the fourth. Casey was sitting in the dugout this time, watching as his substitute, Bill Cunningham, played center field. Ruth hit a tremendous drive behind the monument near the bleacher wall, but Cunningham raced behind the slab and made a sensational catch.

This time, winning the series was worth $4,470 to each Giant. But the most significant result of the Yankees' defeat in four games was an argument it caused between the owners of the team, Colonel Jacob Ruppert and the magnificently named Colonel Tillinghast l' Hommedieu Huston, who was all for dispensing with Miller Huggins as manager of the Yankees.

Huston, who had been a contractor and engineer during the Spanish-American War, was already far along with plans for Yankee Stadium, which was opened the following year. But by then Ruppert had resolved the argument by simply buying him out.

Fate was about to play a perverse trick on Stengel, too. Having played only a minor role in the Giants' two consecutive successes over the Yankees, and having reached the advanced baseball age of 33, he suddenly was projected into the limelight in 1923 as the Yankees and Giants won their third straight pennants and faced each other for the third straight year—this time with the new Yankee Stadium ready for its prime tenant, George Herman Ruth.

Ruth had rebounded dramatically from his "off" year by hitting 41 home runs and batting in 131 runs, while the Yankees finished 16 games ahead of Detroit. But now, like star-crossed lovers, he and Stengel were headed for each other in the World Series—and Casey was headed for a "fairly amazing" surprise after the series.

As the series opened—the first one ever broadcast by radio, with Graham McNamee at the microphone and a record crowd of 55,307 in the new concrete stadium at 161st Street and River Avenue in the Bronx—Stengel went to right field not knowing two things: He was about to live the most memorable moment of his career as a ball player, but 30 days later his career as a Giant would abruptly end.

However, he had more on his mind that October than either Babe Ruth or the Yankees' new stadium. He, the "team bachelor," had met a girl, and her name was Edna.

Chapter

Edna

Edna Lawson was one of those fearsome combinations: beautiful but smart. She was a tall, willowy brunette accountant when she met Casey Stengel at a baseball game in 1923, and he was playing right field for John McGraw's Giants. They were married on August 18 the following year, and then Edna followed baseball teams around the circuits of a dozen leagues for 41 years while the fortunes of Casey and his teams fluctuated wildly.

Her thinking, though, never strayed far from their home at 1663 Grandview Avenue in Glendale, California, and she practically commuted from it to baseball games all over the country. So, whether the year was 1925 and Worcester was in third place in the Eastern League under a rookie manager or whether it was 1955 and the New York Yankees were in first place under a patriarch—the house, the palm trees, the swimming pool, the Oriental furnishings, the playhouse in the garden were all there awaiting the return of Charles Dillon Stengel.

It all started on a kind of blind date at the Polo Grounds. She had gone to the game with Mrs. Emil Meusel, the wife of the ball player best known as Irish Meusel, who in fact was of Alsatian descent and who had played with Stengel in Philadelphia as well as in New York. Casey was one of the few bachelors in the lineup—the "team bachelor," in some ways—and when McGraw removed him from the lineup in the seventh inning in order to send in Jimmy O'Connell for defensive purposes, he changed Stengel's life.

O'Connell was sent in because of "that fence," Edna said years later, referring to the difficult carom shots that bounced off the short right-field fence in the Polo Grounds and that made right field an obstacle course at times for a pair of legs as uncertain as Casey's had become. Anyway, when O'Connell went in, Stengel went out. He went straight to the clubhouse, showered, dressed and then appeared in the box-seat section reserved for the players' wives and guests, where Edna Lawson was sitting with Mrs. Meusel. All four went out to dinner after the game, and that was the beginning of that.

"Just think," he would say 40 years later, "if I hadn' been taken out of that game, Edna might've wound up with somebody else."

Edna, in fact, almost did wind up with somebody else, since she had an "understanding" at the time with a young doctor. But she wound up with Casey, and from the first day became the gyroscope of his life. He was already 34 years old and had led the life of a galloping nomad. But Edna wasted no time providing him with a base of operations that he never relinquished.

The base was in Glendale, where she had been raised while her father, a building contractor, had constructed some of the early movie sets, Glendale being one of the early capitals of silent films. As a schoolgirl in the seventh grade, she and her classmates would stop to watch scenes being shot while on their way home from school. Later, as an 18-year-old, she began to get into the act, so to speak, as did other people in the town who were being trotted in as extras.

"I was a good dancer," she recalled, "so they put me in western dance-hall scenes. Once I knocked over the whole set. Nobody made much money in those days. The most I ever got was 85 dollars a week. But I acted with Lillian Gish and Hoot Gibson and other stars. I guess I photographed well, but it wasn't for me."

In 1924, her father built something else, not far from the movie sets he used to build: a house. And Casey and Edna moved into it as a wedding present and settled down.

It was a big two-story house on a street lined with palm trees, a street that sloped upward to the foothills of the Sierras. And wherever Casey roamed around his acres for the next half-century—to the flower gardens, the tennis court, the pool out back, the orange and lemon trees—he could look over his shoulder and see a majestic gray mountain peak looming up a couple of miles away.

Better yet, wherever he roamed outside the acres—New York, Florida, Japan—he could know that Edna was worrying less about batting averages than about the windstorms that occasionally blew dust all over their living-room drapes.

The only thing missing was children, a fact that encouraged Casey to dote on teen-aged baseball players after he had become a manager or on the hordes of Edna's relatives who lived nearby. Her brother Jack and cousin Margaret lived in houses not far away, and "Uncle Casey" became the paterfamilias of a booming, traveling, enterprising clan of Lawsons.

Thriving, too. When Casey later invested in some oil-well properties along with Al Lopez, Randy Moore and several other baseball cronies, they literally struck oil and the cash started to flow. When Edna's family set up a bank in Glendale, more cash flowed. When they invested in real estate, they found Glendale expanding and their dividends multiplied, too.

The strength of the Stengels' life together, though, rested not so much on their taste for the good life, nor their increasing ability to finance it, nor the riot of adventure that they seemed to incite from the start; it was more the fact that each thought the other was a card, and each was right.

Casey, for example, liked to sit by his wife's elbow at home, in hotel lobbies, in railroad stations or in airport terminals and make impertinent asides as she described the windstorms, rainstorms and even forest fires that created household emergencies back in Glendale.

For one thing, Edna was a tireless interior decorator who always was remodeling the house into "Chinese rooms" and other exotic styles with imported Japanese beds and the like. For another thing, he could tweak her with the impunity of a man who fully appreciates a woman's business skill and often lets the world know it. After all, she had been a professional accountant and actress when they met, and she revived her skills later by managing apartment-house properties and serving as chairman of the board of the company that operated their bank's headquarters building.

"Tell 'em about the time you played with Hoot Gibson," he would say, interrupting her at a serious moment.

Or, while she was relating a plan to save both an insurance company and herself some money by caching the family silverware in the swimming pool to protect it from dust and fire, he would ask off the back of his hand in a stage whisper: "What good silver? Do we own any?"

He conceded, though, that an ill wind might blow some good in Glendale. He used to have a room in the house, he said, that was so flawless that Mrs. Stengel in exasperation finally gave it to "some relation." So now, he went on, he was stuck with a Chinese room and a Japanese bed, inspired by a baseball junket to the Far East.

"That Japanese bed of mine," he said, "the one that took two years to build—it had to be so perfect—I wish the storm would blow that thing away."

Edna was undismayed by his flippancy. "One advantage," she replied with a sly grin, "is that Casey doesn't have to look for his room any more. He just looks for the Chinese room."

Even during the baseball season when he would leave this California oasis for eight months, she would try to keep one foot in Glendale while following the baseball trail herself. One reason was that nobody could keep up Casey's whirlwind pace, anyway—up at dawn; meals taken on the run; long afternoons and, later, long evenings in stadiums; drinking with the Giants or Braves or Toledo Mudhens or "my writers" until 2 or 3 a.m.

Another reason was that her roots were deep in Glendale, and she simply liked it there. When the bank was established, she sold most of the stock for it and enlisted the most depositors. She also rang doorbells and made speeches to help her brother in his campaign for mayor of Glendale and, she said a trifle triumphantly, "of course he won."

When she finally would hit the baseball trails with Casey, though, she traveled in full plumage and rivaled him for energy and zest. She had a rich, smart, expensive wardrobe and the long, lean figure to go with it. She indulged herself in dramatically ornate hats. Her jewelry was usually glittering, and she was as vivacious and outspoken in a high voice as Casey was in a low voice.

But, whether at home or on the road, Edna was a tower of strength and a buffer shielding him from the world. She undertook to answer his stacks of fan mail, setting up a little office wherever they traveled and drafting replies to letters for him to sign, separating the autograph requests from mail that required information; getting him to sign baseballs that were sent to them, then repacking the baseballs and often paying the return postage; adding to their Christmas list, which grew into the thousands, and in general performing the work of a staff of secretaries and stenographers.

When the World Series became a regular part of their life—long after the 1923 World Series the first year they had met—Edna sifted through hundreds of requests for tickets, often from persons who simply put the bite on them or who were willing to pay if Casey could produce the seats.

One day there came a knock on the door of their suite in the Essex House in New York during a World Series, and she opened it to find a man and a 3-year-old boy standing outside. It would mean a lot, he said, for the boy to have a ticket to that game that day, so he had simply called for it. Edna forked over two tickets.

"I thought he was a friend of Casey's," she said later. "I assumed Casey had promised him tickets and he *was* just calling for them."

The confusion was understandable, since Casey tended to be as imprecise about the mechanics of some things as she was precise. One of his closest friends in baseball was Al Lopez, who was a catcher for 24 years and a highly successful manager at Cleveland and Chicago for 17. They were boon companions, and yet, Lopez recalled, "I don't ever remember getting a letter from Casey during all that time."

"We might not see each other for a year or so," he said, "and we would not write to each other. But we could always resume the conversation when we got around to it, without any loss of communication."

Besides this stream-of-consciousness quality of Stengel's friendship, Lopez detected one overriding characteristic of life with Casey: "He was warm. I mean, on the ball field, he had one great goal: to teach. But as a friend, he was simply warm."

The crevasse in his personality was noticeable to others, too. With ball players, he could be short, he could be brusque, he could even be mean. With "civilians" like his sister Louise, who lived alone in Kansas City in later years, he could be devoted to the point of doting. He would simply stop off at Kansas City en route from East Coast to West Coast and see that she was provided for. With a blind man brought to him in a ball park, he could be gentle to the point of letting his visitor run fingers over that great stone face in order to picture it and frame it in memory.

That is, he could be careless about the fringe details of friendship like writing letters; but he cared. He did not go to church as Edna did each Sunday, checking the schedule of masses and attending faithfully; but he was compassionate. She would worry about a meal; he would merely eat it.

In a word, Edna kept the books. She even preferred this type of administrative duty to some of the more prosaic household chores, like cooking.

"I never really liked to cook," she said, looking back on the early years of their marriage. "I was never what you would call a good cook. Oh, I could cook, all right; but not really well. And yet we always seemed to have great crowds of people around, so I'd have to cook. We'd plan a quiet Sunday at home, with maybe my brother or some other close member of the family, but before long other people would start to drop by the house. The Irish Meusels lived up the street and they would show up, and I might not even have enough to go around, really. Casey didn't mind; he loved crowds. But I worried."

Edna worried about other people's bookkeeping, too. Years after she and Casey had settled in Glendale, she expressed interest one day during spring training in the fact that this writer had a room with a kitchenette with a refrigerator in the Colonial Inn at St. Petersburg Beach.

"When do you defrost the refrigerator?" she asked, sensing a flaw in mid-sentence.

"When do I do what?" I asked.

"Defrost the icebox," she shot back. "Do you keep anything perishable in it? Oh, ice cream, oranges and things like that, eh. Well, I'll take care of that."

Bright and early the next morning, a knock at the door introduced the assistant housekeeper of the hotel, who announced: "Mrs. Stengel sent me. She told me to defrost your refrigerator, and to send your ice cream over to *her* refrigerator until yours is done."

The Stengels supplemented each other like Romeo and Juliet, all right. They liked to globe-trot and they liked little trips to Lake Tahoe and Las Vegas, which were within jaunting distance of Glendale. They liked good food and good drink and horse races, and they liked to eat pancakes—which they did at department store lunch counters. Best of all, they liked each other.

Edna also had an abiding no-nonsense attitude toward his reputation for nonsense, which was already well-established when they met in the Polo Grounds in 1923 and which flourished after that.

"He's not a clown," she would say with emphasis. "He's one of the smartest men in baseball, in business, in anything he'd try. He's given his life to baseball, and baseball owes Casey more than Casey owes baseball."

Later, when he was berated in The Saturday Evening Post as "an angry old man," Edna weighed in with this defense:

"I think I know the man better than almost anyone. I must say that Casey, to me and to my entire family—well, we have worshipped the ground the man walks on.

"When we go out to a restaurant, he walks behind me. He doesn't want any favors. He doesn't call ahead and say, 'This is Casey Stengel. I want a table.'

"The man has never said anything detrimental about any ball player he has managed. Never once did he begrudge anyone in baseball anything or come home and blame any outfielder, infielder or pitcher for losing a ball game.

"He used to say to me, 'Edna, can't you find a place in your business for this player?' He would have liked nothing better than to have ball players come home and stay with us so that he could work with them longer. He might bark and talk out loud, but 30 minutes later he would change.

"Why, Mickey Mantle has called Casey a second father to him. Each and every ball player has meant the best in life to Casey."

In pursuit of her hero, Edna led a kind of limited nomad's life away from Glendale herself. But she kept order wherever they went.

In New York, they customarily lived at the Essex House on Central Park South; in St. Petersburg, at the Soreno Hotel or the Colonial Inn on the beach in later years. She would join him in Florida in the spring, or would accompany him there, and they would share a double suite and keep house while he ran the ball club after he had advanced to managing. If the team opened the season in New York, she would accompany him there for the big day, but was likely to fly home to Glendale when Casey and the boys took to the road a week later.

Then, when they returned to New York, she would fly there for the two-week home stand, often timing her flight from Los Angeles to arrive in New York just as Casey was arriving from, say, Chicago. And they would have a transcontinental rendezvous at the airport, Edna sitting by chattering gaily with the coaches and players while Casey rooted around for his baggage.

Sometimes the exigencies of travel would put a bit of a strain on their relaxed relations. Once, when she was late for a chartered airplane that was transporting his Yankees to New York after a World Series game in Cincinnati, he gave the command to depart without her.

Another time, in March of 1964, his New York Mets spent a weekend in Mexico City on their first "intercontinental expedition" to play exhibition games. They flew from St. Petersburg to Miami, then to Mexico City, and after the weekend—which was a solid success at the box office—they headed back. Everybody was at the airport ready for the takeoff when a hitch developed: Mrs. Stengel, the manager's wife, had lost, misplaced or simply forgotten her exit visa. The airport official was inflexible on the subject and stood by rigidly while she searched her handbags and then her baggage. And while she did, the manager, vexed that the delay to his ball club was being caused by his own wife, quietly fumed.

A taxicab was dispatched back to the hotel and a search there was undertaken; still no visa. And as the manager fumed less quietly and the time passed, a tenseness settled over the party. When the visa was finally found, they took off for Miami, good and late and good and grim.

All the way to Miami, silence enveloped the "manager's seat" on the chartered airliner, where he sat side by side with her, letting her crimes sink in. All the way from Miami to Tampa Airport on the west coast of Florida, he let the silence grow thicker. Finally, they left the plane at Tampa and boarded a chartered bus for St. Petersburg, where the Mets were living, and as they got seated in the front row, the enormity of his response to her faux pas seemed to grow apparent to him. He relented.

"I'll check and see that your bags are okay," he said, breaking several hours of silence in a belated attempt to be solicitous and to make up for the exaggerated strain between them since the airport incident in Mexico. So, he hopped down the steps of the bus and disappeared toward the baggage-loading hatch to the rear. Ten minutes later he returned, trundled on board, sat alongside her and said, in an obvious but overplayed effort to make it up to her:

"Yeah, they're all right. They've got all three of them packed in."

Edna, given her "shot" at him after hours of suffering in silence, made the most of it. Tersely, evenly, unemotionally, yet triumphantly, she replied:

"I had four."

One thing that irritated Casey constantly was the fact that his comfort and wealth were taken for granted, carelessly and anonymously as though he had not labored mightily to achieve both.

"People always say I'm rich and the director of a bank," he said after he had reached a state of considerable affluence, "but they never say which bank."

Well, it was the Valley National Bank, with John E. Lawson chairman of the board and trustee of the Lawson Estate, and Charles D. "Casey" Stengel vice president. The main office was on North Brand Boulevard in the heart of Glendale, and Stengel could be reached there in the off-season through a telephone number with the appropriate exchange of POpular 6.

He wasn't exactly a captain of finance; seven years after it had opened in 1957, the bank listed deposits of 19 million dollars, and the following year edged closer to 22 million. But he was at least a lieutenant, and by September of 1964 the Valley National Bank had a "Toluca Lake Office" in North Hollywood and Casey donned a yellow helmet to break ground for a new main-bank building in a spacious lot adjoining the headquarters.

"We might even strike oil," he said as he dug a golden spade into the ground.

He was finishing his third season as manager of the Mets at that time and the team had just ended a weekend series in Los Angeles. Monday was an off-day, and while the rest of the team flew up to San Francisco to open a series with the Giants on Tuesday, Stengel peeled off to spend a day at home with Edna, their mementoes and their little business empire.

The ground-breaking was accomplished with full flourishes. Cameramen had been alerted, baseball writers traveling with the club had been invited and a small army of businessmen, contractors and relatives from Glendale stood by watching as Casey tried to turn a shovel-full of dirt alongside a cement parking lot.

Then the whole cavalcade drove off to a ceremonial luncheon at a restaurant, where Jack Lawson acted as master of ceremonies and Casey acted as Casey. Lead pencils shaped like little baseball bats were passed out along with matchbooks inscribed "Valley National Bank." Then Stengel packed a couple of dozen writers and friends into more cars for a guided tour of the area before leading the caravan to 1663 Grandview to spend the rest of his "off-day" with Edna in the big house at the foot of the mountain.

There, he climbed into what might best be described as an Oriental cabana outfit, and with a lordly sweep of his hand told his guests in a loud voice to "have a good time for yourselves." He settled into a chair on the manicured lawn alongside the swimming pool, not far from old grandstand seats from the Polo Grounds inscribed "Edna" and "Casey"; directed a band of caterers who soon arrived to set up a steak dinner for 40, and, a fugitive from the circus world of baseball for 24 hours, surrounded himself with the best of both worlds in his own backyard.

Inside the house, Edna cheerfully showed off the family heirlooms— gilded Louisville Slugger bats from each of the 10 Yankee teams that had won pennants, glasses monogrammed with the Yankee top hat symbol in red, white and blue, and hundreds of photographs.

"Look," she cried, as though discovering something, "here's one of Casey and King George."

Sure enough, there was Stengel the outfielder lined up shoulder to shoulder with his touring teammates and other ball players in the winter of 1924 while George V, magnificently bewhiskered and bearded, passed along the line shaking hands. Out of camera range that day stood Edna herself, a bride of three months taking a delayed honeymoon with a traveling baseball troupe.

At the ball park, Edna usually sat in the front-row box just to the right of the dugout, not 30 feet from Stengel as he waddled around in the pin-striped uniform with No. 37 printed across the back of the shirt. She did not keep "official" score for him, as Johnny Keane's wife did all during the years Keane managed in the minor and major leagues. But she paid strict attention, whether her companion was a close friend like Dorothy Heffner, the wife of the Met coach who later became manager of the Cincinnati Reds, or Joan W. Payson, principal owner of the Mets.

One night when Casey was running the Yankees, Edna's maid at the Essex House suggested that it might rain and that Mrs. Stengel might better wear rain gear to the game. Edna did, and walked into Yankee Stadium 30 minutes later under glowering clouds. Then she noticed "a lot of people and policemen around, down near the box behind the dugout on the first-base side." She guessed something was up. She was right. The Duke and Duchess of Windsor were soon escorted into her box, and for the rest of the cloudy evening the son of George V sat alongside the wife of the former outfielder, Casey Stengel—30 years later.

"They were great," Edna recalled. "They asked about the game, and the Duchess kept talking with me about it all the time."

"You know, she was from Baltimore," Edna concluded, establishing a good case for the Duchess on the odd chance that she might turn out to be a red-hot Oriole fan.

Casey's fortunes in baseball gyrated, but Mrs. Casey remained fairly stoical, even when the Yankee years were followed by the Met years. It was a little like going from knighthood to serfdom, but Edna was unruffled.

"The major difference," she said, "was that Casey and I used to have a reunion of our family during the World Series. We'd even have a formal dinner in the hotel for all our relatives and friends. But we adjusted to the Mets very well."

The final adjustment was made in the spring of 1965, his last as a major league manager.

First, Edna strained her back and had to stay home when he flew to St. Petersburg for spring training for the third week in February. Then, a week later, three young prowlers forced their way into the Stengels' home. She woke up and called the police, who arrived a few minutes later and arrested the intruders, but Edna had slipped getting out of bed to make the call and had injured her back again.

Finally, she flew to Florida two weeks later to join Casey, endured the 3,000-mile flight well, but was immediately racked with back pains when she landed, and spent most of the time in St. Petersburg in bed. Casey made a notable adjustment, too. He had been his old night-time self until then, conversing and drinking far into the night with his baseball friends. But when Edna arrived in distress, he stopped carousing with the boys, babied her for weeks and waited on her with the gallantry of a bridegroom.

Edna returned the devotion four months later when their baseball lives unexpectedly reached the turning point.

She was back home one week before his 75th birthday when he fell on July 25 and fractured his left hip. She still wasn't feeling too chipper herself and had intended to stay home until his birthday. But when George M. Weiss, president of the Mets, telephoned the news to her, she set out for New York.

She arrived the next night at 11:30 on a United Air Lines jet from Los Angeles. Dorothy Heffner, Harold Weissman, the Mets' public relations director, and I met her. She was worn out and half-sick herself, but she took time to thank the crew members who had looked after her during the five-hour flight. Then she walked down the long corridor at Kennedy Airport to Mrs. Heffner's car outside, posing for pictures on the way and even sitting in a phone booth as though chatting with Casey in the hospital.

It wasn't until they were getting into the car for the drive into Manhattan that she was told Casey would have an operation early the next morning, and it wasn't until then that she broke into tears.

"Oh, dear," she said, weeping freely, "do you think I'll get to see Casey before they take him in for the operation?"

She did get to see him, though he was under heavy sedation and was sleeping. But for months after, she spoke of one happy memory that night that outlived the apprehension and anxiety. He had told the nurse to ask Edna for three things: his electric razor, his toothbrush and the lump of clay he'd been using for his hand exercises to strengthen his right wrist, which he had broken at West Point two and a half months earlier.

One month later, when Casey made his farewell appearance at Shea Stadium, she was there in the familiar spot alongside him, dressed to the nines and proudly carrying his baseball shirt—No. 37—into retirement. Six weeks later, back home, she drove him to Dodger Stadium for the World Series, at which Casey was scheduled to throw out the first ball. She had two worries: whether there would be an elevator to take him up and down five flights to his seat, mending hip and all, and how to get an aspirin tablet into him to ease his pain. She finally disguised it in a Coca-Cola while he signed autographs, posed for pictures leaning on a cane and answered dozens of questions from radio reporters who lugged tape recorders into their dugout-level box.

That's the way life with Casey always had been, since the day they met at the Polo Grounds with Irish Meusel and his wife. Edna Lawson was chief of staff, financial wizard, homemaker and housekeeper, traveling companion, executive secretary, auditor of the family books and girl friend. In short, the woman behind the man behind the baseball team.

For their 40th wedding anniversary—August 18, 1964—they posed in a hansom cab in Central Park, she chucking him affectionately under the chin while he tried to look abashed. They had it reproduced in a golden tint and sent it out that December as a Christmas card to their mile-long list of friends, with the single word: "Joy."

That was the quality of their feeling for each other, beneath his crustiness and her smart energy. They liked each other, and the "rube" from Kankakee did not let her forget it for long after the day McGraw took him out of the game and into her life.

"They tell me," he said with an air of discovery one day after 40 years of marriage, "that your cream pie is very good."

Another time—a typically whirlwind day in St. Petersburg in the spring —he cut through the fanfare and noise that surrounded them all the time and put things in the perspective that had taken shape the day of the blind date in 1923. He popped his head out of the dugout at Al Lang Field and searched through the Mets' box, where Johnny Murphy, the club's vice president, sat with Lou Niss, the traveling secretary, and Bill Dickey, the old Yankee catcher who was batting consultant to the Mets. Casey seemed to be ticking off a crowded agenda in his mind, and then suddenly he found himself face to face with his wife, sitting in the front row.

He did a double take, without breaking stride, added her to the mental "agenda," pointed toward her and said: "And you want to see me when the season's over, right?"

Edna Lawson, perhaps thinking of those drapes covered with dust back in Glendale, nodded and smiled and said, "Right."

Chapter

5

This Is the Way Old Casey Ran

The Roaring Twenties had some of their most roaring moments in the Polo Grounds, at 155th Street and Eighth Avenue, in upper Manhattan. There, stock brokers, politicians, actors, Gibson Girls and mobsters would abandon the cares of the spiraling stock market and the escalating warfare of the Prohibition feuds for a few hours' fantasy in the home of John J. McGraw's Giants.

There, George M. Cohan would sit, untroubled and unmolested by his public, and watch the titans of New York baseball, the Giants, play the seven other teams in the National League. There, Ethel Barrymore, the prima donna of the grandstand, would observe carefully and intelligently, tracking the ball games on a scorecard as meticulously as the critics of the day would scrutinize her performances on stages downtown. There, Al Jolson would appear from a runway behind first base, dressed magnificently in the high fashion of the affluent of the theater, walk deliberately around the perimeter of the grandstand behind home plate, acknowledge the cheers and shouts of "Hi, Al," by clasping his hands over his head in a victory salute as though he were Jack Dempsey and had just knocked out Luis Firpo, and slowly make his way to a reserved seat behind third base.

Then, with perhaps 50,000 persons seated in this island alongside the Harlem River, famous umpires like Bill Klem would station themselves behind home plate and "the batteries for today's game" would be announced. The advent of radio broadcasts and public address systems relieved umpires of the duty of turning to the throng and bellowing this information, plus changes in the lineups during the game, such as "For New York, Lindstrom now playing third base." But as late as 1928, Klem maintained his role as narrator at least in spring training games, in Sarasota and other cities on the west coast of Florida, where major league teams had been exercising for 15 springs. And nearly 40 years later a professional waiter named Pat Pieper still sat on a camp chair near the screen behind home plate at Wrigley Field in Chicago, keeping track of the supply of new baseballs, often narrowly escaping foul balls that bounced off the screen and conferring with the umpires on pitching changes, which he would then announce to the crowd by a hand microphone in monosyllables that were often hard to decipher and that were sometimes several pitches late.

The Polo Grounds fans of the twenties would get their money's worth by direct participation, too. They kibitzed their heroes loudly, reserving special vocal effects for the more celebrated comics like Casey Stengel, who would be goaded into histrionics by good-natured booing no matter which team he happened to be playing for that season. Stengel always rose to the occasion, turning to the grandstand and bowing low with exaggerated courtesy.

Sometimes, he would make the afternoon exceptionally worthwhile by demonstrating his unusual talents for pugnacious behavior and, later, wounded sensitivity. In 1922, his first full season with the Giants, he experienced one of his better moments in both respects, in addition to exhibiting another peculiar talent: an ability to plague the team that had most recently traded him.

In this case, the visitors were his old, unlamented teammates, the Philadelphia Phillies. And for their appearance in the Polo Grounds, Stengel had preened himself with extreme care. "The full treatment," he had instructed the barber, and then he settled back for a haircut, shave, shampoo and double dose of hair tonic.

Right on schedule that afternoon, his well-groomed head became involved with the Phillies, who remembered his insultingly rapturous farewell to Philadelphia baseball the season before. Phil Weinert, the Philadelphia pitcher, let one of his fastballs fly straight toward the Stengel haircut, and Casey promptly hit the dirt. But he bounced back up with delighted fury, swinging away at Weinert. It was an exceptionally bruising fight, and the umpires finally were forced to send an SOS to the police to break it up.

At that point, Stengel's talent for wounded sensitivity took over, as he recalled later with some pleasure because he had spread the discomfort from Weinert to McGraw, the great reformed brawler of the Baltimore Orioles who now kept order on the Giants with piety as though brawling were tasteless.

"That will cost you 75 dollars," McGraw bellowed. "That fight was the dumbest thing I ever saw you do."

"But what could you expect," he added, wildly misjudging Stengel's pregame grooming rituals, "what could you expect from a cheap lout who comes to the park smelling like cheap gin."

When the baseball season ended, McGraw, Stengel and the rest of the denizens of the Polo Grounds sometimes put their violent little world on display for people across the country who suffered the double disadvantage of not living near the Giants' ball park and of not yet living in a time when television would bring the ball park to the country. They even put the show on the road in faraway places, earning themselves six weeks or so of globetrotting and introducing the "national game" to an international audience that a generation later would start to send Japanese, Cuban and Latin American ball players back to America in return.

McGraw, in fact, had organized the first overseas barnstorming tour in the winter of 1913-14. It was an ambitious project that featured the Giants and Chicago White Sox, and that carried them around the world. Eight months later, World War I started and baseball junkets were out of the question for several years. But, in 1922, a former ball player named Herb Hunter, who had visited Japan and had business contacts there, put the globetrotters back in business.

He organized an Oriental trip in the fall of 1922, starring half a dozen members of the Yankees and Giants, who had just met in the World Series—including Stengel, who had been a "busher" at the time of the first tour nine years earlier but who was now a veteran of 10 seasons in the National League and who was fresh from his famous tiff with Weinert.

They toured Korea, China and Japan, bringing Stengel into touch with Oriental styles that would find their way into his home 20 months later after he had met and married Edna Lawson. In fact, two winters later, in 1924, Edna accompanied him on another barnstorming trip, this time to England, Ireland and France, where he played baseball and met crowned heads of Europe like George V while Edna, who had been married to him during the baseball season that year, celebrated a delayed honeymoon.

Later, the trips abroad became more glamorous and more significant. In 1931, Frederick G. Lieb, the writer, directed a tour that lasted six weeks and that featured six players who later were elected to the Hall of Fame: Lou Gehrig of the New York Yankees, Rabbit Maranville of the Boston Braves, Frankie Frisch of the St. Louis Cardinals and Lefty Grove, Mickey Cochrane and Al Simmons of the Philadelphia Athletics. Lieb had been offered $25,000 for Babe Ruth's appearance with the company, but Ruth was committed elsewhere, though he did make it to Japan with Connie Mack in 1934.

Lieb's tour was a resounding success in promoting baseball and in promoting profits. The players generally got expense money and a free trip abroad, but Gehrig also collected $5,000 this time as a world-famous "name." In Japan alone, the team played 17 games before 450,000 persons. Professional baseball had not yet been organized in Japan, but baseball was already "the fall sport" the way football was in the United States, and the big leaguers had no trouble lining up Japanese college teams and an "All-Nippon" amateur team as opponents.

"They played a lot more baseball then in Japan than they did in the United States," Lieb recalled later. "We went to Yokohama one Sunday to see a Buddhist shrine, and the entire shoreline was choked with ball games, so crowded that the outfielders from one game would overlap with the fielders from another. And the roads were nearly clogged with ball players on bicycles going to games that were held in rapid sequence—one would follow another as soon as the diamond was clear. One day at 6 o'clock in the morning, we even saw bank clerks and other business men playing a game before they went to work—that's how baseball had taken hold in Japan."

Baseball became such a popular export, though, only after it had survived the Black Sox scandal of 1919 in America and had taken hold in the new stadiums like Ebbets Field, the rebuilt Polo Grounds and the Yankee Stadium in New York, with towering new personalities like Babe Ruth, Rogers Hornsby and Walter Johnson. And Stengel, who was 33 years old and who ran on unsteady legs in 1923, was about to live his most memorable moment as a player in a World Series that included the most towering personality of all, Ruth, and the stadium he had just "built."

The Giants had won two straight World Series over the Yankees, but now the worm was about to turn. The Yankees had swept through to the American League pennant by the runaway margin of 16 games over their nearest pursuer, the Detroit Tigers. Yankee Stadium had gotten off to a resounding start in its first year, and it was about to share the "first million-dollar World Series" with the Polo Grounds.

McGraw fired the opening salvo by outraging the Yankees' owner, Colonel Jacob Ruppert, the beer tycoon and National Guardsman, by refusing to allow the Yankees' prize rookie, Lou Gehrig, to play. McGraw's permission was needed because Gehrig had played the season at Hartford, Connecticut, and had been called up by the Yankees after September 1, the traditional cutoff date for eligibility in a World Series.

Properly piqued, the Yankees took the field October 10 with everything going for them—the new stadium, the goading of two straight defeats to the Giants, McGraw's "ungenerosity" on Gehrig and the booming bat of Babe Ruth. They also had Waite Hoyt on the pitcher's mound, but by the ninth inning Hoyt had been relieved by Joe Bush, the score was tied 4-4, and Casey Stengel—of all people—was coming to bat.

Stengel, batting left-handed, as usual, hit a line drive toward the opposite field over the head of the Yankee shortstop, Everett Scott, and between the left fielder, Bob Meusel, and the center fielder, Whitey Witt, who were pulled around toward right in normal defensive alignment against a left-handed hitter.

"I didn't think the ball was hit too hard," said Fred Lieb, who was covering the game in the press box, not far from where Graham McNamee's first broadcast of a World Series game was building to a fine crescendo. "It looked to me like a single."

But, with Witt shaded far over toward right field, the ball skipped through center field unmolested on two bounces and caromed off the fence 450 feet from home plate. Witt finally overhauled it and threw it to Meusel, who was chasing it, too. But a hundred yards away, old Casey Stengel was churning around the bases, amazed that his "single" had met clear sailing and excited that he might break the stalemate in the game and just plain worn out from all that running. Later, he recalled saying—or thinking—to himself, as the crowd of 55,307 followed him around the bases with roars: "Go legs, go; drive this boy around the bases."

Rounding third, he half-lost a shoe, but he staggered on anyway as Meusel fired a long relay to Scott and Scott fired on to home plate. Finally, as Wally Schang, the Yankee catcher, reached for the ball, Stengel, one shoe flopping and both feet dragging, pitched himself toward the plate, collapsing in a heap at Schang's feet.

Damon Runyon described the incident in these words:

> This is the way old Casey Stengel ran yesterday afternoon running his home run home.
>
> This is the way old Casey Stengel ran running his home run home to a Giant victory by a score of 5 to 4 in the first game of the World Series of 1923.
>
> This is the way old Casey Stengel ran running his home run home when two were out in the ninth inning and the score was tied, and the ball still bounding inside the Yankee yard.
>
> This is the way—
>
> His mouth wide open.
>
> His warped old legs bending beneath him at every stride.
>
> His arms flying back and forth like those of a man swimming with a crawl stroke.
>
> His flanks heaving, his breath whistling, his head far back. Yankee infielders, passed by Old Casey Stengel as he was running his home run home, say Casey was muttering to himself, adjuring himself to a greater speed as a jockey mutters to his horse in a race, saying, 'Go on, Casey, go on.'
>
> The warped old legs, twisted and bent by many a year of baseball campaigning, just barely held out under Casey until he reached the plate, running his home run home.
>
> Then they collapsed.

Anyway, he was safe with an inside-the-park home run, and the Giants now had a 5-to-4 lead over the Yankees that McGraw wisely protected by escorting Stengel to the bench and sitting him down while Bill Cunningham took over his defensive post in center field. The Giants held on, and Stengel was suddenly the toast of New York, though Edna Lawson's father, reading newspaper accounts of his wobbly dash around the bases, asked her:

"What kind of old man are you marrying? He looks as though he should be in an old man's home."

Two days later, however, Casey was back in center field and the series was back in Yankee Stadium after a one-day switch to the Polo Grounds. The Yankees had recovered their poise in the second game, as Herb Pennock pitched them to a victory over the Giants and Ruth trumped Stengel's open-ing-day ace by hitting two home runs—which was the story of Stengel's life.

But now, for the third game, a record baseball crowd of 62,430 filled Yankee Stadium and watched Sad Sam Jones shut out the Giants for six in-nings while Art Nehf was shutting out the Yankees for six. So, when Stengel advanced to the plate in the seventh, he found the score tied again as it had been 48 hours earlier and he found the entire Yankee bench hooting, catcall-ing and in general riding him for his theatrical performance in untying it.

This time, Stengel made certain that he would not have to undergo the torture of running the bases. He lifted one of Jones' pitches into the right-field bleachers for his second home run of the series, and having nothing better to occupy his thoughts as he plodded around the bases this time, he artfully thumbed his nose in the direction of the Yankees' new dugout.

"I made like a bee or fly was bothering me," he said, "so I kept rubbing the end of my nose, with my fingers pointing toward the Yankee dugout."

Ruppert, whose pitcher had allowed only four hits against six off the Giants' pitcher, was stung, not only by the final score of 1 to 0 and the way it had been decided, but by Stengel's impudent ounce of revenge in broad day-light. He indignantly told Landis, who was watching from a box seat, that Stengel had insulted players and fans alike.

"I heard about that in a hurry," Stengel recalled. "Commissioner Landis called me over and said he didn't like that kind of exhibition before 60,000 people, and he told me, 'If you do that again, I promise you one thing: You won't receive a dollar of your World Series share.' "

To emphasize the point, Landis fined Stengel $50 on the spot. But Stengel did not know at the time that the Judge also had refused sterner punishment and had put off the furious Ruppert by saying: "Well, Casey Stengel just can't help being Casey Stengel."

As things turned out, Babe Ruth just couldn't help being Babe Ruth, either. His bat was still booming after Stengel's two great moments had come and gone. Casey batted .407 in the series with two home runs, while Ruth hit .360 with three home runs, and the only two games the Giants won were won by Stengel's home runs. Ruth, though, belted one as late as the sixth game, by which time the Yankees had a secure lead in the series and were winning their first championship in an unmatched line of world championships in baseball.

The smart talk described the series as "four games for the Yankees, one for the Giants and two for Stengel." But Casey, upstaged in his finest hour by the king of the upstagers, said the score was "three for Ruth and two for Stengel." He even found that a contract he had signed during the series for a stand-up vaudeville skit was promptly topped by a much better one Ruth signed after the series. And the crowning indignity came when Casey was invited to dinner at the home of Bill Slocum, the writer, and later that evening was taken in to meet Slocum's young son, Frank, who 35 years later became an assistant to Ford Frick, the third Commissioner of Baseball. The little boy was sleeping but his father woke him up, assuring Stengel that he would be thrilled to meet a real live ball player especially one who had been so eminent in the World Series. But, Casey said years later, the tot knew his heroes. He rubbed his eyes sleepily, shook his head, blinked, looked at the craggy face of Charles Dillon Stengel and burst into angry tears, wailing, "I want to see Babe Ruth."

In spite of these little setbacks to his new fame, Stengel had reached a peak of sorts and had also pocketed $4,112 as the Giants' share of the series pie, while Ruth and the Yankees collected $6,143 each. But less than a month later he picked up *The New York Times* on November 13 and read:

> True to his promise to rebuild the Giants from the bottom up, Manager John J. McGraw last night engineered one of the biggest trades of his career. In exchange for Billy Southworth, outfielder, and Joe Oeschger, pitcher, of the Braves, the Giants' manager sent to Boston Shortstop Dave Bancroft and outfielders Casey Stengel and Bill Cunningham. Bancroft will become manager of Boston to succeed Fred Mitchell.

Years later, Stengel would reflect on the irony of the trade—coming just after his most flamboyant performance in a World Series, it made him more or less an extra added attraction in an exchange that really focused on Bancroft as a manager. "Nobody," said one observer of the trade, "regarded Stengel as a likely person to become a manager in those days."

The Times' account of the trade conveyed in full phrase the ornate language used by baseball owners even then to rationalize dealings that might have perplexed or angered their public. The report went on:

> Involving as it does the captains, Bancroft and Southworth, of two National League teams, the deal is the most sensational of recent baseball history. Bancroft is probably the leading shortstop in the game and Southworth is one of the best outfielders. Stengel, by winning two games single-handedly with home runs, was the great hero of the late World Series for the Giants. Cunningham is a coming outfielder, and Oeschger is the pitcher who won fame on May 1, 1920, by pitching the longest game in the history of baseball—a 26-inning contest to a 1 to 1 tie against Leon Cadore of the Brooklyn Robins.
>
> The deal was completed in the offices of the Giants at about 6:30 last night. Manager McGraw and President Charles A. Stoneham represented the Giants, and President Christy Mathewson and Judge Emil Fuchs, vice president, were present for the Boston club. Bancroft, who was first consulted to make sure that he was willing to become a major league manager, was also there when McGraw made his announcement to the newspapers.
>
> The Giants are giving up one of the best shortstops in baseball, if not the very best, but they are getting in return an outfielder who will effectively solve McGraw's outfield problem. With Meusel in left, Southworth probably in center and Youngs in right, the Giants will have an outer cordon vastly stronger than anything McGraw has had

in many years.

To fill the vacant shortstop position, McGraw said he would use Travis Jackson, the 20-year-old sensation from Little Rock, who made good overnight last summer.

Still, the Giants were trading away some of the permanent fixtures of their palmiest days in the Polo Grounds, and McGraw now undertook to defend, or at least to explain, the depth of his shake-up. His explanation, though, was couched in remarkable terms of piety, self-sacrifice and platitudes, and might be considered a prototype of the circular, almost devious, language that baseball officials lapsed into to explain why last season's demigods were next season's expendables.

"The New York Club," he said, softening his Little Napoleon tones, "realizes that in giving up Mr. Bancroft it is losing the best shortstop in baseball without a doubt. We have several reasons for making the sacrifice, the three particular ones being as follows:

"For the good of baseball and with the desire to do something big for my old friend Matty, and finally to give to Bancroft the opportunity which is due him to become a big league manager."

Having thus sacrificed his own pleasures for the good of baseball, his old friend Matty and finally, "Mr." Bancroft, McGraw turned to the other elements in the trade, including his World Series hero of a month earlier, plain old Casey Stengel.

"We also," he said, "have exchanged outfielders Cunningham and Stengel for Pitcher Oeschger of the Boston club."

That seemed to McGraw to cover the Stengel situation, and before anyone could delve more deeply into it, he waved the flag of past Giant glories even more hallowed than the 1923 World Series. He turned the forum over to Mathewson, the All-America boy of McGraw's early years with the Giants almost 20 years before.

"What do you want me to say?" Mathewson asked with a smile, and then, pointing to Bancroft, the only one of the expendables who had been invited, he said: "Here's my statement."

"And a good statement, too," chimed in McGraw patronizingly.

"Matty is the only man in baseball who could get Bancroft away from me," he went on smoothly, ignoring stern statements he had made after the Giants had lost the series to the effect that he would trade anybody on the club except Frankie Frisch, Ross Youngs and Travis Jackson, because on these young turks he was staking his chances for a fourth straight pennant.

The Times, at least, gave Stengel a measure of praise even if McGraw felt constrained to dust him off rather lightly.

"With Bancroft go two other prime favorites of Giant fans," it reported. "Except for Frank Frisch, Casey Stengel was the most popular and colorful of all the McGraw gladiators. After a career with Brooklyn, Pittsburgh and Philadelphia, the veteran, then a second-string outfielder, was thrown in as ballast in the deal that brought Johnny Rawlings to New York in June, 1921. After spending the rest of the season on the bench, the oldtimer was suddenly placed in the outfield in 1922 and came through with flying colors."

Flying colors, indeed. "It's lucky I didn't hit three home runs in three games in the series," Stengel remarked after being advised of the most sensational trade of recent baseball history, "or McGraw would've traded me to the Three-I League."

Then, in a letter to his longtime friend Long George Kelly, he wrote: "It's just as well. We were in two World Series while I was with the Giants and they gave us watches, rings, fobs, cuff links and necktie pins. If we win another, the only thing left to give us is earrings and old Casey would look great walking around with earrings bobbing out of those big sails of his, wouldn't he?"

Still, earrings or not, the switch from the Polo Grounds to Braves Field in Boston was a trip to the salt mines, and it meant as drastic a change in Stengel's day-to-day fortunes as his earlier trips from Brooklyn to Pittsburgh, Pittsburgh to Philadelphia and, in reverse, for a change, Philadelphia to New York. From a winner, he now went to a loser.

The Braves, who had made baseball history in 1914 by winning the pennant and World Series after standing last on July Fourth, had subsided since the "miracle team" days. While the Giants were winning three straight pennants between 1921 and 1923, Boston ranked fourth, eighth and seventh, and after McGraw traded Stengel and Bancroft to Boston, the Giants made it four straight pennants while Stengel and Bancroft promptly made it from first place in New York to the cellar in Boston.

So, when Stengel went south in February 1924 for the first time with the Braves, he left the heyday of New York baseball for good, as a player, at least, to the new generation of young men like Frisch, the Fordham graduate, "which has gone to college and is so smart." He also left the little luxuries of life with a winning team, as he discovered when he checked into the Braves' training camp at St. Petersburg, Florida, and was quartered in the Beverly Hotel.

What he discovered was Rube Marquard, Cotton Tierney and three other boys on the club, making six Braves in all in one hotel room, dormitory style. He later recalled how this communal style of life had contrasted with the calculated comfort of life with the Giants, even in little ways, like fighting for the bathroom the half-dozen shared.

"I had to give those guys the elbow," he said, as matter-of-factly as Custer discussing the demands of frontier survival. "Banny didn't want anybody late for morning practice, and I didn't want to be the one."

By the time the Braves had returned north and started the season, though, he had made the adjustment to the rigors of second division life and was in mid-season form, "with flying colors," as *The Times* chronicled on May 7:

> Casey Stengel, veteran outfielder of the Boston Braves, was fined $100 and suspended indefinitely yesterday by John A. Heydler, president of the National League, for disgraceful (sic) conduct in Monday's game with Brooklyn in Ebbets Field. Stengel was ejected from the

game by Umpire Jack Powell after a heated argument over the arbiter's decisions on strikes. Stengel defied the umpire for several minutes and took his regular post in right field until a threat that his action would forfeit the game persuaded him to depart.

Life in Boston offered one compensation besides the opportunity to raise a ruckus on visits to Brooklyn, where Stengel had raised his first ruckuses in the big leagues: Since the Braves were hurting for players, a 34-year-old outfielder with creaking legs was more likely to get into baseball games than he had been, say, in the Polo Grounds. So Stengel found himself in great demand in Boston, appearing in 131 games—more than he had played in any season since 1917 in his last year in Brooklyn. He hit .280, a decline of 59 points in one year and 88 in two years, with 5 home runs and 39 runs batted in. He also ran out half a dozen triples and 20 doubles—and except for one single in 12 games at the start of the following season, 1925, they were the last hits he ran out as a major league player.

On May 12 the next spring, *The New York Times,* under a headline that read, "Casey Stengel Buys The Worcester Club," reported from New Haven as follows:

> The Worcester Eastern League baseball club was sold today by A. H. Powell and G. H. Andrews of this city to Casey Stengel, the Boston National League outfielder, it was announced here tonight by J. Harmon Bronson of this city, who acted as agent for Powell. Stengel will be president of the club and playing manager, and will take charge of the Worcester organization on Friday. He will bring with him from the Braves the following players who have been awarded to the Worcester club through sale or option: Pitchers Batchelder, Muich and Ogrodowski; Outfielders Sperber and Wilson, Infielder Thomas and Catcher Cousineau. Eddie Eayrs, present manager of the Worcester club, and 3 players are likely to be disposed of.

Actually he was taking over Worcester as an agent for Boston, the parent club, but Charles Dillon Stengel had crossed a Great Divide—a divide greater than indicated in that paragraph. Though he played ball for Worcester in 1925 and for Toledo in 1926, 1927, 1928, 1929 and 1931, he ended a chapter of his professional life that May 12 as irrevocably as he had ended one the day 15 years earlier when he had put aside his frock coat, walked out the door of Western Dental College and headed for the ball park in Kankakee, Illinois. He might be listed afterward as a "playing-manager," even a "playing-manager-president." But he was out from under the shadow of more durable outfielders like Youngs and Meusel and of more "promising" managers like Bancroft, and he graduated almost imperceptibly into the small group of wheelers and dealers who hired, fired and exchanged baseball talent.

He even made the adjustment without changing too many of his stripes.

"He looked exactly the same as he did 35 years later," recalled Ken Smith, who was then a sports writer for *The Hartford Courant* and who later became director of the Baseball Hall of Fame. "The Eastern League was a good league, too. Lou Gehrig had played for Hartford two years before, and Leo Durocher was on the club then.

"I went by the bench one day when Worcester was playing in Hartford and asked him who was pitching and catching for him that day. It happened that he was going to use two guys with alliterative names—Wentz and Woock. And he made the most of it. He looked at me, raised his eyebrows and said, 'W-W-Wentz and W-W-Woock'—rolling his W's if you can roll a W."

Thirty years later, Smith reminded Stengel of that early meeting in both their careers, and Casey, brandishing his unusual memory for places, people and situations, recalled it in detail.

"Even his best friend might have reservations about Casey as a manager," Smith observed, analyzing the impact that Stengel began to have on the game in his new role in Worcester in 1925 and that continued for 40 years. "But he was one of those guys who mastered the details from the start. You know, one of those managers who watch the other team's batting practice. He was a marvel at manipulating player traffic."

He was also an unreconstructed marvel at getting into trouble, despite his new and presumably more dignified station in baseball life.

Just 29 days after becoming manager at Worcester, he was suspended as manager at Worcester. Not only that, but he dragged a rival manager along with him into limbo, probably setting an Eastern League record for provoking trouble. Stengel and Bill McCorry, the manager of the Albany team, were suspended, indefinitely, according to a straight-faced news report of the day from Albany, "as a result of their actions in the game here yesterday. Stengel threw a ball into the grandstand and McCorry threw a bat at a pitcher."

Still, Stengel found that even occasional frolics like this one did not relieve the tedium of playing 100 games in the outfield for Worcester, despite the rewards of a batting average of .320 plus 10 home runs, or of watching the team's 25 other games from the manager's perch in the dugout, despite the rewards of the club's third-place finish. He was simply too far from Broadway. But returning to Boston would be no solution, even if the Braves would countenance—and finance—such a move. He mulled the problem over briefly, then made a decision with characteristic mischief and, as things turned out, with characteristic results.

Reversing the unusual process that had made him president of the Boston farm club who had "hired" himself as a manager, who in turn had "hired" himself as a player, he simply released himself as an outfielder, fired himself as a manager and resigned as a president. Judge Fuchs of the parent team, observing the comic-opera scene from the club's sedate offices in Boston, was not amused. Later, though, he conceded the delicious irony of it all and joined in the applause and laughter that trailed his executive-clown as he left Boston and Worcester.

He was not between jobs very long, though his exit from the big leagues was now—temporarily-confirmed. The following spring, 1926, being a "free agent" for the first time since Larry Sutton had approached him in Aurora for the Dodgers 15 years earlier, he signed on as manager of the Toledo club of the American Association at the behest of his old friend McGraw, who owned the team and ran it as an adjunct of the Giants. Now he was back in the Middle West, he would spend six seasons in one place for the first time in his career, he would manage a baseball team to a league pennant for the first time and he would head back toward the major leagues again as an experienced field manager.

In fact, in his first season in Toledo, using players "sent down" from New York by McGraw, he made good almost immediately. He began to outdistance —outlive would be too strong a word—his reputation as a clown. He accepted "trouble" players from the major leagues. He directed them and molded them into a triple-A minor league team that for a time threatened to win a pennant in the American Association the first time around.

Bill Veeck, the imaginative genius who built the Cleveland Indians into a sensational money-maker in 18 months a generation later, and who liked to point out that his name rhymed with "wreck," was a boy of 10 when Stengel joined Toledo. Veeck's father was president of the Chicago Cubs, and Bill used to follow him around the circuit as he inspected the minor league holdings of the Cubs. "He was never necessarily the greatest of managers," Veeck Jr. said one spring day in 1966, reflecting on Stengel's career, "but any time he had a ball club that had a chance to win, he'd win."

He evidently got such a chance in his second season at Toledo, in 1927. His team won 101 games, lost 67, swept the pennant and defeated Buffalo, five games to one, in the "Little World Series," while Babe Ruth and "the greatest Yankee team" of all time in many views, were cementing the Yankees' dominance on the major leagues—the dominance that had begun to be asserted in Stengel's final season in New York with the Giants.

Stengel the manager had arrived, so to speak; but his "colors" as a troublemaker were still flying, as *The New York Times* observed on September 7 that season when the Toledo Mudhens came pounding down the homestretch of the season. The headlines said "Casey Stengel Suspended" (which may have become a stock head by then) and the story, under a Chicago dateline, said:

> Casey Stengel was suspended indefinitely by President Thomas J. Hickey as a result of an attack by the fans on Umpire Derr, following the first game of the Labor Day bill in Toledo with Columbus. Stengel, whose club has been on a losing streak, was charged with having incited the fans after the umpire had rendered a close decision at first base. Several hundred spectators rushed from the stands and attacked the umpire, who was forced to retreat in the dugout, where police reserves came to his rescue.

As gaudy as this incident appeared in cold print, Stengel had an even gaudier year two seasons later, when the Mudhens had slipped from first place to sixth and were in a headlong collapse to eighth.

On May 23, 1929, it was reported from Toledo: "Casey Stengel tonight surrendered to police when he learned that a fan with whom he had an altercation in the grandstand before today's game with Indianapolis had preferred a charge of assault and battery. The spectator charged that Stengel had struck him on the jaw during an argument over a ball that had been fouled into the stand during batting practice. The spectator was excluded from the park and his admission money refunded to him. Stengel was released on his own recognizance."

On July 7, 1929, from Columbus, Ohio: "POLICE RESCUE STENGEL. A near-riot of baseball fans was precipitated today when Manager Casey Stengel of the Toledo Mudhens rushed from his dugout and knocked down Third Baseman Boone of the Columbus American Association team. Stengel claimed that Boone had held McCurdy at the plate. Police quelled the crowd and escorted Stengel to the clubhouse and later to a taxi."

On July 13, 1929, from Chicago: "Casey Stengel, manager of the Toledo team, was reinstated today by order of President Thomas Hickey of the American Association. Stengel was suspended Monday for striking Third Baseman Lute Boone of Columbus during the Toledo-Senator game Saturday."

The *pièce de résistance* was a footnote to the above report, recalling in a kind of throwaway line that Stengel and Sammy Bohns of the Minneapolis club had been suspended after a "general fight" in the Fourth of July game at St. Paul, in addition to a "general fight" in the Seventh of July game at Columbus. "Near riots resulted from both encounters," it related, as though routinely summing up all the near-riots of the weekend in which Stengel might have had a hand.

Time was running out for Casey in one respect, though, despite his seeming durability as a main-event fighter on the ball diamond: His days as an active player were nearing an end. He played in only 20 games for Toledo in 1929, none in 1930 and two final ones in 1931 (he made two doubles and a single in eight times at bat). From then on, he would be either a coach, a manager or unemployed.

Already, though, he had begun to make a reputation—to say nothing of money—as a Trader Horn who operated at the highest minor league levels with one foot in the majors and one in the sticks. He was a natural judge of potential who could size up a dubious or marginal or troublesome player in the act of falling out of major league grace; then, as a manager, he could play a leading role in rehabilitating the refugee; and finally, as a front-office man, he could resell him back to the majors for new value in cash. It worked with untried players, too, and at Worcester and Toledo it worked to the tune of three-quarters of a million dollars. Part of Stengel's share of these profits went into stocks—the kind he advised his players to buy one day in Toledo because their impending trips to the bush leagues would profit the nation's railroads so heavily.

If horse sense was emerging as the dominant Stengel trait, some of it may have rubbed off from Allie Reuben, whose securities company helped local interests in Toledo to buy the club and the ball park, Swayne Field, from McGraw and who later became the owner of the Hasty House Farms. He also became one of Stengel's closest friends, and when the ball club finally buckled in the crash and went into receivership, Reuben was appointed Receiver.

"Mrs. Reuben and I persuaded Casey and Edna to move into the Park Lane Apartment Hotel in an apartment opposite ours," Reuben recalled, "and enjoyed their company greatly. Edna was sweet and understanding and always took a constant, deep interest in looking after his personal welfare."

One of the things that Edna did during those years in the minor leagues in looking after his personal welfare was to sit in direct line of fire between disgruntled fans and her man. As the Toledo club began declining after the opening days of instant success, the line of fire became withering.

"McGraw's brother was traveling secretary of the club," Edna said, looking back on life in Toledo, "and he suggested I sit in the bleachers to get away from the booing and noise around the dugout. But it didn't faze me."

Edna had good sporting blood at ball park or race track. She did not cry over spilled milk either then or during visits to race tracks that she and Casey made during their long friendship with the Reubens, who crossed their path in Chicago, Florida and other horse ports of call around the country. However, in the late twenties, Stengel was becoming concerned about gambles of a different type than baseball flesh or horse flesh.

The stock market crash in September 1929 and in subsequent months cost him much of his embryo fortune, which had been abetted by his wife's business sense and interests. But, with a base of operations securely rooted in Glendale and with a baseball reputation more securely rooted than ever after his 5-year term as a minor league manager, he was in business to stay. After all, Trader Horn was still at the crossroads looking for talent, as *The Times* reported on April 5, 1930, from Memphis, where the Giants were ending their spring training:

> This was another off day in their exhibition schedule, but John McGraw's boys found time hanging as heavy on their hands as the pick and shovel gang trying to get some rest at an army rest camp.
>
> With Mr. McGraw himself presiding as athletic director, severest critic and chief grounder-slapper, the Giants used Chickasaw Park for a training grounds again today. The practice lasted longer than yesterday's and also covered more ground, since the outfield had lost its resemblance to the Louisiana muskrat marshes and the outfielders were able to range far and wide for fly balls.
>
> In addition to Manager McGraw and the Bancroft-Meusel coaching system, the Giants had Casey Stengel to urge them on. Casey is Toledo's manager, and his presence symbolized to the Giants Toledo, to which point Giants are sometimes shipped. Often when a Giant felt like standing still on one spot long enough for a few deep breaths, the sight of Stengel looking in his direction was enough to send him sprinting after a fly.

The "ogre" from Toledo had a sharp eye, too. Ken Smith recalled that when he and Casey visited the Giants' camp at San Antonio the following spring, Stengel walked in, sighted a player he had never seen before and said on the spot, *"I'll take him right now."* The player was Hal Shumacher, who was soon en route to a career as one of the Giants' best pitchers of the nineteen-thirties.

It was only a matter of time before an ogre with sharp eyes and two decades of baseball experience would be called to work in a big league park again. The time came after Stengel's Mudhens had finished third in 1930 and eighth in 1931. The franchise was collapsing in the Depression but Stengel was rounding out seven seasons as a manager in the high minor leagues after 14 seasons as a player in the major leagues. He was ready for a big plunge. And the call came, as it had come on the fateful day in Montgomery 20 years earlier, from Brooklyn.

Chapter

6

Still
In the League

Western civilization may have had more unusual organizations than the Brooklyn Dodgers, but not too many spring to mind. They won the pennant in the interloping American Association in 1889, switched to the entrenched National League in 1890 as Club No. 26 and promptly embarrassed both leagues by winning the pennant over there. So, with the pennants—or streamers—of two rival leagues flying from the masthead, the Brooklyns embarked on a career in big-time baseball that made them instantly famous, frequently hilarious and almost always poverty-stricken.

In fact, the wife of the second owner of the club, Charles H. Ebbets, was reported to have taken in the team's laundry to save money, while Mr. Ebbets sold tickets to the ball games. It was a raggedy, rickity, rollicking baseball team that changed names almost as often as it changed uniforms, and for considerably less compelling reasons.

At the turn of the century, the Dodgers were known as the Bridegrooms, because the team's sizable bachelor corps had paraded to the altar almost en masse during the off-season. They became the Superbas because their manager, Ned Hanlon, ran a billiard academy on the side with the sensational name The Superba and he felt that if anything deserved the implied glories of such a name as the pool hall it must be the ball club. When Wilbert Robinson appeared as manager in 1914, they naturally became the Robins, though their long-lease nickname through all these changes had been Trolley Dodgers, in tribute to the terrifying maze of streetcars that crisscrossed Brooklyn. And even when the club migrated in 1957 to Los Angeles, where trolley cars presented nowhere near the threat that speedy automobiles did, the name Dodgers migrated along with it.

By whatever name, though, the Brooklyns developed baseball's outstanding talent for slapstick. Where other teams may have been accident-prone, they grew disaster-prone. It didn't matter who happened to own them—Charlie Ebbets, an amiable, worrying architect who sometimes went into bars and took a poll on who should pitch the next afternoon, or the Brooklyn Trust Company, which carried the club for years as a kind of irredeemable liability and which tried to ride out the Depression years later by requiring its board of directors to rule whenever the manager suggested spending $6,000 to meet the waiver price on a ball player being peddled by another club.

The Dodgers' ranged from Uncle Robbie, who had worn a handlebar mustache in the eighteen-nineties, to Stanley "Frenchie" Bordagaray 30 years later, who at various times owned a racehorse, a small black mustache and a Van Dyke beard.

They once boasted a pitcher named Clyde Day who came from Pea Ridge, Arkansas, delivered outstanding hog calls in public and even dived fully clothed into the fountain pool outside the Chase Hotel in St. Louis to win a bet.

They tended to be so bad on the playing field most seasons that it became commonplace for one wit to ask, "How are the Dodgers doin' today?" and for his straight man to reply, "Great, score tied in the sixth and three men on base." To which the sage responded: "Which base?"

So, all things considered, it was a marriage of exceptionally true minds on January 4, 1932, when Casey Stengel rejoined the Dodgers. He had entered the major leagues in 1912 by way of Brooklyn and, after 14 years as an active player with four teams and seven years as a player, coach and manager in the minor leagues, he re-entered the majors that day as a Dodger coach.

"Charles D. (Casey) Stengel, former Giants and Brooklyn star outfielder and in his playing days one of the most colorful figures in baseball," reported *The New York Times,* "has been engaged by the Robins to serve as head coach and first lieutenant to Manager Max Carey for the 1932 campaign.

"Stengel returns to the Brooklyn club exactly 20 years after making his major league debut in Flatbush. A fiery fellow with ever a talent for showmanship, he soon became a popular idol in Brooklyn and played a prominent part in the Robins' capture of the National League pennant in 1916.

"Subsequently he was cast adrift, but after serving a season in Pittsburgh and another in Philadelphia, he came to the Giants in 1921 to stage a sensational comeback for John McGraw, for whom he helped to win a pennant that year, as well as in the two seasons following.

"In all, Stengel appeared in four World Series, one with Brooklyn and the other three with the Giants, his outstanding achievement being a pair of home runs with which he brought down the Yankees in two games of the 1923 series. In 1924, though traded to Boston, he indirectly won a pennant for McGraw by beating the Robins in a 10-inning battle with a single with the bases filled. That defeat put the Robins out of the race and sent the Giants on to their fourth straight pennant."

The report, having established Stengel's unusual qualifications for rejoining the Dodger circus, which he had helped to establish in his earlier days, then cast a long shadow into the future.

"In 1926," it said, "Stengel went to Toledo as manager, winning a pennant in 1927 along with the 'little World Series' title and gaining wide renown not only for his ability in developing young players but in rehabilitating veterans whose major league playing days appeared to be over."

Since Brooklyn offered the greatest opportunities in baseball for a genius at rehabilitating broken-down ball players, Stengel's appearance on the scene amounted to a remarkable instance of the office seeking the man. He lost no time analyzing the situation in appropriate terms, either, saying: "We may lose more games than anybody, but we can out-drink anybody in the league."

Casey's departure from Toledo in the American Association had been dictated by the ravages of the Depression, which collapsed the Toledo management, and his transfer to Brooklyn had been arranged by Max Carey, his old sidekick at Pittsburgh, who was "the best base-stealer I ever saw," but who, unfortunately, could steal no bases for his wayward Dodgers as manager in 1932.

Still, with Stengel prowling the coaching lines, Carey goaded his club into third place that season while the Chicago Cubs won the National League pennant and the Giants, the arch-rivals from across the East River, finished sixth. But when the Giants shot up to first place the following year and the Dodgers subsided to sixth, Max Carey's hours as manager were numbered—and there in the middle of the debris stood his old admiring sidekick.

On the morning of February 23, 1934, Stengel was summoned to the New Yorker Hotel, stood at the bedside of J. A. Robert Quinn, business manager of the Dodgers, who had been as sick as the club, and, at 8 a.m., was handed a contract to replace Carey as manager. He signed it.

"The only unexpected feature of the whole affair," wrote Roscoe McGowen, "was the fact that Stengel was signed for two years, as Uncle Wilbert Robinson had only a one-year contract before he was dropped in 1931 and Carey also worked on a single-season basis."

Stephen W. McKeever, who was president of the Dodgers and chief keeper of the club's deficits, said that Stengel would be paid $12,000 a season. Then Stengel, five months short of his 44th birthday, stepped into another suite in the hotel to leave Quinn with his worries, stood before a swarm of newspapermen for two hours, accepted congratulations, fielded questions and basked in the opening moments of his new career as the manager of a major league baseball team.

He was not overpowered by the cheerless prospect of running the Dodgers. "Maybe this means that the Dodgers have gone in for the N.R.A.," he quipped in the best Will Rogers fashion. "You know, 'New Riot Act.' "

A few days later, he hied his club off to spring training at Orlando. He had an undistinguished infield of Sam Leslie, Tony Cuccinello, Lonnie Frey and Joe

Stripp, plus one "set" outfielder, Danny Taylor, and one pitcher of consequence, Van Lingle Mungo. It was, as he had acknowledged, a new riot act.

The "act" had its moments. Bill Terry, the manager of the Giants, provided one by needling Stengel in his opening days with a question of calculated
rhetoric: "Is Brooklyn still in the league?" And, sure enough, five months later
Brooklyn was still in the league and, though sunken in sixth place, stood
between the Giants and the St. Louis Cardinals, who went down to the final
two days of the season tied for first place.

To make matters worse for Terry, the Giants had led the league by six
games on Labor Day. But in the last hours of the season, they dropped six of
their final seven games to the Boston Braves, Philadelphia Phillies and
Dodgers—all timid souls who turned tiger at the right moment. Stengel's boys
completed the rout, reaching up from sixth place to knock the hated Giants
from first to second as the Cardinals, the Gashouse Gang of Frank Frisch,
roared on to win the pennant.

Mungo, the madcap right-hander with the humming fast ball, was all
business the first day, halting the Giants, 5 to 1. The next afternoon, the
Dodgers gave Casey a day to remember by overpowering the Giants again, this
time 8 to 5, and as the Giants fell from the top of the league, all hell broke
loose. Hordes of Brooklyn fans had stormed the Polo Grounds on that tumultuous afternoon, as Stengel paced the dugout and the third-base coaching box,
hoisting banners that taunted Terry with the words: "Yes, We're Still In The
League."

And when the game, and the season, ended a few hours later, they
swarmed onto the field, hoisted Stengel and Al Lopez onto their shoulders and
carried them off the field like triumphant Roman proconsuls. Even when
Stengel left the clubhouse later, he was besieged by his adoring public. Throngs
of cheering and shouting Brooklynites jammed into the subway with him
when he headed for home, trapped him jubilantly and kept him from getting
off at his station, until he rode to the end of the line and fled in joy—and relief.

Yes, the New Riot Act was still in the league, but just barely so. The
Dodgers carried the momentum into the following season, and struggled into
fifth place, but then receded to seventh in 1936, and their principal contribu-
tion to the American Way of Life lay somewhere between the Marx Brothers
and the Ringling Brothers.

One day, Frenchie Bordagaray, "the only player in the major leagues with
a mustache," and one of the blithe spirits of the game, managed to get to
second base against Chicago with Stengel's wondering approval. The customary stance of a base-runner leading off second is a tense crouch, from which he
can spring back to the safety of the base or leap toward third, if the opportunity arises. But not so Frenchie. He meandered toward third base a bit, then
stood waiting for the pitcher to get back to work, all the while amiably tap-
ping his foot in a pleasant rhythm. He promptly was picked off when the
pitcher wheeled and fired the ball to the shortstop, Billy Jurges.

Stengel roared from the dugout as though shot out of a cannon and began berating the second-base umpire in spades. But Bordagaray turned to his manager and insisted with the fine equanimity that, no, he actually had been tagged out. When they got back to the dugout, Stengel immediately turned his fire on Frenchie, who was sitting on the bench surveying the splendor of the afternoon. "I *saw* your foot on the bag," Casey thundered, "so how could Jurges tag you out?"

Bordagaray, without a care in the world, replied pleasantly: "It was this way, Case. I'm standing near second base doing a tap dance. I guess he just tagged me out between taps."

Actually, Casey wasn't too surprised by Bordagaray's unusual insouciance. In the spring of 1935, when he joined the Dodgers in Orlando for spring training, he had made an incredible splash for a rookie by trying to steal home with two outs in the ninth inning one day and the Dodgers trailing Detroit by one run. He was out, and Stengel approached him with awe after the game and asked: "Are you crazy?"

Frenchie, who evidently regarded the question as a compliment, replied: "You ain't seen nothing yet." It proved to be an understatement.

Bordagaray later went on to a distinguished career as a musician, performing on the washboard with the famous Mudcat Band of the St. Louis Cardinals alongside Bill McGee on the fiddle, Bob Weiland on the jug and Lon Warneke on the harmonica, while Pepper Martin directed the ensemble in clubhouse concerts.

"Another time," Stengel recounted later during a conversational review of life with the Dodgers, "we bought this here pitcher, George Earnshaw, for $7,500. And he was a good pitcher, but he hadn't been going so well. So the first day he was with us, I called him over and said, 'You pitch batting practice for the next 11 days.'

"Now, Earnshaw hit the ceiling, and he had pitched for Connie Mack in Philadelphia when they had Grove and were so good, and all those other guys like Cochrane and Foxx and Simmons. And he said to me, 'Batting practice for 11 days, the hell you say.' And I said, 'That's right, Mr. Earnshaw, you will pitch batting practice for 11 days. You're too good a pitcher to waste like this sitting around, and you'll see in a few days you'll be getting the ball in there.'

"So, sure enough, he commenced pitching batting practice and he was gettin' the ball over and he was so mad he could've fired it through a wall. And after he got in shape that way, I put him in one day against the St. Louis team, which had Frisch as a manager, and he struck out 11 of them. The only thing was, they got a couple of men on base and the batter hit one toward Bordagaray in the outfield and he tried to catch it down here. But the ball went right under his glove and everybody scored and they won, 4 to 2.

"Earnshaw was so mad at Bordagaray he chased after him in the clubhouse and wanted to beat on him, and there was hell to pay after pitchin' battin' practice for all those days, which would've turned out so well except for the guy with the mustache."

Besides Frenchie, the bane of Stengel's existence in Brooklyn was one outstandingly loud-mouthed fan who camped in the grandstand behind third base on many days and spent pleasurable afternoons raising the roof in stentorian tones, aiming a steady torrent of invective toward Stengel, who in addition to managing the team was still doubling as his own third-base coach.

"But it was all right," Casey said, sounding like Voltaire defending unto the death the right of his critics to torment him. "It was okay, he paid to get it." Still, he couldn't help marvel at the bellower's intractable view of the Stengel strategy, particularly when it involved the simple act of juggling the talents of a catcher like Babe Phelps, "which could hit the ball real good but wouldn't be too safe behind the bat as catcher until maybe the eighth or ninth inning and we were ahead."

One day, Casey started Phelps as the Dodgers' catcher and Phelps responded by hitting a home run with the bases loaded in the second inning. By the ninth inning, however, "he'd let in a bunch of runs and they caught us, so this guy behind third is hollering at me: 'If ya'd saved Phelps for the ninth, we wouldn't be in this mess.' "

Stengel, amused at the incongruity of the abuse, shook his head and marveled. "He's hollering at me," he said, "and this guy has batted in four runs already, which he forgot about by the ninth inning."

On another occasion in 1934, the famous Dean brothers—"me and Paul" —descended on Ebbets Field with the St. Louis Cardinals and throttled the Dodgers during both halves of a doubleheader. Dizzy opened the massacre by mowing down the Dodgers on exactly three hits. Then his younger brother Paul took over and mowed them down on exactly no hits.

Stengel, who had watched both games from the solitary splendor of the third-base coaching box, was walking toward the clubhouse after the Deans had finished their chores and chanced to run into Dizzy, who had dressed in his civilian clothes after the first game to watch Paul in action.

"Wasn't that something?" Diz whooped at him. But Casey just snorted and continued down the runway leading to the Dodgers' locker room. Then as the crowning indignity, the bane of his existence, the basso profundo of the grandstand, his constant heckler, leaned out of the seats along the passageway and yelled at Stengel:

"That's okay, Casey. You played a doubleheader today and didn't make one mistake."

"Yes," Casey recalled 30 years later, reviewing life with the Dodgers one rainy day in St. Petersburg, Florida, "I didn't see a base runner for 18 innings, so I *couldn't* make any mistakes."

It is true that during his tenure nobody took a telephone pole and battered their way into Ebbets Field through the center-field fence, as 500 fans had done one day in 1924 in a gallant effort to watch the heroes of Flatbush. Nor did any of Stengel's men simply disappear one night, as Boots Poffenberger did later, only to wind up in Maryland. Nor did a man perched on a window ledge of the Gotham Hotel in Manhattan reply, as one did in 1938 when urged not to jump but to spend a nice afternoon at a ball park watching the Dodgers: "I'd rather jump than watch the Dodgers."

However, the team was terrible enough for the board of directors not to want to watch it particularly, either. So, on October 3, 1936, just after the Dodgers had finished seventh and Stengel had finished his third season as a major league manager, a statement he had made three seasons before came back to haunt him: "Every one of the gentlemen directing this club wanted me to be the manager."

Now, every one of the gentlemen directing the club decided that they wanted him to be the ex-manager. So, on that October day, with the Yankees facing the Giants in the World Series, it was the Dodgers who stole the spotlight. One hour before the official announcement was distributed at World Series press headquarters at the Commodore Hotel in New York, Stengel was called into what he thought was a conference about some player exchange. But to his surprise—since his contract still had a year to run—he was advised by Jim Mulvey and Joe Gilleaudeau, two vice presidents of the Dodgers, that he was now an ex-manager.

Otto Miller, who had been a catcher on Brooklyn's last pennant-winning team in 1920, and Zach Taylor, also a catcher from the old days, were similarly released as coaches. But Casey was the only one of the trio with the remarkable distinction of being dropped and being paid for not managing a team at the height of a depression by a club that was hard pressed to pay even its people who worked.

"They told me the club hadn't done so well," he said. "It hadn't made much money. And they had decided unanimously to make a change. They didn't say who would follow me, though.

"But what I'm interested in now," he said, showing his chronic interest in the economics of any situation, "is the three-year contract into which I entered in good faith and the feeling that there was good faith on the other side. I've got a year to go on that, you know, and I'm going to be curious, not only about whether I'm to be paid off, but how."

The situation was loaded with pure Dodger irony. When Max Carey had been relieved in 1934, he still had a year to go on his contract as manager, and the Dodgers were just as penniless. But the board, fishing frantically for something that would attract paying customers, had decided to pay him for not managing while Stengel took the reins. After one season, Stengel had been called in by Steve McKeever, the club's president, and, with Mulvey and Gilleaudeau smiling their approval, had given him a new contract for three seasons—now that the club had fulfilled Max's contract and presumably had to worry about paying only one manager at a time. And McKeever had sealed the deal by saying: "Casey Stengel will manage the Brooklyn ball club as long as I have anything to say about it."

He still had something to say about it two years later, but evidently his resolve had weakened under the aimless wanderings of the club in the lower reaches of the National League and its blossoming reputation as the best horse-laugh in baseball.

Again—as when the Giants of 1923 shifted to a new generation of players like Travis Jackson and when the Toledo franchise wavered in 1931, spilling Stengel into Brooklyn—Casey was being engulfed by events pretty much beyond his control. A few weeks later, a new day would begin in Brooklyn baseball with the arrival of Leo Durocher, and 15 months later a new era would begin with the arrival of Larry MacPhail. The fact was that the club was in hock, and John Drebinger summarized the situation on November 5 as follows:

> The peremptory dismissal of Casey Stengel in the middle of the recent World Series almost took the play away from the contending Yankees and Giants.
>
> The very manner in which the Dodgers ousted Stengel a month ago took the wind right out of the sails of even the supposedly best-informed chroniclers. All sorts of wild rumors followed this, the most persistent being that the club was about to be sold and the new owners wanted the decks cleared to name their own manager. Most prominent among the supposed purchasers was Colonel T. L. Huston, who was reported to be heading a syndicate which planned to install Babe Ruth as manager.
>
> Others mentioned as possible successors to Stengel include Dutch Reuther and Zach Wheat, also former Brooklyn favorites, as well as Max Carey, who in the spring of 1934 suffered a fate similar to that which befell Stengel by being dropped with a year of his contract to run.
>
> In baseball circles, however, it is being accepted as a foregone conclusion that the new pilot will be Burleigh Grimes, veteran spitball pitcher and onetime Dodger ace who closed his active major league career in 1934 and spent last summer managing the Louisville Colonels in the American Association.

He was right. Burleigh Grimes, the old spitball pitcher, did succeed Stengel as manager and chief sufferer of the Dodgers' unpredictable shenanigans on the field. However, Colonel Huston, the onetime partner of Colonel Ruppert as owner of the Yankees, did not reappear with a syndicate of purchasers. Mac-Phail did, and showed his class by immediately borrowing $50,000 from the harried board of directors to buy a first-baseman, Dolph Camilli of the Phillies. Babe Ruth arrived, but not as manager. He became a coach in 1938 and helped to draw attention to the "new" Dodgers, but even the Babe was overtaken by events in Flatbush. It was Durocher who became the manager after Grimes had sweated and fretted through two seasons, and then the Dodgers began to do something they had rarely done from the time that Stengel arrived as a rookie player in 1912 to the time he arrived as a rookie manager in 1934 and to the time he departed—for good—in 1936: succeed.

As Stengel left, he received the answers to the two questions that had been troubling him. He was paid, all right, for not managing in 1937; and he was paid, as before, by regular checks, which he accepted happily and put to use immediately.

With Casey gone from Brooklyn, the Dodgers fired a final salute in his direction: they showed the world that they could finish in the second division just as hopelessly without him as they had with him. They ran sixth in 1937 under Grimes, while the Giants and Yankees ground out their second straight pennants, with the Yankees emerging into their post-Ruth, or Joe DiMaggio, era.

As for Stengel, he spent 1937 in a flamboyant display of his immense talent for making the best out of a royal mess. He was in the somewhat precarious position of being out of it all, after three fairly unsuccessful seasons with a loser. Instead, though, he settled back and enjoyed himself. He commuted on a reasonably regular basis between Glendale, where he basked in the sunshine, and Brooklyn, where he would deposit himself in the grandstand of the stadium, which was mortgaged half a million dollars' worth. Then treating himself to several bags of peanuts, and having nothing better to do, he would establish himself several rows from his successor's roost in the dugout and watch a ball game.

Some people thought Casey made his excursions to Brooklyn simply to irritate the management that had recently humiliated him. But it was more likely that he was just combining his outstanding talents: a zest for mischief; a need to be near the center of a hurricane; a longing for baseball, the only professional activity that interested him absorbingly; and an unmatched ability to land on his feet when dropped from high places.

He exhibited this last talent, as well as a remarkable Midas touch, by taking the Dodgers' $15,000 that season and, besides investing some of it in peanuts at the ball games, investing much of it in oil. It proved a deal of handsome proportions, even for someone like Stengel who was addicted to grandiose schemes.

The contact was Randy Moore, a former outfielder who had some in-laws drilling for oil near the little town of Omaha, Texas, and who let some of his old baseball cronies in on a good thing. Stengel, with Dodger money freshly in hand, lined up along with Al Lopez, his catcher and confidant; Johnny Cooney, an outfielder for the Dodgers; a pitcher named Watson Clark, and one or two other players. They literally struck oil, and so, while Stengel collected his checks during that idle summer of 1937 from a team that owed $1,200,000, his fortune was being made 2,000 miles away (though the Dodgers kept sending his salary checks by mistake to a bank in Omaha, Nebraska). And in a few years, that money in turn would be invested in California real estate, and ultimately the Valley National Bank would rise in Glendale with Edna's family in control and with a likeness of Stengel's stooped figure carved into the front doors and with his imprint all over the place.

The baseball scene that Casey surveyed from the grandstand of Ebbets Field that season, though, was changing fundamentally.

The excitement that Ruth had imparted in the early 1920s had rescued the game from a decline that was inevitable after the Black Sox scandal of 1919. Now, a generation later, baseball turned to other things to last out the Depression and to prepare itself, financially, at least, for an international crisis that was already spiraling.

Ruth hit his last home run in the major leagues in 1935, but he was in the position of an Old Master whose work survives him many times over. In 1927, at his peak, he hit 60 of the 920 home runs in the big leagues; in 1935, he hit 6 out of 1,325. A whole generation of "sluggers," as the big-batsmen were called, would be compared to the Master: Lou Gehrig, Jimmy Foxx, Hank Greenberg, Joe DiMaggio and Ted Williams in the American League, and Mel Ott, Johnny Mize and Joe Medwick in the National. Great new pitchers like Carl Hubbell, Lefty Gomez, the Dean brothers and Red Ruffing began to succeed Lefty Grove, Waite Hoyt and Dazzy Vance. Teams like the Yankees had reached the million mark in attendance in 1920 with the advent of Ruth and had played before a million or more persons in eight other seasons since then, and in 1937 were still drawing 998,148 persons at home.

The Yankees paid a lot of bills by drawing big on the road, too, but the pattern of success was irregular, and teams like the Cincinnati Reds, the original professional baseball team, drew only 411,225 in 1937. But even they were already adopting revolutionary new gimmicks to get people besides Casey Stengel out to the ball park.

In 1933, the major leagues had played their first All-Star game, asking the fans to elect the best performers, then pitting the best of the American League against the best of the National League. The inaugural game was played in Chicago in 1933, with 49,200 customers present, with the American League winning, 4 to 2, and with Ruth, naturally, hitting a home run.

In 1935, the first big league game was played at night, with Larry Mac-Phail throwing the switch in Crosley Field, Cincinnati, with the Philadelphia Phillies and Reds the opposing teams and a capacity crowd of 30,000 in the seats. In 1938, MacPhail, who was by then running the show for the Dodgers, introduced night baseball to New York after buying $72,000 worth of lighting equipment from the General Electric Company—on the cuff. Undaunted by the enormity of his own thinking, he staged a carnival on the night of June 15, with the Dodgers playing his old team, the Reds, and with Jesse Owens, the Olympic sprinter, racing several ballplayers. Then, as the *pièce de résistance,* when the game finally started, the Reds' young left-hander, Johnny Vander Meer, who had pitched a no-hit, no-run game four days earlier, pitched another.

Ladies Day was becoming a runaway success, too. It flowered most riotously, as might be expected, in Brooklyn, where two men were arrested one afternoon for trying to take advantage of the new promotional generosity by disguising themselves as women and getting by for just the tax. Another man brought suit against the Dodgers, alleging that he had been trampled in a Ladies Day rush. But in spite of diversions like these, Ladies Day began to interest wives in what was going on inside the fences of baseball parks, and when this interest was stoked by daily radio broadcasts of the games—especially when MacPhail installed Red Barber behind a microphone in Ebbets Field in 1939—Ethel Barrymore and other hard-core lady fans began to have a lot of company in the grandstand on those summer afternoons.

Things were going so well at this time, too, for Charles Dillon Stengel, the financial investor and former manager, that he even considered severing his ties to baseball to enter the oil business. But the petroleum industry was spared that revolution when Bob Quinn, who had been business manager of the Dodgers during Casey's tenure in the dugout and had gone on to Boston in 1935 as president of the Braves (or Bees, as they were called for a time), suddenly offered him the job as manager at Boston. The offer came in October, as soon as his idle season ended. It was no outstanding favor, since the Braves had been right down there with the Dodgers, running eighth, sixth and fifth the previous three years after not finishing higher than fourth in 20 years.

Casey, mercurial as ever at the age of 47, promptly accepted, ended his year in exile and headed for Boston. He succeeded his old friend, Bill McKechnie, stayed six seasons, finished fifth one year and seventh four straight years, and was saved from the worst standing in the league only because Philadelphia ran a colossal string of five consecutive seasons in last place.

Life was not so raucous as it had been in Brooklyn, but it had flashbacks to the good old days. He owned no ball players with racehorses or mustaches, but he did own one who had fought a draw with a catfish.

"I got me a young first-baseman, in the hospital after a fight with a catfish," he said wonderingly.

The ball player, George Metkovich, had hooked the fish in the Manatee River in Florida, then had become absorbed in trying to extract his hook when the fish fired a parting salvo, ramming a feeler fin through his foot. For the rest of his career, notably with both the Braves and the Red Sox in Boston, Metkovich carried the nickname "Catfish" as a memento.

But the Boston years were not too amusing in most ways. Stengel had neither a batting champion, home run king, runs-batted-in leader, or pitching ace. Even after the Braves moved to Milwaukee 15 years later and to Atlanta 10 years after that, their "short history of the Braves" included these sentences: "There have been many great pitchers in the Braves' organization. Cy Young won the last of his 511 games while a member of the team, etc." Warren Spahn had not yet achieved prominence when Stengel managed the club and, though a renaissance of sorts was just around the corner for the Braves, the Stengel administration went rapidly downhill.

In his first season, the club won 77 games and lost 75, the first time since he had become a manager in the big leagues that his team had won more games than it had lost. But if he had any fears about prosperity, they were soon dispelled. The next year, the Braves slumped from fifth place to seventh by winning only 63 games and losing 88. They improved fractionally the next year, winning 65 and losing 87. But they reversed the course again, going 62-92 and finally 59-89, with rain and postponements intervening on six days that final season, 1942, to prevent an even worse showing.

The situation was actually worse than that—just losing games; Stengel was beginning to lose money. He had invested $50,000 of his own money in the Braves, being now something of a capitalist in baseball circles and having, as usual, an insatiable craving for getting involved. But then one night in April 1943, just after he had come north to open the season, with players beginning to disappear from baseball to enter the military services and a kind of bewilderment settling over the game, he was snatched from the stagnation of life in the second division by one of those dramatic acts of fate that popped up so often and ruled so much of his life.

He was crossing Kenmore Square in the rain and fog when he was struck by a taxicab, knocked down and hospitalized with a broken leg.

"No one but me," he said later, "could get hit by a taxi, break a leg and wind up in the maternity ward."

His admittance to the maternity ward was simply in the nature of an emergency, but Casey's pals on the ball club and on the Boston newspapers immediately barraged him with letters and messages of condolences addressed to him "care of the Psychopathic Ward." Someone who disagreed with his overall genius even sent him a citation as "the man who did the most for Boston baseball this year"—by spending the season flat on his back while the team struggled up one notch to sixth place.

At least, wrote Dave Egan in *The Boston Record,* "no one did more for Boston baseball."

Well, Boston baseball may not have done more for anyone, either. It was not just that Stengel got paid for not managing, for the second time in seven years. Nor that he and his "partners" were finally bought out by Louis R. Perini, the construction man, who eventually transferred the club to Milwaukee. Nor was it that the Stengel legs picked up another scar of battle, a knot and a limp, both of which he retained. It was, rather, that the accident in Kenmore Square put him on the sidelines in Boston for good—just before the axe fell, most insiders believed. Otherwise, he might not have shaken loose from an increasingly difficult situation, beat a retreat back to the minor leagues and been ready when the most remarkable change in his fortunes arrived five years later.

At first, though, he seriously considered getting out of baseball, as he had during his year in exile in Brooklyn. After all, he was 53 now and the war was spreading all over the world and both he and his profession were forced into some eclipse because the drain on manpower had already begun to result in spectacles like a one-armed outfielder (Pete Gray) in the major leagues and a batting average of .309 (George Stirnweiss) that was good enough to win the American League title.

In fact, some of the best baseball—and football, for that matter—was played in military camps during World War II. Maxwell Field, at Montgomery, Alabama, organized one such baseball team by an ingenuity and determination that might have made its pilot-selection boards jealous. It frequently played four night games a week in Crampton Bowl, plus Sundays, and had no difficulty finding starting pitchers for such an arduous schedule. At one time its pitching staff consisted of two professional right-handers and two professional left-handers: Mel Parnell, who became one of Stengel's irritations when he pitched for the Boston Red Sox later; Royce Lint, who became the property of the Pittsburgh Pirates; George Turbeville, who had already pitched for years under Connie Mack at Philadelphia, and Bill McCahan, who joined the Athletics after the war and pitched a no-hit game against Washington in 1947.

The Bainbridge Naval Base in Maryland once furthered its baseball fortunes by trading some water-survival equipment, which it did not need, to another base for an outfielder, which it did need.

In spite of such aberrations in the pattern of the game, though, Stengel was pried out of his "retirement" in May 1944, by Charlie Grimm, his old friend, who was managing the Milwaukee Brewers in the American Association but who wanted to accept a job managing the Chicago Cubs and needed a fill-in for himself back in Milwaukee. The season was already underway and available managers were scarce, but there was good old Casey Stengel, a manager and available. So Grimm sent an SOS to Glendale, and Casey, as a favor to his old pal, limped from the side of the swimming pool, headed back east and took over at Milwaukee.

As things turned out, he was about to be rewarded a hundredfold for doing Grimm the favor. The Milwaukee team was no patsy. It tore the league apart, winning 91 games and losing 49, and winning the American Association pennant.

Somehow now, all the tricks Stengel had acquired on the way up from Kankakee 35 years earlier began to crystallize: how to evaluate baseball talent, how to invest in a winner, how to resurrect a loser, how to buy low and sell high, how to manage a baseball team in one league and still spend time and money wheeling and dealing in another.

The Brewers were owned by Bill Veeck, who had followed his father around the Chicago Cubs' holdings 20 years before as a little boy and who had run across Stengel in his early days as a manager at Toledo in the same league. Now Veeck Jr. was an executive himself, and, more than that, he was a Marine in the Canal Zone. So he and Stengel ran the club through a brisk correspondence that, years later, Veeck said astonished even him.

One day during the 1944 season he received a letter at his post in the Canal Zone in which Casey announced that he would trade Jim Pruett, a catcher with a reputation for having an exceedingly weak throwing arm. Casey even predicted when and to whom he would sell—or peddle—Pruett. Veeck was amazed, since he saw no chance of such a deal, whether the war had weakened the will of rival club owners or not.

He was even more astonished, though, to learn five months later that Pruett had caught two games under the interested gaze of a scout for the Philadelphia Athletics, and moreover had caught five runners off base with a throwing arm that seemed like the greatest rifle since Daniel Boone. The Athletics promptly coughed up $40,000 and took Mr. Pruett and his rifle home to Philadelphia.

Stengel later let Veeck in on the machinations behind the deal, which Veeck was being advised of through communiques between Milwaukee and the Canal Zone.

"He had carefully set the stage," Veeck recalled. "He had encouraged the notion that Pruett had a weak arm, weaker than he actually had. He didn't even use him behind the bat too often, just nourished the idea that Pruett couldn't throw. Then, he got Pruett primed for the Philadelphia scout—well-rested, warmed-up and hungry as anything. He was an instant success, because he was really better than Casey had let on. But that's the way Casey had been brought up as a minor league manager: his biggest job was probably developing players to sell somewhere. And he got awfully good at it."

He got so good at it that he caught the eye of another old friend, George M. Weiss, who had been administering minor league clubs and systems for the New York Yankees since the old Eastern League days of 1925, when Stengel managed his first team. Now, in 1945, Weiss had a weak team at Kansas City in the American Association and he went to Casey with the same appeal for a favor that Grimm had floated the year before.

Stengel by this time had accepted the cheers for his whirlwind success at Milwaukee but, being an interim manager, had then resigned and bowed out after the briefest and most successful pinch-hit job of his career. He gave Weiss the same respectful ear he had given Grimm. And, where he had done Grimm the favor of taking over a pennant-bound team the year before, he now did Weiss the favor of taking over a cellar-bound team—but a cellar-bound team owned by the Yankees. Besides, he was back home with a Kansas City team for the first time in 35 years. The team, the Blues, plunged into seventh place, but Stengel had now made contact with the organization that was to change his life. All he had to do was wait.

The wait lasted three years, and he spent them in the Pacific Coast League as manager of another Triple-A team, the Oakland Oaks. The league was no pushover, listing among its managers, in addition to Stengel, such professionals as Paul Richards, who later had several careers as a manager and executive in the majors; Lopez, who later achieved the best career record of games won and lost as manager of the Cleveland Indians and Chicago White Sox; Bobby Bragan, later the manager at Pittsburgh, Milwaukee and Atlanta; and Bill Kelly, later a superscout for Stengel when both labored for the New York Mets.

The Oaks had so many veteran players that they were called "the nine old men," in the manner of Franklin D. Roosevelt's Supreme Court. The old men did splendidly for their 56-year-old manager, who was making his debut on the Pacific Coast in a league that included Los Angeles and Hollywood and that made it easy for Edna Stengel, for once, to keep her man within a reasonably short radius. In the long season made possible by the weather on the Coast, they won 111 games and lost 72, in 1946, finishing second. In 1947, they won

96, lost 90 and ran fourth. But in 1948, they dominated the league, winning 114, losing 74 and taking the pennant for Oakland and Stengel.

Casey had now managed at Worcester, Toledo, Milwaukee, Kansas City and Oakland for 12 seasons in the Eastern League, American Association and Pacific Coast League, 11 of the 12 seasons being in the highest category below the majors. He had managed at Brooklyn and Boston for nine seasons in the National League. His minor league teams won 1,037 games and lost 924. He had won two pennants 20 years apart in two Triple-A leagues.

It was a good place to stay, to ease into retirement. But now, without warning, Stengel's world turned upside down.

The New York Yankees had dropped from first place in the American League to third that season. The 16-year reign of Joe McCarthy had ended, and in one season the club had played under McCarthy, Bill Dickey and Johnny Neun before Bucky Harris took over for 1947 and 1948. Postwar attendance zoomed to 2,373,901, and the Yankees' position of dominance, established with Ruth three decades before, was now being challenged before the largest crowds in sports history.

The Yankee scouts on the West Coast, Bill Essick in Los Angeles and Joe Devine in San Francisco, passed the word to New York, where George Weiss had been installed as resident director of the Yankees' empire by Dan Topping and Del Webb, who had recently bought control of the club after a public row with their partner, MacPhail. Webb, moreover, played plenty of golf with Brick Laws, owner of the Oakland club, and heard much about the glory of the nine old men and the ringleader. Then, Gene Bearden, one of the *young* men developed at Oakland, began to pitch his way to considerable fame as the star of the Cleveland Indians' dramatic playoff victory for the American League pennant.

So, it was the "tenth old man" of Oakland who got the call from the Yankees on Sunday, October 10, 1948, and who, the next day, more solemn than usual, boarded an airliner and headed for New York.

1910: Charles Dillon Stengel, resplendent in bowler and three-quarter coat, poses with his classmates at Western Dental College in Kansas City. He gave it his best shot for two winters, then decided that his heart was really in baseball. Besides, lefthanded dentists had a much less certain future in 1910 than lefthanded ball players. America lost a dentist, but gained a wizard.

Casey spent his first six major league seasons as an outfielder for the Brooklyn Dodgers before his 1918 move to Pittsburgh.

He became a player, coach or manager on sixteen professional teams, and played the outfield for five of them in the big leagues, including John McGraw's New York Giants from 1921 through 1923.

1948: In three years as manager at Oakland in the Pacific Coast League, his teams won 321 games and Casey went first-class. Next stop: New York.

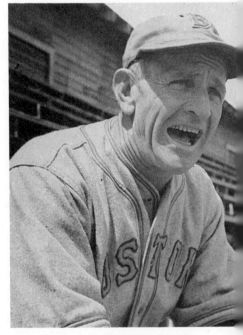

But he already knew managing in the big leagues had its downside. In six seasons (1938 through 1943), his Boston Braves never ran better than fifth. He and Bob Quinn (left) check the talent and look shocked.

Happy times: But after he took charge of the Yankees in 1949, they won
five straight World Series and a legend took shape. Dan Topping (left)
and Del Webb salute the winners in 1950.

After the summer's wars, he went
home to Glendale and harvested
some of his California grapefruit.

Casey seems solemn after
knocking off Charlie Dressen's
Dodgers in the 1952 World Series.

The art of intimidation, 1952: Once he carried an umbrella to home plate to suggest it was raining too hard. But a poncho in Yankee Stadium?

The era of the Yankees: ten American League pennants in twelve years, and Phil Rizzuto (left) and Joe Page help Casey raise the roof.

The United States Senate had heard Daniel Webster and Henry Clay, but not Casey Stengel—until July 9, 1958. The Professor testifies, Mickey Mantle dozes, Ted Williams and Stan Musial sign.

Two generations of Yankees spent spring training in St. Petersburg, Fla. So old No. 37 bows to their public as the Yankees pull up stakes in 1959 and head north for one more summer's campaign. He was, Branch Rickey said, "the perfect link between the team and the public."

Sticky moment in the 1960 World Series: Stengel leaves the mound in the fifth game and also leaves catcher Elston Howard and Art Ditmar to ponder the Pittsburgh power.

For half a century, they traveled the baseball trails together: Casey Stengel and Edna Lawson, who were married in 1924. Above, in 1960, Casey turns 70 and Edna beams.

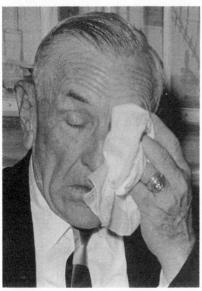

He wasn't overcome by emotion very often. But he was when the New York writers threw a farewell party for the Professor in 1960 after the Yankees had dropped him because he was too old.

Well, he was two years older in 1962 when he started a new career as manager of the Mets, the new team in town. In spring training in St. Petersburg, he remembers the good times with his superpowers of Yankee years, Roger Maris (left) and Mickey Mantle. The Mets even beat the Yankees that day, but Casey knew it didn't count.

September 2, 1965: Hail and farewell, as Casey retires at Shea Stadium.
"I chased the balls that Babe Ruth hit."

Bowie Kuhn, Lindsey Nelson and 55,000 fans cheer for the legend one more time in Shea Stadium, and the Professor gets his rewards.

August 18, 1968: It is exactly 44 years since they were wed, and they seal it with a kiss.

August 8, 1970: Now he is 80, and Whitey Ford and Yogi Berra (right) bestow uniform No. 37 on the man who wore it so grandly.

Frederick G. Lieb, who saw his first baseball game in 1904, spent a lifetime writing a history of the sport—including this piece of history inscribed at Huggins-Stengel Field in St. Petersburg.

Chapter

The Year the Yankees
Won the Pennant

On May 11, 1944, *The Sporting News,* the weekly journal of baseball, reported the results of a poll of 151 newspaper writers on the subject: the "most" in major league managers. Leo Durocher, for example, was voted the most pugnacious. Connie Mack was voted the best-liked. Bill McKechnie the most studious. And Casey Stengel, who that season was not even in the major leagues, was voted the "funniest."

He received four times as many votes as the runner-up, Jimmy Dykes, and six times as many as the No. 3 man, Charlie Grimm, who played the banjo and was considered exceptionally funny even by Stengel. Still, no one came close to Stengel, the onetime bow-legged outfielder for the Dodgers, Pirates, Phillies and Giants, the brawler and practical joker who later cemented his reputation as a clubhouse comic by directing the exceedingly funny—and spectacularly—unsuccessful—Brooklyn Dodgers.

Consequently, it came as a distinct shock to most persons when Stengel appeared suddenly in New York in October 1948, and was introduced as the new manager of the New York Yankees, the most exceedingly unfunny—and spectacularly successful—baseball team in history.

It was as though the State Department had borrowed Emmett Kelly from Ringling Brothers and introduced him as the government's new Chief of Protocol. It was universally regarded as an interim step between Yankee dynasties, as when John XXIII was elected Pope a dozen years later and was considered by most persons a "transition Pope." And the results in Stengel's case were almost as surprising.

For one thing, the Yankees, like Old Man River, had just kept rolling along, winning 15 American League pennants and 11 world championships, principally under two of the more straitlaced managers in the game, Miller Huggins and Joe McCarthy. But then, adjusting to the lean days of World War II, and later emerging from them, the Yankees slipped. They finished third in 1944 after winning three straight pennants, then dropped to fourth in 1945, edged back to third in 1946, went all the way back to first in 1947, but then sank again to third in 1948 under Stanley R. (Bucky) Harris, who had been installed as manager by Larry MacPhail. Finally, after a sensational brawl in public, MacPhail had been bought out for $2,000,000 by his partners, Dan Topping and Del Webb, and Harris had abruptly lost his patron.

So the Yankees were struggling to recapture their equanimity and Rock-of-Gibraltar quality in the fall of 1948, when Stengel flew to New York in response to an invitation from the new owners of the Yankees. He arrived on Sunday night, October 10.

Everybody's attention in baseball at that hour was fastened on the World Series, which was being played between the Boston Braves and the Cleveland Indians. The Indians in 1948 had enjoyed a remarkable renaissance under Bill Veeck, the promotional wizard who would later send a midget named Eddie Gaedel to bat when he owned the St. Louis Browns (Gaedel walked on four straight pitches) and who had stormed Cleveland with so many stunts that the team performed before an average of more than 40,000 persons every time it appeared in Municipal Stadium in 1948.

The Indians' magic touch lasted right up to the final hours of the season, which found the club in a tie with the Boston Red Sox. Finally, after winning a tumultuous playoff for the American League title, the Indians swept into the World Series and, on the day after Stengel arrived in New York, edged out the Braves, 4 to 3, before 40,103 persons in Boston and brought the championship back to Cleveland.

It was a gaudy finish to a gaudy season. Lou Boudreau, the boy manager and shortstop, led the Indians to their first championship since Tris Speaker's team had defeated Wilbert Robinson's Brooklyn Dodgers 28 years earlier. Joe Gordon, "the sterling second-sacker whom the Yankees cast adrift in 1946," according to one report of the final game, hit a home run in the sixth inning. And Gene Bearden, the young left-hander developed by Stengel at Oakland in the Pacific Coast League, saved the game while Cleveland routed Boston's pitcher, Bill Voiselle, with the great young left-hander Warren Spahn pitching in relief for the Braves.

It was a difficult act to follow. But the next day, October 12, the Yankees followed it with Casey Stengel.

It was a cloudy, rainy day, and the World Series was still dominating the front pages, though Allison Danzig wrote in *The New York Times* that "now that the World Series has come to an end, football holds the center of the stage for a run through November." Columbia, it seemed, was preparing to open a long home stand that Saturday against the University of Pennsylvania, and

"New York hasn't seen any bigtime football for some time."

At the St. James Theatre off Times Square, Ray Bolger had just opened in "Where's Charley?" and Brooks Atkinson noted that the dancer made "a mediocre show seem thoroughly enjoyable." Tony Pastor and his orchestra were holding the fort at the Paramount, with a new singing star, Vic Damone. Vito Marcantonio was running for a seventh term in the House of Representatives from his district in East Harlem and *The Times* asked in an editorial whether the electorate would "vote Russian or vote American."

Harry S. Truman was whistle-stopping his way across the country against Thomas E. Dewey, while George C. Marshall headed for the opening of the United Nations General Assembly meeting in Paris, saying the country was "completely united" in foreign policy—though the Presidential campaign indicated otherwise. And Great Britain at that hour was asking for a censure of the Soviet Union over Andrei Y. Vishinsky's disarmament proposals, charging that Vishinsky actually was obstructing disarmament.

The Alger Hiss-Whittaker Chambers controversy was at its height, too. And stylists were reporting that Persian lamb collars on women's coats were about to make a solid "bow" for the fall season. It was Columbus Day. Yom Kippur began solemnly at sundown. And at the 21 Club, one of the toniest nooks in town, Dan Topping stood before a phalanx of microphones in the glare of spotlights raised by swarms of photographers and television cameramen and introduced the new manager of the New York Yankees.

"Meet the new manager of the Yankees," wrote John Drebinger in *The Times*. "Charles Dillon (Casey) Stengel, onetime hard-hitting outfielder, manager of both major and minor league clubs, sage, wit, raconteur as glib with the wisecrack as the late Johnny Walker."

True, but the man brought 2,700 miles to take over the American League's most successful team had never played, coached or managed for a single inning in the American League. And, to compound his innocence, he had been flown to New York, had been taken directly to the Waldorf-Astoria that night, had signed a two-year contract and now, 36 hours later, had been put on display like one of the wonders of the world in the broad, artificial daylight of a high-toned nightspot.

To present a united front for such an incongruous occasion, the Yankees also put Joe DiMaggio on display alongside Stengel. The great centerfielder was going on 34, had suffered a painful charley horse in his frequently bruised legs during the closing weeks of the season, had almost single-handedly salvaged something better for the Yankees as they finished third behind Cleveland and Boston, and now was explaining that he planned to visit Johns Hopkins for a medical checkup to determine whether an operation would be required on his right heel to remove a bone spur similar to the one that had been removed from his left heel two years earlier.

That was symbolic enough, and bad enough: that the central figure in the Yankee dynasty on the field appeared to be in fading health. But his presence was intended to allay a worse suspicion: namely, that DiMaggio regarded the appearance of Stengel as a menace to his own ambition to manage the Yankees. But the Yankee Clipper, as he was called, smiled broadly, engagingly and convincingly as he stood shoulder to shoulder with Stengel. No, he said, he had no managerial ambitions.

"You know me, boys," he said. "I'm just a ball player with one ambition, and that is to give all I've got to help my ball club win. I've never played any other way."

Clarence (Brick) Laws, owner of the Oakland team in the Pacific Coast League and Stengel's most recent employer, also stood in the front ranks in another show of force and unity. He had released Stengel from his obligations at Oakland so that he could accept the Yankees' offer, which Casey said had not been made until that Sunday despite the fact that he had been reading speculation about it on the Coast for nearly a month.

One other Stengel "connection" with the Yankees was suggested. Precisely 25 years earlier, to the day, he had hit the home run for John McGraw's Giants off Sad Sam Jones to defeat the Yankees, 1 to 0, and tighten the 1923 World Series, just two days after his inside-the-park home run had won the opening game. The Yankees eventually took the series, four games to two, but the implication now was that, a quarter of a century later, the Yankees had decided that if they could not beat Stengel, they might as well join him.

None of this symbolism overcame the fact that the Yankees in reality had reached out into left field, so to speak, for a celebrated comic as their field leader in a strange new context for both, and not even Stengel could find the words to dispel the misgivings that had settled over the party at "21."

In fact, with the first words he uttered to acknowledge his accession to power, he fell on his face verbally. With tape recorders, microphones and cameras all switched on from a common cue, the man of the hour said: "I want first of all to thank Mr. Bob Topping for this opportunity." That was all right, except that Mr. Dan Topping should have been thanked for this opportunity instead of his brother Mr. Bob Topping, whose marital difficulties with Arlene Judge, the film actress, formerly Dan's wife, had put both Toppings in headlines even before Stengel had arrived.

Cries of "Cut!" and "Hold it!" drowned out whatever else the Yankees' new manager had in mind for his opening sentence. Then, after everybody had rewound the equipment, Casey took another cue and made another start.

"This is a big job, fellows," he said, with no trace of his usual plunges into slapstick, "and I barely have had time to study it. In fact, I scarcely know where I am at."

Then, turning to the Yankee "situation," he delved into generalities and said: "There'll likely be some changes. But it's a good club and I think we'll do all right. We'll go slow because you can tear down a club a lot quicker than you can build it up."

The performance of all concerned was not entirely convincing.

"Most observers," recalled Drebinger, "always kindly disposed toward the engaging Stengel, were viewing his forthcoming assignment with some misgivings. Casey's rows with umpires stand as classics, one of his most brilliant performances having occurred one day when he strode to the plate, bowed to the arbiter and doffed his cap, from which a sparrow escaped. Just what he plans to spring out of his cap for the Yankees next spring is a matter which gives much food for speculation."

The next day, Casey made his first move as manager of the Yankees: he signed Jim Turner, a onetime milkman, pitcher for the Boston Braves and manager at Portland in the Pacific Coast League, as a coach, his first appointment. He made two moves, actually, as *The Times* noted, and the second became a much more characteristic one:

"Last night Casey went into a huddle with George M. Weiss, general manager of the Yankees. It is a fair guess that there will be many such sessions in the next few weeks, for all interested parties realize there is much work to be done before the Yankees can ever hope to reclaim their baseball leadership."

Ben Epstein wrote in the New York *Mirror:* "One can get better odds naming the Yankees' opening-day lineup than the 1949 opening-day manager. Such a smart-alecky attitude is sneered at as right unneighborly by the ownership. Yet Casey Stengel will be the fifth candidate to have stabbed at this morning glory since 1946."

Sure enough, the 1949 season became an unending series of huddles between Stengel, Weiss, Topping and a platoon of physicians and surgeons who were summoned in a struggle to rescue the Yankees from an epidemic of breakdowns—while their new manager, a 59-year-old man, struggled to put nine sound young men on the field.

Joe DiMaggio missed the first 65 games because of the bone spur on his heel, then missed two more weeks in September because of a virus infection that weakened him right through the final inning of the season. The back-up sluggers were hobbled, too—Tommy Henrich (wrenched knee, three broken vertebrae), Charley Keller (chronic back ailment) and Yogi Berra (broken finger). Seven men played first base at one time or another—Henrich, Johnny Mize, Dick Kryhoski John Phillips, Billy Johnson, Fenton Mole and Joe Collins. Third base was shared by Johnson, a part-time first-baseman, and Bobby Brown, a part-time medical student, who, it was suggested, might have helped the team more with scalpel and bandage than with bat and glove. Two accomplished midgets played shortstop and second base—Phil Rizzuto and George Stirnweiss—with support from Jerry Coleman, a Marine Corps Reserve pilot who shuttled between the Yankees and the Marines for years. Berra, an outfielder, was made a catcher. And Johnny Lindell, a pitcher, was made an outfielder.

Every day when he arrived at the stadium, Stengel would check with the team's trainer, August R. Mauch, to determine the number of able-bodied men before putting nine names down on his lineup card, which he then would sign in his mid-Victorian script with flowing letters as though it were a historical document. He put down the names of the three "middle" batters—Henrich, DiMaggio and Berra—supposedly the anchor of the lineup, only 17 times as a unit in 154 games.

Ten years later, Stengel started 100 different lineups to get through a schedule of 154 games, and was both hailed as a Merlin among managers and criticized as a meddler. But he had been "platooned" himself as an outfielder 40 years earlier, and whatever his excesses as a juggler of men later, he platooned players as a manager that first year of the epidemic with the Yankees out of dire necessity.

Mauch, a trim man who wore white slacks and tennis sneakers, held degrees as a Doctor of Naturopathy and as a Doctor of Chiropractics, had treated professional baseball players, college swimmers, football players at all levels, George M. Cohan, Jimmy Durante and even George Bernard Shaw, and played a calculated hand of contract bridge, besides.

He was the trainer for the football Giants in New York for 17 seasons, the football Yankees for 4, the baseball Yankees for 16, New York University for 6 and Manhattan College for 12. He eventually trained eleven baseball pennant winners, eight World Series winners, two National Football League champions, six American League All-Star teams, one National League All-Star team and one All-Star team each in the N.F.L. and the All-America Football Conference.

He once helped keep Cohan dancing on stage for weeks while the entertainer was suffering with a sprained ankle, a pulled hamstring muscle and a case of influenza. Shaw visited him at the McAlpin Hotel's roof club in 1926 for massages. Durante called on him for help during his Copacabana appearances in 1940. And Admiral Richard E. Byrd—who "looked a little pale when he came back from the North Pole"—was a fairly regular patient starting in 1927.

But Mauch said without hesitation that the busiest year in his career was 1949.

"Every day I'd walk into Stengel's office," he recalled, "and I'd say, 'Your star outfielder is hurt and can't play.' And he'd say, 'Thank you, doctor.' He never blinked an eye. He grew tougher later, but that year he was gentle. If the team was on a winning streak, he might howl and shout, but he was mild when we were losing or when we were hurting."

The Yankees grew so accident-prone that even Mauch became a casualty in a far-fetched way. The team was in Boston near the end of the season and Charley Silvera, a second-string catcher, was in a doughnut shop when he noticed Mauch walking by. So Silvera picked up two doughnuts, put them over his eyes, peered out through the holes and rapped on the window. Gus was so amused by the spectacle that he began to laugh—and walked into a parking meter, breaking two ribs.

"Joe DiMaggio had a pain in his heel like the pain of a hundred carpet tacks," Mauch said. "He had a flock of tiny calcium deposits that had to solidify into one before the pain would stop. We could have filled a Fibber McGee closet with all the contraptions that shoe companies sent us to correct the problem. They sent shoes with half-soles in the front and iron bars in the rear to act as a cradle for Joe's foot. People who had had bone spurs sent advice and even medicine."

One day DiMaggio stepped out of bed and discovered that the pain in his right heel had gone. It was already late in June and the Yankees were struggling to keep pace with the Boston Red Sox of Ted Williams, Bobby Doerr, Dominic DiMaggio, Ellis Kinder and Mel Parnell, a talented bunch who played under the stern hand of Joe McCarthy, who had led the Yankees in their heyday. The Yankees had an exhibition game on June 27 against the Giants, and DiMaggio walked into Stengel's office while Casey was fiddling with his lineup card and said without warning: "I think I'll give it a whirl tonight, Case."

"Great," Casey croaked, "you can play as long as you want. Just let me know when you're ready to quit."

Instead of taking a "mild workout," as expected, DiMaggio played the whole game. The next night, against the Red Sox in Boston, he got back into the regular lineup, hit a single his first time up and a home run the second, then hit two home runs the next day and another the day after that.

Before the last one, he had hit a long ball that just missed being a home run, and McCarthy had shot out of the dugout waving his arm and scowling toward the pitcher's mound. He was growing weary of DiMaggio's theatrical comeback. He retreated into the dugout, and just had time to sit down before Joe rocked the next pitch even farther, and this time there was no doubt that it was a fair ball—or that the Yankees had started to revive.

Still, few sane persons would have gambled on the Yankees' health or luck or ability to survive. "If Casey pulls this one out," said Bill Dickey, the onetime catcher who was then a coach, "he's a Houdini."

"It was hard to believe," Mauch said, "but Casey would take a guy out of the lineup and the substitute would do better than the original. He moved players around, he switched positions, he did everything, and everything seemed to work."

Berra, a 23-year-old who had been paid $90 a month when he signed with Norfolk in 1943 and who later became celebrated as "Mr. Berra, which is my assistant manager," hit 20 home runs and batted in 91 runs. Allie Reynolds, the part-Cherokee "Chief" from Oklahoma who later struck oil, had been acquired from Cleveland in exchange for Joe Gordon after the management had consulted DiMaggio on the league's toughest pitchers; he won 17 games for Stengel and lost 6—though he finished only four. But a young left-hander with great speed, Joe Page, finished what Reynolds started most times, appeared in 60 games and won 13 as one of the new breed of heavy-duty relief-pitching specialists.

Somehow, with emergency performances like these and with heavy reliance on intuition and Gus Mauch's wizardry in the trainer's room, Stengel brought the Yankees home on September 26 in a tie for first place with the Red Sox and with one week to go in the season.

When the Yankees arrived in Grand Central Terminal that Sunday night, they were astonished to find a crowd of 7,000 persons jamming the station waiting for them, including Mrs. Johnny Mize, the wife of the veteran first-baseman the club had bought from the Giants (who was injured, of course), and Mrs. Babe Ruth. A detail of policemen had to escort the players out through side exits through the cheering mob, and as they did, Stengel said above the noise: "We're still up. Tomorrow we'll have them on our home ground, and tomorrow's a big one."

It was a big one, all right. Before 66,156 persons in Yankee Stadium, the Red Sox took the league lead by scoring four runs in the eighth inning and beating the Yankees, 7 to 6. The game ended in a monstrous argument when Johnny Pesky slid across home plate on Bobby Doerr's squeeze bunt as Ralph Houk lunged to tag him out and the home-plate umpire, Bill Grieve, called him safe.

The Yankees lost the game, the league lead and $500 in fines on one play—$150 each for Houk and Stengel and $200 for Cliff Mapes, an outfielder who wasn't even in the game but who was tactless enough to ask Grieve as the players and umpires headed for the dressing rooms: "How much did you bet on the game?"

Four days later, after the Yankees had played three games against the Philadelphia Athletics, the Red Sox still clung to a one-game lead with two to go—two to go against the Yankees in New York. And as the teams staggered toward the climax of an improbable season, *The New York Times* paused in its coverage of the world scene to say, in an editorial titled "Days of Anguish":

> In times like these, we customarily repair to the classics for what calm we can discover. We like the soothing cadence, marching though it does to doom, of the Ernest Thayer lines:
>
> > Oh, somewhere in this favored land
> > The sun is shining bright.
> > The band is playing somewhere, and
> > Somewhere hearts are light.
> > And somewhere men are laughing, and
> > Somewhere children shout . . .
>
> Charity and the fear of laying a hex on Casey Stengel lead us to draw a veil, temporarily, over the last line of this masterpiece. We will not believe that our Casey has struck out until the baseball mathematicians say the Yankees are impossible.

The Yankees were almost impossible from the first inning on the fateful day, Saturday, October 1. It was "Joe DiMaggio Day," and close to $50,000 worth of gifts were showered on the Yankee centerfielder, who was still pale and drawn from his siege of virus infection. But as 69,551 persons crammed Yankee Stadium, with the Red Sox needing one victory to win the pennant and the Yankees needing one defeat to lose the pennant, Stengel sat in the dugout before the game and said: "I think we've got 'em. I feel it in my bones."

But the Yankees, who felt fatigue and pain in their bones, fell into all kinds of trouble at the start when Allie Reynolds lost his control and gave up four runs in the first three innings. But somehow, six innings from losing it all, they scraped together enough hits here and there to survive, as though having been through hell every day of the season, why be panicked now? And when Lindell hit a home run in the eighth inning, they went ahead, 5 to 4, with Page pitching in relief and saying later that he kept looking out to center field to his dog-tired idol, DiMaggio, and thinking: "If he can play the way he feels, I can pitch forever."

"And so, it develops," John Drebinger wrote after the game, "that those battered Bombers with their countless aches and bruises, weren't ready to be rolled into a boneyard after all. At least, on this final day of the American League championship season, they are still standing as well as their formidable rivals, the hale and hearty Bosox."

And, on the final day, 68,055 persons filled the stadium as the teams met in the final game of the season—winner take all. It was 1 to 0, Yankees, until the last half of the eighth inning, with Vic Raschi pitching for New York, and, after each team had fired a kind of spasmatic parting shot in its last turn at bat, it was 5 to 3, Yankees.

"We had had 72 injuries that season," recalled Gus Mauch, whose ribs were still taped following his collision with the parking meter in Boston. "I mean, 72 injuries that kept a man out of the lineup. And when Henrich caught the foul ball that ended that last game and gave us the pennant, Bill Dickey jumped up in the dugout and cracked his head on the roof. That made 73."

"That was the most fighting team I ever saw," Mauch said. Stengel, said many people, "did it with mirrors." It was, said Henrich, "a team of destiny."

The "team of destiny," though, still had to get through the World Series, and the National League was providing an opponent with almost as pronounced a flair for melodramatics and "destiny." The St. Louis Cardinals had already begun selling and distributing tickets for the series, then lost four straight games to the sixth-place Pittsburgh Pirates and the eighth-place Chicago Cubs. That gave the Brooklyn Dodgers a last-minute chance, and while the Yankees were squeaking past the Red Sox on the last day of the season in New York, the Dodgers were squeaking past the Phillies, 9 to 7, in 10 innings on the last day in Philadelphia.

What would they all do for an encore? On October 5, the first day of the World Series, 66,224 persons packed Yankee Stadium to watch Don Newcombe allow the Yankees five hits and strike out 11. But Reynolds allowed the Dodgers two hits and struck out nine. They were scoreless until Henrich led off the last half of the ninth inning, with Newcombe keeping one eye on Joe DiMaggio in the batter's circle and letting the count on Henrich slip away to two balls and no strikes. He got the next pitch over and Henrich hit it into the right-field seats.

The next day, Preacher Roe, a left-handed country boy, allowed the Yankees six hits while the Dodgers made seven off Raschi and Page. Brooklyn won this time, 1 to 0, before 70,053 persons.

In the third game, they were still tied, 1 to 1, after eight innings in Ebbets Field before 32,788 fans. Then the Yankees scored three times in the visitors' half of the ninth; the Dodgers scored twice on two home runs in their half and lost, 4 to 3.

In the fourth game, the Yankees rushed to a lead of 6 to 0 inside five innings, then gave back four runs and Stengel had to call in Reynolds to protect what was left of his lead. Reynolds did, striking out four of the final seven batters he faced.

Finally, in the fifth game, the Yankees treated Stengel—after an unholy season of one suspense after another—to the luxury of a nine-run lead. Gil Hodges, who in a later World Series would receive the prayers of an entire congregation in Brooklyn during a batting slump, hit a three-run home run in the seventh, and Stengel, his season not yet over, wearily signaled Page into the game. Page stopped the Dodgers, the Yankees won their 12th World Series, the triumvirate of Topping, Webb and Weiss won its first—and Casey Stengel completed his tumultuous debut in the American League.

What had Houdini wrought? Had he done it, as so many people believed, with mirrors? Had the Yankees simply revived after a dormant period? Had justice triumphed? Had tomfoolery triumphed? Had Gus Mauch conquered adversity with Band-Aid and rubbing alcohol?

"It was," said Arthur E. (Red) Patterson, 17 years later, "part of the greatest rebuilding job in baseball. Between 1948 and 1953, Topping and Webb gave Weiss the authority and the money, and Weiss rebuilt an organization. Stengel had been hired with the complete respect of all three. They didn't think he was a clown or a buffoon. They knew that he had a record in the minor leagues that maybe nobody else could match—making out with old players, new players, finished players, professional players. And they brought him to the Yankees with their eyes wide open. He was no diversion to keep the public amused enough to forget the club's collapse."

Patterson, looking back on the year that the Yankees won the pennant between surgical operations, puffed on a cigar in a handsome office on the fifth "level" of Dodger Stadium, the only ball park in the major leagues with Sandy Koufax on the pitcher's mound and palm trees rising over the bullpen fences. He had preceded Stengel by three years with the Yankees, as public relations director and road secretary from 1946 until midway through the 1954 season, then had switched to the Dodgers and jumped the continent with them in 1957 to Los Angeles, where Stengel lived 15 miles from the new home of his old rivals of the 1949 World Series.

"Stengel," Patterson went on, "took a few veteran ball players who required special treatment, like Joe DiMaggio, Charley Keller and Tommy Henrich. Kids who needed encouragement and experience, both at the same time, like Gil McDougald, Whitey Ford, Billy Martin, Mickey Mantle. Several established stars whom Weiss bought when things got rough, like Johnny Mize, Johnny Hopp and Enos Slaughter.

"How do you get all these elements to work together, to succeed together? His minor league background made him a natural. Hank Bauer, for example: Casey played him only against lefthanded pitchers early in his career until Bauer became established, and then played him against all kinds of pitching.

"I think he was the father of the two-platoon system. And he was criticized for it. But in defense of the platoon system, he'd say: 'If I still had DiMaggio, Keller and Henrich at their prime, I wouldn't platoon. But I don't.'

"And the 73 famous injuries. It would be like this: During one double-header in July of 1949, just after Weiss had bought Mize from the Giants for $40,000, Mize played first base, so Henrich was bumped to right field. In the first game, Henrich crashed into the wall and broke three vertebrae. He was carried out on a stretcher. In the second game, Mize dived to make a tag, threw his shoulder out, and for the rest of the year all he could do was pinch-hit. So now, both first-basemen were out.

"Not only did Stengel make changes that paid off in situations like that, but he made the Yankees more popular, more likeable than they ever had been. They always won everything but love. But then, when they were hurt, they won the public, too."

And if the sleight-of-hand had not worked out, would Stengel's wandering road from Kankakee have ended 40 years later in New York?

"They would have forgiven him, I think, considering all the injuries, because he did a good job of rebuilding," Patterson said, "and they would have given him the next season to finish the job."

Still, Edna Stengel kept 1949 apart in its importance to his career, which at least won a reprieve of sorts by the margin of one game. When, 17 years later, he was elected to the Hall of Fame chiefly because of his success with the Yankees, she wiped tears from her face in St. Petersburg and said: "I can't get over it. This is greater even than winning the World Series in 1949."

Stengel, hard-nosed in financial, economic and "career" matters despite his insouciance in most other things, regarded 1949 as a milestone for good reason. He entered his 60th year during that difficult season; he was operating in a new league in an unforgiving city; he had an unbroken record as a manager of losing baseball teams in the major leagues; and he was on the brink of seeing the great opportunity of his lifetime obscured by his firm reputation as a fair major league player, an accomplished minor league manager and an outstanding practitioner of horseplay at all levels. He was, as *The Sporting News* had reported, the "funniest" manager in the game. And, until 1949, that stood as his most enduring claim to fame.

"No skipper," wrote Arthur Daley, "was ever handed a more formidable task than the Ol' Perfessor. The Bronx Bombers just didn't have the ball players they once had in profusion. But for 148 of the 154 games they were in the lead. There is no escaping the fact that the major part of the credit for this astonishing performance has to go to Stengel."

"Watching Professor Stengel manage a pennant-contender club for the first time in his career," he observed on another occasion, "seems to reveal talents few believed he possessed. Yet, he must have had them all along. . . . Certain it is that he didn't learn it all overnight when they named him to lead the Yankees."

The talents that Stengel brought with him to New York had one outstanding thing going for them: George Weiss, general manager of the Yankees and their prime minister for almost a quarter of a century, had implicit faith in his old friend from the Eastern League days. And he gave the Stengel talents wide room in which to maneuver.

Weiss, after conferring with Stengel during the earliest days of their joint stewardship, mailed more than 30 contracts just before the 1949 spring training season, indicating some new directions the Yankees would take. Raises were awarded to several players who had endured the team's defeat in 1948 with some distinction, like Berra, Henrich and Bob Porterfield, the young pitcher who had won his letter almost as soon as he had been elevated from the minor leagues. But most of the other players received "conditional" contracts. That is, a certain sum was to be withheld, every month, its payment remaining optional with the manager—Stengel. The option was exercised if the player hustled, kept himself in good physical shape and went all-out—in the opinion of Stengel.

With this much control of the situation in his hands, Stengel had less trouble surmounting any dugout opinions that he was chiefly a theatrical personality. Money was one thing that the ball players didn't think was funny. The only rub, though, was that the platoon system made it difficult for some players to play steadily enough to please Stengel without the strain of being injected into the lineup in pressure situations.

Once the contracts had been mailed, and returned, Stengel shifted his command of the personnel onto the field from the opening day of spring training. He instituted double practice sessions—two a day—and organized Yankee workouts on what was called "the most elaborate scale since the days of Miller Huggins."

Having lashed himself to the mast, so to speak, Stengel made certain that he could not escape the Yankees' fate in 1949: the club had his stamp, required his approval, played his type of game. By the margin of that one game, it survived the plagues that visited it during the season and he survived with it.

"If we had lost," he said, after "we" had won, "I would have offered to resign in case the club wanted to get somebody else. You know, I am getting along in years, and this was a pretty rough season for a man of my age."

He also acknowledged the mutual dependence he and the players had shared, and would share for the next dozen years, when he said:

"This is the greatest ball club a man could manage. We've been one happy family from the time spring training started. There has never been a sour note in the clubhouse, on the bench, or on the field. A really great bunch of fellows, and I am indebted to them for the way they came through for me. They won it. Not me."

After a riotous celebration at the Biltmore Hotel, and with the World

Series victory behind them, the "greatest ball club" dispersed for the winter. John Drebinger, surveying 1949 in sports, wrote:

"In the first few postwar years, such sports as baseball and racing soared to fantastic heights, chiefly because, aided by prevailing conditions, they were better equipped to break away from the barrier. Folks went to ball games because there wasn't much else to do and they plunged on the horses in staggering amounts because there wasn't much else to do with their money, it still being something of a trick to buy an automobile, a refrigerator or even an extra pair of shoes. With the fourth postwar year, however, the final leveling-off resulted.

"Outstanding in achieving the totally unexpected were the Yankees, who, making a mockery of the baseball experts' forecasts and flashing an utter disregard for an unprecedented total of injuries, swept to a pennant and world championship as well. The Bombers started the year with a manager, Casey Stengel, who never spent a day in the American League and closed it monarchs of all they surveyed."

As the monarchs of all they surveyed headed home for the winter, their manager and his wife flew from New York to California, then stepped down at Glendale to find a cheering crowd whooping it up on the steps of the City Hall. They were driven in an open car strewn with flowers through the downtown business district, passing under a banner that stretched across the street reading: "Glendale, Calif., is proud of Casey Stengel."

It was one year almost to the day since he had left the job at Oakland for New York. And now the "healthy" Yankee returned, stood in front of his cheering townsfolk and neighbors and Edna Stengel's relatives and, when the noise had quieted down, told the throng in vintage Stengel understatement:

"I'm tired. I've been pretty busy."

Chapter

8

The 12 Most Splendid Years

When Babe Ruth died on August 16, 1948, the United States reacted as though a great American institution had fallen, as indeed it had. It was not just that Ruth had dominated an industry for most of his 22 years in it; nor that he had played in 2,503 major league baseball games, gone to bat 8,399 times, made 2,873 hits, scored 2,174 runs and batted .342. Nor that he had excelled as a pitcher before becoming a great hitter. Nor that he had rescued the professional game from its decline after the Black Sox scandal of the 1919 World Series; nor that he had "built" Yankee Stadium and the modern Yankees.

But, by hitting 714 home runs and revolutionizing the image of baseball, he had elevated the game itself, raised the sights and salaries of all players along with his own, increased the revenue of all clubs and captured the public's imagination to an incredible degree.

So it seemed fitting when he died to signal the passing of an institution, not simply the passing of a man. The *St. Louis Post-Dispatch* caught the mood and the significance of the moment in a remarkable editorial that did not lament his death nor even mention his name, but that simply symbolized—almost photographed—his meaning to the national life. It was titled "Bambino" and it said:

> There he stood, a great tall inverted pyramid at the plate. At the top were two of the broadest, most powerful shoulders the bleachers had ever seen. His slender legs hugged each other and his feet came together like the dot of an exclamation point. He was not fussy. No nervous swinging of the bat. No uneasy kicking of his shoes. No

bending over. No straightening up. Just a deliberate getting set. Maybe a little motion at the wrists—that and a death watch on the man on the mound.

Then the first pitch. Low and outside. Everybody tense except the inverted pyramid. Another pitch—low and away. Were they going to walk him? With two on and the winning run at bat, a walk was the play. Then a third pitch. The pyramid gathers himself, steps into the ball and swings—all in one motion. Before the crack of the blow reaches ears in the stands, the ball is lofting away on wings. It rises right of second, arches higher and higher over right field and drops into a sea of upraised hands for another home run. The Babe is jogging around the bags, two runs scoring ahead of him.

Another game won for the New York Yankees, another game nearer the American League pennant and still another World Series. Jogging on, around second, up to third as the din rises, now spikes down on the plate and home again—home for all time.

Two months after Ruth died, the passing of the "institution" was followed by the passing of the Yankees into the era of Casey Stengel, the "funniest manager in baseball" and something less than an institution at the time. And the transition was accompanied by widespread misgivings. In fact, few baseball seasons marked the end of an era more graphically than the next one, 1949, when the Yankees under Stengel played without any "big" man for their first 65 games until Joe DiMaggio recovered from an operation, then juggled line-ups perilously until they squeezed out the pennant on the final day of the season.

The team had moved from institution to improvisation. And, after recovering his breath, his calm and his poise, such as they were, during the winter of 1949-50, Professor Stengel headed for St. Petersburg, Florida, in February of 1950 feeling like a man who had won a reprieve—but who was not certain how long it would last.

"Our improvement for 1950," he said, lapsing into the double-talk that had become a kind of institution itself, "will be the strength we added to what was our strongest department: the bench. There, too, lies our material for trades. Any club offering us a starting pitcher will find us willing to deal."

A few days later, in a fine display of the second-guessing that had been forced upon him during the hectic 1949 season, when every new day offered a new emergency, he reflected:

"Everybody we talked trade with wanted Johnson"—Don Johnson, a promising 23-year-old right-handed pitcher—"and this prompted me to take another look at him myself. He must be good, and if he is, we can use him."

The fact was that Casey could have used anybody with sound health and effective major league experience to prevent a recurrence of the panic of 1949. He looked enviously at pitchers like Bob Kuzava of the Chicago White Sox and Ray Scarborough of the Washington Senators as possible additions to his Big Three of Allie Reynolds, Vic Raschi and Ed Lopat. But, meanwhile, he was beginning to experience the kind of trouble that descends on all teams when they win, before they can start worrying about losing.

Yogi Berra, the young catcher who had led the club in runs batted in, with 91, had been offered a slight raise over his salary of $14,000, but wanted more. Bobby Brown, Tommy Byrne and Raschi wanted more, too. Eventually, Berra signed for $20,000 and Raschi for $30,000, and everybody else got into line. Then, shortly after all hands were present and accounted for in spring training, the inseparable Joes—Page and DiMaggio—were shaken up in an automobile accident on the causeway leading to St. Petersburg Beach.

The holdouts and minor scrapes were not defeats in themselves, of course; but Casey was trying to regroup a team that had survived 73 "out-of-the-line-up" injuries the season before. So the health and conduct of the troops at spring training assumed exaggerated importance.

He briefly considered imposing a curfew to protect the players from themselves, but then reached back in his memory for precedents and discarded the idea.

"Uncle Robbie even put in a curfew," he said, reflecting on the rough-and-tumble days of Wilbert Robinson and the Brooklyn Dodgers of 35 seasons before. "But he soon called it off. A curfew may be all right when you had a lot of good ball players like McGraw had on the Giants, Robbie would say, but with this bunch it just won't work."

Stengel's problems continued at a galloping pace right through his second season as a manager of the Yankees, a team that for two decades during the Ruth-Gehrig era had presented a calm, unruffled, imperturbable face to the world but that now, despite its dramatic salvaging job the season before, was still picked to finish second behind Boston.

Joe Page suddenly lost his effectiveness and George Weiss, the power behind the shaky throne, had to go shopping for an experienced relief pitcher; he got one, Tom Ferrick, from the St. Louis Browns. Tommy Henrich added a battered knee to the club's medical log and was out most of the season; Weiss bought Johnny Hopp from Pittsburgh in September to take his place.

But the move that paid off the best—and for the longest time—was the elevation of a 21-year-old left-handed pitcher from the Yankee farm at Kansas City in midseason to Yankee Stadium: Edward Charles Ford. He was a short, fresh-faced New York City boy who had attended Manhattan Aviation High School, played sandlot ball with the Police Athletic League and the Kiwanis League, and had started his professional career at Butler in the boondocks leagues in 1947 by winning 13 games and losing 4. By the time the Yankees brought him up two and a half years later, he was about to enter military service for two years—but before he did, he pitched in 20 games for them, started 12, won 9, lost one, completed 7 and wound up with an earned-run average of 2.81.

He still autographed baseballs "Ed Ford," but he was already beginning to be called Whitey Ford and, having helped stabilize the situation in a few months in 1950, he went off to the Army. When he returned in 1953, he won

18 games, lost 6 and resumed a career under Stengel that never included a losing season.

When the trading, promoting, and wheeling and dealing were finished in 1950, the Yankees somehow were leading the league again at the end of the final day, with Detroit, Boston and Cleveland in that order behind them. In the National League, the Philadelphia Phillies—who had won only one pennant in 81 years—held a seven-game lead on September 23 and seemed in no danger of not winning their second in 82 years. But they won it the hard way. They lost 9 of their final 13 games, let their lead dissolve to one game, then had to play 10 innings on the final day of the season at Ebbets Field before defeating the Dodgers on a home run by Dick Sisler, with a young right-handed pitcher named Robin Roberts outlasting Don Newcombe.

There were extenuating circumstances, apart from the fact that the Phillies had finished last in the league more than half the time in the previous 30 years. They had lost two bright young pitchers, Bubba Church and Bob Miller, to injuries and had lost their 21-year-old left-handed pitching star, Curt Simmons, to the Army. Simmons, in fact, was inducted during the pennant run in September and got back to watch the World Series by special dispensation. And what he watched was a massacre of sorts in which the Yankees extracted maximum value out of the World Series debut of Ford, who ironically entered the Army just after the series instead of just before it.

The Phillies, living up to the descriptive cliche, the "Whiz Kids," engineered a surprise as the series opened, and nearly got away with it. Their manager, Eddie Sawyer, started Jim Konstanty—more elegantly known as Casimir James Konstanty—against Stengel's choice, Vic Raschi, in the opening game. Konstanty had set a major league record by pitching in 74 games that season, winning 16, losing 7 and starting none, and, in fact, he had never started a game for the Phillies.

Konstanty not only started, but almost finished, this one. He allowed four hits until he left for a pinch-hitter in the eighth inning, after coming close to one of the great coups of baseball history. But Stengel had horses, too. Raschi allowed the Phillies only two hits and won the game, 1 to 0.

The next day, Roberts tangled with Reynolds for 10 innings until Joe DiMaggio, after six straight pop-ups, popped one into the upper grandstand in left-center field in Philadelphia.

The third game, in Yankee Stadium, went to the Yankees by a score of 3 to 2, and not only put the Phillies three games behind but also marked the seventh straight time they had lost a series game by one run—having lost the final four of the 1915 series to the Red Sox by one run.

They finally managed to break that streak the next day against Ford. Instead of losing by one run, they lost by three. The score was 5 to 2, the Phillies also lost the series and now suddenly "the funniest manager in baseball" had taken two consecutive world championships and was beginning to build a new "institution" for the Yankees.

However, institutions like the old Yankees needed titans like the old Yan-

kees. Nine members of the club had made the All-Star team that season—
Byrne, Raschi, Reynolds, DiMaggio, Coleman, Henrich, Rizzuto, Berra and
Stengel; even Dickey and Crosetti were there as coaches, and Turner pitched
batting practice. But in spite of this saturation of talent, the American League
had lost the game, 4 to 3, in 14 innings and, far more important, none of the
army of Yankees on hand seemed to represent a new link in the line of titans
that had stretched from Ruth to Gehrig to DiMaggio, who was nearing the end
of his career.

Nevertheless, Stengel pitched his camp early the following February in
Phoenix, Arizona, occupying the training base of the Giants, who had switched
with the Yankees that year and who were now advancing on St. Petersburg. It
was the Yankees' first penetration of the Far West, and they not only found
gold there but also brought gold there. Phil Rizzuto, the smallest member of
the club, who had once received milk money of 20 cents during a tryout with
the Yankees, arrived with a contract worth $50,000, the third highest in the
team's history after Ruth's $80,000 and DiMaggio's $100,000. The feeling was
that Rizzuto may not have been precisely a titan but that he was worth it. He
had played in all 155 games in 1950, had hit .324 and had made exactly 200 hits.

Stengel, always sensitive to the bread-and-butter factors of baseball, arrived with a new two-year contract himself. It was worth $65,000 plus bonuses
and it made him the highest-paid manager in history. He was 60 years old,
though, and was still impressed by that fact as much as anybody else.

"The only question," he said after the 1950 season, "concerns my health. I
was sick during the spring but I feel fine now. I will pass up most of the winter
dinners and hope to be ready for 1951. If my health does not hold up, there's a
clause in my contract permitting me to step down."

He had talked of retiring after winning in 1949 and again after winning in
1950, but had not been taken too seriously; a few years later, though, when he
talked of retiring after *losing,* he was to find "sympathizers" in the Yankee
hierarchy.

Nevertheless, he made it to Phoenix in 1951 in fine fettle and was on hand
on February 21 when the advance guard of the Yankees descended on Arizona.
It was a four-man delegation consisting of four pitchers—Raschi, Porterfield,
Spec Shea and Tom Ferrick—with Dan Topping in command. The caravan
had set out by railroad from New York on a Sunday night, detoured for a
party in the Cameo Club in Chicago, basked in the warmth of an outpouring
of admirers at Tucumcari, New Mexico, and pulled into Phoenix to a full-blast
welcome from the mayor, natives in cowboy regalia, a hillbilly band and
Casey Stengel.

The manager had been on the scene since February 15 with Dickey, Crosetti, Turner, Henrich and Johnny Neun, "inspecting rookies." In particular,
they were inspecting a short, brutally strong blond from Oklahoma, who
looked many days like the missing candidate for the institutional lines of
succession.

"Mickey Mantle," wrote James P. Dawson in *The New York Times,* "rookie from Commerce, Oklahoma, will be the subject of an extensive experiment in the Yankee training campaign. No less an authority than Manager Casey Stengel revealed this information today, one of those rare days when rain dampened activities in the Valley of the Sun.

"Stengel said he would work the 20-year-old Mantle in center field, and immediately speculation arose over whether the Yanks regarded the rookie as the eventual successor to the great Joe DiMaggio."

The great Joe DiMaggio added a bit of urgency to the situation by declaring that he intended to retire after the 1951 season. That gave Stengel one season to groom a replacement, and if the replacement was to be Mantle, who had played at Independence, Kansas, in 1949 and at Joplin, Missouri, in 1950, then the grooming process suddenly became a quandary.

"The husky blond," according to one flowing report, grasping the problem well, "has the speed of a deer, the swinging power of a seasoned hitter and the throwing arm that compares with anything in camp right now. But he is both a delight and a problem. Should Casey play him or let him ride the bench after a jump from Class C at Joplin, Missouri?"

Mantle had a problem, too. He had osteomyelitis in his left ankle and, in fact, was 4-F in the military draft. He was not in the lineup, in any event, when Stengel shepherded his team west for a 21-day, 12-game swing through his home state of California, a cavalcade that started with this batting order; Rizzuto, shortstop; Coleman, second base; Berra, catcher; DiMaggio, center field; Bauer, right field; Mize, first base; Gene Woodling, left field; Billy Johnson, third base, and Reynolds, pitcher.

It was a great show, except that Stengel's affinity for catastrophe flashed on, even while the team was playing games before Governor Earl Warren, Hollywood stars like Max Baer and Hollywood stars unlike Max Baer, huge, glittering crowds—and ambitious, tough teams from the Pacific Coast League. DiMaggio repeated his announcement about quitting. Mantle, in spite of his osteomyelitis and 4-F rating, was notified by a draft board in Oklahoma to report for an examination. Reynolds developed sinovitis in his elbow on the opening day of the tour. And the Yankees, after winning six games, immediately lost four straight to minor league teams.

Somehow, they made it north for the start of the regular season at Yankee Stadium, then went to Washington for the ceremonial opening, which had been rained out and which now, consequently, had been rescheduled as a doubleheader. President Truman, a southpaw, wearing an infielder's mitt on his right hand, threw out the first pitch; Reynolds caught it on the bounce, and the Yankees lost both games to the Senators, 5 to 3 and 8 to 4.

Mantle appeared in 96 games for the Yankees and 40 for their farm team at Kansas City that season, and was still being groomed, so most of the burden fell on the "old pros" behind DiMaggio. The "old pros," though, were a little frayed around the edges. Berra led the club in runs batted in, with 88 (Gehrig had batted in 175 in 1927), and a rookie infielder named Gil McDougald was the only .300 hitter on the roster. But the Yankees had so much momentum that they rolled right through the Cleveland Indians (15 times in 22 games) and the Boston Red Sox (7 times in 8 games in September alone) and won their third straight American League pennant.

The high spots were a pair of no-hit games pitched by Reynolds: against Cleveland on July 12, by a score of 1 to 0, and against Boston on September 28, by 8 to 0. The games had one thing in common: Reynolds' catcher was Yogi Berra, the short, blunt St. Louis boy who was growing side by side with Stengel in Yankee folklore, and who was becoming a national character as Casey's "assistant" in later seasons and who was to follow him into high places during the next 15 years.

Stengel instinctively liked the primitive nature-boy qualities of Berra, who became a kind of hero lovably caricatured as "Yogi Bear" and who was constructed along such lines of fireplug simplicity that baseball writers sometimes sent waiters to his table in restaurants with notes addressed to Yogi's dinner partner, saying: "Who's your ugly friend?" He even displayed a Stengelese flair for philosophy couched in doubletalk, remarking on one occasion during a discussion of baseball sagacity: "You can observe a lot just by watching."

But Berra had flourished artistically and financially, rising from $90 a month at Norfolk in 1942 to $5,000 a month a dozen years later. One season he caught 151 games out of 154 played by the Yankees and Stengel usually wrote "Berra" first on his unpredictable lineup cards the way the First Lord of the Admiralty might write "Gibraltar" first on a list of things-to-count-on during the threatened dissolution of the Empire.

DiMaggio was about to leave the Yankees' empire, and Mantle had not yet established his place in it, but there was Berra anchoring things and winning a place in Stengel's affections that no other ball player ever quite matched. On the day that Reynolds pitched his second no-hitter, though, Yogi unaccountably gave Stengel and the rest of the Yankees, to say nothing of Reynolds, a moment of runaway excitement. With two outs in the ninth inning and Reynolds one out from baseball history, Ted Williams swung and lifted a towering foul ball off to the side of home plate. Yogi drew a bead on the ball, carefully tossed his mask out of the way, waited—and dropped the ball. Now Reynolds was still one out from baseball history but, with Williams still "alive," he also was one pitch away from seeing the ball disappear toward right field.

If Yogi's error was astonishing, what happened next was incredible. While Reynolds, Stengel, Berra and everybody else held their breath, Williams lifted an identical foul ball to the side of home plate. But this time Berra clutched it to preserve Reynolds' no-hitter.

"I thought Reynolds was gonna catch that one himself," Stengel said, shaking his head over the incident years later.

"I called for the same pitch the second time," Yogi recalled, reviewing the technicalities. "Fastball across the letters and tight. And Reynolds pitched it right there."

"I'll tell you where Berra was pretty good as a ball player," Stengel said. "People don't understand it. He put time in on the sport; he knew everything about different sports. He'd like to sit and watch. Berra was pretty good, too, watching pitching. He was very good when he saw them careless. Berra was pretty good making them do it. I thought he was wonderful in jacking up Raschi. He was very good in doing the same thing to, you might say, Reynolds. I thought he was one of the best catchers. When he started, he couldn't do it. He couldn't go out and pick up a bunt. Now, in the World Series he's proved it. He's quick, he could get out—he looks awkward to get a bunt—he knows, it's a suspicion, if you watch the hitter, whether the man's gonna bunt or isn't gonna bunt."

If that analysis wasn't entirely clear, Stengel's reliance on Berra was, especially since the Yankees' chances of winning a third straight World Series were blocked by the Giants, who got into the series through a succession of feats that many persons regarded as the most improbable in the history of baseball. The Giants lost 11 games in a row as the season started and were still 13½ games behind in mid-August. But, under the goading of Leo Durocher, they caught and tied the Dodgers on the final day of the season, then defeated them in the third and final game of a playoff series when Bobby Thomson hit his famous three-run home run off Ralph Branca in the last half of the ninth inning.

The World Series started the next day and was a bit of an anti-climax, though the Giants won the opening game and appeared en route to certifying their nickname of "Cinderella Team" once and for all. But the Yankees, by now old hands at the perils of the "short series," made it three straight championships by winning four of the next five games.

Three things transcended even the fact that Stengel had gone 3-for-3 as a Yankee manager: A rookie named Willie Mays played center field for the Giants in the series; he was flanked by Henry Thompson and Monte Irvin, giving the Giants the first Negro outfield in the major leagues, and on October 10, the day the Yankees won the series, Joe DiMaggio played his last game. Two months later, on December 11, DiMaggio went by the Yankee office on Fifth Avenue and wrote this valedictory message to Weiss:

"Mr. George Weiss—They will come and they will go, but with you at the helm there will always be Yankee pennants."

It wasn't a bad prediction, even though the Yankees were still being troubled by the fact that DiMaggio's successor, Mantle, was being plagued by two chronic weaknesses: He was prone to knee and leg injuries and he was prone to strikeouts.

In fact, during the following season, 1952, Mantle's first as the "big man" of the club, he set a record by striking out 111 times. However, Berra set a record by hitting 30 home runs, the most ever hit by a catcher, and the Yankees individually and collectively set or tied 33 records, hit 129 home runs, won the club's 19th pennant and Stengel's fourth straight, and equaled Joe McCarthy's streak of four titles from 1936 through 1939.

But some distant shadows were already falling across the Yankees. They were forced to seven games in order to defeat the Dodgers in the series, then had to win the final two games to do it, which they did by scores of 3 to 2 and 4 to 2. Duke Snider hit four home runs for Brooklyn, and Pee Wee Reese and Jackie Robinson demonstrated the advantages of "old-fashioned" baseball by pulling a double steal and otherwise running aggressively against the Yankees for Charlie Dressen. Stengel, though, still had the horses to pull him through the thickening competition. Berra and Mantle each hit two home runs; Mize got off the bench after three games to hit three. And Billy Martin, a graceless youngster with few classic talents but all kinds of brass, hit, ran, fielded and plain pestered the Dodgers into submission.

Martin, a scrawny 165-pounder who had enthralled Stengel at Oakland, scrambled back into Casey's affections in 1953, too. He hit .257 while the Yankees were winning their fifth consecutive pennant, a record for one club and for one manager. Then, in the World Series against Brooklyn, Martin hit a cool .500; Carl Erskine struck out 14 Yankees in the third game; Ford made his first World Series start in the fourth game after two years in the Army, and lost; Mantle hit a home run with the bases loaded in the fifth game, and the Yankees won it all when Martin singled over second base in the last half of the ninth inning in the sixth game.

The series, noted Frederick G. Lieb, came close to being the first $3,000,000 series in history, and Ford C. Frick, the Indiana farm boy, sportswriter, broadcaster and president of the National League who had succeeded Happy Chandler as commissioner in 1951, commented in a rousing understatement: "Receipts of $2,979,269 aren't hay." Television fees, already becoming a significant part of baseball revenue, totaled $925,000; radio brought in $200,000; a pregame TV program was worth $100,000; each Dodger got $6,178 for losing, and each Yankee, including Stengel got $8,280 for winning.

However, it was temporarily the last winning share for each Yankee after an unparalleled string of five years in which regulars like Berra collected $30,000 apiece in World Series checks alone; in which the Yankees had somehow made the transition from the McCarthy-DiMaggio era to the Stengel-Berra-Mantle era, and in which Stengel had parlayed his wits and Yankee depth in players into the most successful span in baseball history.

The Professor also had blossomed, during this rush of prosperity, into a more indulgent type himself—less primitive than in his earlier years, less imperious than in his later years.

Even the image of "Casey the Clown" was being soft-pedaled to some extent. When one of the most famous trick pictures of his career was taken, showing him as a Swami peering wide-eyed into a crystal ball, his old friend and boss Weiss was not particularly amused. He still did not want the Stengel image to be presented in ludicrous terms.

When Mantle started the 1953 season in Washington by hitting a fastball thrown by Chuck Stobbs over the bleachers in Griffith Stadium, Red Patterson rushed outside the park with a tape measure. He found a boy who had chased the ball into the yard of a house across the street, brought it back, paced off the distance back to the 50-foot-high bleacher wall, added 69 feet for the depth of the bleachers and 391 feet to home plate, and calculated that the ball had traveled 565 feet. The ball and bat later were enshrined in Yankee Stadium, were stolen and were eventually returned. But Patterson's principal memory of the incident was Stengel's admonition to him to promote all possibilities, saying of Mantle: "I want to make that boy some money."

When the Yankees got into an extra-inning game in Philadelphia one night, missed their train and went instead by chartered bus to the Broad Street Station, the old man saw that all the seats on the bus were taken and croaked: "You fellas played hard and you're tired." So he stood alongside Gus Mauch, holding onto the vertical metal pole. His concern for his troops took an odd turn. The bus driver tried to go through a tunnel that was too low, the top of the bus struck the roof of the tunnel and, in the grinding crash that followed, the metal pole broke and fell on Mauch, with the 62-year-old manager still gripping it.

He carried his compassion a step too far, perhaps, in the spring of 1954 when he declared, as the Yankees opened spring training in search of an improbable sixth straight pennant. "If the Yankees don't win the pennant, the owners should discharge me."

Having crawled out that far on the limb, he analyzed the situation further: "Perhaps I should be worried, but I'm going to tell you why I'm not worried. I still hear the other clubs moaning that we keep coming up with new players. Well, why wouldn't they moan? I would, too, if I were in their shoes. We have come up with three tremendous youngsters this spring—Bill Skowron, Bob Cerv and the young pitcher, Bob Grim. I would say as of now all three have definitely established themselves with the club.

"Right now I would have to say my infield has been shaky, the pitching, especially the left side, has been wild and a lot of the regulars, excepting Yogi Berra, have yet to start hitting."

Having thus switched from the pitchers of the left side to the hitters of the left side without punctuation in mid-sentence, Casey then led his club into the training exhibition season, in which they proceeded to win 8 games and lose 16. Now it was Topping's turn not to be worried.

"I don't think there's any reason to become unduly alarmed just yet," the Yankees' owner commented, sounding duly alarmed. "Casey doesn't seem too greatly disturbed, so I don't see why I should be."

Nevertheless, there was cause for at least curiosity, if not concern. Mantle's right knee was troubling him again, and the Yankees had begun to resort to the hit-and-run, the bunt and opposite-field hitting, all old-fashioned remedies, to neutralize the ailments that had begun to creep into their pattern of play. On the opening day of the season, April 13, a golfing enthusiast named Dwight D. Eisenhower threw out the first ball, Bucky Harris presided over the Senators' dugout and his successor in the Yankees' dugout, Dr. Stengel, platooned 19 players like a football coach. However, in the 10th inning, the Senators' 35-year-old first-baseman, Mickey Vernon, hit a home run to beat the Yankees, 5 to 3. Eisenhower, who had a golfing date in Augusta the next day, stuck it out to the end, called Vernon to the Presidential box and shook the hand that shook the Yankees.

The 27,160 persons at the game in Griffith Stadium had seen the beginning of the end. Five months later, Casey got around to acknowledging his position on the limb, too.

"I got a shock this morning when I looked at the standings," he admitted. "We could have been 4½ games out. Instead, we're 8½. That frightens me. It should frighten the owners, too. Something will have to be done or the Yankees will not be the Yankees."

The optimism of his view in the spring had now shifted to pessimism in September, and not just because the Yankees were losing for the first time in six seasons. Now he was grumping about the long-range view and was intimating that the "owners" had better start becoming alarmed, as he was. But they were the same owners who had relied on his *not* being alarmed a few months earlier. So a tug of war was setting in, one that would intensify gradually during the next seven years—the second "half" of the Weiss-Stengel administration—as the club inevitably meandered in the one direction open to a club at the top: down.

Would he be back as manager the next year?

"I won't talk about that because I don't have to talk about that," Casey replied, sounding a bit crotchety, and giving an answer that he would repeat almost annually (and petulantly) for the rest of his career.

Yet, a week later, on September 19, the Yankees won their 100th game— the first time they had won 100 under Stengel and the first time in 40 years that a team had won 100 games and still lost the American League pennant. They lost it, all right, as the Cleveland Indians won 111 games behind the remarkable pitching of Bob Lemon, Early Wynn, Mike Garcia, Bob Feller and Art Houtteman. The Indians' remarkable pitching, though, did not prevent an even more remarkable upset in the World Series, which the Giants swept in four games.

But the lasting significance of the 1954 season was that, after five years, the Yankees' dominance was broken. The next seven years would produce five more pennants but only two more World Series victories, and already the competition was gathering as the Yankees' rivals began to spend big money for bonuses to entice young ball players who formerly had wanted only to wear the magic pinstripes.

The Yankees still had flair, though, and on September 23, one week before the season ended, instead of sawing off the limb that Casey had crawled out onto in the spring, they awarded him a new two-year contract for 1955 and 1956 at $80,000 a season. It was his fourth contract with the Yankees, and as it was tendered everybody naturally recalled his admonition that "if the Yankees don't win the pennant, the owners should discharge me."

"I meant what I said then, and I still feel that way," he said, pocketing the contract.

"We talked him out of it," Topping said.

"We were beaten in a good fair way by Cleveland," Casey went on, summing up the decline and fall of his heroes. "They had the pitching, the power, the bench. My job now is to better the Yankees. The Yankees are not gone. We'll have to change our methods somewhat."

As things turned out, the Yankees changed their methods somewhat less rapidly than their ex-victims changed theirs. Perhaps the Yankees had less reason to change, considering their record of success. Perhaps they had grown too attached to the methods that had bred such success. Perhaps they were just growing older together. Whatever the reason, fundamental changes were taking place in baseball outside their sphere of influence. The Boston Braves moved to Milwaukee and the St. Louis Browns were reincarnated in Baltimore in 1953; the Philadelphia Athletics became the Kansas City Athletics in 1954; the Brooklyn Dodgers migrated west to Los Angeles and the New York Giants to San Francisco late in 1957. Yet, Yankees attendance, which had reached 2,281,676 in Stengel's first year, went down with only minor adjustments to 1,428,438 in 1958, then crept up to 1,627,349 in 1960—but still totaled 600,000 below Casey's first season, in spite of the fact that the Dodgers and Giants had left town and the Mets had not yet arrived.

Outwardly, the Yankees were still one big, mostly happy family and the patriarch was still the old man in uniform No. 37. He still, as his fortunes began to ebb slightly, showed a soft spot for the young players, who were inheriting the "situation."

Whitey Ford, who was maturing into a prosperous Long Island suburban-ite and one of the most effective pitchers in the club's history, named his pet poodle "Casey." Mantle allowed that Casey "used to get mad at me sometimes" but rated him one of the smartest baseball men ever, and "about the funniest person I've known." Bobby Richardson noted that Stengel used to twit him when he first came up to the Yankees by saying: "Look at him. He doesn't drink, doesn't smoke and he still can't hit .250." But when the dedicated young Baptist from South Carolina was about to earn his letter a few seasons later and got a hit in the final game of the season, Stengel telephoned the club statistician from the dugout, ascertained that Richardson's average had reached .301 and took him out of the game to preserve it.

Bill Veeck recalled that whenever the Yankees played in Cleveland, he and Casey would have breakfast together, and one morning Stengel said over the toast: "I blew a ball game last night."

"How so?" Veeck asked.

"Well," Stengel said, "our kid shortstop, Kubek, slipped on the wet ground chasing a line drive in the ninth and two runs scored and they beat us, 3 to 2."

"How was that your fault?" Veeck persisted, and he was surprised when Stengel said:

"Yeah, well, after the game I said to the kid, let me see your spikes, and he showed them to me. They was the same ones he used in high school, all worn down and no spikes left to run on. So it was my fault, I should've asked sooner."

Ten years later, Veeck added that he had learned that Stengel then had told Kubek to get a pair of new shoes at once and charge them to him—$26.

Another day the young left-hander Bob Kuzava found himself sitting alone in the dugout with the manager, who had squirmed the night before while Kuzava was giving up the winning run in the last inning.

"What did you throw that fella?" Stengel asked.

"A curve ball," Kuzava said.

And where did it break?

"Right across here," the pitcher said, motioning across the waist and over the plate.

"If it breaks over the plate," Stengel said, delivering one of his briefest lessons on the art of pitching, "it ain't a curve."

One day in St. Petersburg, Casey enacted one of his more memorable performances at the behest of a group of New York writers who enlisted him in a practical joke. The victim was John Drebinger of *The Times,* an accomplished extrovert who relished and perpetrated many pranks himself despite the fact that he was hard of hearing and, in fact, wore a hearing aid that became a prop in clubhouse horseplay. Casey was headed across the outfield at Huggins Field—later renamed Huggins-Stengel Field in tribute to his 12 splendid years with the Yankees—and it was decided to conduct the daily press conference in pantomine without advising Drebbie. Casey gave a virtuoso performance. He pointed, roared silently, waved his arms and mouthed exaggerated imprecations—while his old friend bent his head, shook his earphone, frantically cranked the control knob on his chest and finally removed the "faulty" equipment, trying to tune in the great man.

Another day, Harry Harris, first-string photographer for *The Associated Press,* dropped by the dugout at Huggins-Stengel Field and found the old manager sitting alone. Harry had heard that it was wise to avoid Casey on days when he wore Mexican sandals in the dugout; it meant he was probably suffering a "morning-after" grouch. So, spotting the sandals, he began to beat a strategic retreat. But Casey shouted after him and summoned him back, saying he felt lonely and wanted to talk.

"You look grim," Harris said tentatively. "Did you lose your best friend?"

"I sat up all night," Stengel said. "One of my relatives died."

"Close?"

Casey took a deep breath, sighed remorsefully and replied with a wink: "Old Grand-Dad."

Stengel's understanding of the aberrations of human nature had frequent opportunity to develop on the Yankees, who were such a clamorous lot off the field despite their cool efficiency on it that the management once hired private eyes to shadow the ringleaders. That was Keystone Comedy stuff out of Stengel's own days as a mischief-maker 40 years earlier and, although he was instinctively against such surveillance, he went through the motions of enforcing the club's will, especially when off-duty pranks were followed by on-duty setbacks.

One such setback came in 1955, the year after the Yankees lost the pennant. This time, they won seven fewer games but out-distanced Cleveland in a difficult race and went into the World Series with Mantle and Hank Bauer hobbled by injuries. The Dodgers, who had led the National League by 13½ games, swaggered into the series under their second-year manager, Walter Alston, lost the first two games, but made history by winning four of the last five, principally on the stout pitching of Johnny Podres, and won their first series after eight defeats and their first against the Yankees after six.

Having dropped a pennant and a World Series now in successive years, Stengel recouped some of his losses in 1956. Mantle had his strongest year, winning the so-called Triple Crown by leading the league in batting average (.353), home runs (52) and runs batted in (130). But in the World Series, the last to be played by the Dodgers in Brooklyn, the Yankees lost the two opening games, then had to go the full seven again before winning—for the first time in three years.

The redeeming feature, apart from the victory itself, was the comeback of Don Larsen, a man who, in Stengel's words, "liked to drink beer" and a man who had run into a tree one night in St. Petersburg that spring. Casey sized up his man and played down the incident but told Larsen that the next time it would cost him a bundle of money. Larsen got the message. He won 11 games and lost 5 that season, then on October 8, with the World Series tied at two games apiece, the 27-year-old right-hander from Michigan City, Indiana, paid Stengel back before 64,519 persons in Yankee Stadium.

Twenty-seven Dodgers went to bat and Larsen, pitching mostly fastballs to Berra, got all 27 out for the first perfect game in World Series history. His 96th pitch was a shoulder-high fastball that Dale Mitchell, a pinch-hitter, looked at and that Babe Pinelli, the home-plate umpire, called Strike 3. That ended the game and Pinelli's career as a balls-and-strikes umpire, since he retired after the series. The box score read like this:

October 8, 1956

BROOKLYN (N.L.)						**NEW YORK (A.L.)**					
	ab	r	h	o	a		ab	r	h	o	a
Gilliam, 2b	3	0	0	2	0	Bauer, rf	4	0	1	4	0
Reese, ss	3	0	0	4	2	Collins, 1b	4	0	1	7	0
Snider, cf	3	0	0	1	0	Mantle, cf	3	1	1	4	0
Robinson, 3b	3	0	0	2	4	Berra, c	3	0	0	7	0
Hodges, 1b	3	0	0	5	1	Slaughter, lf	2	0	0	1	0
Amoros, lf	3	0	0	3	0	Martin, 2b	3	0	1	3	4
Furillo, rf	3	0	0	0	0	McDougald, ss	2	0	0	0	2
Campanella, c	3	0	0	7	2	Carey, 3b	3	1	1	1	1
Maglie, p	2	0	0	0	1	Larsen, p	2	0	0	0	1
a-Mitchell	1	0	0	0	0		26	2	5	27	8
	27	0	0	24	10						

a-Called out on strikes for Maglie in ninth.

Brooklyn.................................0 0 0   0 0 0   0 0 0—0
New York ....0 0 0   1 0 1   0 0 x—2

Errors—None. Runs batted in—Mantle, Bauer. Home Run—Mantle. Sacrifice—Larsen. Double plays—Reese and Hodges; Hodges, Campanella, Robinson, Campanella and Robinson. Left on base—Dodgers 0, Yankees 3. Bases on balls—Maglie 2. Struck out—Larsen, 7; Maglie, 5. Umpires—Pinelli (N), Soar (A), Boggess (N), Napp (A), Gorman (N), Runge (A). Time—2:06. Attendance—64,519.

The jubilation caused by Larsen's perfect game was still loud seven months later, on May 15, when Mantle, Bauer, Johnny Kucks, Ford and Berra gathered with their wives at the Copacabana in Manhattan to celebrate Billy Martin's birthday. The party broke up after a fight in the men's washroom, in which a Yankee non-fan was the loser and in which nobody claimed to be the winner. Accordingly, the Yankee management levied equal fines of $1,000 each ($500 on Kucks, who was less affluent), and a few weeks later, Casey's boy, Martin, the guest of honor and roommate of Mantle, was traded. The gang was beginning to break up.

Two seasons later, Casey was to criticize "cut-ups" on the team publicly, the day of indulgence having ended with Larsen in the spring of 1956. But before the gulf began to widen, Stengel and his young adults went through more rough-and-tumble days.

For the second straight year, in 1957, they were carried to the full seven games in the World Series, after winning the pennant by eight games. Their opponents were the Milwaukee Braves, who won their first pennant since being transplanted from Boston four years earlier. The series was exciting, almost hysterical, with Lew Burdette pitching three victories for Milwaukee and Ford, Larsen and Turley one each for New York. Spahn also pitched one for the Braves, and now the Yankees had gone four years with only one World Series success and were, by their own standards, at least, wavering.

They were still wavering in 1958, winning only 92 games, but the rest of the league was wavering worse. After two months, nobody was playing .500 ball except the Yankees, who played little better than that the rest of the way and who, as the World Series opened in Milwaukee, were described by Lieb as "still in their slump" and frequently acting "like a team in a trance."

Becalmed as they were, they lost three of the first four games to Spahn (twice) and Burdette. But somehow, they pulled it out, with Turley pitching in all three remaining games and winning two of them for a team that batted .210. It was a bittersweet victory—the third straight series in which they had been extended to the limit, and the last they would ever win for Stengel.

In fact, his job wavered with the club that season and even though the club won, the wear and tear was beginning to tell. For five years, Stengel's teams had won five straight pennants and championships; for the next five, they won four pennants but only two series. And the worst was yet to come. In 1959, they not only wavered but also collapsed, winning 79 games and losing 75 for a playing percentage of .513, the lowest for a Yankee team in 34 seasons.

The Chicago White Sox filled the vacuum by beating out Cleveland for the pennant and later George Weiss looked back and analyzed the debacle:

"It was the only year we lost decisively in 12 years of operation. Criticism went on all year and, as a sensitive man, I think that Casey would have quit if it hadn't been for his great desire to beat McGraw's managerial record. Most of the criticism was against his two-platooning, but the fact is that we lost that year because of constant injuries to key players like Bill Skowron, Gil McDougald and Andy Carey. Stengel had his first-string lineup intact for less than a month. That was the sole reason we lost."

Maybe Weiss knew that was the sole reason and maybe Stengel felt it; but more and more, they were holding a minority position in the Yankee scheme of things. For the first time, Weiss recalled, he even met resistance in a manpower matter. He suggested trying to acquire Ned Garver from Kansas City, but nobody in the front-office superstructure would second the nomination. The handwriting was on the wall, and even Stengel, whose eyes would be 70 years old the following season, could read the message.

The Yankees of 1960—Stengel's 12th and last Yankee team—were built around old pros like Mantle, Ford and Berra; new young players like Richardson, Clete Boyer and Elston Howard, who had been the Most Valuable Player in the International League in 1954 and who became the Yankees' first Negro player; and Roger Maris, the left-handed-hitting outfielder who had just been acquired from Kansas City. Stengel was still brooding over the front office's critical appraisal of the previous season when the team fell two games behind Baltimore in September, but the boys rallied round the flag with a 15-game winning streak that won the pennant—No. 10 in 12 years.

Casey opened the door to second-guessing by starting Art Ditmar in the World Series against the Pittsburgh Pirates instead of Ford, who was nearly 32 years old now and who had won only 12 games and lost 9 in a disappointing season. Ditmar lost. But then the Yankees scored—"wasted" might be a better word—26 runs to win the next two games before losing the two after that.

So, Pittsburgh held a lead of 3 games to 2 on October 12 when the action shifted back to Forbes Field. Ford, who pitched better with four or even five days of rest, had had only three; but he assured Stengel that morning that he felt all right. The Yankees had backed him in his previous game with 10 runs and now, before 38,580 persons, they backed him with 12 as he pitched his second shutout and evened the series, 3-all.

After the game, Mayor Robert F. Wagner sent a telegram to Stengel saying: "Our city solidly behind you and hope that you will stay with the Yankees and win the series next year."

Casey also received a petition from the New York newspaper writers—"my writers"—asking him to remain as manager as long as his health would permit. He replied:

"I've been here 12 years and when a feller stays as long in one place he gets a lot of people mad at him and he gets mad at a lot of people when they blame him for blowing the tight games."

The tightest of tight games was still ahead of him, unfortunately.

The fateful day was October 13, with 36,683 persons sitting and standing in the Pirates' old stadium. Pittsburgh scored four runs in the first two innings, routing Stafford and Turley, who had started and who threw only 20 pitches, the 14th of which was hit for a two-run home run by Rocky Nelson. But in the fifth inning Skowron hit a home run and in the sixth "my assistant, Mr. Berra," hit a three-run home run, and the Yankees scored four times, chasing Vernon Law and Elroy Face. And now the Professor had a one-run lead in a series in which 72 runs had already been scored with more to come.

But as cheap as life seemed in Forbes Field that afternoon, nothing could have prepared Stengel for what happened in the final two innings.

First, the Yankees added two runs in the top of the eighth, making it 7 to 4. But in the home half, Gino Cimoli singled and Bill Virdon hit a double-play grounder toward Tony Kubek, the long, strong Wisconsin boy who "threw like a girl" but who, in Stengel's description, "made the play."

Tony never had a chance to make this play, though, and for want of a good bounce a grounder was lost and, a few moments later, for want of a grounder, a series was lost. Virdon's grounder took one final hop off the hard Pittsburgh infield—one of the hardest in the major leagues—and struck Kubek in the Adam's apple, then bounced away for a hit. He was rushed to a hospital, while the Pirates rushed to one of the most unlikely climaxes imaginable. Dick Groat singled; Jim Coates replaced Bobby Shantz for Stengel on the pitcher's mound; Bob Skinner sacrificed; Nelson flied out; Roberto Clemente hit a grounder right of the mound for the "third out," but Coates failed to cover first base and Virdon scored the second run of the inning.

Then Hal Smith, a onetime Yankee prospect, knocked the ball over the left-field fence and it was suddenly 9 to 7, Pittsburgh.

Things would have been bad enough if the game had ended there, but Stengel's nightmare was just beginning. Richardson opened the ninth inning with a single, Dale Long pinch-hit a single and Harvey Haddix replaced Bob Friend as the Pirates' pitcher. Maris fouled out to the catcher, but Mantle singled to right, scoring Richardson and sending Long to third, and it was 9 to 8.

Suddenly, it almost ended when Berra hit a rifle shot down the first-base line that Nelson somehow grabbed, almost doubling Mantle off the bag. But Mickey dived back in ahead of the tag, while McDougald, running for Long, scored the tying run.

Yogi Berra's son Larry was watching on television back home in New Jersey when Bill Mazeroski, a 24-year-old West Virginian, led off the Pittsburgh half of the ninth with the score tied, 9 to 9. He saw Ralph Terry throw one ball, then he saw Mazeroski hit the next pitch toward the wall in left field and, Larry said, "I thought, if only my father could catch it." But Yogi was watching it, too, as it sailed over the wall for a home run, abruptly making the score 10 to 9, giving Pittsburgh its first World Series victory in 35 years, giving the Yankees their seventh defeat after 18 victories, and giving Casey Stengel, who had won seven World Series in 12 seasons, his third defeat—and his last.

"I can't believe it," said Yogi in the stunned clubhouse.

"I'll never believe it," said Dale Long.

Chapter

Commence
Bein' Amazin'

When Harry S. Truman's Secretary of Defense, Louis A. Johnson, was enduring heavy criticism during the early days of the Korean War, he likened his position to that of another national figure. "I am reminded," Johnson said, in a thrust at his critics, "of the bleacher fans at the Yankee Stadium who credited the victories of the team to the players and always blamed Casey Stengel for temporary setbacks. So it has often been with me."

Having thus phrased his defense in terms that would be unmistakable to the nation, Johnson stood his ground until replaced at the Pentagon on September 12, 1950. His allusion, however, grew increasingly more accurate as the years went by. One decade and one month later, while the bleacher fans at Yankee Stadium were still talking about the bizarre climax to the World Series of 1960, in which the Pittsburgh Pirates nipped the New York Yankees by one run in the last half of the last inning of the last game, Johnson's fate befell the man he had selected to illustrate the slings and arrows of outrageous fortune.

The Yankees assembled their highest echelons of executives at the Savoy-Hilton Hotel on Fifth Avenue in New York—all except Del Webb, co-owner of the club with Dan Topping, who was in Los Angeles, where Casey Stengel had started his trip East in 1948 to become manager. In 12 years, the Yankees had survived the postwar transition on the most lavish scale ever known in professional baseball. They had won five consecutive world championships, they had won ten American League pennants in 12 seasons, they had won seven World Series. But most of their success had come during the first half of the Stengel administration; the club had not won a series since 1958; it had just lost one to a team rated far below it in man-to-man ability, and Professor Stengel, now presiding over a less serene dugout, had just turned 70 years old.

Topping, puffing somewhat nervously on a cigarette, opened the momentous meeting by reading a prepared statement that was considered a model of diplomatic, euphemistic language that the denizens of Washington might have envied.

Two years earlier, he said, Stengel had "quite reluctantly signed a new two-year contract with the understanding that after the first year he could retire if he desired to do so. Keeping in mind his possible retirement, the Yankees set out to develop a program for the eventual replacement of Casey."

Under the club's profit-sharing plan, he added, Casey would be relieved of his burdens with "an amount exceeding $160,000 to his credit to do with as he pleased."

As for reports that Stengel's retirement signaled a wholesale shakeup that would also hasten the retirement of George Weiss as general manager at the age of 65 and that would hasten the ascension of Ralph Houk as manager at 41, Topping parried the pitch. He said merely: "We decided to let this be Casey's day."

It wasn't exactly Casey's idea of a "day," however. With evident agitation and anger, the Old Man faced the turbulent gathering of writers, broadcasters and photographers who were recording the milestone and left no doubt that the owners had given him no choice on forestalling "his day."

"I was told that my services no longer were desired," he said, breaking the pattern of minced words. "Yes, sir, Mr. Topping and Mr. Webb paid me off in full and told me my services were no longer desired because they want to put in a youth program as an advance way of keeping the club going. That was their excuse—the best they've got."

He insisted that the first he had known of the impending "eventual retirement" was three days earlier, when he had met Topping and Weiss just after the World Series had ended in Pittsburgh. Now it was October 18, and now the "understandings" reached in the preceding 72 hours were being rapidly obscured in recriminations. The three men, according to some front-office people, had shaken hands on the timetable. But then, it was intimated, Edna Stengel had raised the family hackles and goaded Casey into resisting. In any event, he was resisting as flamboyantly as he had done everything else since arriving in the major leagues as a rookie outfielder in 1912.

"If I had been offered a new contract," he said, "I would have wanted certain changes made. I would have wanted to have known who was the boss. When Weiss was the boss, I wanted a player and he would go get him for me. They say they need a new manager for a new system and a new organization. They don't want the old way. Mr. Webb is letting Mr. Topping run the ball club. I don't want to return to an organization where I don't have the authority.

"I want to run the players on the field. I want to discharge the players and tell them who to get rid of. I want to play the players I want and not the players they want. If I manage, I must manage with full authority."

Was he suggesting that the front office had interfered with his authority?

"Just once," he replied, in a mild non sequitur. "They got rid of one player, but they got him back for me."

The inference was that the "once" involved Ralph Terry, the young right-handed pitcher who had been traded to Kansas City in 1957 but who then had been reacquired two years later—and who subsequently was traded again to Kansas City.

"When I heard their demands about this new program they were trying to build," he went on, oscillating unhappily between chagrin and righteous indignation, "I told them, 'If that's your program, gentlemen, don't worry about Mr. Stengel. He can take care of himself.' "

Could a man of 70 direct a big league team effectively?

"It depends," he said, "on what you can instill into a ball club and how you run the club. The results—a pennant in 1960—prove it."

He softened at that point to speak warmly of the team, which won the pennant by taking 15 games in a row in September just after he had returned from a brief illness. But then he bristled, noted that he would be under contract for 13 days more, until November 1, and said: "I never will return to the Yankees."

That made it unanimous. It was a little like the night the Titanic sank, since Stengel and his old idol, mentor and boss John J. McGraw had dominated—or, at least—embroiled New York baseball for 40 years since the turn of the century. And like the iceberg that punctured the Titanic, only a fraction of the penetrating mass was visible above the surface. Lurking beneath the turbulence of Casey's departure were powerful personalities—one going and one coming.

The one going was Weiss, who had helped direct Yankee affairs for a quarter of a century and who, with Stengel, had dictated them for half that time. The one coming was Ralph Houk, 41 years old and a generation younger than the Old Guard, the man whose personality was to dominate Yankee affairs on the field and in the front office in the era that was starting the day the Weiss-Stengel era was ending.

Houk was a Kansas farm boy who had entered professional baseball in 1939 in the lowest minor leagues as a catcher. Three years later he entered the Army as a private, served with great distinction for four years in the "Recon" penetration units of the Rangers, emerged as a major in 1946 and stepped up to the Yankees' highest affiliate, Kansas City. He was a competitor, but not overly productive as a batter, hitting no home runs in his major league career, and in fact going to bat only 158 times.

Later, when he failed to select Dick Stuart to the American League All-Star squad, Stuart upbraided him as a "third-string catcher." Stuart was being caustic, though his appraisal was realistic enough, since Houk lived in the shadow of the man the newspapers called "the incomparable Yogi Berra." That was true enough, too, since both had arrived on the Yankee scene at about the same time after the war. But Berra made the "big team" and stayed with it throughout the Stengel years—the only player who did so—while Houk went up and down between the Yankees and their minor league teams three times.

"My annual job," recalled Red Patterson, who was road secretary of the Yankees after the war, "was sending Ralph back to Kansas City. Once, though, he refused to go back down unless the Yankees gave him some incentive for not quitting altogether. And he told me, 'If you think I'm kidding, here's my airline ticket home.' Sure enough, he showed me one. So the club gave him a $500 raise, and he went to Kansas City. But he came that close to leaving for good."

It was ironic, since 10 years later Houk was waiting in the wings while Stengel and Weiss, the men who had sent him "down," were going through their final acts as Yankee headliners. It became even more ironic, after he had first succeeded Stengel as manager and later Weiss as general manager, that he elevated Berra to the manager's job in 1964 and, one season later, deposed him in favor of Johnny Keane of the St. Louis Cardinals. Then, when Keane was deposed a season and a fraction later, Houk returned as field manager.

Houk's strength through all these fluctuations, obviously, was not his ability with a baseball bat or catcher's mitt, though he was respected as a player. It was, rather, his qualities of leadership, the same qualities that had made him a war hero. He was rough, blunt, decisive and sound in tactics. When the Yankees sent him to manage their club at Denver in 1955, he guided the team to third place, then to second place two years in a row, and he went on in 1957 to win the American Association playoffs and the "Little World Series" against the pennant-winner of the International League.

He came back to the Yankees in 1958 as a coach, but his reputation as a successful manager was already established. Moreover, at Denver he had managed the young Yankee prospects like Bobby Richardson and Tony Kubek, who began to struggle a bit under Stengel's demanding style of managing in the late fifties. To make the conflict decisive, Houk was receiving offers to manage other major league clubs—and was, with justification, exerting an upward pressure on the patriarch of the dugout.

The other protagonist in the situation was Weiss, who had brought Stengel to the Yankees late in 1948 and who had shielded him from pressures of this kind, especially in the later years, like 1958, when the pressure seemed to be growing irresistible. Like Houk, Weiss was a man to be reckoned with, except that he had been a man to be reckoned with for more than 40 years, since becoming the impresario of baseball in New Haven, Connecticut.

Damon Runyon, upon contemplating the memorable features of covering a Yale football game, once wrote:

> New Haven—what fond memories the name conjures—
> Elms. The Campus.
> More elms. George Weiss.

It was no exaggeration. Weiss had fashioned a career in the business side of baseball as powerfully as Stengel had fashioned his career in the artistic side of baseball, and at about the same time. He was the son of a "fancy-grocer" in New Haven and got his first job as a "front-office" man while student manager of the New Haven High School baseball team in 1912. Five years later, while still studying at Yale, he became manager and master of the New Haven Colonials, a semipro team that promptly began to make life difficult for the professional team in town, which played in the Eastern League—but never on Sunday, because of regulations on organized sports.

Weiss immediately filled the vacuum by scheduling such Sunday attractions for the Colonials as an All-Chinese team, a Bloomer Girls team, and a team led by the great Ty Cobb, who insisted on a $350 guarantee to make the side trip to New Haven from either Boston or New York, where his Detroit Tigers were similarly kept idle on Sundays. When Weiss forked over $800, Ty was impressed and came back often—with no written guarantee.

His Colonials became studded with famous athletes like Charlie Brickley and Eddie Mahan, the Harvard football heroes, and Wally Pipp, Walter Johnson and Cobb from the big leagues. Once they even defeated the Boston Red Sox, 4 to 3, with Babe Ruth playing first base for Boston in "the greatest baseball attraction ever offered New Haven fans." That was in 1916, the year Boston won the World Series, and in another exhibition Ruth pitched for the Red Sox while Cobb, playing for Weiss, nicked him for a single and double and the Colonials tied the world champions, 3 to 3. After that, evidently to forestall such spectacles—a "semipro" team defeating the best in the major leagues—the National Commission of baseball ruled that only three members of a championship team could participate in post-season exhibitions.

"In 1919," Weiss said, "the New Haven club apparently decided to stop fighting us, too. They came to me and said, 'You want to buy the club for $5,000?' I had to borrow the $5,000, but I did."

Ten years later, he moved up to the International League as general manager at Baltimore, succeeding Jack Dunn, who had died after falling from a horse. Weiss arrived in Baltimore with the Depression, and cash was becoming tight, but he sold eight players to the major leagues in three years (while Stengel was selling players to the majors from the American Association). Then, in 1932, the telephone rang and Jacob Ruppert invited him to join the Yankees.

He rose from farm director to secretary to general manager and vice president. He was voted "major league executive of the year" 10 times. He brought his old friend from the Eastern League days, Stengel, back from the Pacific Coast in 1948 to manage the Yankees. He was the power behind the greatest throne in baseball.

But now, in October 1960, the throne behind which Weiss stood was tottering. Why?

"The Yankees," commented Frank Lane, a baseball impresario himself, though a dedicated critic of the Establishment, "had one great thing during the

Weiss and Stengel years: players. They had been hunted up by great scouts like Joe Devine, Bill Essick and Paul Krichell. They had built a great farm system with teams at Newark and Kansas City and Denver that were almost of big league caliber.

"But, by the nineteen-fifties, the competition was beginning to increase. The other clubs, with the postwar attendance boom and all that going, began to spend big money for young players. I was chairman of the major leagues' bonus committee in the early fifties, and we put through two bonus rules—the idea being to require a free-spending team to keep a boy who got, say, $6,000 for signing. They had to keep him on the varsity roster. But the rich teams like the Yankees weren't the ones who did the big spending. Weiss just did not believe in big bonuses.

"The Yankees had always been in a strong position with young players, anyway, and the young players would flock to the Yankee farm teams. But now the minor leagues were beginning to fade, with television cutting into their attendance, so it became harder to maintain strong minor league systems. Even then, the Yankees were slower with bonus money than the others—they simply didn't meet the competition for talent.

"To be fair about it, the Yankees not only wouldn't spend big money for bonus players, they couldn't. They couldn't afford to carry a first-year man on the roster because their roster was already loaded with professionals. The less successful teams, having less to lose than the Yankees, obviously would suffer less if they carried a few extra rookies. A few years later, when the rookies had matured, their teams wouldn't suffer at all—while the Yankees' professionals would be that much older.

"When the player draft was set up in 1964, giving the lowest teams first pick of talent, the Yankees were against that, too. But by then they had lost their monopoly on players. It's unlikely that any club will ever again dominate the game the way the Yankees did for those 12 years. They were spoiled by success."

Still, nothing succeeded like success on the playing field, and for the first half of the Weiss-Stengel term of office, the Yankees succeeded. The second half was different. Casey grew older, for one thing, and his competition was growing smarter, for another. Then he tended to become more arbitrary with younger, inexperienced players—the kind he had doted on during the first years. Then his platooning, born of necessity, had become almost a compulsion—partly because he was an all-out manager of the McGraw school and partly because he was driven to even heavier platooning as his teams inevitably lost their absolute, five-for-five touch.

Phil Rizzuto looked back years later and confessed that he "did not enjoy" playing for Stengel particularly.

"He had two tempers," the little shortstop said. "One for the public and writers, and one for the players under him. The players were frequently dressed down in the dugout and clubhouse. He could charm the shoes off you, if he wanted to, but he could also be rough. And after the first couple of seasons, he began to believe he had as much 'magic' as the newspapers said he did."

"In later years," recalled Tony Kubek, "Casey's platooning probably became rougher on the young players. He was more difficult with them then. I played five different positions before settling at shortstop, but even then I figured he platooned me less than some of the others."

Richardson described how, after his arrival from Denver in 1955, "I had my first taste of real platooning, Casey Stengel's specialty. If I started in a game, I'd be pulled out almost immediately as a pinch-hitter was sent to the plate in my stead. If I did get to bat once in a game, I was so tense that I tried too hard." Two years later, Bobby was so discouraged that he considered quitting baseball, but "Ralph Houk talked me out of it."

John Blanchard became another case of frustration, appearing in one game in 1955 (his fifth year in professional baseball), then waiting four more years before getting back to the Yankees, then playing less than a third of a season until 1961—when Houk, another frustrated catcher, became manager.

In one World Series game, Clete Boyer was removed for a pinch-hitter the first time he went to bat.

The outstanding "angry young man," though, was probably Norm Siebern, an outfielder and later a first-baseman who had led the American Association in eight categories, batting .349 with 24 home runs, before "sticking" with the Yankees in 1958. Stengel, though, tended to describe him in somewhat neutral terms—coolly, some thought—and appeared dubious of Siebern's talents. When Bob Turley went into the ninth inning one day with a no-hitter, Julio Becquer of the Washington Senators looped a fly into short left field and it fell in front of Siebern for a single. Should he have caught the ball? the manager was asked later. "Shouldn't anyone?" he asked in return. Siebern wept at the criticism. After two years on the Yankees, he was traded to Kansas City.

The ultimate in second-guessing the manager occurred after the World Series of 1960, when Stengel started Art Ditmar, who lost, instead of Whitey Ford, who later won twice—both times by shutouts. The Old Man's critics had a field day speculating on the results if Ford had been rotated into three starting assignments instead of two, and they were still speculating a week later when the 12 most splendid years came to an end at the Savoy-Hilton.

It was evident that day that even the most carping criticism could not by itself have shaken down the castle that Weiss and Stengel had built. After all, they *had* won ten pennants and seven World Series in a dozen years. But Casey *was* 70, his contract *was* expiring, the club *had* slipped a bit on the field and the Yankees *were* in danger of losing their heir apparent, Houk, to another club.

"I guess this means they fired me," Stengel said as his "day" drew to a close. "I'll never make the mistake again of being 70 years old."

"The first person to call Casey after the Yankees let him go," Edna Stengel recalled later, "was Bill Veeck, saying, 'Don't do anything until you check with me.'"

Casey did nothing, all right, despite the interest shown by Veeck, by the Kansas City Athletics, the San Francisco Giants and other baseball people. He just said, when he had calmed down, "My own plans are indefinite." Then he headed for Glendale, the swimming pool, the hacienda with its Japanese bed and Chinese room and orange bushes and tennis court out back—and the Valley National Bank.

A couple of weeks later, the decline and fall of the empire was complete. Weiss followed him into "retirement," headed for his country home in Greenwich, Connecticut, and figured he would never make the mistake of being 66 years old again, either.

So, there they sat, a continent apart. Weiss puttered around the house on Round Hill Road, made a pass or two at his hobby of handicapping horses, "played a little golf," and got in Hazel Weiss' way until she complained one day to a friend: "I married him for better or worse, but not for lunch."

Stengel, meanwhile, was puttering around the house on Grandview Avenue, resuming his mild duties as vice president of the bank, sitting in the sun and getting in Edna's way.

"How did we pass the time?" Edna mused five years later when the question was put to her as the lady of the house. "Casey started out on January 6th with a broken back that took place in Toluca Lake while watching the completion of our second bank. It was finished the end of January, and Casey spent most of his days just watching and waiting to move into his new quarters. Then on May 4th my back also went out, a disc condition, that lasted for months all through 1961 and more. I for one spent the entire year in pain, giving baseball little thought. Matter of fact, when he turned down Detroit and other offers to manage in the majors, I was sure he would not take another baseball position."

Casey, though, was not so sure. At least, he hedged his bets, saying at the time:

"By the time the season's over, I'll know what's going to happen to myself in baseball or whether I don't want to go back into baseball. Right now, I can't tell you just what I'm going to do. I don't think I'll become an actor, although I will be interested naturally in watching baseball games. I can't just take baseball and cast it away. No, I can never do that."

George Weiss' recollection lay somewhat in between. "He couldn't make up his mind," he said later, reconstructing the mood. "My impression was that his wife was encouraging him not to return."

In February, the telephone rang in Weiss' home and he heard the voice of a New York stockbroker named Donald Grant. He had an invitation that would add a chapter to the professional life of the team of Weiss & Stengel. He was calling for Mrs. Charles Shipman Payson, nee Joan Whitney, the sister of John Hay Whitney and the matron of Manhasset, Long Island, the mistress of the Greentree Stable and a longtime, incurable New York Giant fan.

Joan Payson had been put on a collision course with Grant, Weiss and Stengel almost as soon as Walter O'Malley took the Brooklyn Dodgers west to

Los Angeles and Horace C. Stoneham took the New York Giants west to San Francisco in the fall of 1957. Mayor Robert F. Wagner had decided on the spot that it was unthinkable for New York not to have a team in the National League, and he had asked his friend, William A. Shea, an energetic and successful lawyer, to start thinking about the unthinkable.

Shea tried to inveigle the Cincinnati Reds, Pittsburgh Pirates and Philadelphia Phillies to take up residence in New York. Then he enlisted Branch Rickey, the old Deacon of baseball in St. Louis, Brooklyn and Pittsburgh, to join him in forming a "third league," the Continental League.

Dwight Davis, the New York financier, had checkbook in hand as a potential angel for New York's entry in the Continental League, and he, Rickey and Shea all converged on Joan Payson as a possible partner, too. Mrs. Payson's resistance, which was not too high anyway where baseball was concerned, gave way completely when the American and National Leagues voted late in 1960 to expand from eight to ten teams each—the American League adding Minnesota and Los Angeles, and the National League adding Houston and New York.

Two strategic jobs had to be filled before New York's new National League team could take shape: general manager and manager. For a while, Rickey himself was a prime contender for the former, and his prime candidate for the latter was Casey Stengel. However, Rickey was holding out for substantial authority to buy players by spending in the neighborhood of $5,000,000— no strings attached. Mrs. Payson, by now the grande dame of the enterprise, was dissuaded by her advisers from being too free with blank checks, so Rickey backed off—and George Weiss marched in. He had a prime candidate for manager, too, one who "drove the World Series off the front page," he said later.

"We arrived in New York," Edna Stengel related, "and were driven from the airport in a Rolls-Royce. Casey wondered about it, so I said to him: 'You're returning to baseball in New York, Casey. We might as well go first class.' "

It was the fifth time in nearly 50 years that Stengel had marched on New York: In 1912, eagerly, to join the Dodgers; in 1921, jubilantly, to become a Giant; in 1932, gratefully, to coach the Dodgers; in 1948, solemnly, to take over the Yankees, and now in October 1961, apprehensively, to direct the Mets.

The Meadowlarks, Joan Payson preferred. But the Mets they were, and by any name they would strike apprehension into the heart of even a battle-scarred manager like C.D. Stengel. The reason became clear on October 10, when the "expansion teams" stocked their rosters by selecting players from the rosters of the eight regular clubs—from the unprotected, or nonexempt, portions of their rosters, in any event. And the nonexempt players available to the Mets resembled "bargains" at a rummage sale—Hobie Landrith, a 31-year-old catcher from San Francisco was No. 1. Then things went from bad to worse. For the established fixed price of $125,000 for "outstanding" talent, the Mets selected such outstandingly mediocre players as Jay Hook, an electrical engineer, from the Cincinnati Reds; Bob Miller from the St. Louis Cardinals, Don

Zimmer from the Chicago Cubs and Lee Walls from the Philadelphia Phillies.

For $75,000 apiece, they added Landrith and 15 others, mostly retreads, and for $50,000 they picked up a pitcher named Sherman (Roadblock) Jones from Cincinnati and a minor league outfielder named Jim Hickman, who had hit .249 at Portland.

The total tab was $1,800,000, an overprice of the wildest sort. And it was as something less than a conquering hero that Stengel returned to New York to take charge of the ragamuffins, Rolls-Royce or no Rolls-Royce—especially since the Yankees, under young Houk, had just made a smooth transition into the post-Stengel era by winning the smashing total of 109 games, losing only 53, winning the World Series and capturing the attention of the nation for weeks by the stirring home-run rampages of Roger Maris (61) and Mickey Mantle (54).

Stengel's mission with the Mets lay precisely astride that obvious fissure in New York baseball. On the one side, the Yankees were lords of all they surveyed—and any new team in town would inevitably live in their shadow for years, maybe decades, maybe forever. On the other side, the Mets were as inept a baseball team as the United States had ever seen—"the worst club in baseball history," said Veeck, whose credentials were unassailable, since he had once owned the St. Louis Browns.

That was the "artistic" situation, and Weiss and Stengel did not have to strain their genius to decide that they could not rival the Yankees on the field for a long time. But they could also sense the golden opportunity beyond: namely, that New York held an immense reservoir of National League interest, and that the Yankees could never draw on that reservoir, nor replace it. The year after the Dodgers and Giants left town, Yankee attendance had actually dropped—from 1,497,134 to 1,428,438. Then Maris and Mantle helped revive it in 1961, up to 1,747,736—but that was the high-water mark, and it was still half a million below the immediate postwar years.

That was the "commercial situation," and Weiss and Stengel did not have to strain their genius to decide that they *could* rival the Yankees there. And they did. They made no pretense to glory on the playing field; in fact, they made the Mets a "mirror image" of the Yankees, and they proceeded to capitalize on the image.

Where the Yankees were successful as ball players, the Mets became monumentally unsuccessful. Where the Yankees were cool cats, the Mets grew up as warm ugly ducklings. Where the Yankees were institutional, the Mets lunged into the public domain. The Yankees, on top, had everything to lose; the Mets, on bottom, had everything to gain. And they set out to gain it with those Yankee renegades, Weiss and Stengel, who discovered now that the same public that had criticized them in the later Yankee years was clamoring to adopt them in their new roles, to idolize them—to support them at the box office.

Weiss gave full credit for this support to two things: "The latent interest in the National League after the Dodgers and Giants left, and the energies and personalities of people like Casey Stengel and Mrs. Joan Payson."

Two years later, Weiss would add a third asset to his list, Shea Stadium. But for the first two years of their existence, the Mets were forced to play in the old Polo Grounds, where Stengel had played two generations earlier to the cheers of Ethel Barrymore and Al Jolson and where demolition men were waiting, along with the Mets, for the ball club to vacate the premises so that a housing development could rise on John J. McGraw's sacred acres.

The idea was the Mets would entertain the public with a kind of Circus Maximus. The aim: to keep the people docile until times grew better. The ringleader: Casey Stengel, who would run the show by doing what had come naturally since his days of mischief-making at Western Dental College.

"Yes sir," he said, as he took charge, capturing the mood to the letter, "come see my amazin' Mets, which in some cases have played only semi-pro ball."

The Mets responded nobly. Their opening game, April 10, 1962, was a night game in St. Louis; it was rained out. As things turned out, that was the Mets' finest hour. The next night it did not rain, unfortunately, and in the first inning Roger Craig, the Mets' first starting pitcher, committed a balk with Bill White on third base and they were behind, 1 to 0, before they had even struck a blow in their own defense. Stan Musial, who was 41 and the nearest thing in age to Stengel on either team, got three hits; the Mets made three errors, the Cardinals stole three bases and scored 11 runs, and the Mets scored 4. A whole new concept in losing baseball games was unfolding before the eyes of the man who had tried to keep his sanity running the old Brooklyn Dodgers.

Then Casey packed everybody off to New York to give the big city its first look at its new baseball team. It was, appropriately, Friday the 13th. It had rained and the field was muddy. Only 12,447 people paid their way into the Polo Grounds, and after Mayor Wagner had hoisted the first pitch toward the wet infield, the Mets unwaveringly pursued their destiny.

In the second inning, on a ground ball by Smoky Burgess of the Pittsburgh Pirates, Charley Neal made a spectacular stop at shortstop, then slipped in the mud. Don Hoak doubled to right and Bill Mazeroski hit a fly to right-center. Gus Bell crabbed to his right toward the ball, Richie Ashburn drifted to his left. Bell waved him off, Ashburn stopped short, Bell stopped short and the ball fell for a triple. Three wild pitches let in two more runs later, and the Mets lost the game, 4 to 3.

In fact, they lost nine straight and Casey began to wonder. "This sets up the possibility," he said, "of losing 162 games, which would probably be a new record, in the National League, at least." The chance for "a new record," evaporated, though, on April 23. The Mets finally won one, beating Pittsburgh, 9 to 1, and celebrated in the clubhouse as though they had won the World Series, amidst shouts of "break up the Mets."

"We didn't start with the idea that we were going to be as bad as we were," Weiss said in July of 1966, when the team had become one of the wonders of the baseball world by climbing into ninth place after four seasons of almost unbroken tenancy of tenth place.

One reason for his chagrin was that nobody started with the idea that any team could be that bad. The Mets scored runs, all right. Ashburn hit .306 and Frank Thomas hit 34 home runs, batted in 94 runs and was struck by pitches eight times—giving him undisputed possession of first place in offensive departments of all kinds. But the nine other teams in the league scored runs against the Mets in lavish numbers. Craig lost 24 games, allowed 35 home runs, gave up 261 hits; Alvin Jackson "led" the club in earned-run average, allowing 4.4 runs a game. The Mets won 40 games, lost 120, played before 922,530 customers at home (876,780 on the road) and began to be called "my amazin' Mets" by Stengel, who meant that he, at least, was amazed.

He may have been amazed most by the commercial success of the club despite its spectacular lack of artistic success. For, after drawing 922,530 persons in the Polo Grounds the first year, the Mets vaulted over the million mark in attendance, toward two million, and stayed there.

As Branch Rickey diagnosed the situation, the "perfect link" between the ball club and the public was Stengel.

Everything he did for the Mets, he did with fanfare. Every picture he posed for, he posed for with gusto and expressiveness. Every speech he made, he delivered with vivid "image." He emphasized the fact that the Yankees had "fired" him and that he now had been reincarnated as the Great White Father of the Amazing Mets, who were everything the Yankees weren't—warm, lovable, comically unpredictable, splendidly unsuccessful Sad Sacks.

Now, in a stunning postscript to his professional career, he returned to tie up all the loose ends of his rambling life in baseball. He brought to the Mets his sense of humor and sense of histrionics from the earliest days of his playing career, days of umbrellas, flashlights, birds-under-hats, manhole covers, grapefruit dropped from biplanes, the works. He brought his playing sense, as taught by Robinson and McGraw. He contributed his business sense from the wheeling-and-dealing days in the minor leagues. He excelled in the arts of distracting the public, arts he had polished to a dazzling shine in Brooklyn and Boston a generation earlier. The only phase of his career that went slightly against the grain was the Yankee era. But he even borrowed from that—the strategy of mass platooning and the awareness of Yankee haughtiness that now, with the Mets, became the most obvious and effective foil of all.

From the start, he skillfully blended all these strands of his life into one towering Met mountain. All roads led to my amazin' Mets. Even the name helped forge the link to the public: it was chosen in a public contest, and when Joan Payson decided that the best name submitted by the public was "Mets," somebody said, "Let's go, Mets." When a banner day was held to translate this spirit into slogans, one bright banner-maker paraded around the Polo Grounds with a lace-curtain version that said: "Let us proceed, Metropolitans."

When Stengel was placed before the public as the spirit behind this spirit, he demonstrated again the great characteristic of his 50 years in the shifting fortunes of baseball: his adaptability to disaster or success, depending on the roll of the dice. He had adapted to success with the Yankees; then to runaway disaster with the Mets. Now he was to go full cycle and convert disaster into success, or at least to make people forget about the disaster long enough for success of a sort to crystallize. He was bugged by only two things during this great public relations campaign: his age, which was a mixed blessing, and the fact that the Yankees had "fired" him after his proudest achievements. But even here, he could exploit the axiom that two minuses make a plus.

When the Mets unveiled him as their first manager, they staged the great event with a tragedian's sense of drama. They hired the same hall the Yankees had hired to dismiss him, Le Salon Bleu of the Savoy-Hilton. The date was October 2, 1961, almost a calendar year since the Yankees gave him his "day." Now the Mets were giving him another "day," and they rang up the curtain with theatrical splendor: After everybody had been seated, the Old Man entered to a standing ovation. Score: Mets-1, Yankees-0.

"My health," said the Professor, exorcising one of the chief demons at the start, and also betraying his own concern over the subject that had concerned the Yankee brass a year earlier, "my health is good enough above the shoulders, and I didn't say I'd stay fifty years or five years.

"Most people are dead at my age, and you could look it up."

Now he had sounded an echo of his parting shot at the Yankees, which had been: "I commenced winning pennants when I came here but I didn't commence getting any younger."

And to demonstrate that, a year later at the age of 71, he had commenced getting younger indeed. He parlayed his unveiling on October 2 into a triumphal ride down Broadway on Thanksgiving Day in the 30-degree cold of Macy's annual parade, waving his arms to the throngs on the sidewalks as though he wished Glendale were only this splendidly warm and calling everybody to "come out and see my own amazin' Mets."

Besides Hippodrome showmanship of this personal sort, Stengel showed an incisive knowledge of the mechanics of newspaper production, and he used this knowledge to cultivate "my writers," who welcomed him with open arms as the man who had resurrected their own spirits after the Dodgers and Giants had traduced the public by leaving town.

On days when his amazing Mets were, for some reason, amazing, he simply sat back and let the writers swarm over the heroes of the diamond. On days when the Mets were less than amazing—and there were many more days like that—he stepped into the vacuum and diverted the writers' attention, and typewriters, to his own flamboyance. Then he would hold forth at interminable length with stories, anecdotes of half a century before, Uncle Robbie, McGraw and you could look it up, all in highly quotable and lovable Stengelese.

He even scheduled daily press conferences at 12 noon in spring training in order to provide sparkling copy before his team had had a chance to boot a few in practice. And he carefully distinguished between morning newspapers and evening newspapers, with the precision of the dean of the Columbia Graduate School of Journalism. He knew their various writers, requirements, even deadlines. When *The New York Times* switched its Yankee and Met writers in the middle of spring training, an event that might have gone unnoticed for at least a day or so in the commotion of the training camp, he gave it sly notice during dinner in the Fort Lauderdale airport restaurant while both groups of writers were gathered following a Yankee-Met game.

"I made a mistake there in the seventh inning," he said, with exaggerated sincerity, "and it cost us the ball game. But you see, I was upset at the time and simply blew the play. I was sitting there thinking that Mr. Durso was going to leave us after the game and Mr. Koppett was going to switch over from the Yankees, and I just forgot to give the sign for the play."

So, the perfect link to the public was formed, and it grew stronger as the team grew zanier. True, the Stengel style caused irritations in the clubhouse, as it had on the Yankees. After all, if Bobby Richardson felt nervous about making a mistake, how nervous would, say, a Marv Throneberry feel about making a mistake, especially since he had earned the nickname "Marvelous Marv" through sensational mistakes at first base? Or Charley Neal, who pounced on the first grounder of 1963 and threw it over first base for an error while Curt Flood of the Cardinals circled all the way to third base and the Mets launched an eight-game losing streak at the start of their second season? Or Roger Craig, who looked like Slim Summerville and even pitched a little like him, losing 18 straight games? Or the whole ball club, which lost 22 in a row on the road before winning?

But if the Stengel manner kept some players on edge—in the lineup one day, out the next—it also covered a multitude of sins, and that was his great service during the Mets' formative years. By the time the boys played, and lost, the final home game of 1963, the final game ever played in the Polo Grounds, they had exhibited their antics before 2,002,638 cash customers in two years and they had already succeeded the Yankees as the toast of New York.

The irritations slackened as this type of success increased, and as Stengel realized that he was managing a team with screaming limitations. At first he had expected the sophisticated maneuvers that separated the men from the boys in baseball. Then, he began to appreciate the fact that the main problem was not so much in executing the finesse as in just catching the ball. So he relented. He still platooned players wildly, but chiefly because he had to do so in order to muster the isolated talents available to him.

"You didn't see them sending up a left-handed hitter for Hornsby, did you?" he would shout during the long evenings of bourbon and soda with his writers.

He was amazed, all right, having spent 12 years with Yankee players who were Old Masters compared with his New Breed. But he grew tolerant as the hopelessness of the player situation sank in.

"He knows," said one observer, "that the kids are giving 100 per cent, but that their 100 per cent just isn't enough. So he has stopped trying to beat more out of them."

He showed one outstanding flash of his old petulance—not over an inept play in the field, but over a flip remark about his years with the Yankees. The remark was dropped during a team dinner in spring training by Duke Carmel, one of the less inept Met players, a player, in fact, with a breezy personality and a promising future as a left-handed-hitting first-baseman and outfielder. But his future with the Mets ended when he tweaked Stengel about the Yankees and how anybody could win with a team like that, right? He may have been right, but he was wrong about Casey's reaction. A few days later Carmel was shipped to the minor leagues, and although Stengel tried to rationalize the move on baseball terms, few people in the Mets' camp doubted that Carmel had lucklessly gibed in one of the Old Man's unforgiving areas.

The Mets, meanwhile, moved from one trivial success to another. Losing eight straight games at the start of 1963, for example, was better than losing nine straight in 1962. Winning 51 games and losing 111 was better than winning 40 and losing 120. Winning four games on a 14-game road trip was better than winning three; in fact, it was a club record. Ten victories for a pitcher was better than eight, and it, too, was a club record. For a new team, of course, everything is a club record. But with Stengel providing the translation, even the molehills began to look like mountains.

So convincing was the Met mystique, and so willing to back it with cash were the customers, that the Yankees even broke tradition in 1964 in a wild attempt to counteract their new crosstown rivals. They named Yogi Berra manager, replacing Houk, who in turn was elevated to the front office as general manager. Yogi, after all, was cut from the same cloth as Stengel. He had been Casey's "assistant" manager; he was a lovable Met type, despite his great ability as a ball player; he was warm. He even won the pennant for the Yankees in the final weekend of the season, but he proved—to nobody's surprise but the Yankees'—to be no Stengel when it came to saying, doing or creating funny things, not even when reprimanding Phil Linz for playing the harmonica on the team bus. He was simply Yogi Berra. And Yankee attendance, which had dropped from 1,747,736 the year before the Mets were organized, dipped to 1,493,574 the year they took the field, and to 1,305,638 the year Yogi was installed as the "counter-agent."

The Mets, meanwhile, had moved into their resplendent new stadium that spring—Shea Stadium, just north of the World's Fair and just south of LaGuardia Airport in the parkway-studded section of Flushing, Queens. They even lost their opening game as gloriously as they had lost their previous openers. The date was April 17, 1964; the score was 4 to 3, Pittsburgh; the attendance was 50,312. And in addition to the new stadium, "which has moving stairs for the people," in Stengel's description, the Mets also had a legion of other assets and conversation pieces that far overshadowed the Yankees' best efforts at matching them.

They had one All-Star player, Ron Hunt. They had a future All-Star player, perhaps, in Ron Swoboda, a muscleman from Baltimore with the build of Li'l Abner and a Chinese step-grandfather. They had a teen-aged pitcher

named Jerry Hinsley, who drank milkshakes, had never seen New York before, had thrown only to his twin brother in high school and who was instructed by his teammates to "knock down" Willie Mays the first time he ever
faced the great man. Hinsley did so, sending Mays sprawling with a head-high
fastball; but when Willie rocketed the next pitch off the fence in right-center
for a triple, the rookie analyzed the problem like a true Met and explained:
"They didn't tell me what to throw him on the *second* pitch."

They also had extra added attractions like the Astrodome in Houston,
which the Mets visited three times a summer for nine games and which boasted
a plastic roof 208 feet high at its apex behind second base. Stengel saw it for the
first time in May 1964, as he stepped down from the Mets' bus outside the
huge, circular white structure. He was impressed, having come a long way
from the wooden stands in Washington Park, Brooklyn, but he also was manager of the Mets, who were in the throes of an epidemic of sky-high, futile pop
flies. "Hell," he said, upon being advised that there was no danger any fly ball
could reach the dome, "I got four guys on this club right now who could pop it
straight up to the roof."

The Mets also had the added attraction of a National League pennant race
that was even more sensational than the American League race that Berra was
winning, and they were soon to play prominent roles in it. Six teams all had
shots at winning, even though the Philadelphia Phillies held a 7½-game lead
with only two weeks to go and then began printing World Series tickets. In
fact, they distributed the first batch after losing two straight to Cincinnati in
the next-to-last week of the season. That evening they made it three straight.
Then Cincinnati went to New York and knocked over the Mets five times in
one weekend while the Phillies kept losing to Milwaukee.

By the time the Mets had reached St. Louis a week later, with three games
to go, the Cardinals, Phillies and Reds were tangled in a free-for-all, and while
the Reds were playing the Phillies in Cincinnati that weekend, the Cards were
host to the Mets.

Johnny Keane, who was then manager of the Cardinals but who was
about to switch to the Yankees right after the World Series in a spectacular
rotation of managers, watched Al Jackson shackle his Cardinals, 1 to 0, that
first night, defeating the Cardinal ace Bob Gibson.

"In the runway under the grandstand after the game," Keane recalled, "I
ran into Casey. We had two games left to play, and the pennant was at stake.
He shook his head at me, and just said: 'You've got a job to do.' "

The Mets won the next day, too, and were leading as late as the fifth
inning of the final game of the season Sunday, October 4. Then the tide receded, the Cardinals rallied, the Reds ironically blew their game in Cincinnati to
the Phillies (who had lost 10 straight while blowing the pennant themselves)
and St. Louis snatched the pennant.

But hours later, the Old Man, his hair neatly combed to the side, sat in the
lobby of the Chase Hotel in St. Louis, surrounded by well-wishers who had just
seen him nearly score the coup of the decade. He sat politely charming a circle

of nuns who gathered round him on a stone bench, presenting autograph books on behalf of their school children back home, giggling "Oh, Mr. Stengel," at his tall tales and beaming as he orated with complete satisfaction on the feats of "my amazin' Mets."

The amazin' Mets, despite all their heroics in St. Louis, still finished last—for the third straight year. But they were the most successful last-place team in baseball history, and the "perfect link" to their public was secure.

"Since Khrushchev was fired," wrote Russell Baker on the editorial page of *The New York Times,* borrowing the "perfect link" to dramatize a point in geopolitics, "the Reds have had the same problem the New York Yankees had after firing Casey Stengel. Fan interest has sagged, and the players seem more interested in playing the harmonica than in helping the Reds win the moon and the World Series."

Chapter

10

Kankakee
To Cooperstown

Jesse Owens ran, Yogi Berra batted and Warren Spahn threw baseballs in the bright sunshine of February 27 in St. Petersburg, Florida, as the New York Mets opened their fourth spring training circus while Charles Dillon Stengel stood like a ringmaster behind home plate bellowing: "Yes sir, come see the amazin' Mets."

There was something for everybody as Stengel started his 55th—and last —year in a baseball uniform that resplendent day in 1965. And it was difficult to tell who was more impressed by the staff of celebrities crowded around the Old Man in baseball knickers with "New York" embroidered across the chest and "37" across the back of the shirt—the 1,000 persons who crowded the small, wooden grandstand of Huggins-Stengel Field or the 21 young pitchers and catchers who staged the first workout of the season.

They all followed the all-star coaching staff through three hours of exercise and batting practice on a magnificently sunny day with the temperature rising to 65 degrees and a light wind blowing across Crescent Lake beyond the palm trees past the centerfield fence.

No banners were unfurled. But wild ovations greeted Professor Stengel as he crossed the infield to open the festivities. And cheers were sounded when Berra, deposed as manager of the Yankees four months earlier, opened his career with the Mets by donning a catcher's mitt to warm up a 19-year-old pitcher.

The 26 players on hand ranged from Mike Buist, who was 17 years old and 57 years younger than Stengel, to Spahn, who was 43 and who had won

108 games in the major leagues before Buist went to kindergarten.

Stengel started the day with an administrative announcement: After conducting two workouts a day all during his career, he would hold just one a day for the 1965 Mets. His reasons were appropriately vague.

"We had a meeting," he said, "and Mr. Spahn was for one workout, and we had two men who had amazing records with the Yankees and one of them preferred one workout and the other two. I was for one or two."

"And the consensus," he added in one of the charging non sequiturs that had made him pre-eminent as a 20th century logician, "was for one."

When this matter had been settled, Casey turned his New Breed over to Owens, who was 51 years old, who weighed 14 pounds more than his Olympic weight of 165 and who was listed on the roster as "track coach" but who described himself as "the Drillmaster."

Promptly at 10 a.m. the great sprinter took his post at the head of Stengel's young army, wearing white sneakers and a gray sweat-shirt with "Ohio State Athletic Department" printed in bright red letters across the front. Then, just 29 years after he had won four track-and-field gold medals in the Olympics, he led the Mets, who had never won anything but wealth and fame, through one lap around the field. He finished a solid first.

This was followed by "bicycle" leg exercises, body bends, pushups and sprints, and Jesse, who ran the 100-yard dash in high school in 9.4 seconds, commented that he would be pleased if his charges ran it in 11 seconds or less. "They enjoyed it very much," he said, without confirmation, after 25 minutes. "I even had old Spahn running."

He then turned the squad back to Stengel, who watched every pitcher throw five minutes of batting practice while the deputies on the Professor's staff conducted fielding, pitching and bunting drills around the fringes of the field to the delight of the fans, who feasted on a kaleidoscope of celebrity baseball. On one practice field they could see Berra, who a year earlier had been managing the lordly Yankees, still wearing his familiar No. 8; Spahn, the greatest left-handed pitcher of modern times, his $70,000 contract still unsigned but nevertheless flashing his famous No. 21; Eddie Stanky, No. 54, the onetime "brat" of the old Giants, living up to his new title of director of player development by directing his players in the art of stopping ground balls. And, at the center of the whirlwind stood Casey Stengel, who had first gone south for training one spring when William Howard Taft lived in the White House.

Now, he was starting his last spring training, though none of the people watching, nor his celebrated coaches, nor the teen-aged Mets realized it. For that matter, *any* season in the previous 30 might have been the "last," a decision being dictated by the lure of oil money, wayward taxicabs in Boston, the pressure of life with the Yankees, or simply old age. But constitutionally, emotionally, compulsively, like Sarah Bernhardt, he had resisted. And while each season might have been "the last," each season seemed to lead into yet another.

The previous September, Edna Stengel had shown friends through her house full of treasures in Glendale, the rows of tumblers and old-fashioned glasses inscribed with the red, white and blue Yankee emblem and top hat, the gilded World Series Louisville Slugger bats, the pennant rings and championship ash trays, the ceremonial sword bestowed by Dan Topping. And she had said, in a kind of whisper: "Whether this is the last year or we go on, it's been worth it."

A few days later, Casey popped up at a press conference to announce that he had signed for another year as manager of the Mets at an increase in pay and, dressed brilliantly in a suit of expensive Italian silk, said slyly: "I have a one-year contract, as I've always had with the Mets, and an increase in pay which makes me very happy that they would want to give it to me. It was a very splendid raise. I believe I can use it—this suit's a little old. I might get a new wardrobe."

Then he hopped off to the airport, climbed aboard a jet bound for Milwaukee and rejoined his players for the final week of the season, while Branch Rickey was saying in St. Louis that here was the perfect link between the club and the public.

Stengel at 74 ranked somewhere between the Pied Piper and Santa Claus, and once shorn of the pressures and second-guesses of the Yankee years, the public followed him almost blindly as the Mets bungled along magnificently.

He somehow made everybody identify with the human failings exhibited so relentlessly by the Mets. There but for the grace of God go I. Everybody a frustrated shortstop, like the Mets' shortstop; or a catcher who could not catch the Dodgers when they ran the bases. Everybody a ringmaster, a grandstand manager—even as everybody in St. Louis had been, during Veeck's promotional bomb bursts in the early fifties, when the St. Louis Browns followed strategy dictated by a whole grandstand full of managers. "Grandstand managers' day," it was called, and decisions would be made according to the response of the crowd to large signs hoisted at critical moments during the game, asking: "Infield in—or out?" and "Should we walk him?" The crowd would signify its choice by applause, while a municipal judge sat on the dugout roof in a rocking chair to determine the mob's wishes and old Connie Mack sat grandly in the stands to lend dignity to the occasion.

True, one of Veeck's pitchers, Ned Garver, refused once to pitch with the infield drawn in, as the mass strategy had dictated, but Veeck's assistant, Bob Fishel, got busy on a megaphone and influenced the crowd to reverse its signals. The Browns won the game, 5 to 3, and grandstand managing never had a more glorious day—until Stengel forged the link between the customers and his floundering Mets a decade later.

Casey had the spear-carriers for such an Everyman drama, too.

Take Choo-Choo Coleman, a stumpy, silent, friendly little sign-painter whose real name was Clarence, which may account for the Choo-Choo. He would peer out of the team bus as it wound through Florida's back roads during spring training, recall that he had been paid $1.50 an hour for lettering signs by hand, point triumphantly out the window at a roadside sign advertising a nearby beanery and shout: "There's one, there's one." Ever since the Mets had paid Philadelphia $75,000 for Choo-Choo in the expansion draft, he had astonished people by his lack of any other classical abilities, except maybe his ability to hug the ground lower than any catcher in baseball, crouching close to the dirt behind the bat, diving into the dust to trap balls and in general just making the play by fighting it into the ground. He spent most of his time in the minor leagues, despite his splendidly childlike disposition and an occasional home run—both of which made him a conquering hero to the Mets' public—and then one day, more in wonder than in anger, said: "Mr. Murphy said he was sending me to Buffalo to get in shape." But, added Choo-Choo a trifle impatiently, "that was two years ago."

Boy, was he in shape. Another spear-carrier in the cast was Danny Napoleon, a rookie outfielder who shuttled between New York and way stations like Buffalo while Johnny Murphy, vice president of the Mets, tried to assemble 25 able bodies for Professor Stengel's roster. One day Napoleon ended a long cat-and-mouse chase between the Mets and San Francisco Giants by pinch-hitting a triple that won the game. Stengel led the parade of Mets into the clubhouse, threw his hands straight up into the air and shouted, in praise of Danny Napoleon: "Vive la France!" Then, having astonished everyone by even this meager burst of French, he rendered a typically far-fetched association by adding quickly: "We been giving him so much publicity, De Gaulle oughta give us a free trip to Paris."

When Shea Stadium opened on Friday, April 17, 1964, Stengel sat at the center of this whirlwind as usual, basking in his new diggings, amazed that 50,312 persons had joined in the great occasion, impressed that the Traffic Commissioner of New York, Henry A. Barnes, was circling the field in a helicopter trying to untangle the traffic swarms, pleased that an immense horseshoe of flowers had been delivered to the dugout before the game, distressed that the first hit in the new ball park was a home run by Wilver Dornel Stargell of Earlsboro, Oklahoma, better known as Willie Stargell of the Pittsburgh Pirates—and depleted by the fact that the first game in the new stadium was lost by his Mets, 4 to 3, in the ninth inning.

Casey had now had key roles in opening Ebbets Field, Yankee Stadium and Shea Stadium and in closing the Polo Grounds. But could any of that have prepared him for the home stretch—improbable days like May 26, 1964, when the amazing Mets amazed even him?

They shook off the inhibitions of two years in the cellar of the National League and 20 straight scoreless innings, rattled the ivy-covered walls of Wrigley Field with 17 singles, three doubles, two triples and one home run and disintegrated the Chicago Cubs, 19 to 1.

Nor could it have prepared him for what happened the following day, when Cinderella turned into a pumpkin and the Cubs disintegrated the Mets, 7 to 1.

Nor could any of the preceding have prepared him and his public for what happened four days later back in Shea Stadium: a 10-hour, 23-minute doubleheader with San Francisco that included one nine-inning game and one 23-inning game that required 7 hours and 23 minutes to decide. No major league teams had ever played more baseball in one day in history (Gaylord Perry of the Giants pitched 10 straight innings in relief). The Mets even made a triple play but, having kept their 74-year-old manager on the bench from 1 p.m. until 11:25, to say nothing of stragglers in the crowd of 57,037, they not only set endurance records but also set futility records. They lost both games.

Nor could it have prepared him for the remarkable fact that one of his troops, Ed Kranepool, had played both halves of a doubleheader for the Mets' farm club at Buffalo the day before, then, having been summoned to rejoin the parent team, played both halves of the doubleheader against the Giants—50 innings in two days, at the age of 20.

Nor could it have prepared him for the day his boys led the St. Louis Cardinals by five runs going into the ninth and trailed them by one run going out of the ninth. Nor for the day his pitcher, catcher and third-baseman carefully followed a bunt up the third-base line, watching to see if it would roll foul (it didn't) while Maury Wills, who had been on third base, raced past the dedicated group and crossed the unprotected plate. Nor for the day his pitcher had only one man to get out in the ninth inning to defeat the San Francisco Giants, but that man was Willie Mays, who hit a home run, and then the game didn't end until the 15th—when Jim Davenport hit another home run to win it for San Francisco.

A man made of less stern stuff might have quit the whole farce to tend his ulcers or avocados, or might have slashed his wrists or simply flipped his lid. No. 37 did none of these things. But he began to show, as his 75th birthday approached, a susceptibility to other disasters than the ones perpetrated by his amazing Mets.

On May 10, 1965, he shepherded his wards to the United States Military Academy for an exhibition game against Army, and before the day was over West Point became Phase I of the Old Man's Waterloo. He was walking down a ramp from the cadet gymnasium to enter the team bus for the trip to the playing field when his feet slipped out from under him and he slid heavily along the cement. His right wrist was broken.

However, he returned to the dugout a few days later, wrist in sling, and resumed his role in the eye of the hurricane. Then, on Sunday afternoon, July 25, five days before his 75th birthday, came the deluge.

The sound of 39,288 voices singing "Happy birthday, dear Casey," wafted over Shea Stadium that sunny day as the Mets and Philadelphia Phillies gathered to salute the Professor's diamond jubilee and, almost incidentally, to play a doubleheader. The Phillies were in fifth place, six and a half games out of first place; the Mets were in last place, 24 games out of first place. The guest of honor was in Roosevelt Hospital with a fractured left hip, facing an operation and three weeks of hospitalization, and watching on television as the crowd roared its birthday tribute in a ceremony marked by a message from President Johnson, 35,000 small birthday cakes, one 250-pound cake shaped like the stadium and a serenade by a 60-piece band.

He had arrived in front of the hospital television set by a circuitous route that had started in the Essex House the evening before.

He had gone south seven blocks to Toots Shor's emporium, had joined 38 "old-timers" from the New York Giants and Brooklyn Dodgers for one of the midsummer Old-Timers Day frolics, had had the time of his life jousting with Frank Frisch and other cronies from the good old days, had slipped in the washroom as the clock slipped past midnight, had been trundled into a car and had been driven to a house at 112 Malba Drive in Whitestone, Queens. The car and house belonged to Joseph J. DeGregorio, controller of the Mets, and the logic behind the drive just after 2 a.m. had been this: Though the Essex House was only a few minutes from Shor's, Casey would be alone there in his suite (Edna being in Glendale), and he would be in better position to make his own birthday party if he spent what was left of the night at DeGregorio's, eight minutes from Shea Stadium.

If the logic was a bit twisted, it became apparent early in the morning that so was Casey's left hip. He awoke about 8 a.m. and complained of severe pains. The call went out to Gus Mauch, who also lived in Queens, and the onetime masseur and therapist to George Bernard Shaw and Admiral Richard E. Byrd took one look at his old friend and decided he had a problem.

"I'd never seen Casey in such pain in all the years I'd been with him," the trainer said. "I knew it was more than just a muscle spasm."

He telephoned the Mets' surgeon, Dr. Peter LaMotte, who piloted his Lincoln Continental at a low altitude from his home in New Rochelle, across the Whitestone Bridge, and who made a preliminary diagnosis of a "twisted left hip." He then called for an ambulance from Roosevelt Hospital, and while they were waiting, a statement was drafted for the 39,288 birthday guests eight minutes away in Shea Stadium. It was signed by Casey and it said:

"I know I can't make it to the stadium today. I do feel sorry for all those people who went to all that trouble for my birthday."

When the first bulletin relating his accident was flashed on the electric scoreboard in right field during the second inning of the first game, all those people groaned. They were kept posted by electric message as the X-ray report and later diagnosis were relayed from Dr. LaMotte, and the twisted left hip became a fractured left hip.

There was a bit of a scramble behind the scenes to account for the debacle in reasonably solemn, yet honorable terms. After all, some people would raise an eyebrow over that old-timers' party. Others would suspect a heart condition or stroke, considering the patient's age and the references to pain along his left side. But whatever, any time a 75th birthday party is stood up because the guest of honor has broken his hip, it's an occasion that can't be glossed over.

Accordingly, the word was duly passed after the kind of pause that precedes unhappy news in, say, the Kremlin, that Casey had twisted his hip getting out of the car at DeGregorio's home. The medical relationship between the slip and the one in Shor's has never been established, but either one might have fractured the hip of any ordinary 75-year-old and it did not seem unusual that it would require two such falls to break the hip of an extraordinary 75-year-old.

In any event, with a broken right wrist and a broken left hip within 10 week's time, it was becoming evident that baseball had become a hazardous profession for the Old Man—especially since he went up and down those dugout steps so many times a day just to change pitchers.

President Johnson, who had drawn his message of greeting before the great fall, had nevertheless framed it in words that could have held up under almost any set of circumstances, and they did. "I want to join with your thousands of friends," he said, "in celebrating Casey Stengel Day and commemorating your 75th birthday. Your recent accomplishments have been a source of admiration to all and you have been a living example to citizens of all ages of human vitality and achievement."

Three of Casey's lieutenants accepted the honors for him—Yogi Berra, Don Heffner and Wes Westrum, who was designated "acting manager." Miss St. Petersburg of 1965 presented a plaque. Everybody stood and sang "Happy birthday, dear Casey." George Weiss reported, after visiting the hospital, that Casey seemed "fairly alert and reconciled to the situation, and he thought something was wrong after stepping out of the car." The Mets won the first game, 8 to 1, with the help of an error, then lost the second game, 3 to 1, after returning the favor by contributing an error at a critical moment. And then they prepared to leave for Chicago without the familiar stooped figure wearing uniform No. 37 whom they had followed around like the children of Hamelin following the Pied Piper since they were organized four years earlier.

The next day, as the club left for series in Chicago and Philadelphia, Westrum was named "interim manager," the "interim" referring respectfully to the interim between Casey's accident and the day of decision on his future.

That night Edna flew in from California, and when I met her at Kennedy Airport she was tired, tense and concerned. She had not been feeling well herself because of an eye infection, but now she postponed her own aches and pains and went straight to the hospital, were Casey already was under heavy sedation. The flood of fan mail that she tackled every day was about to be multiplied, as thousands of messages poured into the room on the 11th floor where the former king of the Grumblers lay with a broken hip.

Early the following morning, July 27, "more nervous" than Edna had ever seen him, Casey was wheeled into the operating room, where Dr. LaMotte led a four-man team through a 45-minute operation termed a ball prosthesis. A metal ball, about the size of a plum, was fixed on top of the femur, or thigh bone, at the point where the femur fits into the socket of the pelvis. Then the femur was supposed to perform its customary ball-and-socket movements.

"Knowing the kind of guy Casey is," Dr. LaMotte said, "he'll probably want to be up and around as quickly as possible, and in consideration of his age, I thought this was the best procedure."

"Does he have all his bones?" Edna asked. Then she followed the caravan to his room, noting that he was all drowsy from the anesthesia, cooing softly to him to "go to sleep," and being somewhat surprised when he opened his eyes and said firmly: "Bring me some toothpaste."

While Stengel lay in the hospital, the Mets were careening along under Westrum, a onetime catcher for the Giants whose only managing experience in 25 years of baseball had been with an Army disciplinary barracks at Greenhaven, New York, during the war—tough-to-handle cases, ideal experience for a future manager of the amazing Mets. The club lost six of eight games in Chicago and Philadelphia, including one in the 12th inning when Ron Santo of the Cubs hit a home run minutes after the umpire had announced that the 12th inning was to be the last inning, win, lose or draw. So the Mets, at least, were not rocking the boat.

Eleven days after the operation, Stengel, tastefully dressed in a yellow kimono, held his first post-operative press conference and demonstrated that his fractured hip and fractured English were almost as good as new. In the course of a 45-minute session at the hospital, now 75 years and one week old, he made several things exceptionally clear—for him. He said that he expected to leave the hospital in four or five days, that he did not know if he would return to the dugout that season and that he would not know about the following season until after the current one had ended. "I am the manager of this ball club," he said, a bit testily, as though insuring his franchise, as he had during the late Yankee years, too.

He also made several things exceptionally unclear, but that was interpreted as a sign that he was rapidly returning to normal. He started by umlimbering his favorite adjectives, like "terrific" and "extraordinary." Then, alluding to the platform, blackboard, lectern, overhead lights and "briefing" atmosphere of the conference room, he said: "I thought this was the space program here."

He demonstrated how he maneuvered around the hospital corridors leaning on a tubular stroller known as a walkerette. He even lifted his kimono daintily and showed the 22 stitches in his left hip. He did not dispute a suggestion that they formed a "crescent," though it also was suggested that a more appropriate Met description might be a "boomerang."

He agreed that with the aid of the walkerette he might make it from the dugout to the mound to relieve a pitcher, but when asked if he could do without the stroller, he replied with flawless logic: "If I walk without that thing, I wouldn't need it."

He expressed astonishment at the medical technique used in his operation, saying: "I found out that there's more people alive than me with a steel ball in their leg. Why, I'll walk down the street with that wheel in there. The wheel's working, too."

Then Casey, who was still being called "Doctor" by his close friends in spite of the fact that he now was the patient, also made the following declarations, again displaying his short temper with suggestions that 75 might be a ripe old age for a baseball manager:

• Would he return to managing the Mets that season? "I couldn't tell you," he said flatly.

• Would he be back in 1966? "I always sign a one-year contract with Mr. Weiss, and when the season is over I'll go in and talk with him."

• Had he been watching the Mets' games on television? "Every one of them. Last night it gave me a pain, though. I thought the club was very well run down there in Philadelphia. I thought five or six of them looked very alert."

• What was wrong with the team? "The trouble is, how can you get it better offensively and how can you get it better defensively. I don't know how they're going to straighten it out. I would like somebody to find out how many men were claimed by this ball club and we didn't get them. I'd say outside of two men, we didn't get them. And they say we need you nice fellows to stay in business."

That was a thrust at other teams in the league who had foiled the Mets just when they had been about to claim or draft players, and at the other teams' pious protestations that they needed the Mets and other new clubs to stay in business. He was taking maximum advantage of his convalescence to assume a pose of righteous outrage, and he fired a parting shot when asked whether he had been consulted about sending Danny Napoleon to the minor leagues earlier in the week.

"They've talked to me ever since I've been in this job," he said, irritated. "I'm still the manager of this club."

Three weeks later, that statement stopped being true. Flanked by Joan Payson, Donald Grant, George Weiss, Wes Westrum and Edna, he stepped before microphones on a small dais in the Essex House and said: "If I can't run out there and take a pitcher out, I'm not capable of continuing as manager." And so he formally handed the reins over to Westrum, ended 55 years in a baseball uniform, accepted the title of vice president of the Mets for West Coast operations and became, in Arthur Koestler's words describing a more profound passing, a shrug on the wave of eternity.

But he became a shrug that threatened to outlast the wave of eternity. He had been psyched and brain-washed and almost conned into accepting retirement as a medical necessity, when the Mets' upper echelons prevailed upon the one man, perhaps, who could make such a decision stick—Dr. LaMotte. Now, Dr. LaMotte happened to believe professionally that Casey could no longer manage a baseball team because of the hardships of airplane travel and the movement around stadiums, to say nothing of going out to the mound to change pitchers, as Casey himself had described the hardship in bread-and-butter terms. But he still believed that transmitting this belief to a man as rock-solid as Casey Stengel was not going to be child's play. In a sense, as unfortunate as the whole incident was, it probably spared the Mets' directors a scene with at least some of the rancor that the Yankee directors had provoked five years earlier. Sooner or later, someone would have to decide that Bernhardt had taken her last bow and that somebody had better work up the gumption to notify Bernhardt. Now the issue was transcended by a fractured hip, and the "somebody" was an orthopedic surgeon whom Casey respected. The deed was done.

That still left Casey in complete command of his vocal and theatrical gifts, even if he would have to find a new platform for displaying them. But that was the least of his problems.

On September 2, he made his farewell to the troops at Shea Stadium. He walked out to the pitcher's mound, looked around at the empty seats, posed for numerous pictures, hobbled on a crooked black cane that he had adopted, followed Edna inside as she carried his No. 37 uniform shirt to be enclosed in a glass case in the stadium ("like a mummy," he decided), and made a valedictory to the players in which he told them that "if you keep on, you can be here four or ten years."

Then, on behalf of the players, Galen Cisco mixed a couple of metaphors as neatly as the Old Man, saying he hoped some of the manager's greatness had rubbed off on the team and that "you got us off the ground and I think we can go on."

"I'd like to say one thing," Casey said later, slightly astonished at the phrasing. "That Cisco from Ohio State University seems to have picked up some Stengelese along with way."

Then, he was gone. He faded from the scene of some of his greatest triumphs and some of the Mets' greatest failures, and left. And even in the simple act of leaving town, he went fiction one better. He stopped off in Kansas City for a few days to visit and commiserate with his sister Louise, who was 78 years old and who had just fallen and broken her hip, too.

There were some who predicted that Stengel would wither on the vine in retirement, like some great Prometheus bound to a swimming pool and silent rows of orange and lemon trees after half a century in the front trenches. But five months later, he returned to New York for the first time since his swan song and he could not have created a bigger splash if he had waded ashore at the Battery.

In one sweeping return to form, he re-anointed his successor, Westrum; promised not to haunt Shea Stadium as a second-guesser; expressed doubt that the Mets were on the verge of amazing success; supported the idea of switching Mickey Mantle to first base from the outfield; disclosed that the Yankees and Boston Red Sox once had considered swapping Joe DiMaggio for Ted Williams, and agreed that the worst thing about baseball was that the games were too long. On the last point, he agreed that he had been one of the chief offenders. But, laying aside his two stainless-steel crutches and his one black night-time cane ("which I wear to black-tie affairs"), he noted the following extenuating circumstances:

"You have to have relief pitchers nowadays, and sometimes the other club'd get five runs on us with two outs. So I'd have to go out a couple of times in one inning to change pitchers, and how many guys can pitch nine innings today, anyway?"

Having clarified that point, the Professor rambled on for two hours from "the year I won 103 games with the Yankees and still blew the pennant" to Jim Hickman's chances of playing center field for the Mets in 1966. Casey conducted his rambling tour of baseball in the living room of his suite at the Essex House. He did not ramble far on foot, however, because he had been over-exerting himself and his recovery had been somewhat slowed. But he was clearly beginning to enjoy his new role as elder statesman, though it was still a subject of speculation how well he would adjust a month later when spring training would begin to stir the juices.

Anyway, he still had enough of the old Stengel range to fly East for four sports dinners that week and then to head back to the Coast with Edna to open the new building for the Valley National Bank, C.D. Stengel, vice president.

"Don't let anybody say I'm going to manage the club," he said, nodding toward Westrum, who sat alongside trying to make a gracious adjustment of his own. "I don't want anybody in this city to think I'm going to come in here and tell this man, 'I told you so.' If he asks me for some advice, I'll give it to him."

Then, he flashed his old form as master of the shattered syntax, using Larry Bearnarth as a case in point.

"Now you take Bearnarth," he said, apropos of nothing in particular. "When I was running this here ball club, I was too enthusiastic about Bearnarth. When I saw him at the Polo Grounds the first year, he could do eight or nine things and I said he can pitch in the big leagues. Then he commenced pitching too fast, and some men are amazing that way, but how can you be a starting pitcher that way? We're not talking about Koufax now, and besides he's got Perranoski."

"I was very disappointed," he went on, switching abruptly to his own medical stance. "I was doin' all right with the leg, and I got letters from all over the world, people telling me about their aches and pains. It was very sad."

"Then I tried to do too much," he said, not fully convincing anybody, "and set myself back."

Casey's next, and ultimate, challenge as one of the supposedly content Medicare set among the nation's "aging," came after the Mets had descended on St. Petersburg for their fifth spring training season—their first under another ringmaster. He showed a delicate sense of the occasion—in reverse, for a lifelong spotlight-stealer of his talent. He even gave Westrum a head start.

The "interim" "acting" manager, now the resident manager, arrived late in February and marshaled his men, including some established players like Ken Boyer and Dick Stuart, whom the Mets had bought since the change of command.

Then, one week after Westrum had hung out his shingle, Boyer bounded onto the little porch of the Mets' clubhouse at noon on March 4, glanced at the swarm of persons crowding around the old man with the cane and said: "You'd almost think Casey was in town."

Casey was in town. He had arrived by jet from California a dozen hours earlier, had almost got out of the house in a sports shirt, but then had been forced to change his "uniform" because Edna didn't think he should attend the races later in casual attire.

So then, dressed splendidly in maroon sports coat, dark slacks, white shirt and red tie, and carrying the black, crooked cane, he stood on the porch at Huggins-Stengel Field, held court and saw his amazing Mets for the first time in 1966 in the post-Stengel era.

"This club's got a chance to move," he said approvingly, with no trace of envy or resentment at his spot on the sidelines. "These fellows aren't as green as when I had them. You won 50 games last year, didn't you? Then why didn't you win 60? That's what I'd like to know."

Could the Mets go all the way from last place to the first division, as suggested by Westrum when he got the show on the road without help from the Great White Father?

"I saw it happen once," the Great White Father replied, reaching back a cool half-century to George Stallings' Boston Braves of 1914, who were last in July and still won the pennant and World Series. "That Boston club did it, but they had three pitchers that couldn't do nothing but win ball games."

"He's got a good power man at first base and a young man at first base, and they got the same problem in Los Angeles," he said, switching abruptly to Westrum, Stuart, Ed Kranepool and the Dodgers, in that order.

"He's got Scheffing, who knows about catching, and he's got Berra and he's got himself, which was fairly skilled for several clubs," he continued, ringing in Westrum, Bob Scheffing, Yogi Berra, and Westrum again. "And he got the best prospect from Los Angeles, too."

Now the subject was catching, the Mets' No. 1 problem at the moment, and the "best prospect" was 20-year-old Greg Goossen.

"The last coaches were terrific men," the Professor went on, starting a new paragraph on the coaching situation and saluting Don Heffner and Eddie Stanky, who left to manage the Cincinnati Reds and Chicago White Sox. "Two of them got employed running other clubs; three, counting our man. And now, can you fulfill the job?

"Now you got Virdon, a splendid high-class fella, and there's got to be something wrong with the outfield which he can help those young men. And his roommate at Pittsburgh was Groat, and they beat us out of the World Series and I got discharged."

Having thus covered Bill Virdon, the Mets' new manager at Williamsport, and Dick Groat, who helped beat the Yankees in 1960, the Professor switched back to the Mets, who were running onto the porch one by one, shaking hands and greeting their 75-year-old skipper emeritus with "Hello, Mr. Stengel," and "How you feeling, Casey?"

"McGraw," he said, meaning Tug McGraw, the young left-hander, "has got the earmarks of a splendid big league pitcher. When he's got 2-and-2 on the batter, you might get a foul off him. And having Stuart around would make Kranepool a better ball player, because Stuart bats in 90 runs and Kranepool is only 21 but you don't see him racing around the bases, do you?"

Westrum trotted over, posed affectionately with his predecessor and heard the Professor's final verdict on the 1966 Mets.

"And so," Casey concluded, "the youth got older guys playing in front of them, and that ain't bad."

Later, driving out to the Florida racetrack, he summarized the overall situation.

"They say Koufax ain't signed and Drysdale ain't signed," he said, "and they done fairly splendid last year. And I'm supposed to know all about the English language and baseball and politics, but now all they want is a picture of this here cane."

"Yes, sir, these people down here want to put me in Sarasota," he said, referring to the Circus Hall of Fame. "But you can't get into the Baseball Hall of Fame unless you limp."

And four days later, that's exactly how he did get in. Leaning on the crooked black cane and wearing a shiny blue New York Mets' cap, he unexpectedly limped into the Hall of Fame—the 104th person elected and only the second elected on a special ballot after an extraordinary poll conducted quietly by mail during the previous month.

The secret had been kept even from Casey, in spite of a furor raised because the rules at Cooperstown required a waiting period of five years after a candidate had retired. The idea was to avoid hasty installations based on fervor, passion or enthusiasm, and to allow a respectable time for the eyes of "history" to grow accustomed to the light. But the Baseball Writers Association of America had petitioned the Hall of Fame to waive or ease the rule for Stengel, and the hall had acceded.

The next problem was to get the Professor into position for the announcement without letting the cat out of the bag. The ruse was elaborately staged.

Casey was roused at 5:30 on the morning of March 8 to attend a civic breakfast for the members of the Mets and St. Louis Cardinals, who also trained in St. Petersburg, and Edna recalled that as she combed his slightly tinted reddish gray hair over to the side he had groused mildly about wearing the same suit and shirt he had worn the night before. But she had—innocently, she insisted—pointed out that he had worn them only to dinner in the Colonial Inn and that they would be perfectly neat. So he stepped into the morning sunshine and declared in the first of four speeches he was to make that day that "this club is going to get out of 10th place and go very far upward."

When he was driven out to the ball park several hours later, the car radio was kept silent to avoid any unforeseen leak of the big news to come. He and Edna had been told that they were to make a presentation to Weiss and Westrum, and Casey even rehearsed a little speech en route about what a smart man Weiss was, with that Yale education and all.

When they pulled into the gravel parking lot at Huggins-Stengel Field and walked over onto the grass in foul territory in right field, alongside the clubhouse porch, a spray of red carnations was handed to Edna, ostensibly for her to present to Joan Payson, who in fact was at her home on the east coast of Florida. Ford Frick, who had recently retired as Commissioner of Baseball in favor of William Dole Eckert, a former lieutenant general of the Air Force and a man widely teased as baseball's "Unknown Soldier," stepped before the gathering of newsmen and club officials and said into a cluster of microphones, as Casey stood by to deliver his "Weiss speech";

"We have had a special election and Charles Dillon Stengel was unanimously elected to the Hall of Fame."

The announcement touched off one of the most clamorous scenes since major league baseball teams had begun training on the west coast of Florida 53 years earlier. Edna, still carrying the immense spray of flowers, began to cry and leaned over and kissed Casey on the cheek.

He had just responded to Frick's announcement by saying "Thank you, very much," and now he turned toward Edna and said, in the same tone of acknowledgment as she planted the kiss: "Thank *you*, very much."

Eckert, who had been advised of the election only 24 hours before, shook Casey's hand and expressed cheer for "a great day."

Weiss wrung his old friend's hand and agreed that this was what he had had in mind in December when he had urged the Hall of Fame to "let him smell the flowers now."

"I guess," Casey finally said into the microphones, "I should say a thousand things. Being elected into the Hall of Fame is an amazing thing, and there are so many men which are skilled in various ways. So many noted men have got into the Hall of Fame and I think it's a terrific thing to get in while you're still alive."

Then, after throwing in a few sentences from his "Weiss speech" for good measure, and still leaning on his cane, he marched from the clubhouse terrace to the small bleachers along the first-base line and, without microphone or megaphone, stood before the overflow crowd. They were mostly old people of his own generation, who made St. Petersburg a mecca for the retired, and they had come to sit in the sun and see the Mets' first intrasquad game of the spring.

"They just put me in—if you don't know—the Hall of Fame," he said in a loud, hoarse voice that was promptly overriden by tremendous cheers.

Then, while Mets players three generations younger gathered behind him like an honor guard, he limped to the third-base grandstand and repeated the announcement, to more thunderous cheers.

The holiday, town-meeting atmosphere was fanned by two things: his 55-year career as a player, coach and manager, and the unusual procedure followed to get him into the Hall of Fame. Only Lou Gehrig had been elected through a special vote since the shrine was established in 1939. He was inducted after announcing his retirement on May 2 that year when it was learned that he had been sticken by lateral sclerosis, which ended his life two years later.

Several other giants of the game had been honored under unusual circumstances, too. Connie Mack, who was born during the Civil War and who was a major league manager for 50 years until 1950, was elected with a special "pioneer" group while he was still managing. And Judge Landis was elected in 1944, two weeks before his death. Joe DiMaggio was enshrined in 1955, although he had retired only four years earlier, but as a result of this "haste" the five-year rule was adopted—until Stengel broke his hip and the regulations almost simultaneously.

Edna, signing autographs for fans who leaned over the fence behind first base, wiped another tear or two and said: "I can't get over it. This is greater even than winning the 1949 World Series."

A couple of hours later Casey, curiously serene and uncommonly pleased, slipped onto a stool in the lounge of the Colonial Inn and helped himself to a cocktail. Nat Holman, the pioneer basketball player and coach, who was vacationing at the inn, approached deferentially, introduced himself and was surprised when Stengel said brightly: "I know more about you than you know about me."

Then he launched a discussion of the Old Celtics and how he and some other baseball players used to sneak off at night to watch Holman play. Holman, incredulous, finally beat a respectful retreat and wandered down the mall behind the inn toward the Gulf of Mexico. He stopped outside the Stengel's double suite, where Edna was gabbing with the neighbors, and told her:

"I had a dream in the still of the night. It was of you and Casey arriving in Cooperstown, and there was a Rolls-Royce waiting at the airport, and you entered the Hall of Fame in style."

Edna, in a typical Stengelese recovery from grandeur to the economics of life, shot back: "That's nice. Who pays for the Rolls-Royce?"

The problem did not materialize, though several others did, such as an airline strike, but the Professor and his bride arrived in Cooperstown in a style that would have fulfilled Holman's fantasy, anyway.

Eight days before Casey's 76th birthday, they flew from Los Angeles to New York (on a non-striking airline), switched to a regional line and hopped right back out to Utica, then arrived in Cooperstown by car and swept into the Otesaga Hotel in plenty of time for the induction ceremony. Like three days early.

So by the time Ted Williams arrived for his induction at the same ceremony, Casey was already the toast of Main Street, and the surrounding country could not have been more astonished by his verve if he paddled a canoe across Otsego Lake, jumped ashore like the Deerslayer and begun to stalk Indians with a baseball bat.

This was the Leatherstocking country of James Fenimore Cooper, country that was in the business of "selling history" through a series of museums that chronicled the adventures of the American Indian, the American farmer and the American baseball player. Williams, who had been accused during his magnificent 22-year career with the Boston Red Sox of being uncommunicative, even hostile, immediately communicated the fact that "I know what I want to say" at the installation ceremony, closeted himself in a motel room and composed a speech. Stengel, at the other extreme as a communicator, wrote and even rehearsed a speech, and then, as at St. Petersburg, disregarded it when the great moment came.

In any event, they added a few memorable paragraphs to Cooperstown's history industry on Monday morning, July 25, when they were enshrined in the Hall of Fame in a resplendent ceremony that crowded, thrilled and touched the country village where baseball had been born a century and a quarter earlier.

They staged their performances before 10,000 persons, four times the resident population of Cooperstown, speaking from a platform on the tree-lined lawn behind the Hall of Fame while people sat on folding chairs, stood along the slopes and even perched in trees. The widows of Babe Ruth, Christy Mathewson and Eddie Collins were introduced to loud cheers. Officials of the Yankees, Mets and other teams basked in the sunshine alongside league presidents and baseball brass of all levels. Edna sat in a front-row chair in a bright yellow dress. Dr. LaMotte, as intrigued as anybody over his patient's galloping convalescence, sat nearby, as did George Weiss, watching his lifelong friend "smell the flowers now."

Then the new Commissioner of Baseball, William D. Eckert, a proper, erect, almost guarded man in a dark suit, introduced Williams. He noted that the great left-handed hitter had spent nearly five years "in the service of his country" as a Marine Corps pilot, and Eckert, an Air Force pilot and officer for 35 years, said he was pleased to share that bond with him. He recited some of Ted's remarkable statistics as a slugger: a career batting average of .344, a slugging percentage of .634 (second to Ruth), a 1941 batting average of .406 (making him the last man to reach .400), a career total of 521 home runs, 6 batting championships and 18 All-Star Games.

"It is difficult for me to say what's in my heart," replied Williams, a towering, suntanned curly-haired man, looking like Rock Hudson and sounding like John Wayne. "Today, I am thinking of my playground director, my high school coach, my managers and Tom Yawkey, the greatest owner in baseball."

He went on, in a moving, almost reverent speech, to express "pride and humility" at "the greatest thing that ever happened to me."

Williams, who had been elected to the Hall of Fame in January after the minimum "waiting time" of five years, stirred the crowd by his sincerity and solemnity. He was the 103rd person installed into baseball's colonnade. Then Charles Dillon Stengel became No. 104.

He was introduced by General Eckert as "one of the greatest managers of all time and a great judge of men," and no one, Eckert said, "could get more out of players." Then the Professor was off and running in a great, rambling, splendid reminiscence of his life and times.

"Mr. Eckert," he began, in acknowledgment when the cheering had died down, "and those distinguished notables that are sitting on the rostrum. I want to thank everybody. I want to thank some of the owners who were amazing to me, and those big presidents of the leagues who were kind to me when I was so obnoxious. I want to thank everybody for my first managerial experience at Worcester, which was last in the Eastern League, and where I met that fine fellow George Weiss, who ran the New Haven club and who would find out whenever I was discharged and would re-employ me.

"I want to thank my parents for letting me play baseball, and I'm thankful I had baseball knuckles and couldn't become a dentist.

"I got $2,100 a year when I started in the big league and lived at Broadway and Forty-seventh Street. And they get more money now.

"I chased the balls that Babe Ruth hit. We couldn't play on Sundays, that was the preacher's day to collect. But in Baltimore we played at a racetrack even, and Ruth hit one over my head and Robby said, 'You'd think you'd play back on a guy who swings like that.' So I replied, 'who's Babe Ruth? He's a kid who just came out of that school.' But I backed up 50 feet more and called over to Hy Myers, 'Far enough?' And he said okay. And Ruth hit it way over my head just the same.

"And Grover Cleveland Alexander pitched in a bandbox in those days and still won 30 games. And there was Walter Johnson, who could pitch for a second-division club. And there was Joe McCarthy, whose teams were called lucky in the minor league, and so I told my players at Toledo: 'Yeah, and they'll be lucky until 1999 if *we* keep playing them.' "

Williams, he said, was "the most aggressive batter who ever went up to home plate." And he recalled his own troubles as a manager against Boston, "which is in New England," saying: "Of course, with my English and the Boston English, we had a little trouble understanding each other."

But nobody had any trouble understanding Casey as he roared nonstop through a 21-minute valedictory that ended with the incongruous, incredible statement: "And I want to thank the treemendous fans. We appreciate every boys' group, girls' group, poem and song. And keep going to see the Mets play."

Then the man who had traveled 55 amazin' years from Kankakee to Cooperstown stood with the sunshine reflecting off his hair, carefully combed to the side by his Edna, and heard the cheers roll across the hamlet where Abner Doubleday had started playing the "new game."

Now he was surrounded by the memories of other cheering throngs, and by amazin' baseball players like Cobb, Wagner, Mathewson and Lajoie, who were great when he stepped off the train in Brooklyn in 1912. And players like Ruth, Collins and Johnson, who became great in games in which he played. And managers like McGraw and Robinson, who taught him to teach other players and lead them toward Cooperstown.

He was still surrounded by the criticisms of 55 years, too. He had "overmanaged" players. He had been resented for being too curt with some players in the dugout. He had been arbitrary, self-righteous, rude at times. He had been "the last angry old man" to some. He had even confused people and issues by a colossally egocentric outlook. He had even confused the nation into thinking he was going to retire, but then he had "clarified" his remarks, made at City Hall in New York in July 1965. Then he had broken his hip three days later and retired anyway.

Yet, he was surrounded by the huzzahs of half a century for things uncommonly well done.

"He was short and wiry," wrote Leonard Koppett in *The New York Times,* "and certainly not as strong as most top athletes. He could run fairly fast, threw accurately enough and hit the ball pretty well, but in no respect could he be called gifted. In no physical respect, that is; in mind and spirit, he was as gifted as they come.

"Because he had no children to tutor and lead, his craving to improve through knowledge was directed at the young players working for him. In short, he became a dedicated teacher.

"He didn't always succeed, but he didn't always fail, either. That is why his deepest feelings in all his years as manager of the Yankees and Mets have been involved in 'leaving something behind.' With the Yankees, already successful, it was a desire to 'rebuild'; with the Mets, it was a desire to build from nothing."

"He gave the Mets the momentum they needed when they needed it most," said Arthur Daley, summing up the Professor's final assignment. "He was the booster rocket that got them off the ground and on their journey. The smoke screen he generated to accompany the blast-off obscured the flaws and gave the Mets an acceptance and a following they could not have obtained without him. He and he alone could have done the job."

"Casey," said Ty Cobb a few years before Cooperstown, "deserves to be in the Hall of Fame. He has shown the greatest ability to successfully manage a ball club, and surely deserves credit as the top manager of all time."

"He's probably done more for baseball than anyone," said Eckert.

"I think," said a friend of Lillian Gish, the actress, trying to find words to describe Miss Gish, "she has vanity. She's wonderful and loyal. She's an American institution, and no one would take a crack at her any more than they would at Casey Stengel."

So, surrounded by the deeds that would live after him, the American institution stood in the sunshine of the Cooperstown morning, looking a bit like Cooper's last of the Mohicans, the great wrinkled face thrust toward the cheering crowd.

At least, he was probably the only "American institution" that at the age of 75 had gone out and bought a new tuxedo, a piece of wardrobe equipment not normally considered necessary at 75—in any event, not a new one. But in Charles Dillon Stengel's case, it would add a touch of the splendor necessary for him to commence bein' amazin' all over again.

It was a little like the time Noel Coward and Gertrude Lawrence left the cast of "Private Lives," and their replacements, wrote Brooks Atkinson, were fine—"but something of insanity has gone out of the performance."

APPENDIX

On July 9, 1958, hearings were held in Washington by the Subcommittee on Anti-trust and Monopoly of the Committee of the Judiciary of the United States Senate. The subcommittee was considering H.R. 10378 and S. 4070: to limit anti-trust laws so as to exempt professional baseball, football, basketball and hockey. The chief witness: Charles Dillon Stengel. Following are excerpts of his testimony:

SENATOR ESTES KEFAUVER. Mr. Stengel, you are the manager of the New York Yankees. Will you give us very briefly your background and your views about this legislation?

MR. STENGEL. Well, I started in professional ball in 1910. I have been in professional ball, I would say, for 48 years. I have been employed by numerous ball clubs in the majors and in the minor leagues.

I started in the minor leagues with Kansas City. I played as low as Class D ball, which was at Shelbyville, Kentucky, and also Class C ball and Class A ball, and I have advanced in baseball as a ballplayer.

I had many years that I was not so successful as a ballplayer, as it is a game of skill. And then I was no doubt discharged by baseball in which I had to go back to the minor leagues as a manager, and after being in the minor leagues as a manager, I became a major league manager in several cities and was discharged, we call it discharged because there is no question I had to leave. (Laughter.)

And I returned to the minor leagues at Milwaukee, Kansas City and Oakland, California, and then returned to the major leagues.

In the last 10 years, naturally, in major league baseball with the New York Yankees, the New York Yankees have had tremendous success and while I am not a ballplayer who does the work, I have no doubt worked for a ball club that is very capable in the office.

I have been up and down the ladder. I know there are some things in baseball 35 to 50 years ago that are better now than they were in those days. In those days, my goodness, you could not transfer a ball club in the minor leagues, class D, class C ball, class A ball.

How could you transfer a ball club when you did not have a highway? How could you transfer a ball club when the railroads then would take you to a town you got off and then you had to wait and sit up five hours to go to another ball club?

How could you run baseball then without night ball?

You had to have night ball to improve the proceeds, to pay larger salaries, and I went to work, the first year I received $135 a month.

I thought that was amazing. I had to put away enough money to go to

dental college. I found out it was not better in dentistry. I stayed in baseball.
Any other questions you would like to ask me?

SENATOR KEFAUVER. Mr. Stengel, are you prepared to answer particularly why baseball wants this bill passed?

MR. STENGEL. Well, I would have to say at the present time, I think that baseball has advanced in this respect for the player help. That is an amazing statement for me to make, because you can retire with an annuity at 50 and what organization in America allows you to retire at 50 and receive money?

Now the second thing about baseball that I think is very interesting to the public or to all of us that it is the owner's own fault if he does not improve his club, along with the officials in the ball club and the players.

Now what causes that?

If I am going to go on the road and we are a traveling ball club and you know the cost of transportation now—we travel sometimes with three Pullman coaches, the New York Yankees, and I am just a salaried man and do not own stock in the New York Yankees, I found out that in traveling with the New York Yankees on the road and all, that it is the best, and we have broken records in Washington this year, we have broken them in every city but New York and we have lost two clubs that have gone out of the city of New York.

Of course, we have had some bad weather, I would say that they are mad at us in Chicago, we fill the parks.

They have come out to see good material. I will say they are mad at us in Kansas City, but we broke their attendance record.

Now on the road we only get possibly 27 cents. I am not positive of these figures, as I am not an official.

If you go back 15 years or if I owned stock in the club, I would give them to you.

SENATOR KEFAUVER. Mr. Stengel, I am not sure that I made my question clear. (Laughter.)

MR. STENGEL. Yes, sir. Well, that is all right. I am not sure I am going to answer yours perfectly, either. (Laughter.)

SENATOR JOSEPH C. O'MAHONEY. How many minor leagues were there in baseball when you began?

MR. STENGEL. Well, there were not so many at that time because of this fact: Anybody to go into baseball at that time with the educational schools that we had were small, while you were probably thoroughly educated at school, you had to be—we had only small cities that you could put a team in and they would go defunct.

Why, I remember the first year I was at Kankakee, Illinois, and a bank offered me $550 if I would let them have a little notice. I left there and took a uniform because they owed me two weeks' pay. But I either had to quit but I did not have enough money to go to dental college so I had to go with the manager down to Kentucky.

What happened there was if you got by July, that was the big date. You did not play night ball and you did not play Sundays in half of the cities on account of a Sunday observance, so in those days when things were tough, and all of it was, I mean to say, why they just closed up July 4 and there you were sitting there in the depot.

You could go to work some place else, but that was it.

So I got out of Kankakee, Illinois, and I just go there for the visit now. (Laughter.)

SENATOR JOHN A. CARROLL. The question Senator Kefauver asked you was what, in your honest opinion, with your 48 years of experience, is the need for this legislation in view of the fact that baseball has not been subject to anti-trust laws?

MR. STENGEL. No.

SENATOR CARROLL. I had a conference with one of the attorneys representing not only baseball but all of the sports, and I listened to your explanation to Senator Kefauver. It seemed to me it had some clarity. I asked the attorney this question: What was the need for this legislation? I wonder if you would accept his definition. He said they didn't want to be subjected to the *ipse dixit* of the Federal Government because they would throw a lot of damage suits on the *ad damnum* clause. He said, in the first place, the Toolson case was *sui generis,* it was *de minimus non curat lex.*

Do you call that a clear expression?

MR. STENGEL. Well, you are going to get me there for about two hours.

SENATOR KEFAUVER. Thank you, very much, Mr. Stengel. We appreciate your presence here.

Mr. Mickey Mantle, will you come around?

Mr. Mantle, do you have any observations with reference to the applicability of the anti-trust laws to baseball?

MR. MANTLE. My views are just about the same as Casey's.

CHARLES DILLON STENGEL

Born at Kansas City, Mo., July 30, 1890

Height, 5:10. Weight, 175.
Batted and threw left.

Record as a Player

YEAR	TEAM & LEAGUE	G.	AB.	R.	H.	2b	3b	HR	RBI	AVG.
1910	Kankakee, N.A.	59	203	27	51	7	1	1		.251
1910	Maysville, Bl.Gr.	69	233	27	52	10	5	2		.352
1911	Aurora, Wis.-Ill.	121	420	76	148	23	6	4		.352
1912	Montgomery, S.A.	136	479	85	139					.290
1912	Brooklyn, N.L.	17	57	9	18	1	0	1	12	.316
1913	Brooklyn, N.L.	124	438	60	119	16	8	7	44	.272
1914	Brooklyn, N.L.	126	412	55	130	13	10	4	56	.316
1915	Brooklyn, N.L.	132	459	52	109	20	12	3	43	.237
1916	Brooklyn, N.L.	127	462	66	129	27	8	8	53	.279
1917	Brooklyn, N.L.	150	549	69	141	23	12	6	69	.257
1918	Pittsburgh, N.L.	39	122	18	30	4	1	1	13	.246
1919	Pittsburgh, N.L.	89	321	38	94	10	10	4	40	.293
1920	Philadelphia, N.L.	129	445	53	130	25	6	9	50	.292
1921	Phila.-N.Y., N.L.	42	81	11	23	4	1	0	6	.284
1922	New York, N.L.	84	250	48	92	8	10	7	48	.368
1923	New York, N.L.	75	218	39	74	11	5	5	43	.339
1924	Boston, N.L.	131	461	57	129	20	6	5	39	.280
1925	Boston, N.L.	12	13	0	1	0	0	0	2	.077
1925	Worcester, E.L.	100	334	73	107	27	2	10		.320
1926	Toledo, A.A.	88	201	40	66	14	2	0	27	.328
1927	Toledo, A.A.	18	17	3	3	0	0	1	3	.176
1928	Toledo, A.A.	26	32	5	14	5	0	0	12	.438
1929	Toledo, A.A.	20	31	2	7	1	1	0	9	.226
1931	Toledo, A.A.	2	8	1	3	2	0	0	0	.375
Major league totals		1277	4288	575	1219	182	89	60	518	.284

N.A.—Northern Association
Bl.Gr.—Blue Grass League
Wis.-Ill.—Wisconsin-Illinois League
S.A.—Southern Association
N.L.—National League
E.L.—Eastern League
A.A.—American Association

World Series Record

YEAR	TEAM	G	AB	R	H	2b	3b	HR	RBI	AVG.
1916	Brooklyn.................	4	11	2	4	0	0	0	0	.364
1922	New York	2	5	0	2	0	0	0	0	.400
1923	New York	6	12	3	5	0	0	2	4	.417
World Series Totals............		12	20	5	11	0	0	2	4	.393

Record as a Manager

YEAR	CLUB & LEAGUE	FINISHED	WON	LOST	PCT.
1925	Worcester, E.L.............	3	70	55	.560
1926	Toledo, A.A.	4	87	77	.530
1927	Toledo, A.A.	1	101	67	.601
1928	Toledo, A.A.	6	79	88	.473
1929	Toledo, A.A.	8	67	100	.401
1930	Toledo, A.A.	3	88	66	.571
1931	Toledo, A.A.	8	68	100	.405
1934	Brooklyn, N.L.	6	71	81	.467
1935	Brooklyn, N.L.	5	70	83	.458
1936	Brooklyn, N.L.	7	67	87	.435
1938	Boston, N.L...................	5	77	75	.507
1939	Boston, N.L...................	7	63	88	.417
1940	Boston, N.L...................	7	65	87	.428
1941	Boston, N.L...................	7	62	92	.403
1942	Boston, N.L...................	7	59	89	.399
1943	Boston, N.L...................	6	68	85	.444
1944	Milwaukee, A.A.	1	91	49	.650
1945	Kansas City, A.A..........	7	65	86	.430
1946	Oakland, P.C.L.............	2	111	72	.607
1947	Oakland, P.C.L.............	4	96	90	.516
1948	Oakland, P.C.L.............	1	114	74	.606
1949	New York, A.L.*..........	1	97	57	.630
1950	New York, A.L.*..........	1	98	56	.636
1951	New York, A.L.*..........	1	98	56	.636
1952	New York, A.L.*..........	1	95	59	.617
1953	New York, A.L.*..........	1	99	52	.656
1954	New York, A.L..............	2	103	51	.669
1955	New York, A.L..............	1	96	58	.623
1956	New York, A.L.*..........	1	97	57	.630
1957	New York, A.L..............	1	98	56	.636
1958	New York, A.L.*..........	1	92	62	.597
1959	New York, A.L..............	3	79	75	.513

Record as a Manager

YEAR	CLUB & LEAGUE	FINISHED	WON	LOST	PCT.
1960	New York, A.L............	1	97	57	.630
1962	New York Mets...........	10	40	120	.250
1963	New York, N.L............	10	51	111	.315
1964	New York, N.L............	10	53	109	.327
1965	New York, N.L............	—	31	64	.326
Major league totals.................		—	1926	1867	.508

E.L.—Eastern League
A.A.—American Association
N.L.—National League
P.C.L.—Pacific Coast League
A.L.—American League
N.L.—National League

*Won World Series.
Elected to the Baseball Hall of Fame—March 8, 1966.
Inducted—July 25, 1966.